CHARLES DICKENS'S
GREAT EXPECTATIONS

Great Expectations has had a long, active and sometimes surprising life since its first serialized appearance in All the Year Round between 1 December 1860 and 3 August 1861. In this new publishing and reception history, Mary Hammond demonstrates that while Dickens's thirteenth novel can tell us a great deal about the dynamic mid-Victorian moment into which it was born, its afterlife beyond the nineteenth-century Anglophone world reveals the full extent of its versatility. Re-assessing generations of Dickens scholarship and using newly discovered archival material, Hammond covers the formative history of *Great Expectations'* early years, analyses the extent and significance of its global reach and explores the ways in which it has functioned as literature and stage, TV, film and radio drama from its first appearance to the latest film version of 2012. Appendices include contemporary reviews and comprehensive bibliographies of adaptations and translations. The book is a rich resource for scholars and students of Dickens; of comparative literature; and of publishing, readership and media history.

Ashgate Studies in Publishing History: Manuscript, Print, Digital

Series editors: Ann R. Hawkins, Texas Tech University, USA, and
Maura Ives, Texas A&M University, USA

Exploring the intersection of publishing history, book history, and literary and
cultural studies, this series supports innovative work on the cultural significance
and creative impact of printing and publishing history, including reception,
distribution, and translation or adaptation into other media.

Other Ashgate titles of interest

Charles Dickens's *Our Mutual Friend*
Sean Grass

Lewis Carroll's *Alice's Adventures in Wonderland* and *Through the Looking-Glass*
Zoe Jaques and Eugene Giddens

Elizabeth Gaskell's *Cranford*
Thomas Recchio

Charles Dickens's
Great Expectations
A Cultural Life, 1860–2012

MARY HAMMOND
University of Southampton, UK

ASHGATE

Published by
Ashgate Publishing Limited
Wey Court East
Union Road
Farnham
Surrey, GU9 7PT
England

Ashgate Publishing Company
110 Cherry Street
Suite 3-1
Burlington, VT 05401-3818
USA

www.ashgate.com

British Library Cataloguing in Publication Data
A catalogue record for this book is available from the British Library

The Library of Congress has cataloged the printed edition as follows:
Hammond, Mary, 1960–
　　Charles Dickens's Great Expectations : a cultural life, 1860–2012 / by Mary Hammond.
　　　pages cm.—(Ashgate Studies in Publishing History: Manuscript, Print, Digital)
　　Includes bibliographical references and index.
　　ISBN 978-1-4094-2587-8 (hardcover : alk. paper)—ISBN 978-1-4094-2588-5 (ebook)— .
　　ISBN 978-1-4724-0551-7 (epub)
　　1. Dickens, Charles, 1812–1870. Great expectations. 2. Publishers and publishing—England—History—19th century. 3. Books and reading—England—History—19th century. I. Title.
　　PR4560.H36 2015
　　823'.8—dc23

2014033506

ISBN: 9781409425878 (hbk)
ISBN: 9781409425885 (ebk – PDF)
ISBN: 9781472405517 (ebk – ePUB)

MIX
Paper from
responsible sources
FSC® C013985
www.fsc.org

Printed in the United Kingdom by Henry Ling Limited,
at the Dorset Press, Dorchester, DT1 1HD

In memory of Betty (1922–2012)

Contents

List of Figures

Acknowledgements

In writing a book of this scope one inevitably incurs many debts of gratitude, of many different types. I'll start by acknowledging the generous institutional support I received. In 2012–13 the Arts and Humanities Research Council (UK) awarded me a nine-month fellowship which freed me from teaching duties and made the last part of the research and most of the writing possible. The Faculty of Humanities and the English Department at the University of Southampton both funded several research trips during 2011, and in 2013 allowed me a semester's leave for fact-checking and editing. The following organisations and individuals kindly gave me permission to publish material from their collections: the BBC at the Written Archives Centre, Caversham, Reading; Immediate Media Company London Ltd.; the Henry W. and Albert A. Berg Collection of English and American Literature, the New York Public Library, Astor, Lenox and Tilden Foundations; Commander Mark Dickens of the Charles Dickens Estate; the British Newspaper Archive, (www.britishnewspaperarchive.co.uk); the Serial and Government Publications Division of the Library of Congress, Washington, DC; and John O. Jordan, Director of the Ada B. Nisbet Archive, The Dickens Project, University of California, Santa Cruz.

During the period of research I had the assistance of many dedicated archivists, curators, collectors and librarians, whose enthusiasm for Dickens and for this project made the work a genuine pleasure. My gratitude goes in particular to Peggy Alexander (UCLA Film and Television Archive); Jeanette Berard (Special Collections, Thousand Oaks National Radio Library, Ca.); Retha Buys (Springbok Radio Archives, South African Broadcasting Corporation); Bryony Dixon and Katherine Dixon (British Film Institute); Katrina Dixon (The Lawrence & Lee Collection, Rodgers and Hammerstein Archive of Recorded Sound, New York Public Library); David Francis and Joss Marsh (Kent Museum of the Moving Image); Isaac Gewirtz (Berg Collection, New York Public Library); Helen Hanson (Bill Douglas Centre, University of Exeter); Nick Hiley (British Cartoon Archive, University of Kent); Sue Hodson (Huntington Library, California); Jess Hogg (BBC Written Archives Centre, Caversham, Reading); John O. Jordan and JoAnna Rotke (Ada B. Nisbet Archive, UC Santa Cruz); Karen Nickeson (Billy Rose Theatre Division, New York Public Library); Maria Isabel Molestina (Pierpont Morgan Library, New York); Clare Norton (National Film and Sound Archive of Australia); Amber Paranick (Reference Librarian, Serial & Government Publications Division, Library of Congress); Mark Quigley (Access Archivist, UCLA Film & Television Archive, Research & Study Center); Marcus Riddell (Garrick Club Theatre Archive, London); Jenny Romero (Special Collections, Margaret Herrick Library, Academy of Motion Picture Arts and Sciences, Los Angeles); Florian Schweizer and Fiona Jenkins (Charles Dickens Museum, London); and Jill Sullivan (Theatre Collection, University of Bristol).

Many other individuals freely offered their time, help and support in other ways both large and small. My Southampton colleagues John McGavin, Marianne O'Doherty and David Glover kindly read and commented on drafts of the grant proposal. Elizabeth Karlsen (Producer, Number 9 Films) granted me an interview, answered questions by email, and allowed me to spend a fascinating afternoon watching the filming on the set of Mike Newell's movie adaptation of *Great Expectations* (2012). Kim Varvell of the BBC arranged an email interview for me with George Ormond, Hilary Salmon and Anne Pivcevic, producers of the 2011 TV series. Robert Fraser and his wife Catherine accompanied my partner and I on a pilgrimage to Cooling church, where, undaunted by a bone-chilling February wind blasting across the Thames estuary, Robert recited the first chapter of *Great Expectations* over the 'little stone lozenges', and gave me new insights into the heart of Dickens's novel. On that same trip Sally Hergest gave us a private tour of Gad's Hill before its official opening as a museum, and I found her vast knowledge of all things late Dickens invaluable. Bob Patten, Mike Hammond, David Mayer, Clare Gill and John McGavin all read drafts of various chapters, and I am more grateful than I can say for their astute and generous comments. Klaudia Lee and Ewa Kujawska-Lis offered key insights on Dickens in translation. Helen Hanson, Mervyn Heard, David Francis and Joss Marsh kindly answered questions by email about magic lanterns, and Frank Krutnik advised me on radio adaptations. My thanks also go to Ashgate's anonymous reader, who made invaluable suggestions for improvements to the manuscript, and to my commissioning editor Ann Donahue, who waited a long time for this book and somewhat miraculously continued to believe it would eventually appear.

On a more personal level I'd like to thank Alex and Sarah Hammond, Katie Moy, Bob Brimson, Shelley Cobb, Neil Ewen and Jann Hodges for the much-needed moral support and spells of recreation, and a special thank you goes to my partner Mike for sharing this long journey, for driving when I needed it, and above all just for being there.

I am deeply grateful to you all. In your different ways you have helped to make this book better than I could ever have made it on my own, though any remaining errors and omissions are, of course, entirely my own responsibility.

Introduction

'"Great Expectations" is a book which offends against all the laws of probability, and outrages all the laws of execution; to it the famous lines so often quoted by the enemies of Gothic architecture might be aptly applied. It is full of "Rich windows which exclude the light / And passages which lead to nothing".'
— Anon., review in the *Morning Post*, 31 July 1861, p. 3.[1]

For a story which in 1861 the *Morning Post*'s reviewer thought led to nothing, Dickens's thirteenth novel has done remarkably well for itself. In the bicentenary year of 2012, hundreds of writers, critics, scholars and ordinary (largely middle-class) readers named it as their favourite novel or among their most influential childhood reading experiences.[2] It is the third most adapted Dickens story after *A Christmas Carol* and *Oliver Twist* (in an adaptation oeuvre which puts even Shakespeare and Austen to shame), and it has been recast countless times in new incarnations in fiction, poetry, art, animation, film and popular music. Its reappearances have often coincided with significant historical events, from the silent black-and-white movie version which appeared towards the end of the First World War in 1917, to dramatizations by South African Radio in the 1970s and 1980s during some of the worst years of Apartheid. Its influence has been remarkably pervasive in other directions too; lines from the book have provided titles for a number of post–World War II scholarly works on Victorian literature, including most notably David Musselwhite's *Partings Welded Together: Politics and Desire in the Nineteenth-Century English Novel* (1987) and John Plotz's *Portable Property: Victorian Culture on the Move* (2009). Beyond literary studies the novel lends its name, ironically or otherwise, to numerous Anglophone publications on (among other topics) prenatal care, educational strategy and the analysis of relative economic growth in developing nations. The twenty-first century looks set to mark its zenith: in 2011–12 no fewer than three new major stage and screen versions appeared in close succession to mark the bicentenary, which fell during another period of global economic crisis, and in that same year

---

[1]   Unless otherwise attributed, all quotations from nineteenth-century British newspapers are reproduced with the kind permission of The British Newspaper Archive at the British Library (www.britishnewspaperarchive.co.uk).

[2]   In 2011, 24.9 per cent of readers of the British left-leaning broadsheet the *Guardian* voted it their favourite Dickens novel, well ahead of the 16.9 per cent who voted for *Bleak House* (Alison Flood, '*Great Expectations* voted readers' favourite Dickens novel: orphan Pip's rise through society thanks to his mysterious benefactor wins poll by comfortable margin', *Guardian*, Monday 3 October 2011). In 2012, according to a Folio Society advertisement, *Guardian* and *Observer* readers voted it one of their top four favourite novels published in Folio Society editions. On 2 December 2010 Oprah Winfrey chose *Great Expectations* and *Oliver Twist* as the perfect holiday reading for her Book Club members.

the British Schools' Minister Nick Gibb singled it out as one of the books all British children should have read before they leave primary school at age 11.[3]

This is a very truncated list, but it should suffice to demonstrate that *Great Expectations* has come to represent a remarkable number of different things in a remarkable number of different contexts in the century and a half since its first appearance. It seems able to stand for the enduring popularity of a long-dead author called Charles Dickens, for the perceived timeless excellence of classic English literature on which we might draw when times are hard or national identity at stake, for the major generic concerns of the nineteenth-century novel, for the problematic imperialist assumptions of the Victorians (and their legacy), for the value of learning to count one's blessings, for the dark underbelly of Western capitalism, for hubristic claims to affluence or influence, and for all the occasions on which we wish to signal optimism which ought to be tempered by realism.

The extraordinary multiplicity of possible cultural readings of Dickens's novel underpins the arguments in this book. How, I ask, have we come to load with such significance those 'passages that lead to nothing'? In what ways and for what purposes has the Dickens heritage industry – and a wide range of other industries – managed to create meaningful images for so long out of those 'rich' but opaque 'windows' of its architecture? More broadly still, what can we hope to gain from a collation and analysis of this Victorian novel's many afterlives? These are large questions, and in tackling them I draw gratefully on the work of the many Dickensians, media historians and literary and cultural theorists who have been thinking about them for many years. A large part of this project, indeed, has been to supplement and as necessary offer corrections to the painstaking work of finding, cataloguing and commenting on the many editions and adaptations of Dickens's works carried out by, among others, Adair Fitz-Gerald (1910), Dubrez Fawcett, (1952), Bolton (1987), Pointer (1996), McFarlane (2008), Glavin, ed. (2003; 2012), and many diligent contributors to the *Dickensian*. But, as my list of research questions above suggests, the focus on a single novel has necessitated thinking beyond bibliometrics. What I'm in search of here is something that might begin to turn lists into patterns.

Patsy Stoneman's *Brontë Transformations: The Cultural Dissemination of Jane Eyre and Wuthering Heights* (1995) broke the ground in which this book is rooted in that she too examines the multiple afterlives of iconic novels in film, TV, theatre and numerous other cultural, literary and visual incarnations. Our approaches differ in important respects, however.[4] Her main focus is on the possible ideological functions of these various incarnations. While I also seek to understand what ideological needs my chosen text might serve in each

---

[3]	Richard Garber, 'Every pupil should read Dickens, says minister … (but he's too hard, says the author's biographer)', *Independent*, 6 February 2012. http://www.independent. co.uk/news/education/education-news/every-pupil-should-read-dickens-says-minister-but-hes-too-hard-says-the-authors-biographer-6579525.html [accessed 20 March 2013].

[4]	Patsy Stoneman, *Brontë Transformations: The Cultural Dissemination of Jane Eyre and Wuthering Heights* (Brighton, 1995).

of its different cultural and historical locations, I attempt to add to the textual deconstruction an equal focus on industry history, situating the phenomenon known as 'Charles Dickens's *Great Expectations*' in terms of a pragmatics of publishing (in its broadest sense). Ideology, I suggest, while indisputably part of the Dickens phenomenon, still constitutes only part of its historical make-up.[5] I am further indebted, therefore, not only to the work of the pioneer of Dickensian book history, Robert Patten (1978), and to early cultural studies approaches such as Paul Schlicke's *Dickens and Popular Entertainment* (1985), but also to the more recent work of scholars such as Juliet John, whose *Dickens and Mass Culture* (2010) offers a timely analysis of the intimate relationship between the form of Dickens's novels and the economic conditions of their production. Dickens himself recognised the importance of this relationship to his career, but for the first half of the twentieth century, at least, his unabashed profit motives and their effect on his literary forms made critics deeply uneasy about him.[6] Now, however, as John rightly claims, 'the seriousness with which the public has taken Dickens since his death has forced professional critics to take his work seriously', and she sees Dickens's afterlives in other media as central to this impetus towards his acceptance in academe.[7] This has been a welcome breakthrough in Dickens studies. But can we trace the workings of this entente through the life of a single Dickens text and, if so, what can such an attempt offer us?

Paul Davis was among the first to tackle the cultural history of a single text in *The Life and Times of Ebenezer Scrooge* (1990), and I have built here upon his notion of the novel as a 'culture text' which is still being written, though I hope to explore the impact of different media industries on that process more thoroughly than he, perhaps with more limited access to archives, was able to do.[8] More recently, James Secord's magisterial *Victorian Sensation: The Extraordinary Publication, Reception, and Secret Authorship of Vestiges of the Natural History of Creation* (2001) took the single text focus in a different direction. Drawing on Chartier's concept of 'object study', his claim for the usefulness of investigating a single bestselling text as a 'cultural tracer' is that we might thereby begin 'to understand the role of the printed word in forging new senses of identity in the industrial age'. Yet Secord warns us against thinking in terms of a 'biography of the book' because, he argues, 'books do not have a "life" of their own independent

---

[5]   As Joss March has sensibly pointed out, we need to remember the significance of the fact that all of Dickens's novels were out of copyright by 1920 and that this made him attractive to early twentieth-century adaptors for reasons that had as much to do with economics as ideology. 'Dickens on Film', in John O. Jordan, ed., *The Cambridge Companion to Charles Dickens* (Cambridge, 2001), p. 204.

[6]   K.J. Fielding dates the resurgence of critical interest to the 1940s with the publication of essays by George Orwell and Edmund Wilson, though it is significant that he does not read enduring popularity as a factor. See Fielding, 'The Critical Autonomy of *Great Expectations*', *Review of English Literature*, 2 (1961): pp. 75–88.

[7]   Juliet John, *Dickens and Mass Culture* (Oxford, 2010), p. 24.

[8]   Paul B. Davis, *The Life and Times of Ebenezer Scrooge* (New Haven, CT, 1990), p. 4.

of their use'.[9] Quite so. I take on board the implicit championing of the role of the reader here, and I too investigate and take very seriously the life which its use by readers, listeners and viewers has given to Dickens's novel over time. But if a sensational new book has only a limited chance at life (if we follow Secord and take the term 'sensation' to mean a significant and very public cultural event),[10] the cultural *text* of which a book is but a part has more options. In cases where its use is multifarious, constantly evolving and still endures today, and where the material object called 'the book' forms only one strand of a tapestry of possible uses, the notion of textual biography is perhaps more useful than Secord recognises. *Vestiges* may have had a finite lifespan as a 'sensation', but the 'cultural event' known as *Great Expectations* (like that known as *A Christmas Carol*) has never died or even (quite) lain dormant in over 150 years. The phrase 'Great Expectations' itself now exists, even in some non-Anglophone cultures, as something outside of its basic grammatical function of noun and qualifying adjective. And while as a pair the two words certainly signified something before the publication of the first instalment on 1 December 1860 (or Dickens would not have chosen them), there is little doubt that afterwards the signifier added something new (many things, in fact) to its list of signifieds.[11] I persist here, therefore, in thinking in terms of a 'biography of the text' in the belief that in this case the metaphor might bear some useful epistemological fruit. Like Secord, I use this novel as a 'cultural tracer'; but since, unlike Secord's, my subject leaves traces in cultures far beyond 'the industrial age' in which readers first encountered and responded to it, I must perforce ask an additional set of questions. In tracing as many of the paths taken by this Dickens novel as possible over time, I try to understand how and why and in what ways this 'classic' mid-Victorian text, filled with all the prejudices and assumptions and hopes and fears of its age, has appealed to succeeding generations of adaptors and consumers in so many different national contexts.

In many ways *Great Expectations* is an unlikely candidate for the kind of immortality it has enjoyed. After an initial flurry of interest in the serial had passed it was not as popular in the nineteenth century as Dickens's earlier works, and it took time for it to gain new fans in the twentieth. There are many possible reasons

---

[9]   James A. Secord, *Victorian Sensation: The Extraordinary Publication, Reception, and Secret Authorship of Vestiges of the Natural History of Creation* (Chicago, 2001), pp. 2–3.

[10]   Secord, *Victorian Sensation*, p. 11.

[11]   David Paroissien suggests that the name may have originated in references to 'great expectation' appearing in two works with which we know Dickens was familiar: Sir Philip Sidney's *Astrophil and Stella* (c.1580s) and Milton's *Paradise Lost* (1667). Paroissien, *The Companion to Great Expectations* (Robertsbridge, Sussex, 2000), p. 21. Edgar Rosenberg points out, however, that the phrase was very well known to Victorians and – perhaps more significantly – that Charles Lever had used it in passing in number 7 (Ch. 9) of *A Day's Ride*, just a couple of days before Dickens began the novel that bumped it off the top spot in *All the Year Round*. Dickens had, of course, read the proofs of those chapters while contemplating what to call his new serial. Charles Dickens, *Great Expectations*, ed. by Edgar Rosenberg (New York, 1999), p. 422.

for this, some obvious, some less so. Unlike *A Christmas Carol* it is not able to define and help us to celebrate a public holiday: the fact that its opening scenes take place on Christmas Eve has not made it very successfully into our cultural memory (not least, perhaps, because Magwitch is no one's idea of the perfect Christmas present, and because the novel refuses to fulfil any of the dearest wishes of its orphan child protagonist). Unlike *Oliver Twist* it does not engage polemically with institutional iniquity or the rights of children, despite its obsessions with class prejudice and bad parenting. Perhaps the greatest social iniquity in the text concerns the treatment of criminals, and for a satisfactory exploration of that we have required several (particularly antipodean) recastings. So how and why has it become the Dickens book that (middle-class and largely middle-aged) twenty-first-century readers most often cite as their favourite?

Juliet John puts Dickens's twentieth-century revival down to his novels' formal properties: 'Dickens's popularity and respectability in the post-Victorian period have been mutually reinforcing in the sense that the very qualities that proved problematic to critics for so long – the machinic and formulaic style of his art, in particular – have aided the mass dissemination of his art.'[12] But popularity has not been equally or consistently distributed across the whole oeuvre of his novels since *Pickwick* in 1836–37, and this cannot be explained purely by the relative mass-dissemination ('machinic and formulaic') potential of their respective forms. *Great Expectations* is arguably no less 'machinic and formulaic' than other Dickens novels; indeed, Elizabeth Karlsen, producer of the latest film version directed by Mike Newell (BBC/Lipsync/Number 9 Films, 2012), told me during shooting in 2011 that her team chose this novel for their bicentenary remake because it is among the easiest Dickens to adapt, having a simple tripartite structure, a strong narrative momentum with regular dramatic peaks, and fewer subplots and digressions than almost any of his other works.[13] But, as this book will show, these qualities were not immediately apparent to nineteenth and early twentieth-century theatre, film or radio adaptors; the adaptations of this novel were relatively slow to happen, and when they did, they were not at first particularly successful. 'Machinic' and 'formulaic' properties are a crucial part of Dickens's creative practice, but they are insufficient explanations in themselves for mass dissemination or relative popularity. I suggest here, therefore, that a 'classic' novel's formal and thematic properties need to be situated within the framework of its culture's shifting publishing and reception contexts if we are to we approach an understanding of its power over time and space.

With this in mind, in chapters 1 and 2, I sketch out the importance of the novel's genesis as an emergency measure written at speed to rescue the fluctuating fortunes of Dickens's new journal *All the Year Round* (AYR), situating its first appearance in instalments, its subsequent publication in volume form and its adaptation for public

---

[12]   John, *Dickens and Mass Culture*, pp. 24–5.

[13]   Author's interview with Elizabeth Karlsen (Producer, Number 9 Films) on location in Hounslow, London, 27 October 2011. All material from this interview is reproduced with the kind permission of Ms Karlsen.

performance between 1860 and 1900 in the contexts of periodical publication, international piracy and the circulation of the notion of celebrity authorship in popular discourse. Most critical editions of *Great Expectations* appearing in the last 20 years have, of course, fully acknowledged its important early publication history, Margaret Cardwell's Oxford edition of 1998 and Edgar Rosenberg's Norton Critical Edition of 1999 being among the best of these. Some scholars have, in addition, examined in great detail Dickens's relationships with the theatre (Jordan, ed., 2001; Glavin, 1999; Callow, 2012), or with popular culture in general (Schlicke, 1985; Vlock, 1998). What I hope to add to this scholarship stems from the fact that my 'biography' does not end with the death of the author or the end of the nineteenth century, and it is not limited to just one aspect of (or media response to) the cultural event he created in 1860–61. My interest is primarily in what happens to this 'event' after it has passed out of the control of its author and his publishers.

Rather than repeating at great length an early publication history that is very well known to Dickensians and very widely available to the general reader, then, I use these first two chapters to examine the development in the nineteenth century of a cultural vocabulary coalescing around Dickens's pre- and posthumous fame and to chart its course on both sides of the Atlantic. The early stages of this process have been mapped in intriguing ways by both Robert Douglas-Fairhurst (2008) and Robert L. Patten, whose *Charles Dickens and "Boz": The Birth of the Industrial-Age Author* (2012) has informed much of my thinking here about the relationship between authorial self-construction and emergent modern media. I pick up the story roughly where Patten leaves off, in the mid-1850s, during the 'last phase' of the birth of the industrial-age author.[14] This was a phase during which Dickens might have been emotionally troubled and physically exhausted, but it was one which he nevertheless controlled with all the professional clarity, energy and experience his early experiments with self-fashioning had taught him. The history of *Great Expectations* is filled with the evidence of Dickens's understanding of and active engagement with Victorian publishing and reading practices.

Subsequent chapters explore how Dickens's posthumous fame and the uses to which it has been put have helped to construct *Great Expectations'* global public persona in the new media age. Chapter 3 traces the importance of the Dickens brand to the fluctuating fortunes of Western theatre and to the development of the competing new media of radio, TV and film in the UK and USA between 1900 and 1945. While acknowledging the formal and conceptual relationships between Dickens and the new media as demonstrated by several scholars, I argue here that of equal importance is Dickens's practical applicability to media industry needs, in particular his unexceptionable morality, his familiarity to readers and his availability in the public domain after his copyrights expired. He may well, as Grahame Smith has argued, to an important extent have 'dreamed' the cinema and produced works so easily visualised that their transference to the big screen seemed

---

[14]   Robert L. Patten, *Charles Dickens and "Boz": The Birth of the Industrial-Age Author* (Cambridge, 2012), p. 327.

almost a matter of inevitability (Sergei Eisenstein famously thought so).[15] His humour, his dialogue and the clear character differentiation for which he was well known may have made radio adaptation seem equally natural.[16] The episodic nature of his plots may have lent themselves easily to serialisation on TV, whether or not one subscribes to the Dickens-as-early-soap-opera argument.[17] But, as a focus on the single example of *Great Expectations* is able to demonstrate, the synergy was not smooth, or inevitable, or exactly the same in each cultural or historical location. The posthumous Dickens brand diversifies in important ways, demonstrating a wide range of national, ideological and industrial motivations. This chapter examines the role played by *Great Expectations* in the early struggles for self-definition and legitimisation of these nascent media industries between 1900 and 1945 and explores the very different shapes the recasting took in Britain as compared to the USA, the countries in which these new media industries cut their teeth.

Literature's capacity to shape-shift was not new, of course, even in the early part of the twentieth century. As Rachel Malik has shown, the nineteenth-century novel in general and Dickens's novels in particular demonstrate keen Victorian awareness of the fact that, since readers were becoming 'sophisticated genre-switchers' and competition for their attention and their hard-earned cash was becoming increasingly fierce, fiction developed an ever more flexible internal 'horizon of the publishable' in response, rendering itself comprehensible in a number of different forms: serialised, complete, staged, illustrated, non-illustrated and so on.[18] It is significant, I think, that she feels this generic flexibility applies particularly to *Great Expectations*, forged as it was in the crucible of an author's urgent need for an immediate hit with staying power and a periodical industry undergoing major changes, from the launch of the shilling periodical to the repeal of the last of the 'taxes on knowledge', Paper Duty, in 1861. Malik demonstrates (through a neat melding of the methodologies of literary criticism and book history for which she has argued elsewhere[19]) that *Great Expectations* is exemplary in this respect due to what she calls its unusual 'capsularity':

> This ... involves the development of a number of relatively autonomous stories, which can be lightly coupled or decoupled by the addition or subtraction of a sentence or even a phrase.... It is a compositional practice that presumes

---

[15] Grahame Smith, *Dickens and the Dream of Cinema* (Manchester, 2003). Sergei Eisenstein, 'Dickens, Griffith, and the Film Today', in *Film Form: Essays in Film Theory and The Film Sense*, ed. and trans. by Jay Leyda (New York, 1957), pp. 195–255.

[16] Early BBC radio programmers discussed this issue at some length and listeners enthusiastically joined the debate, as I show in Chapter 3.

[17] Some recent additions to the debate about Dickens and soap opera can be found here on David Perdue's always lively Charles Dickens web page http://charlesdickenspage.com/Soft_Soaping_Dickens.html.

[18] Rachel Malik, 'Stories Many, Fast and Slow: *Great Expectations* and the Mid-Victorian Horizon of the Publishable', *English Literary History*, 79 (2012): p. 479.

[19] Rachel Malik, 'Horizons of the Publishable: Publishing in/as Literary Studies', *English Literary History*, 75 (2008): pp. 707–35.

accelerated processes of multiform publishing (most obviously here, abridgement and anthologization) and translation into other mediatic forms (most obviously here, public performance) that will succeed and sometimes exist alongside each other. It is not of course peculiar to Dickens, though he is an extreme proponent, and it is his dominant method.[20]

The notion that a Dickens novel demonstrated a 'capsular' form some twenty years before the newspaper industry would capitalise on the idea of bite-sized reading with the marketing of the 'tabloid' daily provides intriguing evidence of the relationships between different media and modernity. It also offers proof of Dickens's remarkable creative and professional prescience. But Malik's railway metaphor of the easy 'coupling' and 'decoupling' which *Great Expectations's* 'relatively autonomous stories' makes possible is equally useful, adding to John's notion of the 'machinic qualities' of his prose the intriguing suggestion that some parts, at least, of Dickens's thirteenth novel were more freight than engine, and that that makes them infinitely more dispensable.[21]

I build on the idea of continuities – both industrial and historical – in the first part of Chapter 4, where I trace the fortunes of this novel with its unusually expansive 'horizon(s) of the publishable' as they were defined by – and indeed helped to define – the developments of the four main non-literary media beyond the era of the 'industrial-age author' and into the age of new technologies after World War II. Here, utilising Malik's model of the novel as usefully 'capsular' in form, I examine adaptations for the stage, TV, film and radio in the UK and the USA between 1946 and 2000, considering the *Great Expectations* phenomenon's evolving shapes as these four media industries competed for increasingly diverse national and international markets in this period, and frequently (though not always successfully) used Dickens as a means to do so.

Chapter 5, covering translations between 1860 and 2012, picks up the thread of the novel's non-Anglophone and non-Western lives introduced here, first by returning us to the nineteenth century and the first translations and foreign English-language editions of *Great Expectations* which appeared during Dickens's lifetime, and then by examining its posthumous global spread, helped by its translation into different media in the twentieth and twenty-first centuries. Dickens has had a remarkable life in non-Anglophone cultures, as Professor Ada Nisbet spent upward of 20 years trying to prove,[22] and as more recent work has amply borne out. Standing out among these recent examples are the two volumes of *The Reception of Charles Dickens in Europe*, edited by Michael Hollington (2013), and the essays brought together in the useful volume *Global Dickens*, edited by John O. Jordan and Nirshan Perera (2012), which between them represent more than two decades of increasing interest and specialism in the global Dickens phenomenon.

---

[20]   Malik, 'Stories Many, Fast and Slow', p. 485.

[21]   John, *Dickens and Mass Culture*, p. 124.

[22]   Like Hollington, I have drawn gratefully in this chapter on the Ada B. Nisbet archive at the University of California, Santa Cruz. For more on this ill-fated project and its rich legacy, see John O. Jordan, 'Global Dickens', *Literature Compass*, 6 (2009): pp. 1211–23.

While I cannot hope to offer as thorough an account of global Dickens as has been achieved by all this scholarship, I try to provide a fuller list of translations of this one novel than has ever previously been compiled in an attempt to contextualise its place in comparative studies more broadly.

We will see that while *Great Expectations* was widely translated, bought, borrowed, taught and thus (possibly) enjoyed in some cultural contexts, in others it was deeply problematic, rejected after a translation attempt or two or simply unknown, sometimes for more than a century. This makes it both typical but also – in some contexts – quite unusual in the Dickens oeuvre. Given the novel's uneven Anglophone reception history as mapped out in my first four chapters, I suggest here that one might also read *Great Expectations'* global history dialogically, seeing it as representative of the spread and appropriation of, or resistance to, Anglophone literary culture more generally. But I also suggest that such an analysis can shed light on the novel itself, particularly on its available range of meanings over time. I believe we can trace through this example of a 'classic' Victorian novel's reception in non-Western, non-Anglophone locations an illuminating range of responses to its supposed topicality and the supposed universality (or indeed conservatism, or insularity) of its themes.[23]

Later sections of Chapter 5 take the term 'translation' in its broadest sense, to mean not only 'removal or conveyance from one person, place, or condition to another', but also the 'expression or rendering of something in another medium or form'.[24] Postcolonial and feminist 'writing back', as exemplified by (among others) Lloyd Jones's *Mister Pip* (2006), Peter Carey's *Jack Maggs* (1997), Kathy Acker's *Great Expectations* (1983) and Sue Roe's *Estella: Her Expectations* (1982), is one of the key ways in which this type of translation occurs. Ankhi Mukherjee has characterised rewritings of canonical novels in general and *Great Expectations* in particular as

> a project of denaturalizing, defamiliarizing, and problematizing 'natural givens' in a master text. The constructedness of the literary artifact is seen, in these second comings, as analogous to the constructedness of identity categories and cultural formations: the work of rewriting, then, is to look awry at virtual pasts, interrupt collective identities and the habitual coherence of cultural experience, and confront the social discourse informing memorable acts of literature.[25]

---

[23] Franco Moretti makes a similar point. He tells us that British adults rejected French and most other European novels and the stylistic innovations they offered and instead, as a result of their insular prudishness, they 'read *David Copperfield*, and it serves them right'. Franco Moretti, *Atlas of the European Novel 1800–1900* (New York and London, 1998), p. 158.

[24] OED Online, s.v. 'translation', http://www.oed.com/view/Entry/204844?redirected From=translation#eid [accessed 23 August 2013].

[25] Ankhi Mukherjee, 'Missed Encounters: Repetition, Rewriting, and Contemporary Returns to Charles Dickens's *Great Expectations*', *Contemporary Literature*, 46 (2005): p. 109.

Here Mukherjee introduces an idea which is never fully focalised in her article, but which highlights my concerns in this section: that 'natural givens' and 'the social discourse informing memorable acts of literature' are themselves constructs worthy of attention. If rewritings tell us nothing else, it is that the 'authentic', canonical 'master' text is an illusion, something that must be *constructed* in a particular way in order to be *de*-constructed for a particular purpose. Previous chapters have demonstrated some of the ways in which these constructions have taken place. In the final section of Chapter 5, I examine some of the works bent on deconstruction.

Elsewhere, Mukherjee's article is (albeit implicitly) alert to the dynamics I am suggesting: she begins by reading Julian Barnes's novel about the construction of a national theme park, *England, England* (1998), as an investigation of what she calls the 'specular dualism of originality and replication'.[26] Her conclusions about Barnes's novel are useful:

> We prefer the replica [the theme park called 'England'] to the original [the geographical/ideological location known as 'England'] because it opens up endless possibilities of differential reproduction.... Replication in this sense does not follow the law of recurrence or the logic of compulsive returns but is a mode of inventiveness that, through its reiterative structure, mobilizes narrative instead of arresting it.[27]

The revivification and mobilisation principles she suggests here help to explain – and to illuminate the machinations of – the diversity and number of adaptations and rewritings which *Great Expectations* has engendered in a range of national and linguistic contexts, and to move us beyond earlier models which saw the pleasure of repetition as the most fundamental attraction of an adaptation.[28]

Mukherjee does not refer here to the model proposed by Jay David Bolter and Richard Grusin in 1998, but her analysis is very much akin to it. Bolter and Grusin, motivated by the proliferation of cyber technologies such as video gaming in the 1990s, think in terms not of adaptation or rewriting but of remediation, by which they mean the ways in which each new adaptation of a text 'oscillate[s] between immediacy [in effect, the suspension of disbelief] and hypermediacy [a hyper-awareness of the media through which the information comes], between transparency and opacity'. As they explain: 'Although each medium promises to reform its predecessors by offering a more immediate or authentic experience, the

---

26 Mukherjee, 'Missed Encounters', p. 108.

27 Mukherjee, 'Missed Encounters', pp. 108–9.

28 Thomas Ellis, for example, has argued: 'Adaptation into another medium becomes a means of prolonging the pleasure of the original presentation, and repeating the production of memory.' See 'The Literary Adaptation – an Introduction', *Screen*, 23 (1982): p. 4. For more on fidelity criticism and the struggle to be free of it, see John Glavin's useful introduction to *Dickens Adapted* in the Ashgate *Library of Essays on Charles Dickens* series (Burlington, VT, and Farnham, 2012), and Sarah Cardwell's 'Theory Revisited', chapter 3 in *Adaptation Revisited: Adaptation and the Classic Novel* (Manchester, 2002).

promise of reform inevitably leads us to become aware of the new medium as a medium.' This process depends on the one hand on understanding the adaptation as 'a play of signs', a concept drawn from poststructuralist literary theory, and on the other on reading the media as powerful – and real – 'agents in our culture', self-referential, often self-celebratory, and above all representative of the 'practices of specific groups in specific times'.[29]

For me, the usefulness of this concept of remediation is twofold, since it places equal emphasis on the creative and essentially ongoing process of textual renewal, and the role played in this process by a range of media showcasing their own technical dexterity. First, it enables me to consider the cultural (including industry-motivated) uses to which this novel has been put without shackling me either to technological determinism or to fidelity criticism, which has tended to judge all adaptations through the lens of their likeness to an ('the') original text. Second, and by a logical extension, it enables me to think about the cultural event called 'Charles Dickens's *Great Expectations*', not as an immutable work of art to be kept behind glass and admired from a distance (or, *pace* Nick Gibb, force-fed to schoolchildren to test their attention spans, inject them with cultural capital, or inculcate national pride), but as an Ali Baba's cave of treasures which can be – and, perhaps more importantly, always has been – plundered at will. While Dickens felt as he finished writing *Great Expectations* that he wished everyone could have read it all at once and that the third part in particular worked best as a whole,[30] as an author acutely alert to the vagaries and the plurality of nineteenth-century market forces and badly in need of a hit he had written it to be easily decoupled and recoupled in different ways, to be endlessly remade and remediated. He wrote it in the full knowledge that it would be (*needed* to be), published in serial form, then reissued in three volumes and finally in one; that it had to be of interest to both British and American (and indeed continental European) audiences and to work whether illustrated or non-illustrated; that it could be performed as extracted readings or acted on the stage. He probably also hoped that it would furnish newspaper editors with catchphrases and caricatures, and engender spin-offs in the shape of popular songs, perfumes or bonnets. As a result, after his death it was readily available for theatre, radio, television and film adaptations, and also for cartooning and advertising and pilfering for memorable names and useful stereotypes. Dickens created a 'cultural event' the integrity of which cannot be compromised because its remediation potential was inbuilt. This does not mean all the remediations have been commercially or aesthetically successful, of course; they have not. But even the relative failures are useful, not because they show up the 'superiority' of the 'original' which they are trying to render anew, but because they are filled with historical traces of the uses to which Dickens has been put and the shifting meanings attaching to the 'event' he began in 1860.

---

[29]   Jay David Bolter and Richard Grusin, *Remediation: Understanding New Media* (Cambridge, MA, 1998), pp. 19–20.

[30]   Letter to Forster, mid-April 1861, *Letters of Charles Dickens*, Vol. 9: 1859–61, ed. by Graham Storey, Margaret Brown and Kathleen Tillotson (Oxford, 1965–97), p. 403.

The whole notion of 'compromising' or 'diluting' the aura (to borrow Walter Benjamin's term) of a Dickens text by adapting it is, in fact, another example of the 'constructedness of the literary artefact', in this case a construction of the post-Victorian multimedia age. To John Glavin's provocative question 'Is there anything that a study of Dickens, the novels, can contribute to the study of Dickens adaptations?', I must therefore answer (in opposition to Glavin himself), yes, there is; but only if we add to our obsession with literary forensics, our constant fingerprinting of the texts of the past for incriminating traces of ideology, an equal acknowledgement of the pragmatics of their survival.[31] Not just the text of the novels, but the characteristics which make them responsive to changing publishing and reception contexts are the reason we still have adaptations of them; we must understand these things as interdependent if we are to understand them at all.

Jeffrey Sconce has come to a related conclusion about the interdependence of form and function, noting:

> [I]t may well be that classical Hollywood narrative was but a detour in the textual modes established in the serialized nineteenth-century novel and resumed by television, albeit in a wholly different historical moment of production and reception.... While most literature on Dickens's legacy in the twentieth century has focused on his role in influencing Hollywood's focus on "bourgeois realism," it is in fact Dickens's (and the nineteenth-century novel's) emphasis on serial narrative and episodic emplotment that has proven a more lasting influence on the more lasting narrative technology of our past century – television.[32]

I broadly agree, though I reject both Sconce's teleological assumptions about television and Dickens's natural suitability for it and his conclusions about Dickens's role in perpetuating British cultural authority. 'At the turn of the twenty-first century', he claims, analysing the irreverent *South Park* episode 'Pip':

> the truce negotiated by Selznik [in publicly consulting the British on the casting of his Hollywood film version of *David Copperfield* in 1935] ... has devolved into hollow absurdity. The cultural authority of the British, so long courted by the American culture industry, serves in this context as little more than the fodder for a joke about America's (or more specifically, the typical PBS subscriber's) haughty search for cultural enrichment in the English classics.[33]

As I will demonstrate, *South Park* notwithstanding, the veneration of 'British cultural authority' insofar as it has manifested itself in Dickens has never been without its critics in the USA; neither has it entirely subsided or degenerated into a joke in the recent past. As always, it has merely begun to take different forms; and as always, while some of these have been reverential, some have not.

---

[31] John Glavin, 'Introduction' to *A Library of Essays on Charles Dickens: Dickens Adapted*, p. xvi.

[32] Jeffrey Sconce, 'Dickens, Selznik, and Southpark', in *Dickens on Screen*, ed. by John Glavin (Cambridge, 2003), p. 183.

[33] Sconce, 'Dickens, Selznik and Southpark', p. 172.

Sarah Cardwell comes nearer to articulating my underlying premise in these later chapters when she recognises that we need to move away both from a qualitative comparative analysis of different media, and from the view of literary texts of the past as author-centred 'standard wholes'. For Cardwell, we need to develop a model that views adaptation as 'the gradual development of a meta-text'.[34] My emphasis throughout this book is on *Great Expectations* as a meta-text; I depart from Cardwell, though, in that I suggest the novel has always been one. It has never been a stable original or a fixed signified; it has always been 'in development', creating and enabling a wide range of cultural meanings of which adaptations on the stage, film, radio and TV form a part. Adaptations, that is, merely contribute new layers to a text that has always offered itself for rewriting.

The final sections of Chapter 5 are informed by my analysis of the latest adaptations to remediate *Great Expectations* (both the text and the history of its fame): the novels of the 1980s and 90s, the 2011 three-part TV series and the 2012 film. These sections explore how the many rewritings of *Great Expectations* in a neo-Victorian/postcolonial context have sought to challenge the perpetuation through 'classic' literature of profoundly marginalising national, racial and gender ideologies. As Cora Kaplan has put it, these neo-Victorian 'writings back', while respectful, ask the reader 'to reflect on the power relations of writing and reading that reach across centuries and continents', and to remember that Dickens's novels were not outside, but a part and product of 'the history of Empire and its aftermath'.[35] But here, also, I invoke the literary remediations that playfully celebrate – sometimes in addition to seeking to correct – Dickens's thirteenth novel by briefly discussing some of the most recent adaptations which spin-off its characters: cult genre novels. In 2013 these are still proliferating and serve to keep some aspects of the meta-text alive for a new generation, even as others wither on the vine and Dickens's name as its author begins to fall out of parts of our cultural memory. Despite confident bicentenary claims for the novel's eternal relevance and power, at the time of writing a recent survey has just demonstrated that a third of British people interviewed had 'no idea who wrote *Great Expectations*', something which I did not foresee when I began this book.[36] The next – perhaps the last – phase in the novel's long life already seems to be underway.

A Note on Organisation

It has probably become apparent by now that this book is not organised completely chronologically. This is deliberate: the many turnings and doublings-back I take are

---

[34] Sarah Cardwell, *Adaptation Revisited*, pp. 20 and 25.

[35] Cora Kaplan, 'Neo-Victorian Dickens', in *Charles Dickens in Context*, ed. by Holly Furneaux and Sally Ledger (Cambridge, 2011), p. 87.

[36] Andrew Levy, *Mail Online*, 25 September 2013, http://www.dailymail.co.uk/news/article-2431259/Now-Dickens-wrote-er-Great-Expectations-Third-adults-idea-wrote-classic-novel.html [accessed 12 November 2013].

not meant to confuse the reader, but to suggest sometimes parallel developments. Just as Dickens wrote, thought and did many other things while he was composing *Great Expectations*, so the lives and influences of its many adaptors, readers, translators and rewriters overlapped in inconveniently messy but revealing ways which it seems important to try to capture. This is one more reason to think in terms of patterns rather than lists. I do include lists in my appendices, of course – quite lengthy ones in fact – and these are provided in the hope that, being fuller, they are more useful than previous versions. Still, it would be foolish to speak of this book as comprehensive in any way. For one thing, evidence for the early periods is often fragmentary and sometimes quite sparse, and I have frequently had to infer patterns from nothing more concrete than a widely spaced set of coordinates. For another, the opposite problem obtains for the later periods: there is too much information. I have therefore, in some instances, spurned the famous and the obvious and chosen to focus on adaptations that have not been fully discussed before, and on information that is held in archives rather than on the more readily accessible data available online, in the belief that the reader will find these discussions more immediately (and hopefully enduringly) useful. For this reason, my select list of editions (Appendix A) does not include either the numerous and often substandard reissues of the most significant editions published between 1861 and World War II, or new editions published after 1939, which are readily available on internet sites such as Amazon.com and are still proliferating so fast that to seek to include them all would be to make the Appendix redundant before it ever saw print.

There have been space constraints, too, and for this reason I do not include in Appendix C the many thousands of amateur theatrical productions there have no doubt been of *Great Expectations* over the years, or indeed many of those performed outside of the USA and UK – unless they struck me as particularly significant. It is not that I think them unimportant; it is simply that they are often impossible to trace and any discussion of them could therefore only be skewed and partial. Equally, I do not include North American radio adaptations (Appendix C) beyond the 'Golden Age' of the 1950s, after radio stations proliferated in the different states of the USA and searching for a single episode title becomes almost impossible. Material books have boundaries, after all, and one must stop somewhere. I have decided to set my boundaries around what can be known or at least reasonably inferred from extant records, what professional productions can tell us about official cultural discourses in different national and generational contexts, and how new and/or changing media industries in need of a hit utilise and perpetuate the famous. But, these caveats aside, it has been my aim here to cover as much ground as humanly possible. Perhaps the necessary gaps I have left open will pave the way for future work which, like this book, will also become part of the *Great Expectations* meta-text, if not part of its obituary.

Chapter 1

The Entry of a New Novel into the Western World, 1860–1870

'Mr Dickens's Great Expectations have decidedly disappointed the great expectations raised by themselves'.

—*Hereford Journal*, Wednesday 13 March 1861, p. 5.

Beginnings: 'A very fine, new, and grotesque idea'

The first reference Dickens makes to the beginning of a new story forming in his mind after he had finished *A Tale of Two Cities* are generally agreed to have appeared in a letter of 8 August 1860 written to the Earl of Carlisle, in which he says: 'I am prowling about, meditating a new book.'[1] A few days later he made similar statements to Alfred Wigan, manager of the Olympic Theatre, and on 14 September he wrote to his friend Mrs Richard Watson: 'I ... am on the restless eve of beginning a new big book.'[2] In his biography of Dickens (1871–74), his oldest friend and advisor John Forster gives us something more concrete when he tells us that the germ of *Great Expectations* – what Dickens famously described as the 'very fine, new, and grotesque idea' that, according to the Pilgrim editors, was to become Pip and Magwitch – appeared in a letter to him which they date at around this same time (mid-September 1860).[3] But there are also suggestions that the idea may have been brewing even earlier: Stanley Friedman dates the beginnings of the idea to 1858, when Dickens had been to see James Byron's burletta 'The Maid and the Magpie: or, The Fatal Spoon', in which a character called Pippo is mistreated by a domineering woman and shielded by her kindly husband.[4] Margaret Cardwell, citing a letter to Dickens's manager W.H. Wills, also suggests that the idea may have arisen at the end of 1858.[5] But given Dickens's emphasis almost a year later

---

[1]   *Letters*, Vol. 9, p. 284. *A Tale of Two Cities* was serialised in AYR, 30 April 1859 – 26 November 1859.

[2]   *Letters*, Vol. 9, p. 309.

[3]   John Forster, *Life of Charles Dickens* (London, 1872), p. 800, and *Letters*, Vol. 9, p. 310. There is a possibility, of course, that this 'germ' may have grown equally out of the Pip and Joe story since Dickens describes it in this same letter as 'singular and comic', and since it is this relationship which drives a large part of the story. I am grateful to Bob Patten for his insights here.

[4]   Stanley Friedman, 'The Complex Origins of Pip and Magwitch', *Dickens Studies Annual*, 15 (1986): pp. 221–31.

[5]   Charles Dickens, *Great Expectations*, ed. by Margaret Cardwell (Oxford, 1993), p. xxii.

on the idea being a 'new' one I think this unlikely, unless Forster had performed a greater than usual act of epistolary larceny and claimed that he was the recipient of a letter written much earlier to someone else, or – perhaps less likely – the Pilgrim editors have got the date wrong. But the point is probably moot in any case. Even if the first creative glimmer had occurred much earlier, getting an idea for a new book is not the same thing as beginning to write it, and for various reasons Dickens was not able or willing to act on the idea in 1859 or during the first part of 1860. In a letter to George Lewes dated 20 November 1859, in which he tries to persuade Lewes's partner George Eliot to write a novel for AYR to follow Wilkie Collins's *The Woman in White*, he says: 'My original idea was, that her [Eliot's] story might follow Collins's, and that I might follow her.' But in the next sentence, in attempting to give Eliot more time he has given himself a reprieve also: 'Now, supposing I were to put Mrs Gaskell next after Collins – say for a four or six months' story – would *that* do?'[6] If this plan had come off, it would have meant he himself was under no obligation to begin a new serial until at least the summer of 1861.[7] He had not taken a complete break from writing, of course; he later expresses to Collins his plan of 'coming in to back you up, if I can get an idea for my series of gossiping papers', but here he is clearly referring to the first series of the 'Uncommercial Traveller' articles published in AYR between 28 January and 13 October 1860.[8] After the punishing schedule of producing *A Tale of Two Cities* for his new weekly (a format which he always found hard), Dickens needed a break.

However one interprets the available references to a new story, then, it seems clear that during the last months of 1859 and the early part of 1860 Dickens's mind was not particularly focussed on fiction; as he put it in the same letter to Collins, while he had hoped that 'one of these days, please God' they might collaborate on another story, his ideas even for a collaboration were at that time 'very odd half-formed notions – in a mist'.[9] Only several months later, in August 1860, did he suggest to his publishers that he hoped he would soon be in a position to discuss 'a new Serial Story' with them, at that stage still planned to appear in 20 monthly numbers as of old.[10]

The reasons for Dickens's apparent unwillingness to focus on a major new book were many and genuine, and are too well-known to require much more than a brief reminder here of their relevance to *Great Expectations*' form and themes. In

------

[6]   *Letters*, Vol. 9, p. 168.

[7]   Collins's fifth novel, *The Woman in White* was published between 26 November 1859 and 25 August 1860. Two more serials following Collins's would have given Dickens up to a year's grace.

[8]   Letter to Wilkie Collins, 7 January 1860. *Letters*, Vol. 9, p. 195. This first series of 16 articles was published in volume form by Tauchnitz in Germany on 13 December 1860 and by Chapman and Hall in London on 15 December. *The Dent Uniform Edition of Dickens' Journalism*, Vol. 4: *'The Uncommercial Traveller' and Other Papers 1859–70*, ed. by Michael Slater and John Drew (London, 2000), p. 199.

[9]   *Letters*, Vol. 9, p. 195. Collins and Dickens had collaborated successfully on several projects, sometimes also with other writers, since 1854.

[10]   Letter to Frederic Chapman, 24 August 1860. *Letters*, Vol. 9, p. 294.

1858 he had separated very publicly from his wife Catherine, and he was pursuing (some biographers think unsuccessfully at that time) a much less public infatuation with the young actress who was later alleged to have become his mistress, Ellen ('Nelly') Ternan.[11] This emotional upheaval created others. Dickens was a loyal but at times irrational and intractable friend, and his marital troubles caused a rift between himself and several long-term friends or associates, among them *Punch* editor Mark Lemon, the novelist William Makepeace Thackeray, and his publishers William Bradbury and Frederick Mullet Evans. This particular falling-out broke up the successful magazine *Household Words* (HW), which since 1850 had been edited by Dickens and co-owned by Dickens, Wills, Forster (briefly) and Bradbury and Evans, and brought another level of anxiety in the shape of the launch of its replacement AYR in 1859 in the face of some fairly stiff new competition. In November of that year Dickens also lost his good friend, neighbour and one-time illustrator Frank Stone, and (generous to a fault as well as irascible) made himself responsible for Stone's bereaved family. The emotional rollercoaster continued into the following year and the pressure began to take its toll on his health: throughout the winter he suffered from what he called a 'bachelor' ailment and in the first part of 1860 he had an acute attack of rheumatism in his left side, followed by facial pains which were to dog him throughout the writing process.[12] In the middle of 1860 he had to deal with the death of his younger brother Alfred (who succumbed to pleurisy on 27 July at the early age of 38), and the consequent dependence on him of his sister-in-law and five nieces and nephews under 14 – whom he called (perhaps significantly for the opening pages of *Great Expectations*) 'five little witnesses' to the tragedy.[13] He was also at this time responsible for moving his mother to new accommodation, as she was succumbing to dementia and could no longer be left alone.[14] Simultaneously he was negotiating the sale of his house in Tavistock Square, London, (sold 4 September 1860) and handling the refitting of his Kent country house, Gad's Hill Place (bought in 1856), and he was involved in planning his daughter Katey's wedding to a man of whom he disapproved.[15] For Dickens, personal problems always seemed to have financial ramifications; all these issues meant he had to keep earning, more than ever, and that AYR had to succeed if he and the three other households he was supporting were to stay afloat.[16] Suffice it to say that had tests for stress existed in 1860 and contained the top ten factors which we now associate with it – highest among them bereavement, marital problems, money and illness (not to mention moving house and weddings) – Dickens, now aged 48 but looking and feeling much older, would have scored off the chart.

---

[11]   See, for example, Claire Tomalin, *Charles Dickens: A Life* (London, 2011), p. 327.

[12]   Tomalin suggests this might have been gonorrhoea. *Charles Dickens*, p. 316.

[13]   Letter to Angela Burdett-Coutts, 3 August 1860. *Letters*, Vol. 9, p. 280.

[14]   Letter to Mrs Frances Dickinson, 19 August 1860. *Letters*, Vol. 9, p. 287.

[15]   Dickens's youngest surviving daughter Katey (1839–1929) married Wilkie Collins's brother Charles Allston Collins (1828–73), who was 11 years her senior and sickly, on 17 July 1860.

[16]   The three households were those of his wife, the Ternans, and his mother, whom he had lodged with his sister-in-law and the 'five little witnesses'.

The year 1859–60 was, then, extraordinary in more ways than one. It was not all bad news; despite the lukewarm and in some cases hostile critical reception of *A Tale of Two Cities*, readers seemed to like it and the new magazine had initially done very well. Dickens was delighted with its early circulation as first his own story and then *The Woman in White* ran their courses, and although George Eliot had turned his offer down he had equally high hopes for its successor, Charles Lever's *A Day's Ride: A Life's Romance*, serialised in AYR 18 August 1860 – 23 March 1861. Unfortunately for Lever but fortunately for posterity, this story proved so unpopular with readers that the magazine's circulation began to fall dramatically, and Dickens had no choice but to wade in and attempt to come to the rescue by turning his 'fine, new and grotesque idea' into a novel more swiftly than he would have liked, or his personal circumstances suggested was entirely wise. 'I called a council of war at the office on Tuesday', he wrote to Forster on 4 October. 'It was perfectly clear that the one thing to be done was, for me to strike in.' He wrote a tactful 'business report' to Lever on 6 October explaining the situation, and the deed was done.[17]

Even before circumstances forced his hand, however, Dickens was taking action of another sort that was to have a bearing on *Great Expectations*. Apparently sensing that the new novel would contain elements of his feelings about his life and that given his current state of mind he had better manage them very carefully, on 3 September he 'burnt, in the field at Gad's Hill, the accumulated letters and papers of twenty years'. Evidently he was feeling ambivalent about something, for alongside the joke about the sheer volume of this incoming correspondence there is an unmistakable touch of wry self-awareness as he continues: 'They sent up a smoke like the Genie when he got out of the casket on the seashore; and as it was an exquisite day when I began, and rained very heavily when I finished, I suspect my correspondence of having overcast the face of the Heavens.'[18] What can it have been in his past that might call forth the Genie from the Arabian Knights, which materialises from the smoke to threaten Death?[19] Gladys Storey, on the authority of Dickens's daughter Kate (who was present at the time) reports that Dickens told his children 'letters are but ephemeral: we must not be affected too much either by those which praise us or by others written in the heat of the moment'.[20] Perhaps – given the themes that were shortly to emerge in his thirteenth novel – he was reflecting on paths taken, or not taken, as a result of overbearing influence or misguided feeling. Whatever it was, there was some soul-searching going on in this period of his life; the following month, having started writing *Great Expectations*, he reread his semi-autobiographical *David Copperfield* to be sure of avoiding repetition and found, as he explained to Forster, that he was 'affected by it to a degree you would hardly believe'.[21]

---

[17]   *Letters*, Vol. 9, p. 321.

[18]   Letter to W.H. Wills, 4 September 1860. *Letters*, Vol. 9, p. 304.

[19]   *Letters*, Vol. 9, p. 304, fn2.

[20]   Gladys Storey, *Dickens and Daughter* (1939; London, 1982), pp. 106–7. Quoted in *Letters*, Vol. 9, p. 304, fn.1.

[21]   Letter to Forster, early October 1860. *Letters*, Vol. 9, p. 325.

The pressures put on him by his personal circumstances were exacerbated by the enforced, rapid production of the story that became *Great Expectations*. AYR was a weekly but Dickens much preferred the monthly format and, as Rosenberg has shown, internal evidence from the novel demonstrates that even well into it Dickens was still thinking in terms of the monthly instalments he had originally planned for the book.[22] This means that the working out of the plot had to be done with the utmost self-discipline. He was doing it at top speed, too, an agreement with *Harper's Weekly* of New York under which the instalments would appear a week earlier in the USA than in the UK necessitating the completion of each week's instalment two weeks in advance.[23] Alongside this he continued editing AYR, and even – restless as ever – embarked on a public reading tour in London.[24] However stressful these circumstances though – or perhaps because of them – they resulted in a book that is something of a *tour de force* even by Dickens's standards. Darkly comic, subtly ironic and genuinely moving, it rolls the kind-hearted, misled orphan protagonist of *Oliver Twist* into the abused, lonely child at the centre of *David Copperfield*, gives him a darker road to travel, and lashes him unmercifully all the way. Despite its almost perfect structure and confident execution, it is also in many ways more thematically uncontainable than anything he had ever done before. It is not quite in the same category as the fantastically 'baggy monster' which followed it,[25] but in its own way it too is bursting at the seams, both with dizzying flights of invention to equal anything in his early works, and with the unresolved pieces of its author's later life. These barbed fragments range from renewed memories of the agonies suffered by a sensitive and ambitious child forced into a job he despises, through the strange power of an increasingly deranged woman for whom time and affection are equally meaningless, to an impossible sexual yearning for an inappropriate lover.[26] Whether or not we believe

---

[22]   *Great Expectations*, ed. Rosenberg, p. 409.

[23]   Dickens explained this to Bulwer in a letter dated June 7 1861. *Letters*, Vol. 9, p. 423. He was paid £1250 (£250 more than for *A Tale of Two Cities*) for the rights to the new serial, which appeared a week in advance of the British one in AYR until winter shipping delays meant the proofs could not be given to the artist, John McLenan, in time for the January 26 number. *Harper's* therefore delayed for a week and thereafter published simultaneously with AYR. *Great Expectations*, ed. Rosenberg, p. 399.

[24]   Performed weekly between 14 March and 18 April.

[25]   Sean Grass, *Our Mutual Friend: A Publishing History* (Burlington, VT, 2014), p. 3.

[26]   Elizabeth Dickens was at this time losing all sense of reality and insisting on being dressed in furs 'like a female Hamlet'. Letter to Mrs Frances Dickinson, 19 August 1860. *Letters*, Vol. 9, p. 287. There have been many persuasive explanations for the origins of Miss Havisham, in particular Harry Stone's tracing of contemporary accounts of eccentric women about whom Dickens may have read. See 'The Genesis of a Novel: *Great Expectations*' (1970), reprinted in *Great Expectations*, ed. Rosenberg, pp. 556–63. But, as far as I am aware, to date no one has suggested that Dickens's own mother – who throughout the writing period was undoubtedly displaying the self-absorption, the detachment from reality and the cruel moments of clarity that go with dementia – may have been another powerful influence on Dickens's depiction of Miss Havisham.

there is a bit of Charles Dickens in Pip, these themes may well have reflected some of his own complex emotions at this time in his life. There can be no doubt that they are rescued from an early-Dickens tendency to mawkishness by a very liberal helping of mature, sometimes bitter, self-awareness.

A great deal of critical ink has been expended – much of it brilliantly – on textual analyses of *Great Expectations* which explore these and many other aspects of its construction and effects, and I am content to leave further such analysis to others. What concerns me here is something much less well explored: the fact that the novel is not only a complex formal triumph, but also a remarkable example of a consummate professional's response to an emergency situation in a changing, volatile market. It is therefore particularly rich in evidence of his intimate knowledge both of the business end of literature, and of the process of public self-construction. An examination of its circulation and the range of responses which it generated might therefore tell us a lot about the role *Great Expectations* played in bolstering, maintaining or adjusting the public profile of the phenomenon known as 'Charles Dickens' in this troubled period.

Great Expectations in the Marketplace

Michael Slater claims that the novel 'wonderfully revived the fortunes of *All the Year Round*'.[27] But the slide in sales was not immediately arrested by Dickens's decision to 'strike in', according to the AYR ledger. Following the first half year of the journal's life (it launched on April 30 1859), the date of the first official accounting period on 31 October 1859 shows profits of £626 4s. 3d., rising to £1821 0s. 4d., just a year later. Dickens's *A Tale of Two Cities* and Collins's *The Woman in White* had clearly attracted – and kept – new readers. Lever's serial damage is immediately apparent: total profits fell by almost two-thirds from £1821 0s. 4d. in the half year ending 31 October 1860, to £679 5s. 1d. by 30 April 1861 (a month after Lever's story ended). But despite Dickens 'striking in' he could not entirely stop the leak: profits were down still further to £413 8s. 10d. by 31 October 1861, more than two months after the publication of the final instalment of *Great Expectations* and despite the introduction of the once-popular Bulwer's new serial *A Strange Story* (10 August 1861 – 8 March 1862), which Rosenberg pithily calls 'ectoplasmic hocus-pocus'.[28] It seems that in spite of Dickens's self-congratulatory claims to anyone willing to listen that his new novel was a great success, and even allowing for some considerable delay in registering real-time profits, we may have to acknowledge that not all the recovery was due to *Great Expectations*. Profits did not recover their pre-Lever heights until the half year ending 30 April 1862,[29] by which time Bulwer had ceded centre stage to another Wilkie Collins novel, *No Name* (15 March 1862 – 17 January 1863).

---

[27]   Slater, *Charles Dickens* (New Haven, CT and London, 2009), p. 491.

[28]   *Great Expectations*, ed. Rosenberg, p. 498.

[29]   Patten, *Charles Dickens and his Publishers* (Oxford, 1978), Appendix D, p. 464.

Robert Patten suggests that we might supplement this not entirely convincing evidence of the novel's popularity from the AYR accounts by acknowledging the 'number, size, and kind of editions on both sides of the Atlantic that appeared within a few months of the novel's serialization'.[30] Dickens and his publishers certainly milked the reformat markets for all they were worth: *Great Expectations* was issued in three-volume unillustrated form by Chapman and Hall in July 1861, price 31s. 6d., followed by a further four reissues of this 'edition' that same year. One can be cynical about what new 'editions' are able to tell us, of course: they might merely be separate batches issued from the same warehouse stock, provided with new title pages and called 'new editions' to give the impression of high demand. Chapman and Hall issued five such 'editions' of the first three-volume version and the media apparently took this to mean great popularity, but, as Patten argues, 'the general Victorian usage of the term "edition" rescues Chapman and Hall from any imputation of dishonesty' since it was legitimately used to describe fresh printings from stereotype. In this case, it produced subsequent 'editions' in early August (750 copies), late August (750), September (500) and October (750), all printed from the original.[31] For some reason Chapman and Hall were being cautious and taking care not to overprint, though this led to an irritating temporary scarcity of copies for some readers.[32]

A genuine second edition, corrected by Dickens and printed from a new typesetting, appeared in one volume (the 'Library Edition', price 7s. 6d.) in 1862, in post octavo with vignette title and eight illustrations by Marcus Stone (son of Dickens's late friend Frank and probably being offered a favour here – repeated with *Our Mutual Friend* – since the illustrations are unremarkable at best and Dickens's attempts to get Marcus work as an illustrator elsewhere seem to have fallen on stony ground).[33] A crown octavo 'Cheap Edition' then appeared in November 1863 (price 3s. 6d.) but, as Patten remarks: 'By that time demand was drying up: half the copies remained unsold at the end of the year.'[34] The drying up was remarkably fast compared with earlier Dickens works. This does not necessarily equate to unpopularity: its serialisation in AYR may have reached up to 100,000 readers in the UK and 50,000 or even 200,000 in *Harper's Weekly* in the USA. Equally, since most of the first and over half of the second printing of the three-volume edition had been snapped up by Mudie's circulating library, each may have had up to 30 readers.[35] But there is no way of proving any of this, and it

---

[30]   Patten, *Dickens and his Publishers*, p. 288.

[31]   Patten, *Dickens and his Publishers*, p. 290. The *Caledonian Mercury* of Tuesday 30 July 1861, for example, notes that the first edition is out of print and claims that this is 'a great test of the book's popularity'.

[32]   *Great Expectations*, ed. Rosenberg, p. 399.

[33]   See letters to three publishers – Longman, Murray and Chapman and Hall – on Stone's behalf, 26 November 1859. *Letters*, Vol. 9, pp. 170–71.

[34]   Patten, *Dickens and his Publishers*, p. 293.

[35]   Patten, *Dickens and his Publishers*, p. 292. Robert McParland estimates there could have been up to 200,000 readers for *Harper's* at the height of its fame. McParland, *Charles Dickens's American Audience* (Plymouth, 2010), p. 12. However, the official website gives

is probably more significant that the net result seems to have been smaller profits for Dickens and his publishers. *Dombey and Son* had maintained its popularity to the extent that it sold over 6,000 copies in the one-volume edition and over 2,000 in the Library edition in 1858, ten years after its first publication. By comparison, in 1862 – only a year after its first volume publication – *Great Expectations* sold 3,429 copies in the three-volume edition and 1,995 in the one-volume edition and within a year, as we have seen, demand had dwindled to a mere trickle.[36]

While *Great Expectations* probably did reasonably well on its first appearance, then, it was not – even taking into account the vagaries of publishers' accounting procedures – especially lucrative for Dickens or his publishers in the long-term. [37] In fact, some clever juggling was apparently required in order to realise a return even in the first years of its volume life, since half (225) of the unsold quires of the Cheap Edition were transferred to the Library edition in 1865.[38] The novel seemed to do a little better there, but by June 1866, while *Great Expectations* was continuing to sell in the three-volume edition, it made only half what *Oliver Twist* made in the same half year (£26 8s. 0d. and £53 14s. 3d. respectively). In 1867 a 'People's Edition' of Dickens's works containing *Great Expectations* (9,000 copies) was issued; and in 1868 the novel appeared in the 'Charles Dickens Edition' (22,000 copies at 3s.) with the original eight illustrations by Stone, plus new descriptive headlines provided by Dickens.[39] This was a large printing (it is worth noting for comparative purposes that *Hard Times*, *The Uncommercial Traveller* and *Oliver Twist* were given 18,000; 15,000 and 5,000 copies respectively), but despite the fact that this edition is generally considered to be Dickens's most widely circulated and successful, it is probably significant that it was the least lucrative works (*Great Expectations* and *Hard Times*) that were given the largest print runs, perhaps in the hope that they would attract a new lower-income readership. At any rate, the 22,000 copies were apparently not immediately snapped up at this price: no reprinting of *Great Expectations* appears in the ledger for 1869.[40]

---

us a more conservative estimate of 50,000. http://harpers.org/history/ [accessed 2 March 2013]. J. Henry Harper himself felt that the high circulation during 1860–64 was due to the Civil War, not necessarily to Dickens, since circulation plummeted towards the end of the War and did not recover (in spite of the serialisation of *Our Mutual Friend*, beginning June 1864) until Collins launched in with *Armadale* (beginning December 1864). Harper, *The House of Harper: A Century of Publishing* (New York, 1912), p. 233.

[36]   Patten, *Dickens and his Publishers*, Appendix A, p. 384.

[37]   As Patten warns us, the account books do not make for clear or easy comparative analysis since they do not always record the same things in the same way year on year, and one frequently has to piece together the story from vague or incomplete records. Patten, *Dickens and his Publishers*, p. 351.

[38]   *Accounts of sales of the works of Charles Dickens: Chapman and Hall*, Vol. 2, National Arts Library, Victoria and Albert Museum, F.D. 18.3.

[39]   See *Great Expectations*, ed. Rosenberg, pp. 489–90.

[40]   *Accounts of sales of the works of Charles Dickens: Chapman and Hall*, Vol. 2, National Arts Library, Victoria and Albert Museum, F.D. 18.3.

A variety of editions there certainly was, then, but this tells us only that Dickens and his publishers were working hard to return a profit on the book, not necessarily that it was a significant long-term success. Dickens's aggregate profits for his publications with Chapman and Hall in the years of the various issues of the volume form of *Great Expectations* are revealing. The half-yearly account for December 1860 shows that he earned £250 14s. 1d. In the next two accounting periods his earnings were £265 6s. 7d. (June 1861) and £383 14s. 6d. (December 1861), in line with this period's poor returns for AYR. In June of 1862, his earnings leap to £2,430 13s. 10d., a result, probably, of a combination of initial library sales for the three-volume edition of *Great Expectations* and the rise in AYR income in that period (which was by that time serialising Wilkie Collins). In the next half year to December 1862, Dickens's profits drop to £703 18s. 1d., and by June of 1863 they are back at the pre-peak level of £383 2s. 11d. They do not rise significantly again until December 1864, with the publication of *Our Mutual Friend* in monthly numbers (136,422 of the first number sold) and an increase in AYR income, total profits amounting to £2,490 8s. 10d.[41] The best that can probably be said of *Great Expectations* in the UK, taking into account both serial and volume sales, is that it did better than its predecessor *A Tale of Two Cities*, less well than its successor *Our Mutual Friend*, and not nearly as well as the early works, especially *Pickwick Papers*, *David Copperfield* and *Oliver Twist*.

What emerges from all this is that when it was carefully managed through a judicious release in different formats targeted at different readerships, *Great Expectations* was a steady though not spectacular seller in Britain during Dickens's lifetime, and that's about all we can say with certainty. In fact this early history can probably tell us as much about publishing practices, Dickens's learning curve in a changing marketplace and cultural perceptions about his image as it can about reading tastes. He was learning some hard new lessons here: he may well have rued the decision to release the book in three-volume form for the circulating library market, just as he may have regretted releasing *A Tale of Two Cities* in monthly numbers as well as in weekly serial form in AYR, since he repeated neither of these experiments.[42] He badly needed *Great Expectations* to turn a fast profit (as indeed it seems to have done), but the fast-buck option diluted long-term sales since readers seem to have borrowed rather than bought the novel. The world of print was changing in the 1850s and 1860s; the 'Industrial Age Author' whose birth Boz's arrival on the scene had signalled in the late 1830s was now more mature, much changed and rapidly proliferating, and even 'the Inimitable' suffered the occasional casualty as a result. The early history of *Great Expectations* contains important traces of this shifting 'horizon of the publishable'.

---

[41]   Patten, *Dickens and his Publishers*, Appendix C, p. 461.

[42]   The Pilgrim editors confirm that Dickens's earnings from this monthly serial version diminished month by month, and were in fact a disappointment and perhaps something of a surprise; they claim his profits were 'adversely affected by heavy reprinting of the monthly Parts'. *Letters*, Vol. 9, p. 223.

The market for print was almost as volatile as Dickens's own circumstances in this period. The repeal of Paper Duty in 1861, which made books cheaper for the publisher and therefore the purchaser, helped sales of the bound editions slightly, but there were other factors at work which meant *Great Expectations* in both serial and volume form was competing in a fiercer market than previous works. Some major new players were entering the periodical market at precisely this moment, among them Thackeray's shilling monthly the *Cornhill Magazine* (founded in 1859 and substantially devoted to quality fiction) and its rival *Macmillan's Magazine* (also 1859, though more focussed on social debate). The new monthlies offered longer serial fiction than the weeklies, plus in-depth critical articles, poetry and short stories, and all – crucially – for half the price of the two-shilling or half-crown monthlies they aimed to emulate.[43] The *Cornhill* also had an agreement with *Harper's*, competing with Dickens for writers as well as for a share of his American readership: the *Cornhill* published works by some of Dickens's AYR favourites such as Elizabeth Gaskell, Wilkie Collins and George Eliot. It was also six times the length of AYR, and while it retailed at six times the cost there was no real equivalence since, unlike AYR, it was illustrated by leading artists, it usually contained two new serial novels rather than one, and its production values were high enough to make it an attractive addition to the middle-class parlour. It looked and felt substantial and serious; something AYR – very much modelled on the newspaper format – did not, even when bound in multiple parts. Also significant is the fact that the *Cornhill* was the product of a close relationship between another Industrial Age author, William Makepeace Thackeray, and another entrepreneurial publisher, George Smith Jr. of Smith, Elder & Co., and it depended on contributions from a wide circle of respected and well-known writers and an astute understanding of the needs and preferences of its potential readership.[44] Dickens himself no longer had a corner on this particular market: ironically, while Thackeray was known to have remarked ruefully in the past on Dickens's vast sales compared to his own, in this period there is an emerging sense that where serial fiction is concerned the trend was reversing.[45] Smith had offered Thackeray extremely generous terms for his writing role in the *Cornhill* (£350 a month for two novels to be published in 12 monthly instalments during 1860–61, later profits from the bound book sales to be split equally), terms with which Thackeray was understandably thrilled.[46] The editorship was another matter, however: Smith knew that a big-name author was what the public would expect given Dickens's example, but his first choice of Thomas Hughes, the Christian Socialist author of the popular novel *Tom Brown's Schooldays* (1857), turned him down. Thackeray himself seemed the next best option, and he was subsequently taken on as editor at an additional salary of £1000

---

[43] Spencer L. Eddy, Jr, *The Founding of The Cornhill Magazine* (Muncie, IN, 1970), p. 8.

[44] Eddy, *Founding of the Cornhill*, p. 2.

[45] Patten, *Dickens and his Publishers*, p. 187.

[46] Eddy, *Founding of the Cornhill*, pp. 8–9.

a year. The happy combination of a known name and a quality miscellany at a reasonable price hit favour with the reading public from the start. The first number of the *Cornhill* sold an impressive 120,000 copies and demand remained relatively high, achieving a circulation AYR could seldom match.[47]

It would be easy to overplay the significance of *Macmillan's Magazine* and the *Cornhill*, both as competitors for Dickens and as market leaders. As Linda K. Hughes rightly reminds us, they were just two among hundreds of periodical titles in this period and they rapidly spawned a host of successful imitators. Furthermore, as Hughes points out, the market was much more complex than this, and 'understanding a dynamic system of print exceeds the importance of a mere two titles at mid-century'.[48] Nonetheless, the sheer number of rival new periodicals is a significant factor in Dickens's professional life at mid-century, as is the rapid increase in the numbers of novels on the market, and none of this can have helped the sales of AYR or of *Great Expectations*. The novel's fame, however – as distinct from its sales – is a different matter altogether, and one that deserves our attention since it is through the ways in which both professional and non-professional readers responded to both official and unofficial versions of *Great Expectations* that we can approach an understanding of its impact, find traces of its author's changing public profile in this period, and perhaps detect the seeds of its remediated future.

'Stamped with many degrees of good, bad and indifferent': Readerships and Reviews

Reading patterns themselves had changed since Dickens's first period of self-fashioning as 'Boz' 'the Inimitable' in the 1830s and 1840s. Mudie's was not the only library circulating the novel to borrowers rather than buyers; by this period the UK had many Mechanics Institutes, Reading Societies and other self-help subscription institutions which required well-stocked libraries, and since the 1850 Public Libraries Act had enabled substantial municipal boroughs to construct and equip 'free' libraries through a half penny rate tax, public library provision had also steadily increased across England and Wales. By 1861 there was by no means universal provision of libraries in every borough and many readers were clearly still buying books for personal use, but during Dickens's lifetime, local newspapers frequently mentioned the addition to both public library and other circulating library stock of copies of *Great Expectations*, to the extent that the *Caledonian Mercury* reported confidently on 21 October 1861: '"Great

---

[47]　Linda K. Hughes, 'On new monthly magazines, 1859–60', Branch (Britain, Representation and Nineteenth-Century History), ed. by Dino Franco Felluga http://www.branchcollective.org/?ps_articles=on-new-monthly-magazines-1859-60 [accessed 1 March 2013]. AYR sold an average of 100,000 copies per number, but according to the accounts circulation clearly fluctuated quite widely. *Letters*, Vol. 9, p. 223, fn2.

[48]　Hughes, 'On New Monthly Magazines, 1859–60'.

Expectations" is still the book of the season, and is most in demand at reading clubs.'[49] The book was apparently borrowed almost as often as it was bought, and it was being widely discussed.

An important adjunct to this culture of borrowing – drawing on much earlier precedents, of course, but surprisingly long-lasting – was the practice of sharing; of spreading all or part of a new Dickens novel around groups of readers or listeners as part of a social event. British newspapers sometimes refer to public readings in which *Great Expectations* plays a part, despite some apparently indifferent audiences. On Thursday 22 February 1866, the *Dorset County Chronicle* reported that on the previous Friday a Mr T. Brown had read an extract of the novel aloud to a 'very small' audience (not even large enough to cover the expenses of hiring the Masonic Hall) at the thirteenth series of Penny Readings, Lyme Regis, Dorset. But the *Buckinghamshire Herald, Uxbridge Advertiser and Windsor and Eton Journal* reported on 20 January 1876 that a varied Lecture Hall programme comprising popular songs, readings (including 'selections from Dickens's *Great Expectations*' read by Rev. J. Lee), musical interludes and a closing rendition of God Save the Queen attracted a 'well filled' hall and was 'greatly appreciated'. Perhaps readings from the novel worked better as part of a miscellaneous programme, especially 15 years after its publication; we know that Dickens himself was not convinced by its effectiveness with audiences, producing a reading copy as he usually did for his works but thinking better of ever performing it.[50]

The novel is certainly less dramatic than previous works: it is darker, in some ways simpler, and altogether more contemplative. That did not mean it was not easily segmented, as I will show in a moment (and Dickens in some measure succeeded in his aim to make it more humorous than *A Tale of Two Cities*),[51] but it did mean it was substantially different from what had gone before. The change is reflected in the mixed reception it received from reviewers who, while they seldom agreed, were all more inclined to praise individual characters or sequences rather than the whole. Most critical analyses of the novel's reviews to date have focussed on the larger monthly and quarterly periodicals, but there is a lot to be learned from reviews in smaller regional papers too; they are if nothing else proof of the

---

   [49]   *Caledonian Mercury*, Monday 21 October 1861, p. 2. See, for example, the addition of *Great Expectations* to the stock of the Workington Mechanics' Institution Library (*Carlisle Journal*, Tuesday 2 February 1864, p. 2); the Montpellier Library and Reading Room, a subscription library (*Cheltenham Looker-On*, Saturday 13 August 1864, p. 2); Spencer's Market Place Library, Leicester, subscribers c.300 (*Leicester Journal*, Friday 4 July 1862, p. 5); 'Robert's Select Library' (a Branch of Mudie's), Exeter (*Western Times*, Saturday 14 December 1861, p. 5); Mudie's Birmingham branch (*Birmingham Journal*, Saturday 25 April 1863, p. 4); Goulden's Library, Canterbury (*Kentish Chronicle*, Saturday 25 July 1863, p. 1; also 16 May 1863); Atkinson's Public Library, Kendal (*Westmorland Gazette and Kendal Advertiser*, Saturday 17 August 1861, p. 1).

   [50]   Jean Callahan, 'The (Unread) Reading Version of *Great Expectations*', in *Great Expectations*, ed. Rosenberg, pp. 543–56.

   [51]   Letter to Forster, early October 1860. *Letters*, Vol. 9, p. 325.

widespread attention even a late work of Dickens still received and interesting evidence of the nature of his fame.[52]

Early instalments sounded promising notes around the UK. Responding after the concluding number of the first stage of Pip's expectations (AYR, February 9 1861), the *Bradford Observer* concurred with the *Saturday Review*[53] in feeling that the novel represented a return to form: '"All the Year Round" continues to maintain its position in the very first rank, we may say at the head, of miscellanies of its particular class. The leading tales "Great Expectations", by Mr. Charles Dickens, and "A Day's Ride", grow in interest.'[54] The *Chester Chronicle* agreed: 'The principal tale in the January part of this work is "Great Expectations", by Charles Dickens, in which "Pip" and "Joe" figure conspicuously. The whole of the characters are depicted in the clever, truthful, easy, and happy manner for which Mr Dickens is so justly celebrated, and the materials are thrown together in such an interesting form that no-one can help reading "Great Expectations" with avidity.'[55] The *Lincolnshire Chronicle* also enjoyed the first instalment 'enough to make us wish for more'.[56] But by March 1861 the tone changes with some reviewers. The *Hereford Journal*'s reviewer, for one, was already growing restless: 'Mr Dickens's Great Expectations have decidedly disappointed the great expectations raised by themselves', the reviewer complained; 'the work does not improve with succeeding numbers. The humour is more enforced and exaggerated than ever, and it labours under a manifest difficulty in depicting the feelings and observations of a youth in an inferior position, from his mouth when he is a man, and in a higher station of life. In this instance the difficulty is not overcome.'[57] The *Morning Post* agreed, claiming that the book 'begins well and then disappoints'. This reviewer clearly felt indignant that Dickens had let down his admiring readership and taken their loyalty for granted: 'An outrageously absurd book by a great writer may be regarded as a breach of public confidence', it pronounced, calling the characters 'monstrosities' and the story a 'jumble of incongruities' representative of Dickens's waning powers.[58] In this the *Spectator* fully concurred.[59] The *Derby*

---

[52]   Phillip Collins's *Charles Dickens: the Critical Heritage* (Abingdon and New York, 1986), for example, includes only reviews from the *Atlantic Monthly*, *The Times*, the *Rambler*, the *Dublin University Magazine* and *Blackwood's Edinburgh Magazine*. Rosenberg adds reviews from the *Saturday Review* and the *Spectator* (*Great Expectations*, ed. Rosenberg, pp. 617–29). George H. Ford adds the occasional small paper review and some invaluable responses from non-reviewer readers, but his evidence for *Great Expectations* is relatively thin. Ford, *Dickens and His Readers: Aspects of Novel Criticism Since 1836* (New York, 1965).

[53]   *Saturday Review*, 20 July 1861, pp. 69–70.

[54]   *Bradford Observer*, Thursday 14 February 1861, p. 7.

[55]   *Chester Chronicle*, Saturday 9 February 1861, p. 5.

[56]   *Lincolnshire Chronicle*, Friday 14 December 1860, p. 7.

[57]   *Hereford Journal*, Wednesday 13 March 1861, p. 5.

[58]   *Morning Post*, Sunday, 31 July 1861, p. 3.

[59]   *Spectator*, 20 July 1861, pp. 784–5.

Mercury was kinder, admitting that while 'superfine spleen has been vented against the late works of Dickens', this is his 'latest and best novel' and while not – significantly – the equal of his earlier ones in terms of character creation, here at least 'we have a score of characters as original, as artistically drawn, and more elaborately developed, than any our well-beloved author has before contributed to the world of literature'.[60] The *Birmingham Gazette* called it rather vaguely 'one of the cleverest and most artistic books he has ever written', though admitting that it thought *David Copperfield* was better.[61] The *Leeds Times* laments that while once

> all the world would have read it [a new Dickens story] as it came out ... the great days of Pickwick and Nickleby and Oliver Twist have long melted into the past.... Many stories have been issued by him since, stamped with many degrees of good, bad and indifferent. They still command, no doubt, a considerable and an admiring audience, but it is something much smaller than the universal circle of English readers.... But if the story has its faults, the scenes and characters have their merits.[62]

And so it goes on. The reviewers are divided between relief that Dickens has returned to something of his old form, irritation that he continues to serve up half-baked caricatures from the same old moulds, and confusion about the new direction he seems to be taking. Almost every reviewer finds something to praise – a section that works, a character that is memorable, *something* that she or he feels should or could have been the story's central pivot – but few find the story effective as a whole. For the *Morning Post* this pivot is Magwitch, for *The Times* it is Joe, for the *Saturday Review* it is Wemmick. But overall, as the reviewer for the latter put it: 'It is rather a story with excellent things in it than an excellent story.'[63]

This episodic quality, recognised by most contemporary reviewers and usually seen as a flaw, is central to an understanding of the reception and subsequent remediation of *Great Expectations*. By 1937, famously, Bernard Shaw considered it Dickens's 'most compactly perfect book ... all of one piece and consistently truthful as none of his other books are'.[64] But this assessment was made after the novel had been performing its cultural work for more than 75 years and by this time, as subsequent chapters will show, it had been adapted a number of times in ways that had (as Estella might have put it) bent it into a better shape in the national consciousness. In the 1860s, the novel's fame was of a different stamp; in the face of much more cohesive novels by new challengers such as George Eliot,[65]

---

[60] *Derby Mercury*, Wednesday 24 July 1861, p. 6.

[61] *Birmingham Gazette*, Saturday 13 July 1861, p. 6.

[62] *Leeds Times*, Saturday 21 September 1861, p. 6.

[63] *Saturday Review*, 20 July 1861, pp. 69–70.

[64] George Bernard Shaw, 'Introduction' to *Great Expectations* (New York, 1937), pp. v–xxii.

[65] Ford demonstrates that reviewers felt writers like Eliot had raised the novel form to new heights that was in danger of leaving the old guard – Dickens, Lever, Thackeray – behind. Ford, *Dickens and His Readers*, pp. 181–3.

Great Expectations was an unwieldy whole made up of brilliant 'teaspoons' (as Thomas Carlyle called serial instalments), and it was in teaspoons or even smaller portions that many readers first encountered it.

Throughout its serial run and even afterwards several newspapers printed short sections of the novel, apparently having no trouble with the concept that taking episodes out of context might somehow dilute them. Of course, reviewers in this period regularly filled many columns of their 'reviews' with long extracts rather than criticism (as Appendix D, filled with necessary ellipses, demonstrates); the practice has a long history. But chunks of a new novel, reproduced without the benefit of a line or two of criticism or much preamble at all beyond an indicative title and the author's name, are a different thing, and they were remarkably widespread over both space and time. To give just a few examples, the *Leeds Times* of 6 April 1861, p. 3, reprints the scene in which Mr Wopsle plays Hamlet; a section on Wemmick's marriage to Miss Skiffins entitled 'An impromptu Wedding' was reprinted in the *Worcestershire Chronicle* on Wednesday 31 July 1861, p. 4; the section in which Pip and Estella have tea together after her arrival in London appears as 'Tea at an Hotel' in the *Salisbury and Winchester Journal*, Saturday 24 August 1861, p. 3, and the same section appears in the *Bath Chronicle and Weekly Gazette* on Thursday 1 August 1861, p. 6.

It is hard to know whether Dickens authorised this practice; I have been unable to find relevant letters to any of these papers or their editors in his extant correspondence.[66] But since these extracts can only have worked to advertise the new novel, it would be hard to imagine that even as assiduous a copyright watcher as Dickens could have disapproved of it. Indeed, there were important precedents: George Ford asserts that the phenomenal success of the *Pickwick Papers* after a slow start was as much due to the extraction and reprinting of key Sam Weller episodes by William Jerdan, editor of the high-circulation weekly journal the *Literary Gazette*,[67] as to the invention of Sam himself. Ford also tells us that Disraeli claimed he had never read any of Dickens's novels in their entirety, only extracts in a newspaper.[68] As Dickens must have been very well aware, the practice of reprinting extracts may actually have enhanced a novel's chances of winning readers since the remediation of a passage out of context does not by any means dilute its power. On the contrary, in the case of *Great Expectations*, encountering a chunk of Dickens's observational humour amongst the shipping and farming news and the advertisements for boots has the effect of situating it in a discourse of Englishness – and indeed regionalism – which draws attention to his gift for capturing and satirizing the mundane, highlighting the flashes of humour which can be lost in the general bleakness and occasional messiness of the novel's

---

[66] Dickens did take issue with the 'London Correspondent' of the *Bath Chronicle* in October 1859 over some comments he had made about 'Hunted Down', so evidently such items occasionally crossed his path. *Letters*, Vol. 9, p. 141. He also lost no time in taking the *Eastern Province Herald* to court for piracy (see Chapter 5).

[67] *Literary Gazette*, 9 July and 13 August 1837.

[68] Ford, *Dickens and His Readers*, p. 91.

broader landscape. Such extracts also provide important evidence of the spread and nature of his fame in this period, and the canny ways in which he permitted and perpetuated it.

The short-lived *Kentish Chronicle and General Advertiser* (1859–67) is a particularly good example in this regard. Of course, regionalism is particularly important here given both the novel's partial setting in the Kent marshes, and Dickens's own residence in Rochester among the paper's readership; it should come as no surprise that this modest four-page Saturday paper is both the most frequent reprinter of sections from Dickens's novel, and among those which most often mention Dickens's name. But while it is solidly committed to representing the interests of a specific region, in common with many papers the *Kentish Chronicle* also devotes considerable space to London and foreign news, and this has an interesting effect on the extracted segment and therefore the novel's relationship with the wider world.

The issue in which Mrs Pocket's paternal history is reprinted is a case in point. The paper contains, in this order: articles on various bankruptcies, the departure of Crimea journalist W.H. Russell for the USA where there was the expectation of Civil War, Dickens's new series of readings in London,[69] the Washington Peace Conference, the departure of gold ships to Australia, and the surrender of Messina.[70] It also includes shorter items such as a report on a drowning in the harbour, a story about a man who, having been transported to Van Diemen's land for machine breaking, disappeared without trace and therefore never heard that he had come into a valuable property, and a story about the escape and recapture of a convict from a chain gang in Chatham. The extract about Mrs Pocket's father, the 'accidental deceased Knight' from *Great Expectations*, appears on the back page. It has no introduction, is simply called 'Mrs Belinda Pocket', and rubs shoulders with short items on the 'Newfoundland Fisheries', 'Hints to Sportsmen' and a column on the 'Cause and Prevention of Malaria'. This decoupling (in Rachel Malik's term) and remediation of a small section of the novel has the effect of drawing attention to its humour and rendering it (in high Pickwickian style) a believable oddity of daily life. 'Mrs Belinda Pocket' could easily be a real live English eccentric such as many a newspaper delighted in describing to its readers, and her appearance here among factual articles reflects an element of veracity back onto the novel.

Despite my presentation here of the newspaper items in the order of their appearance for the sake of expediency, I am conscious of the warnings of scholars such as Margaret Beetham and more recently Andrew King, who rightly claims that a 'retrospective panoptical survey' of a popular journal page by page ignores the 'dispersion, disruption and seriality' which are characteristics of real

[69] On this tour he read from 'The Boots at the Holly Tree Inn', 'A Christmas Carol', 'The Trial from Pickwick' and 'the Story of Little Dombey'.

[70] *Kentish Chronicle*, Saturday 16 March 1861. The mention of Messina was surely significant for Dickens followers, since the unification of Italy had been a favourite topic of his in HW.

readers' experiences.[71] No one, that is, regularly reads a newspaper or periodical from cover to cover in one sitting, and most are regular readers and therefore aware of each edition's relationship with other issues of the same title. It is important to think, as King does, in terms of pragmatics (in the linguistics sense), which means analysing an item or a page in relation to its contextual parameters – its references to contexts that can exist in other parts of or even outside the text. In this case, a pragmatic reading is particularly fruitful: in whatever order it is read, the newspaper's content provides topical contexts for the extracted sections from *Great Expectations*. This means regular newspaper readers who were also familiar with the whole novel would probably not have been surprised by its themes. It is impossible to say whether this paper's layout was done, consciously or unconsciously, with *Great Expectations* in mind, but the novel must have seemed very topical for contemporary readers nonetheless, filled as it was, despite its probable setting in c.1807–26,[72] with references to things going on in the real world around them in 1860–61.[73] Potentially, too, this could work in the other direction: a reader who first encountered an extract here might ultimately bring its rich topical contexts elsewhere in the newspaper to bear when they read the novel, using them to fill in some blanks, smooth over some inconsistencies, and give weight to some of the less plausible moments and characters.

This sort of intertexuality is typical of Dickens, as Walter Bagehot's famous 1858 essay on him so perfectly demonstrates. Here, the disconnectedness that so troubled most reviewers is described as one of the novelist's creative strengths and a feature of his extraordinary modernity, and the metropolis itself is likened to the experience of reading a newspaper:

> Mr Dickens's genius is especially suited to the delineation of city life. London is like a newspaper. Everything is there, and everything is disconnected. There is every kind of person in some houses; but there is no more connection between

---

[71] Margaret Beetham, 'Open and Closed: The Periodical as a Publishing Genre', in *Victorian Periodicals Review Special Issue: Theory*, 22, ed. by Laurel Brake and Anne Humpherys (1989): pp. 96–100. Andrew King, 'A Paradigm of Reading the Victorian Penny Weekly: Education of the Gaze and *The London Journal*', in *Nineteenth-Century Media and the Construction of Identities* ed. by Bill Bell, Laurel Brake and David Finkelstein (Basingstoke, 2000), p. 81.

[72] Mary Edminson has calculated these dates; quoted in Anny Sadrin, *Great Expectations* (London, 1988), p. 37.

[73] Dickens's topicality is not a concept new to Dickensians, of course. For example, much has been made of Dickens's reference in the opening pages of *Great Expectations* to the 'universal struggle', a phrase Darwin uses in chapter 3 of *On the Origin of Species* (1859). See, for example, Goldie Morgentaler, 'Meditating on the Low: a Darwinian reading of *Great Expectations*', *Studies in English Literature 1500–1900*, 38, (Autumn 1998): pp. 707–21. But it is perhaps significant that in the manuscript it is clear that Dickens added the word 'universal' as an afterthought, as though to underline the connection between Pip's history and the concerns of the 1850s and 1860s. Page 1 of manuscript of *Great Expectations*, Chauncy Hare Townshend Collection, Wisbech and Fenland Museum.

the houses than between the neighbours in the lists of 'births, marriages, and deaths.' As we change from the broad leader to the squalid police-report, we pass a corner and we are in a changed world. This is advantageous to Mr Dickens's genius. His memory is full of instances of old buildings and curious people, and he does not care to piece them together. On the contrary, each scene, to his mind, is a separate scene, – each street a separate street. He has, too, the peculiar alertness of observation that is observable in those who live by it. He describes London like a special correspondent for posterity.[74]

The idea of Dickens as 'special correspondent for posterity' is a remarkably prescient one, but perhaps equally significant is the reference just two years before *Great Expectations* was serialised to the fractured and compartmentalised nature of modern life; relations exist between disconnected things only by virtue of an accident of geography, and meaning resides in the modern reader's ability to read intertextually. As Rachel Malik has observed: 'The content of newspapers, magazines and fiction at this time suggests readers who are sophisticated genre-switchers.'[75] Dickens's understanding of this sophistication is an important part of his ubiquity and endurance.

The *Kentish Chronicle* might seem to be a particular case. But other papers publishing extracts perform a similar function. The *Hampshire Advertiser*, for example, prints the 20-line 'Tea in an Hotel' extract alongside two articles, one called 'Capital, Credit and Advertising' which claims, tongue firmly in cheek, 'We of the people are not very fond of Dukes; but we'd all like to be Dukes well enough ourselves', the other titled 'The Secret of Charming Manners' in which we are told that '[t]here are people who do excellently well in the country, who astonish us by a general air of unfitness and failure in London society' and which (without attribution) holds up Joe Gargery as an example. Following hard on its heels, the Pip and Estella episode serves to poke fun at the London practice of serving ostentatious, inadequate and expensive teas.[76] This juxtaposition of country and metropolis on almost every page of the provincial newspapers provides an important backdrop for Pip's journeys between two worlds. Characterised by the proud (if often humorous) delineation of regional difference, by ambivalence towards (as well as a grudging acknowledgement of the importance of) London as the centre of culture and commerce, it was a journey that non-metropolitan readers were well accustomed to making via the pages of their daily newspaper, and an interpretive practice that they may well have brought to their experience of reading the novel.

These sorts of extracts are not reviews and they offer no opinion on the novel beyond the assumption that readers will find the extracts amusing or informative. But in decoupling and redeploying bits of Dickens in this way, they are able to use

---

[74]   Walter Bagehot, 'Charles Dickens', in *Literary Studies by the late Walter Bagehot*, Vol. 2, ed. by Richard Holt Hutton (London, 1879), p. 197. From an essay first published in the *National Review*, October 1858.

[75]   Malik, 'Stories Many, Fast and Slow', p. 482.

[76]   *Hampshire Advertiser*, Saturday 10 August 1861, p. 7.

him to underline a particular page's flavour, simultaneously embedding his fame and knowledge of his new novel's themes at the level of everyday discourse. Even readers who had never – and would never – read *Great Expectations* are through these means given an understanding of it almost as though they had.

Remediation and Cultural Response

Great Expectations sits at the interface between the old 'Charles Dickens' brand and its new challenges, and part of its brilliance is that it engages with both at the deepest level of its structure. I am not suggesting that *Great Expectations* is exceptional in Dickens's oeuvre per se; one could easily make the case (as Patten does) that all his novels contain rich evidence of his ability to manage his literary output in full cognisance of a volatile market. But, as several critics have noted, the conditions of its birth provided this particular novel with some especially relevant characteristics, among them a deceptive structural simplicity, an unusual and largely unfulfilled narrative energy, and a certain amount of internal self-contradiction which make the decoupling of certain elements almost essential to its sense. For example, as Anny Sadrin has demonstrated, while *Great Expectations* is indisputably a modern novel by Marthe Robert's criteria in that it is a fine example of 'the self-searching self-questioning literary movement which uses as subject matter its own doubt and belief in the value of its own message', Pip is anything but a modern hero.[77] One might say the same about its setting in the 1810s and 1820s, which comments so astutely on the world of the 1860s. Like its author in this period, *Great Expectations* simultaneously looks forwards and backwards; it both ends (at least twice) and does not end (at least not satisfactorily).[78] No wonder that for contemporary critics it was puzzling. But for ordinary readers and for potential adaptors these qualities make it rich indeed; richer, perhaps, than the parameters of a single novel can easily contain.

Peter Brooks is one among several critics who have sought to explore the workings and effects of the novel's unusual mix of irresistible narrative drive and the strange sense of dissatisfaction it arouses. For Brooks, all texts 'represent themselves as inhabited by energies' that correspond to the hopes, desires, disappointments and incoherencies 'animated by reading'.[79] This particular novel engenders more than the usual share of disappointment and incoherence because,

---

[77]   Sadrin, *Great Expectations*, p. 120.

[78]   Bulwer-Lytton famously persuaded Dickens to change the unhappy ending in which Pip and Estella part forever to a happier one in which they might (or might not) be seen to have a future together. Since so much critical energy has been expended on discussions of the various endings of the novel and the circumstances surrounding them and my interests lie elsewhere, I can do no better than point the reader to what I consider to be the best of these discussions: Edgar Rosenberg, 'Putting an End to *Great Expectations*', *Great Expectations*, ed. Rosenberg, pp. 491–527.

[79]   Peter Brooks, *Reading for the Plot: Design and Intention in Narrative* (Cambridge, MA, 1992), pp. 113–42.

Brooks argues, it contains 'a quadripartite scheme of plots, organized into two pairs, each with an "official" plot or interpretation of plot, standing over a repressed plot', and there is no way all of these can work out satisfactorily: 'As readers we know that there has been created in the text an intense level of energy that cannot be discharged through the official plots.'[80] On one level this dissatisfaction is, of course, precisely Dickens's point: *Great Expectations* is very much about misplaced (libidinal as well as social) energy, and at this point in his life happy endings – or even tidy ones – were very far from his mind. But Brooks's notion of undischarged energies is extremely suggestive in helping to account for the novel's very different effects on various readers globally, and the many different ways in which readers and adaptors have approached it.

Rachel Malik offers a related argument that 'the novel … comprises several different narratives in several different versions, delicately interlinked, narratives which generate their own rhythms and momentums and endings too'. She draws attention to Dickens's own decoupling of the Estella plotline and the 'redemptive death of Magwitch' which ended the (unread) reading version, and also to the 1861 dramatic edition (unlikely to have been written by Dickens, but almost certainly sanctioned by him) in which Magwitch plays a much greater role.[81] For Dickens, the real heart of the novel was the 'very fine, new and grotesque idea' expressed on its dramatic opening pages, and the rest comprised more or less dispensable episodes which were easily decoupled for remediation elsewhere. He was also clearly keen to get it over with, judging by his ambivalence towards its ending.[82] As we shall see, many adaptors have found this 'capsularity' irresistible – and it is testament to Dickens's gifts that by no means all of them have chosen the Pip/Magwitch plot as their pivot. The 'dispensable' elements are rich enough to have fruitful lives of their own.

It is an odd fact of history that there were – as far as anyone has been able to ascertain – no stage versions performed in Britain during Dickens's lifetime. This may be a result of the unperformed copyrighted dramatic version through which he prevented theatrical piracy, and of his apparent lack of belief in the novel's suitability for the stage. But it may also be a result of the novel's intrinsic qualities as they appeared to British readers at the time. *Great Expectations* was not fully visually realised for British readers: an illustrated edition was some time in coming, and when it did the drawings were comparatively sparse (eight as opposed to the 40 with which the American serial readers were first greeted). The widespread use of cartoons playing on the title and characters do not appear until much later (see Chapter 2), and even Charles Lyall's famous cartoon from 1861 of Dickens conjuring up the story from his imagination emphasises the domination of

---

[80]   Brooks, *Reading for the Plot*, pp. 117–22.

[81]   Malik, 'Stories Many, Fast and Slow', p. 484.

[82]   In addition to what Rosenberg puts down to Dickens's 'fatigue' over the issue of the novel's ending, it is perhaps significant also that while he had suggested to Baron Tauchnitz that the novel was likely to run for nine months, in the end he finished it after only eight. Letter to Baron Bernhard Tauchnitz, Mid-November 1860. *Letters*, Vol. 9, p. 340.

Dickens's own mental processes: it shows Dickens pointing to his own head, but the cartoonist has included no images of its contents.[83]

There was not – as far as we have been able to discover – a magic lantern version, though other Dickens novels including *The Old Curiosity Shop*, *A Christmas Carol* and parts of *Pickwick* were highly successful in that form.[84] There was a music hall song by J.A. Hardwick (1861) which played on the titles of both the novel and the British magazine in which it appeared, but it is impossible at this stage to say where it was performed or how popular it was. Recent work on Dickens in the music hall by Allan Sutcliffe makes no mention of a performance of this song (or indeed any nineteenth-century music hall versions of *Great Expectations*),[85] and now, a century and a half later, perhaps the best that can be said of this strange offering is that it must have relied heavily on live performance for the rendering of its comedy.[86]

Beyond the reviews and extracts, cultural references in Britain tended to take the form of references to characters or episodes in the novel which play on the bizarre eccentrics they conjure or the social problems they address. The *Bury and Norwich Post*, for example, reported on a Northumberland Street murder in rooms that resembled Miss Havisham's in their disarray,[87] the *Hampshire Advertiser* referred to Magwitch's situation in an article about penal reform,[88] and several papers reported the use of quotes from the novel (particularly Joe's dialogue) in lectures and public addresses on education, where they were clearly played for laughs.[89] The *Kendal Mercury* mentioned the novel in its round-up of the year's events at the end of December 1861, though the reference is not a flattering one: 'To England it has been a year of "Great Expectations", followed by many disappointments.'[90] And the *Northampton Mercury* got some fun out of Dickens *not* being read:

---

[83]   A copy of this image, 'From Whom We Have Great Expectations', illustration by Mr. Charles Lyall, published by Herbert Watkins (London, 1861), is available to view on the Victorian Web (http://www.victorianweb.org/authors/dickens/gallery/3.html).

[84]   I am grateful to Professor Mervyn Heard (the UK's leading expert on magic lanterns), Bryony Dixon of the British Film Institute, Helen Hanson of the Bill Douglas Centre, the University of Exeter, and Joss Marsh and David Francis of the Kent Museum of the Moving Image for checking their collections for me and sharing their expertise on this point. None has come across an example of a magic lantern version of *Great Expectations*.

[85]   Allan Sutcliffe, 'Dickens in the Music Hall: Part 1', *Dickensian*, 106 (Summer 2010): pp. 101–17.

[86]   J.A. Hardwick, 'Great Expectations: An original (except the title) new comic song', *Comic and Sentimental Songbook* (London, 1861), p. 79.

[87]   'Northumberland Street Tragedy', *Bury and Norwich Post*, Tuesday 23 July 1861, p. 4.

[88]   'The Working of the [penal/convict] system in England and Ireland' (quoted from *Temple Bar*), *Hampshire Advertiser*, Saturday 31 August 1861, p. 7.

[89]   'Witham Literary Institution: Opening of the new lecture hall', *Essex Standard*, Friday 1 November 1861, p. 2.

[90]   *Kendal Mercury*, Saturday 28 December 1861, p. 4.

> At Chatham, where Mr Dickens passed his boyish days, he has, by his readings, rendered great service in augmenting the funds of the Mechanics' Institute. On Tuesday the High Constable, in recognition of this, invited the author of "Great Expectations" to a private banquet, at which most of the local celebrities of the place were assembled to meet him. "Ah, I like Mr Dickens very much," said a Gravesend magnate who was present, "and I should think he's rather a clever fellow, but you see – " he whispered confidentially in the ear of the gentleman next to him " – I don't care about poetry, so I can't say I know much about his writings." Such is fame.[91]

Not always the kind of press Dickens might have chosen, but proof at least of the ubiquity of his works and his persona in culture. Yet this is a curious set of cultural responses compared with the visual, musical and material spin-offs his earlier works had engendered.[92] Where are the Pip polkas and the Magwitch beer mugs? Collins's *Woman in White* spawned bonnets, dances and even a perfume. In Britain, *Great Expectations* seems to have invoked verbal rather than visual responses. Most of these newspapers' references to the novel depend on the assumption of a set of shared intellectual and political concerns ('a year of Great Expectations') or required a great deal of work by the mind's eye ('rooms that Mr Dickens could have used as a model for Miss Havisham's house'). As Margaret Oliphant put it in her review in *Blackwood's Magazine*: 'Mr. Dickens has this time made nothing but a narrative, powerful, indeed, but not pictorial, and from which we cannot quote any one incident sufficiently vivid and distinct to concentrate the attention of the reader.'[93] Even the extracted segments in the newspapers tend to gesture towards the more serious concerns with which they were surrounded: a harbour drowning, a recaptured convict, an emigrant who never learned that he had come into a fortune. *Great Expectations* was not a 'sensation' in the sense in which Secord uses the term. As the latest in a long line of Dickens's offerings, like other works in the latter part of his oeuvre, it was a product which raised particular expectations and either did or did not realise them. The novel's title is a palimpsest of textual and extratextual irony.

In the USA the picture was a very different one. There were neither authorial constraints on dramatization, nor an assumption of *Great Expectations*' effects as largely politically motivated and nationally constituted and, as a result, in 1860 in the USA 'Charles Dickens' was as visual and dramatic a commodity as ever. Several mostly short-lived adaptations appeared shortly after the novel's publication, including a version by George Aiken performed at Barnum's Museum in New York 7–12 October 1861; the immigrant English actress Julie Granville's ('de Margueritte') adaptation on 16 September 1861 at the Walnut Street Theater,

---

[91]   *Northampton Mercury*, Saturday 22 February 1862, p. 5.

[92]   See Frederic G. Kitton, *Dickensiana: A Bibliography of the Literature Relating to Charles Dickens and his Writings* (1886; New York, 1971) for a useful list of songs, illustrations and plays inspired by Dickens's works.

[93]   [Mrs Margaret Oliphant], 'Sensational Novels', *Blackwood's Magazine*, 91 (May 1862): p. 578. See Appendix D.

Philadelphia;[94] Benjamin J. Woolf's adaptation of 7–19 October 1861, performed at the Boston Museum; a version by the Creole actress and poet Adah Isaacs Mencken (who also played Pip), performed 28 March 1862 in Louisville, Kentucky, and also produced at the Howard Athenaeum, Boston, on 9 July 1862;[95] and a version produced by Mencken's friend William Tayleure at the Holliday Street Theatre, Baltimore, around 1862. After that there were no new American adaptations for almost a decade, the next version being W.S. Gilbert's 1871 adaptation (discussed more fully in Chapter 2) performed at the Boston Museum, and Shafto Scott's version called 'My Unknown Friend', performed at Wallack's Theater New York in 1872.[96]

There are several possible reasons for the scarcity of adaptations in the USA in the 1860s, first among them the appalling human cost of (and communications disruption caused by) the American Civil War of 1861–65, and the upheavals of the period of reconstruction that followed. While American theatre continued to thrive, touring was severely curtailed and some Southern theatres never regained their pre-war status. But it seems likely also that despite Dickens's popularity, *Great Expectations* did not strike the right national mood; the war's greatest theatrical hit – for obvious reasons – was an adaptation of *Uncle Tom's Cabin*.[97]

I will return to dramatic adaptations in a moment, but it seems germane at this point to turn briefly to the reviews of the novel in American newspapers by way of providing a context. Reviews were also thinner on the ground than usual in this period, and for the same reason: the papers were full of war news. Where they did appear, reviews offered similar assessments to those in the UK, but with a few interesting differences. One of the longest, the much-reprinted review in the *Atlantic Monthly*, was also one of the kindest, noting both the excitement and the odd disappointment the novel engendered: 'In no other of his romances has the author succeeded so perfectly in at once stimulating and baffling the curiosity of his readers', it mused, calling these surprises 'pleasing electric shocks to intellectual curiosity'. It also felt that while the novel did not represent 'objective reality' and that it would be difficult to conceive of any of the events as actually happening, nonetheless it represented a return to form and, interestingly and unusually for critics in this period, a well-conceived whole: 'The book is, indeed, an artistic creation and not a mere succession of humorous and pathetic scenes, and demonstrates that Dickens is now in the prime, and not in the decline of his great powers.'[98] Compared with earlier novels, that may well have been true;

---

[94]   'Theatrical Record', *New York Clipper*, 21 September 1861, p. 183. For a full discussion, see Malcolm Morley, 'Stages of Great Expectations', *Dickensian*, 51 (Spring 1955): pp. 79–83.

[95]   Morley, 'Stages', pp. 80–81.

[96]   For full information on these productions including cast lists, see Appendix C.

[97]   See John W. Frick Jr., *Uncle Tom's Cabin on the American Stage and Screen* (Basingstoke, 2012).

[98]   'Reviews and Literary Notices: Great Expectations', *Atlantic Monthly*, 8 (September 1861): pp. 380–82.

fully aware of the serious and carefully crafted productions of rising stars such as Eliot, whose works he greatly admired, Dickens was working hard in this period to produce a novel that could be taken seriously and work as a whole, while also still functioning in as broad a range of publishing contexts as possible. It would be surprising if no one noticed the difference, though perhaps it is less surprising that most felt he had not entirely succeeded.

The *New York Daily Tribune* felt that while '[n]o one of the former productions of Mr Dickens is richer in the peculiar qualities which have given him such a wide and solid popularity than the present remarkable creation of his genius', nonetheless there were flaws in the episodic nature of the plot which 'presents a succession of wild improbabilities; and although conducted with more than Mr Dickens's usual finesse, it carries invention to the extreme borders of legitimate romance'.[99] The *New York Times* reported on a preview of the promising early instalments: '"Great Expectations" promises to be one of the cleverest things DICKENS has done. Its opening is very brilliant.' But the review mentioned Thackeray's new novel and a possible new story from George Eliot in equally glowing terms, and perhaps the most significant thing about it is that the names of Dickens, Thackeray and John McLenan are emphasised equally (though George Eliot is mentioned only as 'the author of Adam Bede'); a marker, perhaps, of the paper's understanding of its readers' equal interest in both British novelists and the American artistic talent that helped to bring their work to life.[100]

These papers often announced the American volume publications with particular emphasis on the quality of printing, binding and illustration. The *New York Times*, for example, wrote again in the following year:

> In regard to DICKENS' last work – Great Expectations – almost as many different opinions prevail as it has readers. But whatever opinions may prevail relative to the literary merits of the work, one can be entertained as regards the form in which it is just issued by JAMES G. GREGORY.... The quality of the paper, the clearness of the type, and the beauty of the binding, render each successive volume of the series a work of wonder, as well as a thing of beauty destined to remain a joy forever. In the illustration of Great Expectations, however, we fancy that DARLEY has not quite done justice to himself. He was hurried, perchance; or it may be that he has been sacrificed by the engraver. As in the matter of cooks and meats, it is often that designers and engravers are furnished by different powers.[101]

---

[99] 'New publications', *New York Daily Tribune*, 25 August 1861, p. 2.

[100] *New York Times*, 13 November 1860, no page number.

[101] 'New Publications', *New York Times*, 23 September 1861, no page number. The photogravure frontispiece drawing by Felix O. Darley (1822–88) for Vol. 1 of the Gregory edition of *Great Expectations* was reproduced in Vol. 19 of the Edition de Grande Luxe, ed. Richard Garnett (London: Merrill and Baker, 1900). Walter E. Smith's *Charles Dickens: A Bibliography of His First American Editions 1836–1870* (New Castle, 2012) places Gregory's edition as the second American one behind Peterson's since it was in readers' hands later, though it was deposited with the Library of Congress first.

The *Columbia Democrat and Bloomsburg General Advertiser* likewise praised the cheap edition published by James G. Gregory 'in superb style at 75 cents per volume. It is uniform with the splendid edition offered by the same publisher. Send and get it'. This paper kept its announcement brief, devoting most of the space on the page to reports of soldiers killed, wounded, or captured.[102] The juxtaposition of war news with items on *Great Expectations* was understandably common practice, but the reviews' emphasis on the quality of the publications is also significant, I think: the quality reprinting of his novels was one of the ways in which Americans made Dickens their own, a claim to technical superiority which was to bear further fruit later in film adaptations.[103]

American and British readers had a very different experience of the novel in its first incarnations. As we have already seen, it was not illustrated in AYR and even the first volume editions were ill-provided for by Marcus Stone's eight rather bland drawings.[104] Figure 1.1, for example, gives us a dandified grown-up Pip saying goodbye after his sister's funeral and presents Joe as a bit unkempt, though he is a figure of power and dignity nonetheless.

In the USA, however, the *Harper's* serialisation was illustrated with 40 weekly plates by John McLenan (with breaks on 11, 18, and 25 May 1861, possibly to make room for Civil War scenes).[105] The first Peterson edition was also issued unillustrated (except for a frontispiece illustration of Dickens), but in subsequent Peterson editions 34 of McLenan's plates were reproduced, including the example provided in Figure 1.2 in which Pip (about to leave the forge) is but a child, and Joe a very much larger, stouter and more comical figure.

Perhaps unsurprisingly, the American reviews remarked on the novel's comedy as often as its pathos or its social commentary, the *New York Tribune* describing its 'broad farce' as a necessary 'safety valve' for Dickens's 'farcical fancies', and the *New York Times* promising that it strikes a 'livelier key' than *A Tale of Two Cities*.[106] But the emphasis in many reviews was on the novel as proudly existing in a particularly American version, superior in design and quality to its British counterpart, and perhaps even making up for its author's faults.

Robert McParland has explored the ways in which Dickens's ordinary (i.e. non-professional) American readers prior to the First World War constructed a version

---

[102] *Columbia Democrat and Bloomsburg General Advertiser*, 24 August 1861, p. 3.

[103] Rosenberg makes a similar point about the marked reference to McLenan's importance in *Harper's* announcement of the delay in getting the plates for the 26 January issue, but I believe the point has wider implications and more importance than he gives it (*Great Expectations*, ed. Rosenberg, p. 399).

[104] See Paul B. Davis, 'Dickens, Hogarth, and the Illustrations for *Great Expectations*', *Dickensian,* 80 (Autumn 1984): pp. 130–43.

[105] See Philip V. Allingham, 'Illustrations of Great Expectations by John McLenan', Victorian Web http://www.victorianweb.org/art/illustration/mclenan/ge.html [accessed 12 March 2013].

[106] 'New publications', *New York Daily Tribune*, 25 August 1861, p. 2; *New York Times*, 13 November 1860, no page number.

Fig 1.1   "'Good–bye, dear Joe! – No, don't wipe it off … for God's sake, give me your blackened hand! – I shall be down soon and often'" (*Great Expectations*, Ch. XVIII). Illustration by Marcus Stone for Chapman and Hall, 1861. Scanned image by Philip V. Allingham, courtesy of the Victorian Web.

Fig. 1.2   "'Pip's a gentleman of fortune, then,'" said Joe, "and God bless him in it!'" (*Great Expectations*, Ch. XVIII). Illustration by John McLenan for *Harper's Weekly*, 5 (9 February 1861), p. 85. Scanned image by Philip V. Allingham, courtesy of the Victorian Web.

of the author that suited their own nation-building moment, asserting that 'the wide consumption and reproduction of Dickens by American audiences shaped the development of American literature and culture'.[107] This is an important claim, one that I think we can see working even here among professional reviewers. Dickens both was and was not 'English': his stories provided models from which American audiences could take what suited them, what fitted their own interests and concerns, and also against which they could define the shape and form of their own national differences. In selling the American reproduction rights of his 'capsular narrative' to *Harper's* without stipulating either an illustrator or a

---

[107]   McParland, *Charles Dickens's American Audience*, p. 5.

subsequent publisher for the volume version, Dickens both protected his own interests and enabled future national diversification. As a result, there genuinely was an American 'Charles Dickens', and it was not the same as the British version. Many American listeners were disappointed rather than thrilled by Dickens's 1868 reading tour, and many complained that his mature renditions of the early work, far from bringing his characters to life, actually ruined them.[108] This suggests that the gap between Dickens's late work (and how he wanted his audiences to see him) and America's conception of his oeuvre was significant.

Like their British counterparts, some American newspapers printed extracts. The *Cincinnati Daily Press* printed the extract of Wopsle playing Hamlet. 'One of the most characteristic sketches of Mr Dickens in his most recent novel', it states by way of an introduction, 'is his description of Hamlet, as played in a minor London theatre. He has written fewer chapters more amusing and graphic.'[109] A pragmatic analysis of the text highlights some interesting differences from the British versions of this practice; this extract is surrounded by articles which by no stretch of the imagination can be seen to provide contextual support for the novel's larger themes. The articles on this page cover topics from 'Gunpowder' (in which the United States' principal manufactories are listed) to 'How to Knit Soldiers' Stockings', and they are accompanied by items of war news with a morale-boosting theme, several short humorous sketches and a few individual jokes. The Dickens extract, like these other items, seems designed purely to raise a smile in difficult times. This truly is an extract decoupled from the novel's main narrative engine.

More importantly still – and surprisingly seldom, if ever, discussed – is the fact that the working-class 'penny' morning daily the *Sun* (New York, circulation around 60,000 copies) printed a chapter from *Great Expectations* almost every day between 3 June and 11 September 1861, without attribution to anyone except Dickens, without mention of a 'ready-print' arrangement (an early form of syndication), and seemingly unconcerned about copyright infringement (which was in fact a hit-and-miss affair in the USA in this period).[110]

There are several significant things about this serial version. First, it means the circulation of the novel in 1861 was greater – and reached a lower class of reader in the USA (particularly in Manhattan, this paper's largest subscription base) – than has often been assumed. It might also be significant that the *Sun*, while probably the most conservative of the penny papers in this period, was founded on the principle that ordinary people needed journalism and fiction to suit their literacy levels and interests. Dickens's thirteenth novel seems ill-suited to this purpose. However, an early history of the newspaper explains the serialisation as the result of the paper's takeover on 6 August 1860 by 'Archibald M. Morrison, a rich young man of religious fervour', who turned the paper's journalism in more

---

[108] McParland, *Charles Dickens's American Audience*, pp. 175–83.

[109] *Cincinnati Daily Press*, 7 October 1861, p. 4.

[110] Charles A. Johanningsmeier, *Fiction and the American Literary Marketplace: The Role of Newspaper Syndicates in America, 1860–1900* (Cambridge, 1997), p. 36.

evangelical directions, refused to accept advertisements on a Sunday, and felt that *Great Expectations* would be a good antidote to the ripping (but not exactly Godly) yarns written specially for the *Sun* by authors like H. Warren Trowbridge, Horatio Alger and Walter Savage North.[111] This is an interesting fragment of evidence, suggesting that despite his popularity Dickens was associated with respectability in this period (though this – as Chapter 2 will demonstrate – was considerably less true a decade later). At any rate, his inclusion did nothing to stop the paper's circulation from plummeting; by the end of 1861, many readers had spurned the paper's new preachy format to the extent that in the following year the management had to change again.[112]

Second, unlike the paper's normal serials, *Great Expectations* was not written especially for this publication, so we must also ask if it was a piracy and, if so, of what sort. Internal textual evidence indicates that it follows the *Harper's Weekly* text, not the AYR, but this is not surprising since *Harper's* text was more readily available to the *Sun*'s editors.[113] What is surprising is that neither Dickens nor T.B. Peterson's seems to have made any move to prevent it, though given the summer timing it must have cut into the volume sales. Dickens probably felt that it was out of his hands (he seems to have been remarkably disinterested in this novel after he finished it), and perhaps Peterson's felt they had the competitive edge with their volume editions. We will probably never know for sure. But *Great Expectations'* presence in a newspaper so very different from *Harper's* provides another piece of the reception history puzzle, offering new ways of understanding its cultural impact.

Third, we should pause briefly on the fact that while the *Sun*'s single chapter teaspoons were even smaller than Dickens had intended, formally speaking, the serialisation still works. Tucked away inauspiciously in a couple of columns on the back page among adverts for medicines such as 'Radways' Ready Relief: The Soldier's Safeguard – Safety Against Death!' and 'Mrs Winslow's Soothing Syrup' for teething infants, the individual chapters hold up remarkably well, better by far than the shorter comic extracts printed so widely elsewhere in the USA. Put to the test, context notwithstanding, the drama and interest remain. The fact that readers were not persuaded to keep buying the paper during 1861 may have had less to do with Dickens than with too many tedious articles about prayer meetings and too few about the war.

It is the novel's ability to provide detachable snapshots like this which informs and enables the remediations, and this process continues into the versions adapted in the USA for the stage. None of these stage adaptations seems to have had a very

---

[111] Frank M. O'Brien, *The Story of the Sun, New York, 1833–1928* (New York, 1917), pp. 135, 141–2.

[112] O'Brien, *Story of the Sun*, p. 137.

[113] On page 1, for example, the phrase 'My first *distinct* impression of the identity of things' is used, as opposed to AYR's 'My first *most vivid and broad* impression of the identity of things'. And Pip's father is called Tobias as in *Harper's*, not Philip as in AYR. (Italics mine.)

long run (perhaps as a result of wartime privations), but for however long they lasted they seem to have worked best as crowd-pleasing popular melodrama at a low price. Dickens as serious theatre was some time in the future; in the USA, *Great Expectations* was a new sensation to be treated like any other. Reviewing the play at Barnum's Museum, the *New York Daily Tribune* enthused:

> AMERICAN MUSEUM. GREAT SUCCESS OF THE NEW PLAY, DICKENS'S GREAT EXPECTATIONS. Crowded and delighted audiences, both afternoon and evening. This great drama is greeted with perfect enthusiasm and will be repeated THIS and EVERY AFTERNOON and EVENING at 3 and 7 1/2 o'clock. Who will pay 50 cents and a dollar to see inferior plays when they can witness this magnificent Drama, and see all the novelties of the Museum beside for 25 cents? Popular and attractive as it is, it will be continued but a short time as it must give place to other dramatic novelties.[114]

As Paul Schlicke has reminded us, Dickens's appearance here among popular entertainments is perfectly natural since he had dedicated his life to such things. But his polemical stance on the need for amusements for the hard-working populace had changed over the years, culminating in his own touring stage show of public readings, and given his belief (in the face of Forster's objections) that he might raise rather than lower the novel's status through these performances, he might have been disappointed at the 'low' culture with which he here rubbed shoulders.[115] The adaptation concluded with a comic ballet by Mr W.A. Wood entitled 'The Jolly Millers', and the 'other novelties' scheduled to follow included 'Miss Dora Dawron the double-voiced vocalist' and a family of albinos from Madagascar.[116]

There was nothing Dickens could have done about this: once his copyright agreements had been reached for the first serial and volume publication rights, he had no control over how his image was constructed in the USA. Apparently aware that in many ways their readers were more attached to an earlier, more playful and exuberant (and perhaps in some cases even a pre-*Martin Chuzzlewit* and *American Notes*) 'Charles Dickens', American publishers and dramatists worked hard to realise *Great Expectations* in familiar visual incarnations and to tie it to Dickens's earlier form. The fact that many more different illustrated editions (with far more generous quantities of illustrations) emerged there in the last decade of Dickens's life than appeared in Britain, along with the comic flavour of the illustrations which McLenan produced compared with those of Stone, are features of this attempt. It is significant, too, that the Petersons' edition of *Great Expectations* bore the old name of 'Boz' – a pseudonym Dickens himself had dropped in the 1840s – rather than 'Charles Dickens'. After the sombre tone of *A Tale of Two Cities*, Americans (including McLenan, who also illustrated the earlier novel) seem to have pounced with relief on the return of comic episodes in *Great Expectations*.

---

[114] 'Amusements', *New York Daily Tribune*, Friday 11 October 1861, p. 1.

[115] Paul Schlicke, *Dickens and Popular Entertainment* (London, 1985), p. 227.

[116] 'Amusements', *New York Daily Tribune*, Friday 11 October 1861, p. 1.

How do we explain this preference for the comic? McParland suggests that nineteenth-century America was still a predominantly oral culture and that the prevalence of 'character tags' in the early caricatures, which enabled listeners and audiences to remember his creations without having to read the stories for themselves, may be one compelling reason. Dickens's caricatures may have helped his first American readers to make sense of a dynamic, rapidly expanding cultural environment in which strangers of all kinds speaking many different languages abounded.[117] Despite its American publishers' efforts, though, *Great Expectations* – while a marked improvement on its predecessor – was still, as a late Dickens novel, less easily available for such purposes, and amid the general chaos and suffering of war it seems to have missed its mark with some readers. This might help to explain the lack of adaptations after war broke out. McParland confirms that it was less widely available than earlier books since the circulation of *Harper's* in the South was seriously disrupted by the war. While there was a Confederate Edition published in Mobile, Alabama, by S. H Goetzel & Co. in 1863, and McParland asserts that the novel was popular among soldiers, his examples of readers' testimonies of Dickens's popularity during the war almost all refer to earlier novels, particular *Copperfield* and *Pickwick*.[118] Wartime readers, one memoir testifies, wanted above all 'the wonderful character pieces'.[119]

Once it was out in the world, Dickens himself seemed done with the novel; while he revised it lightly for both the 1862 and the 1868 editions, it is one of only two works for which he never wrote a preface, the other being his least 'favourite child', *Hard Times*. Dickens's manipulation of his own literary persona in this period was accomplished through the tenor of his darker late novels, the unillustrated serialised and first-volume editions, the often sombre journalism including the 'Uncommercial Traveller' essays in the pages of AYR, and the paid public readings by means of which he firmly controlled both the visualisation of his characters and the public's responses to his own fame.[120] This was resulting in an altogether more serious cultural product, a product for a new age. Whether this was a result of his circumstances, his frame of mind or a conscious attempt to meet the new literary challenges he faced, the net result as it appears in *Great Expectations* is a significant one which would be played out in interesting directions after his death.

---

[117] McParland, *Charles Dickens's American Audience*, pp. 124, 168.

[118] McParland, *Charles Dickens's American Audience*, pp. 144–5, 152.

[119] McParland, *Charles Dickens's American Audience*, p. 145.

[120] Jerome Meckier suggests that the 1867–68 public readings 'were designed to offer the kind of author-reader contact that he discovered he really desired: controlled periods of performance and intoxicating applause followed by a return to sobriety in private'. Jerome Meckier, *Innocent Abroad: Charles Dickens's American Engagements* (Lexington, 1990), p. 6.

Chapter 2
Afterlife in the West, 1870–1900

'The best read author in the English language'?

When Dickens died at Gad's Hill on the evening of 9 June 1870, a Press Association telegram instantly wired the news to newspaper editors all over the British Isles, and almost as quickly via the same means it reached the American press and thus Dickens's fans on the other side of the Atlantic. There was certainly, as almost every biographer notes, a shared outpouring of grief in print (along with a few more temperate articles of the 'bit of a shame, he used to be quite funny' variety), but the responses on each side of the Atlantic are interestingly and distinctly different in ways that shaped Dickens's posthumous fame in both literary and non-literary media.

It is fitting that the demise of the world's first and foremost Industrial Age author could so swiftly become a topic of transatlantic news, since it happened through the same means that had propelled him to stardom and through which he and his publishers had managed his international career. In Dickens's relatively short lifetime, devoted as it was to ensuring that as many people as possible could get hold of his writings in whatever form they could be shared, the means through which print, ideas, images and entertainment could be disseminated had undergone the swiftest developments in human history. While the Associated Press was only two years old when he died and Tillotson's Fiction Bureau was still three years (and a full international copyright agreement more than 20 years) in the future, the dawn of prototype syndicates already meant the benefits of increased publicity in the USA for established British authors, and may even have enhanced and in some measure protected the prospects of those just starting out.[1] Situated as Dickens was in the vanguard of many major shifts in printing, distribution and illustration technologies – perhaps most particularly in the last decade of his life when transport and communication improved dramatically on both sides of the Atlantic – he was both a victim and a beneficiary of the rapid unregulated expansion of print in the United States. This, as Patten remarks, 'contributed largely and variously to his phenomenal popularity' whether he was aware of it or not.[2] While he undoubtedly lost out financially to the pirates and 'readypress' merchants in spite of his lucrative agreements with magazines such as *Harper's*, it is difficult to imagine a more fertile ground for the serving up of his 'teaspoons' than a national press that was expanding exponentially to feed an exploding population, increasingly comprised of immigrants. What he lost in income, he gained in fame.

---

[1]   Johanningsmeier, *Fiction and the American Literary Marketplace*, pp. 102–3.

[2]   Patten, *Dickens and his Publishers*, p. 295.

The publication and reception contexts of *Great Expectations* in the 1860s were, as I have already demonstrated, of a markedly different character on each side of the Atlantic. Posthumously, too, Dickens's fame took on a different flavour in each country. Much of the British Press mourned him as a national hero. *The Times* pronounced: 'There is no one, we are sure, of the present day, whose name will live longer in the memories of English readers, or will be more thoroughly identified with the English language, than the author of Pickwick.'[3] The *Manchester Times* claimed: 'Mr Dickens has not merely shown us to posterity, he has shown us to ourselves.'[4] The *Northern Echo* called him 'the People's champion, friend and favourite, the hater of all meanness, the lover of virtue, the most powerful moralist and preacher of the age',[5] and the *Telegraph* promised that 'his memory will be kept green and honoured while the language and the nation shall endure.'[6] The *Illustrated Police News* printed a memorial illustration of Britannia holding up a picture of Dickens's face, with distraught British fans weeping into their handkerchiefs in the foreground. The *Essex Standard* went further in its construction of Dickens as a national icon, clearly annoyed by the French papers which (predictably) did not pay him sufficient homage: 'Whilst all [the French papers] admit the purity and humour of his works, it is evident that their appreciation of them is not so high as here or in the United States – a fact which is not surprising, seeing the difference between the genius of the two nations and the imperfect manner in which his works have been translated into French.'[7] Even the *John Bull* conceded a point or two: 'Charles Dickens has closed his life-work, and though he may not on all points ecclesiastical, social, or political have taken our own view in relation to current events, we desire to offer to his memory the tribute of a genuine admiration.'[8] Death the great leveller, raising Dickens from a plateau of late-career criticism to the status of national treasure. By these measures, reproduced to a greater or lesser degree in almost every section of the British press, recognising Dickens's genius *made* one an Englishman, the more so because of his reception in other English-speaking countries. In June 1870, not to be able to read Dickens in English was suddenly somehow a measure of inferiority.

In the USA, reaction was inevitably slightly different. While, as McParland claims, 'There was a cultural aura around Dickens immediately following his death ... Dickens was someone Americans wanted to read about', the public discussions of his importance – and his life – reflected a particular set of national concerns and circumstances.[9] There were certainly lamentations over his death.

---

[3]   *The Times*, Friday 10 June 1870, p. 12.

[4]   *Manchester Times*, Saturday 11 June 1870, p. 5.

[5]   *Northern Echo*, Saturday 11 June 1870, p. 2.

[6]   *Telegraph* [London], quoted in the *Dundee Courier & Argus*, Saturday 11 June 1870, no page number.

[7]   *Essex Standard and General Advertiser for the Eastern Counties*, Friday 17 June 1870, responding to a *Times* notice of 14 June 1870, p. 12.

[8]   *John Bull*, Saturday 11 June 1870, p. 413.

[9]   McParland, *Charles Dickens's American Audience*, p. 193.

The Ohio *Conservative* announced: 'We believe Dickens was more generally read, and more keenly relished, by the mass in this country even than in Great Britain, for there are few Americans who possess the average common school education who are not familiar with his works.... He was a brave, good and true man, a democrat and friend of the people ... he invigorated the social forces of the world.'[10] But the Philadelphia *Evening Telegraph* took a more pragmatic view: 'A very great humourist he was, but that he is "one of the greatest and most persuasive preachers" we may be permitted to doubt, unless we take the gospel of jollity to be a divine revelation.'[11] As a late work, *Great Expectations* occupied an odd and rather insecure position in this discourse, continuing to chart an erratic course between iconic status as a work of Dickens and both popular and critical devaluation.

On its emergence, *Great Expectations* had been competing in the USA not only with Civil War news, but also with American novels such as Beecher Stowe's *Uncle Tom's Cabin* (1852), which had hit the stage and the national mood simultaneously and much more publicly. It also competed with new modes of production which favoured different types of fiction: the dime novel debuted in 1860, quickly deluging the lower end of the market with cheap, home-grown fiction which became a staple of the working classes and a particular favourite with Civil War soldiers.[12] By 1865, in addition to the explosion of cheaply priced American stories, there was further competition at the higher end from other home-grown writers such as Mark Twain. This nationalist trend continued with the increasing attention given to writers such as Louisa May Alcott, whose *Little Women* appeared in two volumes in 1868–69, and, for the working classes, the proliferation of cheap 'Libraries' of pamphlet-length stories during the 1860s and 1870s.[13] The 'Charles Dickens' whom American readers had embraced as their own back in the 1830s and 1840s – and upon his death continued to celebrate as having embraced – was not quite the same entity as the middle-aged writer whom in 1870 the British press were lauding as a national treasure.

On both sides of the Atlantic there was a tendency (already present in the first critical responses to *Great Expectations*) to see Dickens's talents as declining in his later years; the death announcements and obituaries published in the press overwhelmingly favour the early works, tiresomely repeating the titles of and characters from *Pickwick*, *Oliver Twist*, *Nicholas Nickleby* and *David Copperfield*, and mentioning the novels that came after these – if they mention them at all – as a list of also-rans. The British *Standard*'s obituary is typical, excusing Dickens's literary sins on the grounds that as a young writer, at least, he made up for them:

> It is said that his pathos was often unreal, that his sentiment often became maudlin, his humour was sometimes forced and always grotesque. All this may have been. But, on the other hand, he has erected a gallery of portraits, made us

---

[10] *Conservative* [M'connelsville, Ohio], 17 June 1870, p. 2.

[11] *Evening Telegraph* [Philadelphia], 19 August 1870, 5th ed., p. 7.

[12] Michael Denning, *Mechanic Accents: Dime Novels and Working-Class Culture in America* (New York and London, 1987), p. 11.

[13] Denning, *Mechanic Accents*, p. 12.

acquainted with a greater number of living flesh and blood characters than any other author of our own or other times, with the exception of Shakespeare or Scott. Pickwick and Weller and Pecksniff, and Mark Tapley, and Dick Swiveller, and Little Nell, and the Marchioness, and a whole host of others, have become to us household words, and have entered as it were into the marrow of our language.[14]

The Times concurred: 'While *Pickwick* charms us with its broad humour, it is in *Nicholas Nickleby* and *Oliver Twist* that the power of Mr Dickens' pathos shows itself.'[15] The American *Evening Telegraph* felt the same: 'In the works that succeeded *David Copperfield* there is a gradual but visible decline, until in his latest efforts a noticeable falling off of the old power is observable.... Let anyone read *Oliver Twist*, *Dombey and Son* and *David Copperfield* and then attempt *Great Expectations* and *Our Mutual Friend*, and the immense difference will be apparent at once.'[16]

The last two or three complete novels in particular seem to have baffled readers on both sides of the Atlantic who thought they knew the real 'Charles Dickens' and were awaiting his return. Dickens's second American reading tour (December 1867 – April 1868) had been a resounding success both critically and financially, but it had done nothing to spread the fame of his later works since he had read exclusively from his early ones (*Copperfield*, *Pickwick*, *Nickleby*, *Chuzzlewit*, *Dombey*, *A Christmas Carol* and *Dr Marigold*).[17] Indeed, in the American press there is a great deal of lamentation (stemmed briefly for a while by false intelligence to the contrary[18]) that *Edwin Drood* had been left unfinished at Dickens's death when its early numbers looked so promisingly reminiscent of the early power; 'the opening chapter shows more of the old fire than any of his recent efforts', claimed the *Evening Telegraph* sadly, having lambasted the three latest novels for being substandard.[19] What to do with the later novels in order to ensure they too could capitalise on the author's fame was a problem for publishers in both nations, one which engendered a distinctive set of solutions.

The Construction of a Posthumous Phenomenon

Characteristic of the difference in cultural responses is the fact that sections of the American press devoted a lot of discussion immediately after Dickens's death to the possible fate of his immortal soul. His literary afterlife, for many Americans, was more easily assured than his spiritual one. In Britain, by 1870, he might be

[14]   *Standard*, Friday 10 June 1870, p. 3.

[15]   *The Times*, Friday 10 June 1870, p. 12.

[16]   *Evening Telegraph*, Friday 10 June 1870, p. 1.

[17]   Michael Slater, *Charles Dickens* (New Haven and London, 2009), p. 577.

[18]   The *Sun* (New York) for example, claimed to have had word from Dickens's publishers that they had 'material for three additional numbers and memoranda almost sufficient to complete the narrative'. 14 June 1870, p. 1.

[19]   *Evening Telegraph*, 10 June 1870, p. 1.

widely thought of as a writer whose works one could safely bring home to one's daughters,[20] and sermons preached after his death generally agreed that he was a good man if not necessarily a religious one.[21] But in the USA, as the obituaries and very quickly thereafter the reams of reminiscences and published biographies began to draw the public's attention to the facts of his life (particularly his drinking, lavish entertaining, separation from his wife and rare appearances in Church), the two parts of his posthumous fame – the literary and the personal – became problematically conflated in a public consciousness undergoing a troubled and bloody process of self-definition in the wake of the Civil War. This was a nation facing bitter struggles over racial equality, the definition of citizenship and radical constitutional amendment, and engaging in complex debates about the kind of country the newly re-United States wanted to be and the kinds of icons (political, cultural and religious) which a nation emerging from the brink of disaster ought to erect.[22] Dickens's posthumous fame played a small but important role in these debates, highlighting the problem of how a reforming national identity could accommodate a widely revered but unorthodox outsider.

On 13 July 1870, the *Charleston Daily News* printed an article called 'Death of Charles Dickens: His Habits of Living – Why he Separated from his Wife – Day of his Death', written by an acquaintance of Dickens's who had stayed with him in 1851. This correspondent assured the paper's readership that while Dickens never appeared drunk, he liked to entertain lavishly, and alcohol formed an important part of all such occasions. It also commented that while his works were undoubtedly moral, Dickens himself was not particularly religious and he never read the Bible or went to Church. On 12 June 1870, the *Daily Phoenix* (Columbia, South Carolina) also wondered whether there was evidence from his life and works that he was good enough to enter Heaven.

On 13 July 1870, Colonel Coates Kinney (1826–1904), a Civil War veteran, popular poet, lawyer, journalist and future Radical Republican senator, entered the debate with a stinging attack on these sorts of opinions. His target was the abolitionist Henry Ward Beecher (1813–87), brother of Harriet Beecher Stowe. Dickens had met Ward Beecher during his 1868 American tour and found him 'an unostentatious, evidently able, straightforward, and agreeable man; extremely well-informed, and with a good knowledge of art'.[23] In the divisive months after Dickens's death, Coates found reason to disagree. From his pulpit at the Brooklyn

---

[20]   The *Leicester Chronicle and Leicestershire Mercury* (Saturday, 11 June 1870, p. 8), for example, assured readers that he 'never wrote a line that a mother need hesitate to put in the hands of her innocent child', and this claim appears in a number of the death notices. Frederic G. Kitton, however, pointed out in 1886 that issues about Dickens's morality had also been a problem in Britain earlier in his career. *Dickensiana*, p.xiv.

[21]   The *Belfast News-Letter*, Monday 13 June 1870, also defensively quoted Dickens's last letter to an unnamed correspondent, answering a complaint that passages in *Edwin Drood* were offensive to religious readers.

[22]   Hugh Brogan, 'Reconstruction 1865–1877', in *The Penguin History of the USA*, New Edition (London, 1999), pp. 346–73.

[23]   Forster, *Life*, p. 858.

Plymouth Congregationalist Church, Beecher had claimed after the announcement of Dickens's death that while his Calvinist father would have been prepared to send Dickens 'straight to hell', he himself was more liberal and had concluded that Dickens was a good but 'low' sort who, though not 'distinctively Christian', had perhaps 'done good enough in the world to save him from being utterly damned' (with the exception, naturally, of his opinions on drink). Outraged by the reformist Beecher's claim to be able to judge an author's merits at all, Coates called him a 'conceited and egotistical humbug', fuming: 'He, to sit in judgement of Charles Dickens! He, with his little rhetorical peddling of dogmas, to presume to gauge the brain which conceived "David Copperfield" and "Bleak House", to decide whether he ought to be admitted to heaven or not!' He ended by calling Beecher a 'blatherskite' who, if he lived a thousand years, could do less to spread the Christian doctrine than Dickens was able to accomplish with a single page. He signed himself the 'Xenia Torchbearer' in a call to arms for like-minded Dickens fans for whom politics, religion and literature were best kept separate.[24] The episode serves to highlight the intense feelings about the nature of individual freedom that were circulating during this period, the ease with which Dickens's life, art and politics could be appropriated either as warning or exemplar, and the ways in which his celebrity was refracted through different national and ideological concerns.

But the public debates about the rights of the individual and art versus morality did nothing to revive the fortunes of *Great Expectations*. Kinney, like most other commentators, refers here to Dickens's reputation only in relation to the older works. Perhaps *Great Expectations* – despite its fine-grained exploration of the emptiness of the desire for monetary wealth and its compassion for the maltreated underdog – was antithetical to American concerns in this difficult period. As historian Hugh Brogan puts it, 'for Americans, a sour taste of failure and disappointment' hung about the reconstruction epoch. The themes of *Great Expectations*, although quite at home among the local news in Britain in 1861, seemed much less topical in America at that time, and by the troubled 1870s a novel with failure and disappointment at its heart was even less likely to offer American readers reassurance or pleasurable escape.[25]

Nonetheless, publishers on both sides of the Atlantic did their best to capitalise on the publicity surrounding Dickens's death and to maximise returns on a now-finite if frustratingly incomplete product, and they were largely successful. Critically denigrated he might be, but some of his works still sold in large and – more surprisingly still – in some cases increasing numbers. 'There probably never was a writer of so vast a popularity whose genius was so little *appreciated* by the critics', George Lewis wrote in 1872. 'Were the critics wrong, and if so, in what consisted their error? How are we to reconcile this immense popularity with this critical contempt?'[26] Patten replies that 'the discrepancy cannot be explained', and

---

[24]   *Urbana Union*, 13 July 1870, p. 1.

[25]   Brogan, *The Penguin History of the USA*, p. 373.

[26]   G.H. Lewes, 'Dickens in Relation to Criticism', *Fortnightly Review*, 11 (February 1872): p. 143.

perhaps he is right, but in the 1870s there was little disagreement among the reading public about exactly which of Dickens's books deserved to stand the test of time.[27] To most of them the early works – deemed funnier, or more overtly polemical, or perhaps just more personal – spoke the loudest. Now he was unable to redeem his reputation for himself through a late return to form, posthumously 'Charles Dickens' was a more fractured entity than even Lewes recognised, increasingly divided up along temporal, national, regional and theological as well as critical lines.

Holding his backlist together in the face of these deep fissures was very much in his publishers' interests. Chapman and Hall continued to issue full sets of the works in a steady stream of reformatted reprints, notably the 'Charles Dickens edition' (1867–75); the cheap 'Household Edition' (1871–79) illustrated by new artists; the second 'Illustrated Library Edition' (1873–76); a 34-volume 'Gadshill edition' (1897–98), reprinted from Dickens's corrected edition of 1867–68, edited and introduced by Andrew Lang, co-published with Scribner's of New York and reissued in 1903 as the 'De Luxe Edition' (then again in 1908 and yet again in 1910–11 as the 'Centenary Edition'). As though to ameliorate the possible confusion caused by this plenitude, the book-buying public was then treated to the 22-volume 'Authentic Edition' in 1901–6. It probably didn't help: simultaneously Chapman and Hall issued the 17-volume Oxford 'India Paper Edition' in 1901–2 (with Forster's *Life* added in 1907), and a reissue of this version in 23 volumes appeared in 1903–7 as the 'Fireside Edition' with illustrations by Charles Green, also issued by Henry Frowde through the New York office of Oxford University Press.[28] At least five further editions followed in the next five years.

Some of these editions were part of a complicated set of transatlantic arrangements, probably set up in an attempt to mop up a share of the vast US market. Patten notes that in 1878 Chapman and Hall sold the entire stock of the 'People's Edition' plus 500 sets of the 'Charles Dickens' edition and the entire 'Household Edition' at half retail price to Routledge, who also contracted for use of the stereo and cover blocks for reissuing *Sketches*, *Oliver Twist*, *Chuzzlewit* and *Nickleby* in the USA (proof, if nothing else is, of the strong sense that it was the earlier novels that were likely to do better there).[29] Apart from this example, *Great Expectations* appeared in all these series, sometimes on its own, sometimes shackled to a partner.

Chapman and Hall by no means had the corner on the Dickens UK market, even in this period; several other publishers also offered series, adopting a range of strategies to make their products stand out in a crowded field. The 'Macmillan Edition' in 21 volumes (1893–1925), for example, reprinted the text of the first editions, contained introductions by Charles Dickens Jr., and featured a collection of letters edited by his sister-in-law Georgina and his daughter Kate. J.M. Dent published the 'Temple Edition' in 35 volumes (1898–1903) edited by Walter Jerrold, and the 'Everyman's Library Edition' in 22 volumes (1906–21), provided

---

[27]   Patten, *Dickens and His Publishers*, p. 327.

[28]   Note in author's copy of the Fireside Edition of Forster's *Life*.

[29]   Patten, *Dickens and His Publishers*, pp. 328–9.

with introductions by Jerrold and G.K. Chesterton. There were also editions with new introductions and in some cases new illustrations by Methuen and Co. (1899–1901), Robson and Kerslake (1885), Nelson (1899) and Merrill and Baker (1900).[30] All these publishing houses devoted a large part of their lists to reprints of bestselling or classic authors; Dickens's presence among them is testament to industry perceptions about his continued saleability.

American firms also republished Dickens after his death; both before and after the Chace Act of 1891, which partially protected the copyrights of foreign authors in America, there were dozens of reprints of all shapes and sizes.[31] As in Britain, there were many complete sets such as those by Porter and Coates (1888), Gebbie & Co. (1892–94), Houghton, Mifflin and Co. (1894); and Peter Fenelon Collier & Son (1900). *Great Expectations* was occasionally issued in a separate volume, but in the USA in particular it was usually coupled to another Dickens work, either a novel (often *Oliver Twist* or *Little Dorrit*) or a set of essays or stories such as 'Pictures from Italy' and 'American Notes'. This was probably for reasons of size: *Great Expectations* is shorter than many of the other novels and thus needs some bulking up if it is to help the edition achieve uniformity: an important consideration for most publishers' series or libraries in this period. But it might also be a sign that the novel was not thought capable of doing very well on its own; publishers know very well that not everyone will buy the whole set all at once and it is worth persuading them to buy as many individual copies as possible. As this small sample shows, there was a bewilderingly wide range of variant editions on offer in both the UK and the USA between 1870 and 1900.[32]

A closer examination of the details of the posthumous repackaging of *Great Expectations* for a new generation of readers can provide us with some navigational aids through this vast ocean of editions. In a sense, the constant readjustment of the novel's paratexts which these editions represent is a form of remediation. As Bolter and Grusin explain:

> The goal of remediation is to refashion or rehabilitate other media … popular acceptance, and therefore economic success, can come only by convincing consumers that the new medium improves on the older ones…. Each of those forms takes part of its meaning from the other products in a process of honorific remediation and at the same time makes a tacit claim to offer an experience that the other forms cannot.[33]

---

[30]   See Paul B. Davis, 'Dickens, Hogarth, and the Illustrated *Great Expectations*', *Dickensian*, 80 (Autumn 1984): pp. 130–43, for a discussion of F.W. Pailthorpe's illustrations for the 1885 Robson and Kerslake edition. Davis sees Pailthorpe's illustrations of the novel as among 'the most successful' in their recapturing of the essence of Cruikshank and Phiz (p. 141).

[31]   It is worth noting here that under the 'manufacturing clause', the Chace Act only protected foreign works which had been printed from type set in the USA. The national pride in American workmanship which we saw seeping through in US reviews of American-printed Dickens works was formalised as a protectionist ethos through this legislation.

[32]   See Appendix A for a select list of editions 1861–1939.

[33]   Bolter and Grusin, *Remediation*, pp. 56, 89.

Offering something *new* is vital here, even as it trades and depends on the value of something well-established and (once) venerated. Crucially, too, for Bolter and Grusin the term 'remediation' does not just refer to the radical refashioning of a work into another form such as a play or a film, although this sort of large-scale remediation was, and still is, very much a part of the Dickens phenomenon and *Great Expectations* – eventually – one of its greatest successes. It can also refer to any of the smaller changes or improvements a work or a system undergoes in order to widen its consumer base. Bolter and Grusin suggest: 'We can also consider repurposing in microeconomic terms as the refashioning of materials and practices.'[34] After Dickens's death, publishers competed with each other to refashion and offer to the public a product that was 'closer' to the 'real' Dickens than any other version; a product that could bridge better than any other on the market the widening gulf of elapsed time between his own bygone era and the present. Introductions written by Dickens's contemporaries and by respected critics were one way of remediating his texts for a new set of consumers. They glossed some of the more dated language and concepts, offered or perhaps even created critical legitimisation in the face of a decline in Dickens's cultural value, and often (when they had known him personally) they added an extra element akin to a personal promise to bring the reader closer to the famous author.

The series of Dickens's works that appeared in such large numbers after 1870 used all these methods. Richard Garnett (1835–1906), who edited the Merrill and Baker edition, was Keeper of Printed Books at the British Museum and, as an authority on all textual matters, a much sought-after introduction writer. Andrew Lang (1844–1912), who wrote the introductions to the 'Gadshill Edition', was a self-confessed 'convert' to Dickens when still a child, and later became one of his most important critical supporters at a time when Dickens was largely out of favour.[35] Lang's critical introductions offered new readers ways of understanding and appreciating Dickens from the standpoint of a critic who felt that anyone who did not like him was not only a 'cretin', but was also socially inept – an early example of the use of Dickens as cultural capital.[36] While still a devotee of the early works, Lang was rare among critics in the early twentieth century in feeling that *Great Expectations* represented a return to the novelist's original brilliant form: 'Except [for] *Great Expectations*', he wrote in 1905, 'none of his later tales rivals in merit his early picaresque stories of the road, such as *Pickwick* and *Nicholas Nickleby*.'[37] Well provided for with the backing of respected critical champions

---

[34] Bolter and Grusin, *Remediation*, p. 89.

[35] He was converted by reading *Pickwick*. Philip Waller, *Writers, Readers, and Reputations: Literary Life in Britain 1870–1918* (Oxford, 2006), pp. 189–90.

[36] Andrew Lang, 'Letter to Charles Dickens', in *Letters to Dead Authors* (first published in the *St. James's Gazette*,1886); online edition by Project Gutenberg, ebook 3319, www.gutenberg.org [accessed 2 May 2013].

[37] Andrew Lang, *The Puzzle of Dickens's Last Plot* (1905), online edition by Project Gutenberg, ebook 738 [accessed 2 May 2013].

such as Garnett and Lang, and often supported by companion volumes of Forster's *Life*, the nineteenth-century reprinted editions of Dickens set a trend for guided interpretations of 'classic' literature that continued into the twentieth century with the famous critical introductions written by luminaries such as George Gissing ('Rochester Edition', 1899–1901; reprinted in the 'Harvard Classics Edition' in 1917) and George Bernard Shaw ('Limited Editions Club', 1937). The critical introduction is still with us today in the shape of the scholarly student edition, a staple of modern academic publishing. But these introductions are also a marker of just how strong the publishing industry's sense was by the 1890s that, while sales of Dickens's early works might be healthy, collectively they were very much materials in need of 'refashioning' if they were to survive.[38]

Illustrations were another and perhaps still more important way of remediating Dickens's works for a new readership, and the numbers of illustrated editions proliferated on both sides of the Atlantic after his death.[39] The *Examiner*'s reviewer recognised their importance in a competitive reprint marketplace:

> At the present time, reproductions of the works of well-known authors is very great … as no new opinion is called for on the works of these authors, the new editions can only be judged or treated of upon their own merits as reprints. In the case of the "Household Edition" of Charles Dickens's works, of which "Great expectations" [*sic*] is the latest volume, the numerous illustrations are of course the chief objects to be regarded. The thirty illustrations by F.A. Fraser which adorn this present volume are on the whole rather unequal, many being very good, while others evince a less accurate conception of the author's ideas. Pip, Estella, Joe, and the other creations who form the dramatis personae of this by no means among the best of the great humourist's works, are represented by the artist, occasionally well, occasionally not so well.[40]

Illustrations – as American publishers had recognised even during Dickens's lifetime – were an important part of making Dickens 'new' in a competitive marketplace. Chapter 1 briefly examined the differences between Marcus Stone's illustration of noble Joe and lofty Pip which, breaking the humorous mould established by earlier Dickens illustrators, was a serious and largely realist representation that contrasts sharply with John McLenan's notably more comic

[38]   See J. Don Vann, 'Collected Editions Published After Dickens's Lifetime', in *The Oxford Reader's Companion to Dickens*, ed. by Paul Schlicke (Oxford, 2000), pp. 205–8. This article provides a useful overview of the major series editions.

[39]   Philip Allingham lists four illustrated editions (with plates by McLenan, Stone and F.A. Fraser) between 1861 and 1875, and a further 12 editions with illustrations (by Pailthorpe, Stone, Charles Green, John A. Bacon, Harry Furniss, Charles Pears, H.M. Brock, Gordon Ross and Edward Ardizzone) between 1875 and 1939, but his list does not include the many reprintings by different publishers both of these illustrated versions in their complete forms, and of compilations of the plates in different combinations. See www.victorianweb.org.

[40]   *Examiner*, Saturday 15 April 1876, p. 439.

version. The different visual interpretations continued apace after the novel's first publication.[41] There have been several decades of excellent work on Dickens's illustrators which it would be pointless to repeat here, but perhaps I can usefully add one or two observations.[42] First, a mention of the fact that visual depictions of Dickens's characters and scenes issued separately from his prose continued to be important after his death. Books or booklets of sketches of Dickens's characters detached from the novels were produced in significant numbers posthumously, including *Illustrations to Dickens* (Philadelphia: Pawson & Nicholson, 1890), the *Characters from Dickens* series (London and Manchester: Siegmund Hildesheimer & Co., 1880) from the same publisher which produced *Characters from Shakespeare*, and J.A. Hammerton, ed. *The Dickens Picture-Book: A Record of the Dickens Illustrations* (London: Educational Books, 1910). Frederic G. Kitton devotes a section of his book to this phenomenon, and more recently Philip Allingham has provided a useful brief article on it on the Victorian Web.[43] Robert Patten also mentions the publication of sets of extra illustrations in his chapter in the *Oxford Reader's Companion*.[44] But the phenomenon needs, I think, to be situated in its larger context: as part of a range of remediations in this period which were crucial in perpetuating and 'making new' Dickens's works. Illustrations might work to support a reader's comprehension of a text (particularly useful for a less competent reader), but they can also – like other remediations – work without the text to hand at all; like the 'teaspoons' of text that also appeared independently in newspapers, they were capable of creating a meaning all their own.

Second, we might usefully pause on the processes involved in deciding on the 'right' illustrations for a book. Patten provocatively describes the intertextuality of Dickens illustrations as a form of translation:

---

[41] A full set of illustrations for each of these editions and some thoughtful commentary is provided by Allingham on the Victorian Web.

[42] See, for example, F.G. Kitton, *Dickens and His Illustrators: Cruikshank, Seymour, Buss, "phiz", Cattermole, Leech, Doyle, Stanfield, Maclise, Tenniel, Frank Stone, Landseer* (London, 1899), probably the first comprehensive account of the illustrations. Also F.R. and Q.D. Leavis, 'The Dickens Illustrations: Their Function', in *Dickens the Novelist* (London, 1970), pp. 332–71. This chapter argues (no doubt based on their own insistence in the previous chapter on 'How We Must' read it) that *Great Expectations* needed no illustrations since it was an example of the mature art into which Dickens had by this time 'dragged his reading world' (p. 361). Jane R. Cohen, *Charles Dickens and His Original Illustrators* (Columbus, 1980), gives a thorough account of most of Dickens's illustrators but for some reason largely ignores *Great Expectations*. See also Paul B. Davis, 'Dickens, Hogarth, and the Illustrations for *Great Expectations*', and Alan S. Watts, 'Why Wasn't *Great Expectations* Illustrated?' *Dickens Magazine*, Series 1, Issue 2, no date, pp. 8–9.

[43] Philip V. Allingham, 'Extra Illustrations and Grangerising: A Dickensian Phenomenon,' Victorian Web, http://www.victorianweb.org/art/illustration/dickens/grangerising.html [accessed 3 May 2013].

[44] Robert L. Patten, 'Illustrators and Book Illustration', in the *Oxford Reader's Companion to Dickens*, pp. 288–93.

> Like all translations, they approximate the source, critique it, supplement it,
> and employ a different vocabulary to enact in another language and tradition
> what the source text expresses…. The wrapper designs, frontispieces, vignette
> titles, wood engravings dropped into the text, and full-page etchings or
> wood engravings speak through alternative means, reiterating, amplifying,
> anticipating, and independently interpreting Dickens's prose.[45]

And like all translations, we might add, illustrations require creative decisions
informed by perceptions about market need; each generation has, in a sense, a need
of its own new translation. A glance at one discarded fragment which never made
it into a published edition or a collection of scenes or character sketches might
therefore be able to tell us something about the decision-making processes behind
these 'translations'. The example I focus on here is a small, faint unpublished pencil
sketch by F.W. Pailthorpe, now in the Henry W. and Albert A. Berg Collection of
the New York Public Library, and originally drawn for the title page of the Robson
and Kerslake edition of 1885.[46] Figure 2.1 shows the published title page.

Here, representing the closing of 'The First Stage of Pip's Expectations', the
top-hatted figure of Pip has walked well past the fingerpost on his way out of the
village. He looks back over his left shoulder, but his direction is clearly set and
his body language indicates that while he might be hesitant, he is firmly London-
bound. He looks lonely, certainly, but he does not look like a young man in tears.
The unpublished alternative sketch for the title page, however, shows Pip pausing
by the fingerpost to lean on it, head bowed, with a much more marked sense of
sorrow and regret.

This version is of course more faithful to Dickens's own depiction of this
moment:

> … the village was very peaceful and quiet, and the light mists were solemnly
> rising as if to show me the world, and I had been so innocent and little there,
> and all beyond was so unknown and great, that in a moment with a strong heave

---

[45]   Patten, 'Illustrators,' pp. 290–93.

[46]   Twenty-one watercolour drawings by F.W. Pailthorpe and pencil sketch, Ref.
181044B, the Henry W. and Albert A. Berg Collection of English and American literature,
the New York Public Library, Astor, Lenox, and Tilden Foundations. To date I have found
no published version or mention of this sketch anywhere. Kitton, perhaps the closest
contemporary source, does not mention the sketch in his section on Pailthorpe's 21 etchings
for *Great Expectations* published as additional material in the useful 'Concerning "Extra
Illustrations"' section at the end of his book. It is not unusual to find an unpublished
sketch by Pailthorpe; he seems to have discarded quite a few and the uncoloured ones,
at least, turn up in library collections and come up for sale quite frequently (though the
watercoloured versions are more highly prized). See, for example, the catalogues of the
specialist Dickensiana bookseller, Jarndyce.

Additional Note: Every reasonable effort has been made to trace the copyright holder
of this image. Pailthorpe appears in the UK Census records as 'artist, etcher and designer'
in 1881, but disappears from the Census records thereafter and may have emigrated. There
is no record of a Will in the Probate Registry in London.

GREAT EXPECTATIONS

BY CHARLES DICKENS

Pip leaves the Village

LONDON

Robson & Kerslake 23 Coventry Street Haymarket.

1885.

Fig. 2.1   'Pip leaves the village'. Title–page of 1885 edition, illustrated by F.W. Pailthorpe (London: Robson & Kerslake). Scanned image by Philip V. Allingham, courtesy of the Victorian Web.

Fig 2.2   'Pip Leaves the Village'. Unpublished sketch by F.W. Pailthorpe
(c.1885). Reproduced by kind permission of Commander Mark
Dickens of the Charles Dickens Estate, and The Henry W. and
Albert A. Berg Collection of English and American Literature, The
New York Public Library, Astor, Lenox and Tilden Foundations.

and sob I broke into tears. It was by the finger-post at the end of the village,
and I laid my hand upon it, and said, 'Good-by, O my dear, dear friend!' (*Great
Expectations*, ed. Rosenberg, p. 124).

The rejection of the sketch raises some interesting questions. Why, in 1885, was it felt (either by artist or publisher) that a mildly reflective but determined Pip well on his way to London was preferable to a Pip sobbing over his old friend the fingerpost? It is impossible to be sure, but the final choice of image seems significant in that from the novel's very first page it gives Pip a harder edge and a keener appetite for leaving. Aspiration requiring relocation was perhaps, in 1885, a more understandable if no less complex impulse for a readership by now well accustomed to commuting, and to the undeniable drift of the British population from rural to urban living.

The association of the city with immorality and the countryside with innocence was also a well-established cultural trope by this period, as witness Thomas Hardy's repeated use of this motif in most of the novels between *Far from the Madding Crowd* (1874) and *Jude the Obscure* (1895). Rider Haggard summed up the problem in 1902:

> Everywhere the young men and women are leaving the villages where they were born and flocking into the towns … as a consequence the character of Englishmen appears to be changing, not … entirely for the better. Nature … only appeals to the truly educated … those cities whither they go are full of misery.[47]

In light of such discourses Pip's relative eagerness to get to London in the published 1885 illustration clearly signals to the reader that he will come to no good, and that it is largely his own fault; there is a subtle shift apparent here in the visual interpretation of the novel's themes of social aspiration and city versus countryside. Perhaps, too, Robson and Kerslake recognised that the late Victorian reader's capacity to be moved by a hero's (or indeed any) fictional tears was more limited than it had been 20 years earlier. Andrew Lang certainly thought so: 'One still laughs as heartily as ever with Dick Swiveller', he wrote in *Letters to Dead Authors* in 1886, 'but who [now] can cry over Little Nell?'[48] So – famously – did Oscar Wilde, who claimed: 'One would have to have a heart of stone to read the death of Little Nell without laughing.'[49]

Neither the effort put into illustration nor the remarkable reissue output are proof positive of *Great Expectations*' status in the popularity stakes, of course; the overriding publishing principles after Dickens's death seem to have been comprehensiveness, sensitivity to a changing marketplace and print-based gimmickry. *Great Expectations* was simply swept up in the tide. But there is some evidence that the reissues did not improve its popularity and that it remained an 'also-ran' for some years.

In his work on Dickens's American readers, McParland uses library records to support his claims for the writer's enduring influence there: 'While Dickens

[47]   H. Rider Haggard, *Rural England: Being an Account of Agricultural and Social Researches Carried Out in the Years 1901 & 1902*, Vol. 2 (1902; Boston, 2001), pp. 539–42.

[48]   Lang, *Letters to Dead Authors*.

[49]   Marcia Muelder Eaton, 'Laughing at the Death of Little Nell: Sentimental Art and Sentimental People', *American Philosophical Quarterly*, 26 (October 1989): p. 269.

was not always the most frequently borrowed author in these libraries, he was one who had wide and lasting impact across all classes, ages, gender, and across several decades.' But he seldom records the borrowing statistics for individual novels except (occasionally) the early ones, and *Great Expectations* makes no showing in his account at all beyond an acknowledgment of its presence in library stock.[50] This, as readership historians are well aware, tells us nothing about who actually read it. Recent digital scholarship has, however, been able to reveal a slightly fuller picture of the habits of library borrowers in middle-America. The 41 Dickens books borrowed from the Muncie, Indiana, Public Library between 5 November 1891 and 3 December 1902 also suggest a strong preference for some of the older works, as well as some interesting deviations.[51]

Borrowing Record of Dickens's Works 1891–1902

> *David Copperfield* (80)
> *Nicholas Nickleby* (68)
> *A Tale of Two Cities* (57)
> *A Child's History of England* (52)
> *Little Dorrit* (49)
> *Sketches by Boz* (47)
> *Oliver Twist* (38)
> *Hunted Down and Other Reprinted Pieces* (36)
> *Bleak House* (28)
> *Dombey and Son* (26)
> *Our Mutual Friend* (26)
> *The Holly Tree Inn and Other Stories* (24)
> *Martin Chuzzlewit* (24)
> *New Stories containing Hard Times and Pictures from Italy* (22)
> *John Jasper's Secret: A Sequel to the Unfinished Mystery of Edwin Drood*
>   by Henry Morford (19)
> *Edwin Drood* and *Master Humphrey's Clock* (18)
> *Great Expectations* (16)
> *Barnaby Rudge* (11)
> *Pickwick Papers* (9)
> *The Uncommercial Traveller* (8)
> *Hard Times and Additional Christmas Stories* (6)
> *Christmas Stories* (4)

---

[50]   McParland, *Charles Dickens's American Audience*, p. 87.

[51]   'What Middletown Read,' Ball State University Libraries, http://www.bsu.edu/libraries/wmr/ [accessed 3 March 2013]. The digitised records show that an undated single-volume edition of *Great Expectations* published in Philadelphia was added to the library's stock in 1875 along with editions of several other Dickens works. Judging by the combination of titles bound-in together, it is likely that T.B. Peterson was the publisher.

> *American Notes and the Uncommercial Traveller* (4)
> *American Notes* (1)
> *Edwin Drood* and *Master Humphrey's Clock* (1)

The fact that *Pickwick Papers* – alone among the oft-mentioned 'popular' older works – comes lower on the list of favourites than *Great Expectations* can probably be explained by the number of cheap formats in which it had been available for readers to purchase since 1836; many households would already have owned a copy.[52] But it seems less explicable that *Great Expectations* had even fewer borrowers than *Martin Chuzzlewit*, in which one of Dickens's least flattering portraits of America appeared. Perhaps Dickens's second visit, closely followed by the conciliatory preface he wrote for the 'Charles Dickens Edition' of *Martin Chuzzlewit* in 1868, had effectively smoothed over old grievances. Muncie library patrons, at least, seemed by the 1890s to be more willing to forgive youthful outspokenness than middle-aged gloom; the 'gospel of jollity' obviously still held sway there, bolstered by an interest in European history which put *A Tale of Two Cities* and *A Child's History of England* towards the top of the list.

A comparison with the numbers of borrowings of American authors in this period is revealing. Mark Twain's works were borrowed 746 times in total, *Huckleberry Finn* alone 149 times and *Tom Sawyer* 71 times. Harriet Beecher Stowe's *Uncle Tom's Cabin* had 115 borrowings, and Louisa M. Alcott's *Little Women* clocked up an impressive 555 borrowings. While there is no proof, of course, that these library patrons actually read the books they borrowed, their intentions clearly tell us something: namely, that in the 1890s Dickens books in general could not compete with the home-grown competition, and that *Great Expectations* in particular was more often than not left on the shelf.

In the UK, too, there is evidence that it was not a national favourite in the decade or so after Dickens's death. Frederic G. Kitton's *Dickensiana* quotes an article by Mowbray Morris, first published in the *Fortnightly Review* in December 1882, setting out the sales by title of Dickens's works between 1870 and 1882.[53] The statistics as repeated by Kitton engendered surprise in some quarters; on 17 April 1886 the *North Wales Chronicle* reported that:

> "Pickwick" came easily first; then, and very deservedly, "David Copperfield" but it is astonishing to hear that while "Little Dorrit" ran into a place and was third, "Great Expectations" and "A Tale of Two Cities" came next to "Edwin Drood", the absolute last. Admirers of Dickens, people who make him a special favourite, may well be astonished at this popular verdict, which puts "Little Dorrit" before "Nicholas Nickleby."

---

[52] See Patten, *Dickens and His Publishers*, pp. 326–7.

[53] F.G. Kitton, *Dickensiana*, p. 496. The original was reviewed by the *Publishers' Circular and Booksellers' Record* on 16 April 1886, p. 379. This trade paper not only liked the book but appeared to take no issue with these statistics, though Morris merely gestures vaguely to 'the very best authority' rather than naming his source.

Apparently it was less of a surprise to the *North Wales Chronicle* that *Great Expectations* came joint second-last. And it should not by now be a surprise to us either.

Dickens and *Great Expectations* as 'household words'

As George Ford has shown, Dickens's literary reputation (along with those of other mid-century novelists such as Thackeray and even Eliot) suffered a further decline in the UK in the last decades of the nineteenth century, as critical tastes turned from realism and naturalism to proto-modernists such as James and Conrad.[54] Realism and naturalism both lasted longer in the USA, perpetuated there by home-grown authors such as William Dean Howells and Stephen Crane, but their literary concerns were very different from those of Dickens. One might add that popular tastes had also turned, away from Dickensian humour, melodrama and pathos and towards the Christian Socialism of Hall Caine and the spiritual romances of Marie Corelli in the UK, and the Civil War stories of Ambrose Bierce and 'dime novel' romances of Laura Jean Libbey in the USA. In 30 years the terms of what constituted a bestseller had also undergone a radical change in relation to numbers of copies sold; even Dickens would surely have been astonished by the sales of some of these authors compared with the first sales of his own works.

Sales of his novels before 1900 were one thing, and *Great Expectations* did not do particularly well in this period compared with earlier Dickens works. But the sense of the novel's presence in culture is something else entirely. It sparked references in the 1860s, and by the 1870s the characters and themes of *Great Expectations* had firmly taken their places among the 'household words' Dickens was repeatedly claimed to have provided for his Anglophone public.[55] In 1871 came the news of the death of an eccentric Philadelphia woman, Madame Mazare, who, the *Fife Herald* suggested, might easily have been the model for 'Miss Haversham' [*sic*].[56] It is an indicator of the type of fame *Great Expectations* experienced after its author's death that while the name of the novel's most eccentric female character was widely known, its correct spelling was not. In spite of the wealth of editions available and the hard work publishers, illustrators, editors and preface

---

[54] Ford, *Dickens and His Readers*, p. 52.

[55] The use of this term was widespread on both sides of the Atlantic, editors apparently unable to resist punning on the name of Dickens's journal, taken from a line in Shakespeare's *Henry IV*, 4.3. See, for example, 'The name of Dickens has long ago passed into a household word' (The *Cambria Freeman*, 16 June 1870, p. 1); 'Of his works it is not necessary to speak, or even to name them. They are indeed "familiar in our mouths as household words"' (The *Dundee Courier & Argus*, Saturday 11 June 1870, no page number.); '[The names of his characters] have become to us household words, and have entered as it were into the marrow of our language'(The *Standard*, Friday 10 June 1870, p. 3).

[56] 'Death of an Eccentric Lady', *Fife Herald and Kinross, Strathearn and Clackmannan Advertiser*, Thursday 10 August 1871, no page number.

writers put into remediating Dickens to render him interesting and acceptable to a late nineteenth-century readership, this broad and not entirely accurate cultural 'understanding' of the novel seems to have been remarkably dominant.

The idea that we can 'know' Dickens without ever having read him properly (or even at all) began during his lifetime, as we have seen, and this creative misreading continued for decades – and of course continues still. Cultural appropriation is in fact an important part of the legacy of Dickens in general and, perhaps, of *Great Expectations* in particular; it has at times been one of his least popular novels, yet it is one which has inspired some of the most pervasive cultural references, its surplus energy easily decoupled from the plot as Dickens wrote it and recoupled to situations requiring a powerful moral metaphor (or simply a useful shorthand).

Among the most common passing references to the novel in the late nineteenth century are reports of court cases titled 'Great Expectations', in which the defendant has been caught out lying about his or her financial prospects with the intention to deceive.[57] But the name also enabled plenty of jokes. In 1893 a comic item called 'Their Favourite Novels' appeared in the *Punch* wannabe *Judy: The Conservative Comic*.[58] The paper listed several social stereotypes from spinsters to schoolteachers whom it felt deserved to be gently mocked, and suggested the novels that might appeal to them; *Great Expectations* was suggested as the favourite of the impecunious. The joke is a poor one, but the idea that *Great Expectations* stands for selfish, immoral or even felonious motives as well as for false hopes clearly had a firm hold on the cultural imagination in this period. This was not the case before December 1860.

We probably need to be cautious about claiming that we can confidently map cultural trends by tracing the appearance of keywords in digitised newspapers (exciting as this recent development is), unless we have considered the many and changeable relationships, both official and unofficial, which newspapermen forged in this period. They often shared news items through the wire and even exchanged sheets or plates; cultural drift sometimes owes more to industrial pragmatics or individual human relationships than to the unconscious spread of ideology. We must also remember that we are at the mercy of the choices of the digitising bodies and (currently at least) the speed of the digitising process. But, these caveats aside, online newspaper archives can surely tell us something when a keyword achieves critical mass through repetition and begins to demonstrate potentially significant patterns. There is thus, I venture to suggest, probably some significance in the fact that while the term 'great expectations' was certainly in

---

[57]   See, for example, 'Great Expectations', the *Portsmouth Evening News*, Saturday 23 September 1882, p. 2; 'Great Expectations: a Captain's Reversionary Interest', the *Daily News*, Thursday 7 July 1898, p. 8; and 'Great Expectations not Complimentary to Clifton Folk', the *Western Times*, Saturday 14 May 1904, p. 3.

[58]   *Judy: The Conservative Comic*, Wednesday 4 January 1893, p. 3. For a useful discussion of *Judy*'s political position in this period, see John Strachan, 'Satirical print culture', in the *Cambridge Companion to Victorian Culture*, ed. by Francis O'Gorman (Cambridge, 2010), p. 171.

common usage in a range of eighteenth-century newspapers and continued to be used throughout the nineteenth century, before Dickens appropriated it for the title of his novel in 1860 it tended to be used in a different way: namely, to stand for the dashing of hopes which may with hindsight have been naively high. It was used in this way in political commentary, as in this example which serves as a warning: 'Great expectations are formed from the appointment of General Suwarrow to the command of the army of Italy.'[59] And it was used for reviewing entertainers: 'The great expectations raised of [the singer] Mademoiselle Nau have not been realised ... she was heralded with too much pomp.'[60] It was also often used at mid-century in reports on the Great Exhibition of 1851, where disappointment seemed inbuilt.[61] Less frequently, the phrase appears with better results: 'Last evening, the celebrated Berlin male choristers ... fully realised the great expectations to which the preliminary announcements of the executive committee had given rise.'[62] In all the digitally available newspapers I have examined, published on each side of the Atlantic, the naivety and the sense of riding for a fall which hovered over the term 'great expectations' were already part of cultural consciousness before 1860. But the sharper edges of selfishness, snobbery, shallowness, greed and final bitter comeuppance seem to be almost entirely inventions of Dickens's, and they quickly spread way beyond the confines of his novel.

Jokes and ironically titled court cases continued through the 1870s and 1880s. Then, in the 1890s, came the cartoons. In the General Election year of 1893, *Punch* used the title 'Great Expectations' for a cartoon depicting Chamberlain and Balfour falsely acting like friends over a potential political alliance between the Liberal Unionist Party and the Conservatives which might somehow benefit Ireland (which, unsurprisingly, it didn't).[63] In 1895, the magazine *Pick-Me-Up* published a cartoon strip called 'Great Expectations' which shows a young man receiving a summons from an elderly Uncle from whom he expects to inherit a fortune. The young man arrives excitedly on a Sunday and dutifully begins to nurse the old man, evidently keen to safeguard the terms of the will in which he is named as chief beneficiary. A week later the Uncle is fully recovered and the young man an exhausted, disgruntled (and still poverty-stricken) wreck.[64] This particular joke ran in cartoon form well into the twentieth century, accompanied by a continued use to this day in political cartooning of the phrase and the idea of 'Great Expectations' as representing hopes and plans which are cynical, selfish, deliberately deceptive or false, as well as wilfully or naively blind. These patterns suggest that Dickens's thirteenth novel did not just explore the concept of 'great expectations' as we have come to understand it; it may also have added significantly to its semantic range.

---

[59] *The Times*, Saturday 30 March 1799, p. 2.

[60] *The Era*, Sunday 20 October 1850, p. 11.

[61] See, for example, 'The Great Exhibition', *The Era*, Sunday 10 August 1851, p. 11.

[62] *Morning Post*, Saturday 2 November 1850, p. 2.

[63] *Punch*, Saturday 18 March 1893, p. 132.

[64] *Pick-Me-Up*, Saturday 19 January 1895, p. 254.

Stages of Fame

Remediations also continued on the stage after Dickens's death and finally even emerged in Britain. They are not numerous, but they are worth analysing for the ways in which they try to bend the story to fit a medium which was itself attempting to break traditional moulds in this period. David Mayer has recently suggested through an analysis of Henry Irving's performance as Mathius in Leopold Lewis's *The Bells* (the Lyceum, London, 1871) that this play helped to subtly redefine expectations of the melodramatic tradition in which it operated:

> [T]here are certain givens expected of this genre that ought to be met but which, in this drama and in others associated with the Lyceum, fail to be observed. The omission or alteration of these givens, far from being a liability, brought new and warmly appreciative audiences to Irving's performances.[65]

The first British dramatizations of *Great Expectations* need to be situated in this same moment in theatre history; a moment of cautious innovation and experiment. It was not in itself anywhere near as successful as *The Bells* or similar Irving dramas, for reasons which I will explore in a moment. But its selection for performance, and the forms those performances took, give us important insights into its public profile and the ways in which it was being interpreted in the period immediately after Dickens's death.

The first posthumous professional production that theatre historians know of for sure was an adaptation by W.S. Gilbert which opened on 29 May 1871 at the Court Theatre, just off London's Sloane Square (that is, outside of the main West End theatre district), and ran for two months. Gilbert had several plays performed at this theatre during 1871 and had already had some success as a dramatist of burlesques, which he was becoming known for rendering suitable for a middle-class audience. He was allegedly part of what theatre historian Allardyce Nicoll calls 'a dramatic renascence' in the 1870s, through which

> the audience had increased and become more representative of all classes in the nation; the theatre had found a new ideal which … had vitality and inspiration in it; the dramatic author suddenly discovered that he had walked into a realm spiritually and materially different from that inhabited by the melodramatists and extravaganza writers … [of] fifty years before.[66]

The aim of this revivalist movement in British theatre, according to many mid-twentieth-century theatre historians such as Allardyce Nicoll, was to make the stage respectable again in order to attract a more up-market audience, and thus to give dramatists more aesthetically important work. The inference here, of course,

---

[65] David Mayer, 'Leopold Lewis, *The Bells*: A case study. A "bare-ribbed skeleton" in a chest: *The Bells* and Henry Irving', in *The Cambridge History of British Drama*, Vol. 2: *1660–1895*, ed. by Jo Donahue (Cambridge, 2004), p. 397.

[66] John Ramsay Allardyce Nicoll, *A History of Late 19th-Century Drama 1850–1900*, Vol. 1 (Cambridge, 1946), p. 73.

is that the popular entertainment on which they had been expending their talents up to that point was neither respectable nor critically significant. Allardyce Nicoll argues that Dickens was of particular importance to this movement:

> There were at least eight versions of "Bleak House" [between 1853 and 1892] and numerous versions of "Little Emily", though naturally it was the contemporary writers who most appealed.... Love of incident and grotesque characterisation had appealed in the past; now a deeper psychological note and a franker treatment of intimate domestic life became the fashion.[67]

Despite Allardyce Nicoll's insistence on Dickens's importance based on the number of performances of his works in this period, it is difficult to see how a Dickens adaptation might compete with the style of a playwright like Ibsen. In fact, the truth is adaptations of Dickens's novels were usually competing on the popular stage circuit rather than with the new 'serious' dramas, and thus with money-spinners like Ellen ('Mrs Henry') Wood's *East Lynne*, also published in 1861. This bestselling novel turned out to be one of the late Victorian period's most long-lived and successful theatrical adaptations, lasting on the stage right up to the turn of the century and – on celluloid – considerably beyond.[68]

Resurrecting the long-neglected history of this more popular theatrical tradition, recent scholarship has in fact taken issue with the whole notion of an evolutionary line, posited by historians like Allardyce Nicoll, which places 'vulgar' entertainments such as melodrama, music hall and burlesque in a lump at one end of the nineteenth century, and the establishment of a sophisticated 'serious theatre' which we might critically embrace at the other. Nina Auerbach, for example, argues: 'This paradigm of a rising theatre is itself Victorian in its snobbish complacency and it is, like most snobbish paradigms, wrong.'[69] In an essay in the same collection, David Mayer makes a compelling case for a new reading of theatre history which resists seeing it as having been dominated by the vulgar melodrama until sometime in 1870 when realism entered stage left and the theatre finally became worthy of critical attention. Mayer's work persuades us to see the melodrama, not as serious theatre's underdeveloped progenitor, but as a variegated and highly culturally responsive form in its own right throughout the century. For Mayer '[t]here is no such thing as a "last word" about melodrama; its fascination and its vitality lie partly in the fact that, mutating as it goes and only provisionally defined, it confidently continues to this very day in motion pictures, indifferent to criticism and objection.'[70] Melodrama, that is, was not only always complex and dynamic, but it continued to thrive and

---

[67] Allardyce Nicoll, *A History of Late 19th-Century Drama*, p. 80.

[68] Sally Mitchell estimates that it was seen by theatre audiences in either Britain or America at least once a week for over 40 years. Sally Mitchell, introduction to Mrs Henry Wood, *East Lynne* (1861; New Brunswick, 1984), p. xiii.

[69] Nina Auerbach, 'Before the Curtain', in *The Cambridge Companion to Victorian and Edwardian Theatre*, ed. by Kerry Powell (Cambridge, 2004), p. 5.

[70] David Mayer, 'Encountering Melodrama', in *The Cambridge Companion to Victorian and Edwardian Theatre*, ed. by Kerry Powell (Cambridge, 2004), p. 146.

evolve even after the production of 'serious' dramas began to change the cultural politics of theatre sometime around 1870.

The notion of a responsive, dynamic theatre is an important one given the evidence we have examined thus far of the remarkable pliability and remediability of Dickens's works. His early novels were particularly well-suited to the melodramatic mode, perhaps most especially its 'emotional, rather than intellectual'[71] engagement with social concerns; indeed, as we know, Dickens was widely and successfully dramatized for the popular stage on both sides of the Atlantic throughout his lifetime. H. Philip Bolton's painstaking compilation and cross-checking of as many references to dramatic adaptations of Dickens as he was able to find in over a decade of research demonstrates dozens of versions of almost every Dickens novel occurring during the Victorian period, perhaps particularly during the height of the melodrama's dominance.[72] But Dickens's pliability meant he was able to offer other theatrical possibilities alongside melodrama, a fact which requires us to investigate how the history of his adaptation for the popular stage fit into an evolving theatrical tradition in the 1870s. To what extent could he cross the popular/critical divide in performance during this transitional period? The timing of the first British stage version of *Great Expectations* provides some interesting answers.

Bolton suggests that 'we can trace a decline in the eagerness of the hacks and actors to stage the latest works of Dickens, beginning in 1860 with "A Message from the Sea" and *Great Expectations*'.[73] However we might feel about Bolton's dismissive reference to 'hacks and actors', the facts are undeniable: under-dramatized during Dickens's lifetime, *Great Expectations* was not often considered a natural subject for the stage in the three decades after its author's death. When it was, however, perhaps because of its uncertain status in the popularity stakes or its unusual moral ambiguity, it tended to require some drastic rewriting or a total relabelling. It also, interestingly, seems to mark a significant moment in attempts to change public perceptions of Dickens in performance. After his death, as G.K. Chesterton put it in 1906, 'the world first woke from the hypnotism of Dickens, from the direct tyranny of his temperament, [and then] there was, of course, a reaction'.[74] Part of this reaction after 1870 seems to have involved an attempt to break away from the tyranny both of Dickens's narrative style, and of his customary rendering in performance. Robert Louis Stevenson expressed these difficulties in a letter to his father about a play version of *Great Expectations* he was writing in 1883 (which seems never to have made it to the stage): '[I]t is extraordinary how much of Dickens had to be discarded as inhuman, impossible and ineffective…. I have great hopes of this piece, which is

---

[71]   Mayer, 'Encountering Melodrama', p. 148.

[72]   H. Philip Bolton, *Dickens Dramatized* (London, 1987).

[73]   Bolton, *Dickens Dramatized*, p. 105.

[74]   G.K. Chesterton, *Chesterton's Biographies: Charles Dickens* (1906; Kelly Bray, 2001), p. 7.

very amiable, and, in places, very strong indeed; but it was curious how Dickens had to be rolled away'.[75]

A decade earlier, in 1871, W.S. Gilbert had been equally concerned with breaking an established pattern. He was a lifelong Dickens fan, and in this period he stepped away from the burlesques with which his career had begun and the clever comedies with which in 1870 he was beginning to achieve popular and critical success, and tried something else: to shift Dickens away from popular perceptions about how he ought to be performed. Alan Fischler suggests, probably correctly, that Gilbert's 1871 adaptation of *Great Expectations* was an attempt to engage with more serious philosophical and dramaturgical issues, among them Darwinism and its impact on the traditional love plot.[76] But while there certainly seemed to be some sort of attempt at generic innovation going on, it was by no means as successful as Irving's reconstitution of melodrama with *The Bells* at the Lyceum in this same year. This was not the last time *Great Expectations* was to be settled upon as a useful reconstruction tool at moments of personal, cultural or aesthetic transition, and Gilbert should probably have had little difficulty in finding both humour and more serious themes in the novel equal to the task. He clearly had high hopes for it since it also played at the Boston Museum on 16 October 1871 and was reprised at the Aquarium Theatre on 19 March 1877 with almost the same cast. But in none of these incarnations did it meet with critical acclaim or with particularly long runs, and compared with Irving's contemporaneous treatment of melodrama, it was a flop. Fischler notes that Gilbert himself later dismissed his dramatization as having 'achieved no success worth mentioning'.[77] Still, a two-month run is not insignificant and several critics mention well-filled houses. Dickens's name was a draw, as theatre managers well knew. That this particular Dickens adaptation was something of a mixed blessing provides important evidence of *Great Expectations'* uncertain cultural status after its author's death.

Like most theatrical programmes in the period, the Court's was a varied one with several different types of entertainment on offer in a single evening. The advertisement placed in *The Era* before opening night tells us that the evening was due to begin at 7:30 with 'a new farce by the late T.W. Robertson entitled "Not At All Jealous", after which, will be produced a drama in a Prologue and Three Acts, adapted from Charles Dickens's novel *Great Expectations* by W.S. Gilbert'. The evening concluded with 'A Musical Fairytale' called 'Creatures of Impulse', also written by Gilbert.[78] T.W. Robertson had cut his dramatic teeth adapting Dickens

---

[75]   Robert Louis Stevenson, Letter to Thomas Stevenson, 17 March 1883, in *The Letters of Robert Louis Stevenson*, Vol. 3: October 1882–June 1883, ed. by Bradford A. Booth and Ernest Mehew (New Haven and London, 1994), p. 91.

[76]   Alan Fischler, 'The Descent of Darwinism: W.S. Gilbert and the Evolution of *Great Expectations*', *Dickensian*, 98 (Summer 2002): p. 102.

[77]   Fischler, 'Descent of Darwinism', pp. 103–6.

[78]   *The Era*, 28 May 1871, p. 8. 'The Creatures of Impulse' had debuted at the Court on 2 April 1871. This was only one configuration: a playbill now held in the Pierpont Morgan Library in New York shows that there were several variations of the programme during *Great Expectations'* run, including one which opened with 'a new comedietta in one Act

novels and writing music hall songs, but by the 1860s his innovative social problem plays had become popular and an important inspiration for Gilbert, to whom he was a mentor as well as a friend.[79] Robertson had died a few months after Dickens and 'Not At All Jealous' had its posthumous debut in this 1871 programme, perhaps as Gilbert's tribute to its author. Like most of Robertson's farces, it is likely that it contained a mixture of forms, combining 'the humour of Mr Dickens with the cynicism of Mr Thackeray'.[80] The combination of humour and cynicism may have provided useful support to a new Dickens adaptation which, despite its adaptor's anxiety to create something different, nonetheless evidently struggled to free itself from what one reviewer called 'commonplace melodrama'.[81]

The programme's concluding act may also have contributed to the evening's thematic mosaic. The bad-tempered fairy, star of Gilbert's musical adaptation of his own short story 'Creatures of Impulse' (1870), devotes her time to casting malicious spells designed to make people do unexpected things, and she may have provided useful cross-textual support to the firmly offstage Miss Havisham, whose machinations are dealt with far more lightly in the play script than in the novel. The play's actors also brought with them associations. Edward Righton, who played Joe, was equally at home doing Shakespeare, musical comedy and burlesque, including Gilbert-authored burlesques such as the controversial and popular political satire 'The Happy Land', and he toured widely with these productions. In 1871, Righton was manager of the Court and, along with several other members of the cast of *Great Expectations* – Kate Bishop (Adult Pip/Biddy), Eleanor Bufton (Estella), Maggie Brennan (Adult Pip) and John Clayton (Jaggers) – had appeared in its successful predecessor *Randall's Thumb*, also by Gilbert, which had premiered on 25 January 1871.[82] The cast thus brought to the Dickens production something of an established fan base. This familiarity fed into the evening's programme in other ways, creating still closer associations between its various components: Righton also appeared in 'Which is Which', and Maggie Brennan and Kate Bishop switched roles (Adult Pip/Biddy) with the change of programme.[83] Gilbert's adaptation, like the first serial instalments, the stolen remediated 'teaspoons' of text in newspapers, and the numerous posthumous editions of the novels, clearly interacted in complex ways with a rich set of

---

by Theyre Smith' called 'Which is Which', and concluded with 'Creatures of Impulse'. Pierpont Morgan Library, Department of Music, Manuscripts and Books, Gilbert and Sullivan Collection, Folder No. 1165, Record ID 198686.

[79]   Andrew Crowther, *Gilbert of Gilbert and Sullivan: His Life and Character* (Stroud, 2011), p. 60.

[80]   Charles Eyre Pascoe, *The Dramatic List: A Record of the Performances of Living Actors and Actresses of the British Stage*, 2nd ed. (London, 1880), p. 18. See also Maynard Savin, *Thomas William Robertson: His Plays and Stagecraft* (Providence, 1950), p. 70.

[81]   *Examiner*, 15 July 1871, p. 707.

[82]   Pascoe, *Dramatic List*, p. 285.

[83]   Playbill, Pierpont Morgan Library, Department of Music, Manuscripts and Books, Gilbert and Sullivan Collection, Folder No. 1165, Record ID 198686.

wider musical, visual and verbal contexts which may have helped to construct its audiences' understanding. This understanding may sometimes, of course, have worked alongside previous knowledge of the novel, or at least of elements of its plot as they circulated in cultural discourse.

The tenor of the criticism this version attracted indicates the struggle experienced by Dickens adaptors such as Gilbert to define a commercially and critically successful new role for his works in a shifting theatrical paradigm in this period. The *Examiner*'s conclusion that the piece, while well-received by audiences, was nothing but a 'commonplace melodrama' was justified by its reviewer's belief that the play was dependent for its success on the audience's knowledge of the book, rather than on innovative stage-craft:

> It is not difficult … to account for the partial success this piece has attained, notwithstanding its many and manifest defects, chief amongst which is the absence of any adequate motive to explain the actions of the leading dramatis personae. A large portion of the audience, being familiar with the novel, are in a position to supply the deficiencies of the drama, while remaining unconscious how far they themselves contribute from memory to the illusion. The dramatist who transforms a popular work into a play, over and above the ready-made plot and characters, gets the advantage of the interest and sympathy which the original author has already excited in the mind of the spectator; and this not only explains the popularity of adaptations, both with play-writers and with the public, but it also, in great measure, accounts for their almost uniform inferior quality as works of art. All that the dramatist has to do in such a case is revive the latent impression left by the reading of the novel on which his play is founded; and, but for the assistance Mr Gilbert has received in this way from the audiences which have witnessed his "Great Expectations", the drama would probably have proved a failure.[84]

The extent to which an adaptor can or should assume the audience's prior knowledge of the book was a perennial problem, and Gilbert clearly found it hard to get it right. Unfortunately, especially given his desire to create something new, he relied very heavily on 'the latent impression left by the book', excising a number of the story's principal characters including Miss Havisham and Pumblechook (who are offstage presences) and Compeyson and Wemmick (who have been written out altogether). Some scenes also make little sense without prior knowledge of the novel's plot: Pip and Biddy's conversation about why he wants to be a gentleman appears out of the blue, for example, with no prior reference to or appearance by Estella.[85] The result – taken on its own merits – is strangely flat.

Another problem for many reviewers seems to have been the production's generic hybridity, underlined by the choice of venue and the different and sometimes contradictory theatrical modes which its actors brought to the ensemble company.

---

[84]   *Examiner*, 15 July 1871, p. 707.

[85]   W.S. Gilbert, *Great Expectations: A Drama in Three Acts with Prologue* (1871). British Library, MS. c.132.g.20.

Fun felt the production was 'not likely to prove successful, chiefly because this fashionable little house is eminently unfitted for the representation of sensational drama – and *Great Expectations* is of an extremely sensational turn.'[86] The *Pall Mall Gazette* agreed: 'It may be questioned ... whether success of an enduring kind will attend this wanton trespass of the Court Theatre upon melodramatic paths.'[87] The *Examiner* praised the performances of the actors, but felt that in some cases they would be 'excellent in pantomime but are out of place in a drama'.[88] The *Graphic* thought the book altogether 'unsuitable for representation on the stage' and deplored the excision of some of the major characters, but likewise felt that some of the acting – particularly John Clayton's performance as Jaggers – was 'of very high merit', and that 'while those around him more or less degrade and vulgarise the creations of the novelist, his performance even invests the part with a new interest'.[89] The *Era* is a little kinder, but it too draws attention to the problem of genre, this time seen as a result of lack of continuity and a certain dumbing down in the Court's season. The reviewer thought it odd that the theatre's management had seen fit to replace a sophisticated and successful comedy (*Randall's Thumb*) with a melodrama (*Great Expectations*) and thus ensure that 'sturdy blows are now interchanged instead of repartee', but she or he acknowledged that the 'pit and the gallery' were more likely to be filled by 'the rumour of an exciting entertainment being close at hand than they would be by any report of a light comedy, sparkling with neatly-turned witticisms and revealing the more delicate touches of histrionic art'.

For this reviewer, Gilbert's rising reputation as a gentrifier of the lower theatrical arts notwithstanding, there was no doubt about the kind of audience a Dickens adaptation was aimed at. Since, the reviewer claims, 'cheaper and more comprehensive editions [of *Great Expectations* had] ... extended its popularity', she or he assumed the motive to be a 'pecuniary' one aimed at a lower-class clientele. This section of the audience, rather than booking boxes in the theatre (priced between 1 and 3 guineas) and dressing up for a social occasion, queued for tickets for the benches in the pit (priced at 1s. 6d.) or packed out the gallery for sixpence.[90] This audience already knew the work and went to be entertained by its familiar characters and plot, or indeed (as Mr Wopsle discovered) to heckle and throw orange peel.[91] Quite apart from the class assumptions attached to cheap books, we probably need no further proof of the perceived interrelationship in this period between Dickens, a mass readership and 'inferior' theatrical productions. Gilbert had a long-standing cultural prejudice to overcome.

---

[86]   'Here, There, and Everywhere', *Fun*, Saturday 10 June 1871, p. 232.

[87]   'GREAT EXPECTATIONS', *Pall Mall Gazette*, Wednesday 31 May 1871, no page number.

[88]   *Examiner*, 15 July 1871, p. 707.

[89]   *Graphic*, 3 June 1871, pp. 518–19.

[90]   Playbill, Pierpont Morgan Library, Department of Music, Manuscripts and Books, Gilbert and Sullivan Collection, Folder No. 1165, Record ID 198686.

[91]   I am grateful to Professor David Mayer for details of the pricing structure of theatre tickets in this period.

This reviewer also mourned the loss of Miss Havisham, Pumblechook and Wemmick, and thought the last act in particular 'thoroughly sensational'. The reviewer has a point. Pip is rescued from Orlick in the nick of time by Herbert, Magwitch and Joe. Magwitch is then shot by the police but lives just long enough to hear that Estella is alive and about to marry Pip. This is pure melodrama, dramatic and cathartic, perfectly in keeping with established adaptation traditions which often altered a novel's ending to suit the taste of audiences for happy plot resolutions.[92] But it troubled the reviewers. In *The Era*'s review, as in several others, there is a note of anxiety about the effects of producing Dickensian melodrama in a new theatre (the Court had only opened in 1870), which until this point had deliberately 'devoted [itself] exclusively to entertainments of a refined character'.[93] This was an age when theatre was frequently decried as vulgar, and *The Era* clearly felt a return to Dickens – and therefore melodrama – was a regressive step which completely changed 'the nature of the entertainments which it seemed to be the chief object of the Management to study'.[94]

Dickens, it seems clear, was perceived to be performed not for the 'higher' class of audience, but in order to fill the cheap seats. Breaking away from this entrenched cultural perception seems to have been beyond Gilbert's powers at this point in his career, despite his prescient recognition of the novel's generic innovations, including its subversion of the roles of hero and villain and its inventive use of 'doubling'. Mayer notes that doubling was of central importance to this period's literature and drama, both melodramatic and serious, and the powerful and complex arrangement of examples in *Great Expectations*, constructed as it is around the young and adult Pip, the good and bad benefactors, and the pairs of convicts, parents, love interests and friends, certainly offer intriguing potential for the serious stage.[95] But they resist easy adaptation to the conventions of stage melodrama by which Gilbert seemed creatively (and perhaps financially) bound. The novel's Pip is not tortured by a twin self and wracked with guilt due to a moral transgression (the traditional use of the double in this period) but by the dawning awareness of his own shallowness. In the novel, also, both good and bad 'parents' are punished, but Pip receives no punishment to speak of beyond the dashing of his pecuniary hopes, unless one counts the possibility that he will end up with the bloodless Estella. The final redemption, restitution and moral cleansing which were key parts of melodrama's traditional form during the Victorian period are largely absent from the novel, and therein, perhaps, lay Gilbert's problem, one

---

[92] See Mary Hammond, 'Hall Caine and the Melodrama on Page, Stage and Screen', *Nineteenth Century Theatre and Film*, 31 (Summer 2004): pp. 39–57.

[93] *Graphic*, 3 June 1871, pp. 518–19. *The Times* too had recognised the new theatre's aspirations in a review of *Randall's Thumb*. It commended '[t]he appearance of the theatre, which is constructed with regard for commodiousness and elegance', and noted that 'the names on the programme show that the performance of a somewhat refined drama is contemplated'. *The Times*, Friday 27 Jan 1871, p. 6.

[94] *The Era*, 4 June 1871, p. 11.

[95] Mayer, 'Leopold Lewis, *The Bells*', p. 398.

which Estella's startling declaration of love in Act 3 and the play's happy ending were clearly intended (though almost entirely failed) to rectify. This adaptation seems caught between the novel's inviting thematic innovations and an established Dickensian theatrical tradition, issues which Gilbert struggled gamely to reconcile. He was no Henry Irving; in the end, possibly because he needed a commercial success or simply because he lacked experience, he played it safe, with somewhat disappointing results.

It was not an experience which he seemed willing to repeat with a different Dickens novel, and the revival at the Aquarium six years later was met with an equally lukewarm critical reception. While the *Chelmsford Chronicle* thought the revival 'one of the most promising ventures which the management of this establishment has yet made',[96] *Fun* was less impressed by the revival of a play which had appeared at the Court Theatre 'with scant success', and the review indicates furthermore that this version was not a straight revival but a reworking:

> [I]t might not be amiss to wonder why the management of the Aquarium Theatre, hitherto so awake to a sense of public desires and requirements, should have made a fresh effort with a comparatively distasteful production. If they wish to patronise the author, he has much other and better, i.e. more popular work, and this latter qualification should mean better in its best sense to a theatrical lessee. Better, too, from an entirely different point, we think the other work of Mr Gilbert which saw the light, as it certainly contained much more that was original and less that was purely transcript … we can only regard the new effort at the Aquarium as, in effect, so much talent thrown away, or, to use an expressive vulgarism, gone wrong.[97]

Like the *Examiner*'s reviewer in 1870, this reviewer seemed unimpressed both by the choice of novel and by the liberties Gilbert took with it. The Aquarium itself was probably also an unwise choice of venue. It had opened on 15 April 1876 with 'Jo', an adaptation of *Bleak House* by J.P. Burnett which had proved popular at the Globe. This play was obviously carefully chosen to launch the theatre's much-advertised aim to bring morally sound amusements to the populace, but neither it nor the productions that followed succeeded in attracting the intended audiences. By 1877, when *Great Expectations* reappeared there, the Aquarium was already more famous as a music hall and circus-act venue than a serious theatre, and by the 1890s it was almost exclusively devoted to circus.[98] This revival of *Great Expectations*, like Dickens's reputation more broadly in the period before 1900, balances precariously on the cusp between the culturally acceptable and the vulgar, but in performance it is never quite able to shake off the taint of the gallery and the pit.

---

[96]   *Chelmsford Chronicle*, Friday 23 March 1877, p. 7.

[97]   'Here, there, and everywhere', *Fun*, Wednesday 28 March 1877, p. 122.

[98]   Phyllis Hartnoll, ed., *The Oxford Companion to the Theatre* (Oxford, 1951), p. 29. See also John Sands, 'Sullivan and the Royal Aquarium', Gilbert and Sullivan Archive, http://math.boisestate.edu/GaS/articles/sull_aquarium/index.html [accessed 20 March 2013].

American versions tended to prefer recasting the novel altogether, perhaps in order to escape the unpopularity or the negative cultural connotations associated with its title, or with a better understanding of which parts of it might work on the popular stage. 'My Unknown Friend', a version adapted by Charles Augustus (Shafto) Scott, is announced on the published play script to have played at Wallack's Theater, New York, in 1872. Morley claims that there is no evidence the play was ever staged at Wallack's, but that it does appear to have been staged in Newark, New Jersey, on 6 July 1877.[99] Bolton suggests these could be two different plays.[100] I have found no reviews of either version, but the fact that we have extant playbills and a script (published by Dicks) is significant in itself; we can, I think, accept the intention to perform it as sufficient evidence of a partial revival of dramatic interest in the novel.[101] Scott did not just change the title, he also changed the story. He choose to end it with Magwitch's death, just as Gilbert did and as Dickens himself had done in his unperformed reading version. But here the emphasis is on the Pip/Magwitch matrix and the use of Pip as a controlling narrator, and Scott's references to the novel's doubling effectively render a few of the novel's subtleties which previous versions lack; 'It's plain I'm in love, but with which? Biddy or Estella?', Pip muses in Act 2.

Similarly focussed on Magwitch is a version called 'Botany Bay: an original melodrama founded in part on Great Expectations', adapted by Levin C. Tees and copyrighted in 1881, which finally appeared on 15 July 1893 in Philadelphia. The first third of the novel seems to have offered the richest dramatic potential in the late nineteenth century; the Pip/Magwitch plot is an easily decoupled scenario which appealed to remediators for some years and indeed continues to appeal, particularly in a postcolonial context. Despite some reviewers' regrets, Miss Havisham and Estella had to wait for a shift in cultural focus from penal reform and the male Bildungsroman to the showcasing of female stars and technical prowess in the costume and scenery departments. Stevenson summed up the late nineteenth-century view when he wrote to his father in 1883: 'Miss Havisham is, probably, the worst thing in human fiction.'[102]

In the 1890s, British theatres belatedly picked up on the possibilities a reworking and retitling of the story provided. The first of these was a version called 'Pip's Patron', adapted by William J. Rix, which appeared at the Town Hall in Beccles on 26 January 1892.[103] *The Era*'s review of this production demonstrates an interesting shift in audience response to the novel's appearance on the stage, and its useful listing of the cast (probably the only evidence we have of what the play kept in and what it left out) suggests an emerging critical sense that while a

---

[99]   Morley, 'Stages', p. 82.

[100]   Bolton, *Dickens Dramatized*, pp. 419–20.

[101]   Charles Augustus Shafto Scott, *My Unknown Friend: A Drama, in Three Acts. Being a Dramatized Version of the Novel "Great Expectations," by the Late Charles Dickens*, Dicks' Standard Plays, Number 412 (London, no date). British Library, X.908.4370.

[102]   R.L. Stevenson, Letter to Thomas Stevenson, 17 March 1883, *Letters*, Vol. 5, p. 91.

[103]   'Plays of the Month', *The Era*, Saturday 6 February 1892, no page number.

certain fidelity to the novel might be a good thing, adjustments had to be made if it was to work in performance:

> A large audience pronounced a decidedly favourable opinion on this piece. The author, with commendable soundness of judgement, refrains from a too violent departure from the lines of the famous story. The construction of the work evinces considerable talent, and the situations are designed with a good eye for dramatic effect.[104]

The play clearly focussed on the first section of the novel and on Magwitch since the cast list contains no Miss Havisham. And while in some respects it may have stuck close to 'the famous story', according to the cast list it took the liberty of foregrounding the character of Pepper, Pip's 'Avenging' servant, perhaps by way of ramping up the comedy.

Another and much looser adaptation (perhaps in this case 'spin-off' would be a more accurate term) which has been missed by most chroniclers of the novel's stage history was 'The King's Outcast' written by Gayer Mackay, which opened on Monday 24 April 1899 at London's Theatre Metropole, and went on to play at the Theatre Royal, Sheffield on 5 May, Liverpool's Shakespeare Theatre on 15 May and Dublin's Gaiety Theatre on 22 May 1899. According to the *Standard*'s reviewer, the author acknowledged 'indebtedness to Charles Dickens and "Great Expectations" for an incident in Act 1 and for the characterisation of two of the parts in the play', those of the village Blacksmith Dan Garth (played by Charles Rock) and Kit Garth (played by Miss Sydney Fairbrother), but the reviewer felt 'the obligation extends to some portion of the dialogue throughout'.[105] The *Morning Post* went further still, calling Act 1 'a dead crib' from Dickens and suggesting that this should be acknowledged on the playbill.[106] Gerald Gurney, the play's director, wrote to the paper the following day, respectfully pointing out that it was.[107] There is a sense here, though, that the *Morning Post* was less interested in protecting the copyright and reputation of an author who was by now fading into distant memory than in preventing the audience from wasting their money on a wrongly labelled rehashing of an old story.

These performances, however loosely based on *Great Expectations*, seem to have been popular successes since they toured widely, and the reviews describe packed and enthusiastic houses, and they point to an important sea change in the reception of Dickens and herald a new era in the fortunes of *Great Expectations*. By 1890 Dickens was old news and, while his name was still invoked at times in the press, his books themselves were more widely and cheaply available than ever before, and thus increasingly devalued in the literary marketplace. In the USA a copy of *Great Expectations* was even available free with a purchase of

---

[104] *The Era*, Saturday 10 December 1892, no page number.
[105] *Standard*, Tuesday 25 April 1899, p. 5.
[106] *Morning Post*, Wednesday, 26 April 1899, p. 5.
[107] *Morning Post*, Thursday, 27 April 1899, p. 5.

Enoch Morgan's Sons Co. soap,[108] a marketing gimmick which the Encyclopaedia Britannica was to repeat in Britain a few years later. In fact, the economic and cultural value of Dickens's works was dependent now more than ever on clever remediation. Canonisation as a 'classic' did not happen until the twentieth century, when emergent new media were in need of material that was familiar, popular and morally unexceptionable in order to win audiences and ward off accusations of moral turpitude, and when the novel's themes began to appeal anew to the concerns of a very different age. As G.K. Chesterton put it, looking back from the first decade of the twentieth century: 'The fundamental difference between the beginning of the nineteenth century and the end of it is simple but enormous. The first period was full of evil things, but it was full of hope. The second period, the *fin de siècle*, was even full (in some sense) of good things. But it was occupied in asking what was the good of good things.'[109] *Great Expectations'* remarkably prescient exploration of this very question was to stand it in good stead in the new century.

---

[108] 'Standard authors popular books: Who is your favourite novelist?', advertisement for Enoch Morgan's Sons Co. 'Book Soap', *Evening World*, 20 January 1890, p. 3. The advertisement lists (in this order) *The Old Curiosity Shop*, *Great Expectations*, *Barnaby Rudge*, *Martin Chuzzlewit*, *The Cricket on the Hearth*, *A Christmas Carol*, *Little Dorrit*, *Pickwick Papers*, *The Uncommercial Traveller*, *Master Humphrey's Clock* and *Sketches by Boz*.

[109] Chesterton, *Chesterton's Biographies: Charles Dickens*, p. 3.

Chapter 3
Great Expectations in the New Media Age, 1900–1945

Relative Obscurity 1900–1917

Great Expectations went through something of an adaptation doldrums in the USA in the first decades of the twentieth century. Robert Giddings *et al.* claim that despite the fact that 'it is a linguistic and not a visual creation' (something, as we have seen, that British audiences had always tended to feel about the novel), 'it is a curious fact that it has always had a very powerful attraction to adaptors for stage and screen', and as evidence they cite Bolton's 100-plus entries for the novel in *Dickens Dramatized.*[1] But the number elides the pattern: most of these adaptations are post–World War II. As far as we can ascertain, the novel did not appear again as a full-length play on the professional American stage until 1977, long after several radio, TV and film versions had given it a new lease of life, and even these were relatively slow in coming. There were 'dramatizations' given around the country sometime between 1904 and the mid-1930s by the impersonator Phidelah Rice, and extant promotional materials for these shows claim that his *Great Expectations* was 'an artistic masterpiece'.[2] But reviewers speak of Rice as a 'Reader of Plays' rather than as an actor, which almost certainly meant (as Dickens himself found) that a process of radical excision of parts of the novel was necessary.

Rare 'teaspoonfuls' such as Rice's seem to have been all the traces that remained of *Great Expectations* on the American stage for some years, and we can probably extrapolate from this a lack of public interest in the novel itself. It had never been among the American public's favourites, and there was little in these decades to revive it. This was a new century filled with rapid technological advances and new social debates about sex, morality and gender, with new challenges in global politics, with anti-European sentiments (particularly in the wake of the First World War), and with myriad new home-grown fictional responses to them ranging from the detective novel to the naturalism of Theodore Dreiser. Dickens's gloomy late novel must have seemed to early twentieth-century Americans as though it

---

[1]   Robert Giddings, Keith Selby and Chris Wensley, *Screening the Novel: The Theory and Practice of Literary Dramatization* (Basingstoke, 1990), p. 82.

[2]   *Phidelah Rice* (Boston: Personality Magazine Press, 1904/1932), in 'Traveling Culture: Circuit Chautauqua in the Twentieth Century,' Digital Collection MSC0150, University of Iowa Libraries Special Collections, http://digital.lib.uiowa.edu/cdm/compoundobject/collection/tc/id/42440/rec/1 [accessed 20 April 2013].

belonged to another world.[3] F. Scott Fitzgerald allegedly wrote *The Great Gatsby* (1925) shortly after discovering Dickens, but while *Gatsby*'s themes of class snobbery, social aspiration and unrequited love are certainly reminiscent of *Great Expectations*, Fitzgerald evidently recognized the need to update these themes for Jazz-age Americans and sensibly substituted optimism for moral comeuppance.[4]

Many of Dickens's earlier novels and stories remained popular on the stage, particularly *Oliver Twist,* and other nineteenth-century titles also continued to thrive.[5] Victorian favourites such as Mrs Henry Wood's *East Lynne* continued playing in theatres on both sides of the Atlantic in the early 1900s, as did Harriet Beecher Stowe's *Uncle Tom's Cabin,*[6] and both also transferred easily from the stage to the new medium of film in the teens.[7] Not so *Great Expectations.* Apparently canonised purely by association with the more famous early works, it seems to have survived largely as a set text in schools and colleges.[8] It does not appear as a play listing either in Bolton or in the *Cumulated Dramatic Index* until 1917, when the photoplay from the first American film version was published, and it was not popular with critics even when they began to reassess Dickens's reputation around the centenary of his birth in 1912.[9]

In the UK, *Great Expectations* fared considerably better in ensemble dramatic performance. As a result of the formation of the Dickens Fellowship in 1902 and various Dickens Festivals, its flame was kept burning during a period of general critical disinterest in Dickens.[10] A number of Fellowship productions took place around the country from 1918, including the performance of 'sketches' from the novel, and charity performances helped to swell the number.[11] There is mention of a Dickens Festival production of *Great Expectations* in London as early as

---

[3]   McParland's final chapter mentions two examples of American readers recalling their love of Dickens in the 1920s, but the only works mentioned by name are the Christmas stories.

[4]   Andrew Hook, *F. Scott Fitzgerald: A Literary Life* (Basingstoke, 2002), p. 54.

[5]   Bolton, *Dickens Dramatized*, p. 105.

[6]   See Claire Parfait, *Uncle Tom's Cabin: A Publishing History* (Burlington, VT, 2006).

[7]   See H. Philip Bolton, *Women Writers Dramatized: A Calendar of Performances from Narrative Works Published in English to 1900* (London and New York, 2000).

[8]   Due to differences in State curricula it is difficult to be certain exactly when the novel was first adopted as a school and college text in the USA, but it was certainly well established by 1935. In that year a Study Guide for school teachers was published by the National Council of Teachers of English in order to assist with teaching the novel alongside the film, and it exhorted students to examine the film's 'authenticity'. Walter Barnes, *A Study Guide to the Critical Appreciation of the Photoplay Version of Charles Dickens' novel Great Expectations* (New York, 1935), p. 12. See also Steve J. Wurtzler, '*David Copperfield* and the US Curriculum', in *Dickens on Screen*, ed. by John Glavin (Cambridge, 2003), p. 159.

[9]   Laurence W. Mazzeno, *The Dickens Industry, Critical Perspectives 1836–2005* (Rochester and Woodbridge, 2011), pp. 53–6.

[10]   Ford, *Dickens and His Readers*, p. 171. See also Mazzeno, *Dickens Industry*, pp. 40–56.

[11]   See Appendix C: Stage Adaptations.

1925 and the annual Broadstairs Dickens Festival, at which it was also performed, began in 1937. The enthusiasm of fans, coupled with the continued outpouring of cheap reprints, meant that neither Dickens's name nor that of his thirteenth novel were permitted to disappear entirely from public view in Britain in the first three decades of the new century, despite critical dismissal both of the author and of the fans who from 1905 began publication of the invaluable *Dickensian*.[12] But these diehards were a relatively small group. Even during World War I, when publishers recognised Dickens's potential for cheap reissue[13] and when one might expect a huge revival of interest in a 'quintessentially English' author among British troops, recent research has demonstrated that while Dickens was certainly read in significant numbers by British and Commonwealth soldiers and POWs, he was competing for their attention with newspapers, journals, poetry, sensational Victorian novelists such as Marie Corelli, new novels by thriller writers such as 'Sapper' and John Buchan, and alternative forms of reading such as technical manuals and other self-improvement books.[14] John Middleton Murry's claim that 'a marked revival of interest and admiration of Dickens among the younger generation' began concurrently with the start of World War I may well be true, but it is quite likely that Dickens was simply benefitting, as many out-of-copyright authors did, from the soldiers' demands for – and publishers' eagerness to provide – cheap, light-hearted reading matter to while away the hours at the front.[15]

In light of this evidence of a faithful but relatively small body of popular support during the teens and twenties, it is revealing to examine what was happening to Dickens's official reputation in the UK in this period, including how important he was deemed to be to the next generation of British readers. Both before and after World War I, a series of Education Acts had argued for the inclusion of English Literature in the curricula of both Elementary and Secondary British Schools.[16] In the so-called 'Newbolt Report' of 1921 a specially constituted committee containing several well-known literary critics took a far-sighted view of literature's rightful place in the curriculum. They felt: 'The prevalence of a low view of art, and especially of the art of literature, has been a main cause of our defective conception of national education. Hitherto literature has, even more than science, suffered in the public mind both misunderstanding and degradation.'[17]

---

[12]   See Ch. 3, 'Dickens Among the Moderns (1915–1940)', in Mazzeno, *Dickens Industry*, pp. 62–90.

[13]   A.J.P. Taylor, *English History 1914–1945* (Harmondsworth, 1973), p. 388.

[14]   See the essays on reading practices and book sales in *Publishing in the First World War: Essays in Book History*, ed. by Mary Hammond and Shafquat Towheed (Basingstoke, 2007).

[15]   Mazenno, *Dickens Industry*, p. 63.

[16]   Gillard D. (2011). 'Education in England: a brief history,' www.educationengland.org.uk/history [accessed 2 April 2013].

[17]   Henry Newbolt, *The Teaching of English in England: being the report of the Departmental Committee appointed by the President of the Board of Education to inquire into the position of English in the educational system of England* [The 'Newbolt Report'] (London, 1921), Chapter 1, pp. 9 and 20–21.

They went on to declare their fervent belief in 'the fundamental necessity of English for the full development of the mind and character of English children', and recommended that the Greek and Roman Classics which had long populated literature courses should be replaced or at least accompanied by more enjoyable creative works.[18] This committee was convinced that 'the teacher who means the effect of his work to be lasting will start from what the children themselves enjoy, recognising that even though what they read may be rubbish, their being willing to read at all is a definite asset'.[19] When they went on to gather information on what sort of 'rubbish' school children were reading in their own time, they were pleasantly surprised to find a certain 'catholicity' in the children's taste and that at one school 'Shakespeare, Dickens, Tennyson, [and] Kingsley, rub shoulders with today's boys' and girls' authors'.[20] In attempting to trace the popularity of Dickens, they found that taste could be passed on by a teacher:

> 'Dickens', says one witness 'does not appeal.' 'Scott', says another, 'is not liked, and Dickens not generally, though an enthusiastic teacher can make the class respond.' A third says: 'Among the older boys I have found, beyond question, the favourite author is Dickens', and adds: 'Possibly the fact that I am myself a devoted Dickensian has its influence.'[21]

There is a strong sense here that while Dickens's novels are not yet considered improving 'classics' which should form part of an essential reading list, they are harmless popular favourites which teachers feel comfortable admitting (perhaps especially to government officials) that they have recommended to their students.[22] Dickens is offered here both as a stepping stone to better things, and as a latent marker of a sound national consciousness rooted in the vernacular, a pertinent compromise, perhaps, during this penultimate year of David Lloyd George's Conservative-Liberal Coalition Government (1916–22).

As part of their endorsement of reading for pleasure as well as education, the Committee approvingly included in their report the details of a school library book-sharing scheme set up by London Elementary Schools. Out of 1,776 departments and a total of 2,000,000 volumes in the scheme, the Committee compiled a list of pupils' favourite novels in order of popularity and found that while *Tales and Stories from Shakespeare*, *Robinson Crusoe*, *Arthurian Legends* and *Peter Pan* topped the list, *David Copperfield*, *A Tale of Two Cities* and *A Christmas Carol* also made the top ten. *Oliver Twist* and *Pickwick Papers* made a showing too; Dickens is a demonstrable self-selected favourite among these London children.[23]

---

[18]   Newbolt, *Teaching of English*, Chapter 1, p. 21.

[19]   Newbolt, *Teaching of English*, Chapter 3, p. 84.

[20]   Newbolt, *Teaching of English*, Chapter 3, pp. 84–5.

[21]   Newbolt, *Teaching of English*, Chapter 3, pp. 85–6.

[22]   Eliot and Hardy both feature in the section of the London Evening Education curriculum devoted to 'Aspects of Victorian Literature', for example, but Dickens is absent.

[23]   Memorandum submitted by Mr A.E. Palfery on the scheme for the circulation of books in London elementary schools. Newbolt, *Teaching of English*, Appendix 3, pp. 374–5.

But *Great Expectations* makes no appearance at all. Some children who grew up in the early part of the twentieth century and left memoirs of their experiences mention reading Dickens, but again, few recall *Great Expectations* with any special fondness. An exception is Norman Nicholson (born 1914). At his school in Holburn Hill in London during the 1920s, Nicholson recollects receiving Dickens novels as prizes chosen by his schoolmaster, Mr Wilson, and being persuaded by this to purchase his own copy of *Great Expectations*:

> In 1926, at the Secondary School, I received *Barnaby Rudge*; in 1927, *Dombey and Son*; in 1928, *Nicholas Nickleby*. *Great Expectations*, which followed *Pickwick* in Mr Wilson's scheme [of recommended reading], I acquired in the red, cardboard-backed Nelson's Classics, price One Shilling and Sixpence, a series which became my regular source of Christmas and birthday presents from uncles and friends.[24]

Nicholson recalls *Great Expectations* as representative of 'the darker Dickens' by which he was immediately 'gripped', preferring it to the sentimentality of the earlier novels, but he is a rarity among children. We should note here also that not only was his purchase the result of a rare teacher's personal enthusiasm, but also that he acquired the novel in the cheap Nelson's Classics edition; proof, perhaps, both that the publishers' energetic campaigns to produce memorable Dickens series cheaply in this period had some tangible results, and of the value of calling a book a 'classic' when one is trying to sell it to the socially anxious Board School educated. But this particular novel is neglected in other working and middle-class memoirs recording the presence of Dickens books in the school library or in their own home reading lists. Since mention of it by child readers is so scarce, it seems likely either that it was not considered by teachers, parents and school boards to be suitable reading for children, or that it simply failed to make an impression on many of them.

Great Expectations did find the occasional influential early twentieth-century fan among more mature readers. As we have seen, Lang, Chesterton and Shaw all publicly claimed it an important work. Iris Barry, arbiter of aesthetic taste during the 1920s for the *Adelphi*, the *Spectator*, *Vogue* and the *Daily Mail*, wrote in praise of cinema as an art form in the face of much opposition, and tried to raise its cultural status in her column by comparing films to great works of literature. In November 1925 she found kinship between the World War I epic *The Four Horsemen of the Apocalypse* (Metro Pictures,1921) and *Great Expectations*, a comparison that could not help but endorse the novel as much as the film.[25] Less publicly but equally sincerely, E.M. Forster wrote of it in his personal Commonplace Book (kept between 1925 and 1968): 'Alliance between atmosphere and plot (the convicts) make it more solid and satisfactory than anything else of D. known

---

24   Norman Nicholson, *Wednesday Early Closing* (1975; London, 1975), pp. 143–4. http://www.open.ac.uk/Arts/reading/UK/record_details.php?id=11381[accessed 29 April 2013].

25   Iris Barry, 'What the Public Wants', *Daily Mail*, 21 November 1925, p. 8.

to me. Very fine writing occasionally.'[26] But Forster too is something of a rarity. The Reading Experience Database, which records the experiences of hundreds of British readers between 1450 and 1945, and from which I have extracted some of this testimony, has fewer entries on *Great Expectations* (a total of eight, counting duplicates) than on almost any other Dickens novel. The early novels are, predictably, mentioned far more often by readers – at the time of writing *Oliver Twist* has 70 entries, *A Tale of Two Cities* 73, the *Old Curiosity Shop* 83, *Pickwick* 105 and *David Copperfield* 158. Of the novels, only *Hard Times* and *Our Mutual Friend* have fewer entries (1 and 0 respectively).[27] Even Rose's magisterial study *The Intellectual Life of the British Working Classes*, the result of combing hundreds of primary sources for readers' experiences between the 1860s and the 1960s, can come up with only two references to someone having read – or remembered having read – *Great Expectations*.[28]

How did we get from this readership low point to the situation barely a century later, when readers like Robert Douglas-Fairhurst (an acknowledged Dickens expert) feels the book has always been part of British lives? 'Readers grow up with it', he wrote in 2011. 'Our culture has too.'[29] The answer almost certainly lies in its appropriation by the emerging new media of radio, film and TV which revivified interest in the novel, and its related appearance on school reading lists in the 1930s. What made *Great Expectations* so belatedly attractive to adaptors and curriculum designers after decades out in the cold is a more complex question. Dickens's status as a national icon, his appeal to sentimental notions of 'home' and his happy endings apparently stood him in good stead in Britain during both world wars. We could also with some justification suggest that *Great Expectations*' thematic focus on the emptiness of monetary ambition might have obvious appeal in the USA and the UK during the Great Depression of the late 1920s and early 30s, as it was to do again in the 1980s. But it is important to note that the establishment of the novel's relevance in each epoch lay in the hands of the remediators who took over from the publishers the task of repackaging it for each new audience, and that they each added new layers of interpretation specific to their own skills as well as to each medium and its moment.

One new entertainment medium in particular – film – seems to have been central to a general revival in Dickens's fortunes. On a number of levels the affinity between Dickens and cinema is so close that it appears natural; Sergei Eisenstein was among the first to explore the formal and structural similarities first

---

[26]   E.M. Forster, *Commonplace Book*, ed. by Philip Gardner (London, 1985), pp. 18–19. http://www.open.ac.uk/Arts/reading/UK/record_details.php?id=20749 [accessed 19 March 2013].

[27]   Reading Experience Database, http://www.open.ac.uk/Arts/reading/UK/ [accessed 19 March 2013].

[28]   Jonathan Rose, *The Intellectual Life of the British Working Classes* (New Haven and London, 2001), pp. 111–12.

[29]   Robert Douglas-Fairhurst, 'Among the Greats', *Guardian Review*, 29 September 2011, p. 6.

recognised by the great American silent film director D.W. Grifffith,[30] and David Paroissien claims that Dickens's novels are also akin to the works of the German expressionist film makers of the 1920s in their use of 'details of setting to depict a character's state of mind'.[31] Grahame Smith goes further, using Benjamin's notion that 'every epoch sees in images the epoch which is to succeed it' to suggest not only that Dickens 'dreamed' cinema, but that the cinema and Dickens were created by the same cultural forces and that Dickens's novels are thus intrinsically proto-cinematic.[32]

None of these commentators claim that all Dickens adaptations are good ones, of course, and most have their favourites; an admirer of David Lean's *Oliver Twist* (1948) but not his *Great Expectations* (1946), for example, Smith agrees with Graham Petrie that Lean's earlier film separates out 'the realistic and poetic elements of the text' to its detriment.[33] 'By stripping the novel to the bare bones of its linear narrative', Smith explains, 'the film loses almost all possibility of density of effect and thematic complexity', and in his opinion this is a result of the fact that while all the late novels possess 'panoramic riches', they also possess 'intellectual complexity and it is doubtful that their translation into film has ever been attempted by an artist with even remotely the vision and imagination of Dickens himself'.[34]

These are all tempting explanations for the attraction Dickens has held for filmmakers, though Smith's unfavourable comparison between Dickens and Lean as auteurs is probably more personally revealing than historically useful. Cinema as a medium is much more collaborative than the average novel, and this was perhaps particularly so in the heyday of the 'Hollywood studio era' which (even in Britain) was as much dominated by finance, competition and market forces as by individual artistry (though artistry certainly played a crucial part). Where *Great Expectations* adaptations are concerned, notions of visual/spatial psychology, proto-cinematic editing and artistic imagination are unable to account fully either for the final forms the products took, or for their performance in the marketplace. In fact, for various reasons, in the first three decades of the twentieth century, filmmakers seem to have chosen to ignore *Great Expectations*' potential for psychological realism (and indeed many of its other innate qualities), focussing most consistently on its classic Victorian melodramatic motifs: the repentant sinner, the cross-class romance, the cruel parent, the triumph of love. As a result, they could not help but foreground the creakiest parts of Dickens's plot. Even Lean's film was subject to forces outside his control, though he did a better job than some others of controlling them.

---

[30]   Sergei Eisenstein, 'Dickens, Griffith, and the Film Today', pp. 232–3.

[31]   David Paroissien, 'Dickens and the Cinema', *Dickens Studies Annual*, 7 (1978): p. 69.

[32]   Smith, *Dickens and the Dream of Cinema*, p. 1.

[33]   Smith, *Dickens and the Dream of Cinema*, p. 123. See Graham Petrie, 'Dickens, Godard and the Film Today', *The Yale Review*, Vol. 64, December 1974, pp. 185–201.

[34]   Smith, *Dickens and the Dream of Cinema*, pp. 124 and 175.

To consider these forces is not to make excuses for the adaptations' demerits, but to seek ways of thinking about them which might move us beyond the baldly comparative. *Great Expectations* was not the same cultural entity (or rather entities) in the 1920s and 1930s as it had been in the 1860s, and its re-emergence on the global scene was mediated through the different tastes of individuals and cultural communities, and the developing needs and institutional constraints of new media industries. As Lea Jacobs suggests, in the 1920s in the USA, 'Film producers ... had to steer a course between the minority whose tastes might be epitomized by the hip and irreverent *Smart Set* [a magazine founded in 1900 by the satirical writer and critic H.L. Mencken] and the vast majority who remained loyal to Norman Rockwell and the *Saturday Evening Post*'.[35] Radio adaptors wrestled with similar market appeal issues, and both media were subject to budget constraints, various forms of censorship and the limitations of their own particular technologies.

Dickens presented attractive solutions to some of these problems. Not only was he easily carved up into palatable chunks to suit different scheduling constraints, but all his novels were out of copyright by 1920 and most of them were known titles with familiar plots and characters, and they were thus prime targets for nascent industries in need of remediable material that came with a low price tag and a fair chance of attracting audiences. His Victorian Englishness also represented a widely recognised guarantee of respectability in the West, as well as a set of imperialist assumptions that set the scene for future non-Western challenges. The relationships between the formal properties and historical forces that projected *Great Expectations* back into the spotlight are not always straightforward or equal, but their synergies and their tensions can tell us a great deal about some of the cultural assumptions and industry machinations behind the process of Dickens's canonisation in the late colonial period prior to World War II.

Rebirth on the Screen 1917–34

Great Expectations' first outings on film in the pre- and early sound eras, along with its comeback in the professional theatre, provide important coordinates in its journey from relative obscurity to global icon. Eclipsed by David Lean's critically acclaimed and globally significant film of 1946 (discussed more fully in Chapter 4), these adaptations are often listed but hardly ever examined, either by Dickens scholars or by film and theatre historians. McFarlane, for example, mentions the 1917 film in his *Screen Adaptations*, but it does not appear in his filmography for the novel and he does not discuss it. Similarly, while he does devote a section to the 1934 version, he centres it on a discussion of the film's lack of fidelity to the novel, concluding that 'the film has little in common with the anterior text'.[36] I suggest

---

[35]   Lea Jacobs, *The Decline of Sentiment: American Film in the 1920s* (Berkeley and London, 2008), p. 22.

[36]   McFarlane, *Screen Adaptations: Great Expectations, the Relationship between Text and Film* (London, 2008), p. 93.

that these early adaptations are worth analysing in a slightly different way. Viewing them as cultural/historical events in their own right will allow us to venture beyond the matter of their fidelity (or lack of it) to the novel, and to examine the role they played in its changing cultural status.

The first screen adaptation of *Great Expectations* that we know of for sure was what Graham Petrie calls a 'very primitive' 12-minute British version called *The Boy and the Convict* directed by Dave Aylott (Kinematograph Company, 1909), which confined itself to long single takes, carried on the theatrical tradition of focussing on the first third of the novel and provided a double-couple happy ending.[37] Its absence from the *Cumulated Dramatic Index* of that year suggests that this film did not make it successfully to the USA[38] and, like many early Dickens 'shorts', it was not even mentioned by the *Dickensian*.[39] In this and other ways the film was typical of its time. As Petrie notes, in this early period, film art was in its infancy and the theatre's influence was still very much in evidence in performance styles: 'Audiences and reviewers seemed happy with works that dramatized the most familiar characters and events in what was largely still a very theatrical manner, with intertitles (or perhaps a lecturer) providing the basic plot information and summary.'[40] It is probably significant that the film's title avoided a direct reference to the novel whose first third furnishes its main plot; at this time the book's title was not considered much of a draw, and ultimately the story is different enough from the novel to warrant a different name.

The first version (and one of the last Dickens novels) to be filmed under its own title was a 50-minute silent film released on 8 January 1917. By this time every other Dickens novel had been filmed in the UK, the USA or Europe at least once, sometimes many times, and most of those filmed post-1909 make an appearance as published photoplays. *Great Expectations* had been oddly neglected up to this point.[41] The decision to redress the balance was probably a matter of pragmatics: other Dickens novels were playing reasonably well with audiences, and this one was patently under-used. The picture was directed by the Italian film-maker Robert G. Vignola, produced by Famous Players-Lasky and distributed by Paramount, who turned out a staggering quantity of pictures in the teens and twenties.[42] The photoplay is listed in the American publication *The Cumulated Dramatic Index* for that year, but according to this and all other sources I have examined (including the main theatre journal *The New York Clipper*) it did not spark any theatrical

---

[37]   Petrie, 'Silent Film Adaptations Part 1: From the Beginning to 1911', *Dickensian*, 97 (Spring 2001): pp. 13–14.

[38]   I have found no reviews of it in the early American film journals.

[39]   Michael Eaton, '*The Dickensian* goes to the Cinematograph', *Dickensian*, 101 (Winter 2005): p. 233.

[40]   Petrie, 'Silent Film Adaptations Part 1', p. 16.

[41]   Glavin, ed., *Dickens on Screen*, pp. 201–16.

[42]   Illness forced Vignola to withdraw before the filming was complete, at which point Joseph Kaufman took over. *Moving Picture World*, 13 January 1917, p. 252.

revival in the USA and it does not seem to have been popular.[43] It had a 'negative cost' (which means production costs excluding advertising and distribution) of $27,000, a middling budget in a period when average negative costs –according to articles in the *Motion Picture Classic* and the *New York Dramatic Mirror* in July 1917 – ranged from $17, 700 to $41, 350.[44] It did what on the surface seems like reasonable business, making $74,000 in domestic and $18, 000 in foreign sales.[45] But when one factors in an additional 60 per cent outlay in distribution and advertising costs on top of the cost of producing the negative, the profits look considerably less healthy.[46] A year later, D.W. Griffith's propaganda film *Hearts of the World* (Paramount, 1918), by no means his greatest success, would reap what his biographer calls 'very respectable' though not huge profits of $600,000.[47]

The low returns for Vignola's film could be a result of its treatment. As far as we know the film is now lost, but the extant publicity material suggests that it was marketed as a stock period romance framed by – in this period – old-fashioned melodramatic motifs. Melodrama, as we saw in Chapter 2, has always needed to evolve in order to survive. The mode and manner of its use in the 1920s in short weekly film serials such as 'The Perils of Pauline', churned out in their hundreds by the studios and hugely popular with lower-class audiences, raised anew the old spectre of melodrama as vulgar. The feature film, more costly to produce and in search of prestige, needed to work hard to differentiate itself from these serials, which often preceded it in screening programmes.[48]

In 1917 we seem to be witnessing a key stage in a long cinematic evolution through which, according to Thomas Elsaesser, Dickensian melodrama eventually enabled 'a portrayal of existential insecurity and moral anguish'.[49] Elsaesser sees this evolution continuing well into the family film melodramas of the 1940s and 1950s, but Vignola's film of *Great Expectations* seems to be embedded in its earliest and most cautious phase. According to the plot précis, Pip and Estella

---

[43]   It is probably significant that while *The New York Clipper* mentioned it as in production in 1916, it failed to review it when complete, though it reviewed both *Oliver Twist*, directed by James Young (Lasky Company, 1916) and *A Tale of Two Cities*, directed by Frank Lloyd (Fox, 1917).

[44]   Quoted in Richard Koszarski, *An Evening's Entertainment: The Age of the Silent Feature Picture, 1915–1928* (Berkeley, 1990), p. 112

[45]   This note on the 1917 film's profits was written on the back of a typed synopsis by Emery Kanarik for a proposed new film version, dated 31 January 1941. It can be found in folder GE 1917: L. Huff – J. Pickford, 665, Margaret Herrick Library, Academy of Motion Picture Arts and Sciences, Los Angeles.

[46]   Koszarski, *An Evening's Entertainment*, p. 114.

[47]   Richard Schickel, *D.W. Griffith and the Birth of Film* (London, 1984), p. 360.

[48]   Ben Singer, *Melodrama and Modernity: Early Sensational Cinema and Its Contexts* (New York, 2001), p. 222.

[49]   Thomas Elsaesser, 'Tales of Sound and Fury: Observations on the Family Melodrama', in *Home Is Where the Heart Is: Studies in Melodrama and the Woman's Film*, ed. by Christine Gledhill (London, 1987), p. 48.

fall in love early on in the film and Miss Havisham keeps them apart due to her opposition to Pip's low social status (a long-standing melodramatic tradition on the stage), and it is this that motivates his desire to be a gentleman. But the real barrier to their happiness is Pip's fear that Estella will spurn him once she knows the truth about Magwitch being his benefactor. Instead, Estella shows her 'finer qualities' (in other words, she is not a snob like her adoptive mother) and helps Pip to arrange Magwitch's escape. Finally, though the plan fails: 'Over his dead body there arises the vision of a new romance as the two young lovers do homage to the better side of this remarkable man's character.'[50]

There is nothing particularly innovative here (indeed, there are shades of Gilbert's 1871 adaptation in the smoothing out of the book's narrative and thematic complexities to fit the requirements of the safest melodramatic modes), and the cinematic competition that year was fierce. The serial melodramas continued to proliferate, giving appreciative audiences some gutsier heroines who bested a villain every week (even if they were returned safely to domesticity at the episode's end). Buster Keaton and Stan Laurel both made their screen debuts in this period. Charlie Chaplin was already a star. Just as significantly, the highest grossing films that year were lavish costume dramas such as *Cleopatra* starring the vamp Theda Bara, and homespun yarns such as *Rebecca of Sunnybrook Farm* starring 'America's sweetheart' Mary Pickford. On the stage in Britain, 'home front' dramas such as G.B. Shaw's satirical *Augustus Does his Bit* (1916) and Mrs Arthur Hankey's patriotic *A House-Warming in Wartime* (1917) were more popular than melodramas.[51] In the USA, Jesse Lynch Williams's *Why Marry?* (1917) received the first Pulitzer Prize for drama, and its cynical modern attitude to traditional relationships was representative of the rupture in nineteenth-century theatrical mores that the war helped to bring about.[52] None of this suggests favourable conditions for a *Great Expectations* revival. By 1917 the USA had entered the war, and the prevailing cinematic taste both there and in the UK was for comedy, westerns, adventure serials and patriotic historical epics that showcased the cinema's technical wizardry. Period romance and melodrama both remained popular, but in order to attract audiences they had to work harder than this adaptation seems to have done to appeal to modern tastes.[53]

There were clearly hopes for a success: as a result of Famous Players-Lasky's international distribution deals, the film was shown as far afield as Australia and

---

[50] Playbill for theatrical release containing six stills, two cover images of the principals, and synopsis. *Great Expectations 1917* (clippings file), Billy Rose Theatre Division, New York Public Library.

[51] Heinz Kosok, *The Theatre of War: The First World War in British and Irish Drama* (Basingstoke, 2007), p. 31.

[52] Don B. Wilmeth and Christopher Bigsby, eds., *The Cambridge History of American Theatre*, Vol. 2: *1870–1945* (Cambridge, 1999), p. 318.

[53] See Michael Hammond, *The Big Show: British Cinema Culture in the Great War 1914–18* (Exeter, 2005) and Michael Paris, ed., *The First World War and Popular Cinema: 1914 to the Present* (New Brunswick, 2000).

New Zealand (though the runs there were not long),[54] and American trade and fan magazines greeted it with optimism and, on the whole, gave it reasonable reviews. *Moving Picture World* cautiously called it 'an interesting and well-staged subject', adding: 'Many liberties have been taken with the story [but] the essence of this old tale has been preserved.' Following a précis of the plot (for those who did not know – or perhaps could not remember – the novel), the reviewer continued in a vein which shows us something of what viewers expected from their drama in this period: 'It is a good cast. Director Robert Vignola shows some notable settings. One of these is the London streets in which are situated the quarters of Pip. Another is the background where Magwitch takes boat [*sic*] to escape the soldiers. There is suspense following the return of Magwitch.'[55] The trade paper *Motography* concurred: 'Perhaps not as dramatically powerful as *Oliver Twist*', it opined, 'but delightfully absorbing and entertaining. The whole production is a thing of beauty'. Its reviewer concluded on a note of optimism about the film's future: '*Great Expectations* is a picture which people will make an effort to see, the land over, as soon as they hear its name, and when they have seen it they are sure to recommend it to their friends as something entirely worthwhile. It is a production of real class.'[56]

As Lea Jacobs has shown, the trade press needs to be considered as '*producing* a discourse on films and on audiences, not as a *reflection* of what real spectators did with the movies they watched. Many of the critical judgements found in the trade press were framed in terms of a film's potential profitability and appeal in the market'.[57] The invocation of Vignola's film as 'worthwhile' and possessing 'real class' in this particular trade-press review taps into an emerging discourse of intellectual value attached to Englishness, coalescing in particular around classic English fiction. This was to prove important to the appropriation of Dickens for the radio and both the large and the small screen in the coming decades, but in 1917 few actual filmgoers seemed persuaded by it. In an illuminating weekly item called 'What the Picture Did for Me: Actual Criticism of Films by Exhibitors, from a Business Standpoint', *Motography* usefully supplements its construction of potential profitability with reports from real cinema exhibitors on the reactions of real audiences, and while one commented 'A great picture. Attendance good',[58] most exhibitors reported little audience enthusiasm. 'The Dickens style of story does not seem to be popular', commented one. 'It was a picture that the audiences did not seem to care about. The story is too old, perhaps.'[59] Another blamed the

---

54   Item on the showing of *Great Expectations* in movie theatres in Australia: 'What the Movies are Doing', *Free Lance*, 22 June 1917, p. 20. See also advertisement for a two-night showing at the Arcadia Theatre in Auckland, *Auckland Star*, 8 October 1917, p. 8.

55   *Moving Picture World*, 20 January 1917, p. 357.

56   *Motography*, 20 Jan 1917, p. 153.

57   Jacobs, *Decline of Sentiment*, p. 18. Italics original.

58   'H.B. Tull, 'Strand Theatre, Monon, Indiana', *Motography*, 25 Aug 1917, p. 38.

59   'Edward Trinz, 'West End Theater [New York]', *Motography*, 17 March 1917, p. 554.

stars: 'The "Expectations" proved disappointing from the box-office standpoint. It is a fairly good picture but did not draw well. Jack Pickford and Louise Huff do not seem very popular with my patrons."[60] A third complained about the genre: 'Another costume play. Why don't producers quit putting these classics on their regular programs? It fell to me on a Saturday night, and did not pull at all.'[61]

Exhibitors' grumbles notwithstanding, movie magazines engaged in delicate negotiations between cultural disapproval and consumer demand continued to see the adaptation of Dickens as a good thing. *Photoplay* noted with approval that gradually 'the novel classics are turning under the eye of the lens', in this instance praising Frank Losee's performance as the 'slimy yet pathetic wrongdoer' Abel Magwitch and commending Louise Huff as 'the winsome Estella'. These are not descriptions which many people familiar with the novel would immediately associate with these characters, and they help to confirm a sense that this film was an odd sort of hybrid. It seems to have been a melodrama in period costume, aimed at increasing the studio's intellectual capital while simultaneously taking care to offend nobody, and somehow also hoping to cash in both on the proven popularity of melodrama and on a nostalgic appreciation for the author. The review also ends with a vague gesture towards a still-forming generic definition for Dickens adaptation which privileges its educative potential: 'In direction and equipment', it notes, 'there is a pretty fair idea of the period both in material and in deportment.'[62]

The comment reflects the prevailing official climate in relation to cinema in this period. In both Britain and the USA there were considerable anxieties about the new medium's potential influence on the bodies and the morals of audiences, and the idea of film as educative (at least as well as, if not instead of, entertaining) was one way of handling them. The National Board of Review of Motion Pictures was established in New York in 1909, comprising 'persons of culture, judgement, and discretion' and reviewing virtually every picture brought to market. Their task was to eliminate 'vulgarity (immorality or impropriety of conduct), prolonged and passionate love scenes, insufficient clothing, unnecessary and detailed showing of opium joints or dance halls, improper dancing, unnecessary brutality to man and beast, and detailed exposition of crime'.[63] In Britain, similarly, the National Council of Public Morals commissioned a report in 1917 to consider the spread and possible effects of cinema on audiences, particularly children. They reported that cinemas in this period afforded 'accommodation for one in every thirty-seven of the population'.[64] No medium had caught the popular imagination so quickly,

---

[60]   'Mr J. Weil, 'Castle Theater. Downtown house', *Motography*, 3 February 1917, p. 224.

[61]   'A.N. Miles, 'Eminence Theater, Eminence, KY', *Motography*, 22 December 1917, p. 1276.

[62]   *Photoplay Magazine*, April 1917, p. 82.

[63]   Anon., *The Cinema, Its Present Position and Future Possibilities: National Council of Public Morals*, Appendix 1: Cinematograph Censorship Regulations in Other Countries (1917; New York, 1970), p. 324.

[64]   *The Cinema, Its Present Position and Future Possibilities*, p. xxi.

and while the Council concluded that cinema was 'the most democratic of the means of enjoyment at the disposal of our populace' and that it should therefore have State sanction, it also recommended State censorship of the conditions of screening and content of films and suggested that as an antidote to 'silly and sordid melodrama ... more of the best stories and plays of the world's literature should be produced'.[65] In the face of these official opinions, circulating widely on both sides of the Atlantic even prior to their official articulation here in 1909 and 1917, the filming of Dickens's works must have seemed like a safe bet. For a start, they were morally unexceptionable. If well-handled they could even be deemed educative (giving 'a good sense of the period'), and most of the characters were well-known and visually distinct enough to work effectively on the pre-talkie screen. The episodic nature of Dickens's stories also worked in their favour; it meant they could be easily adapted to the early film medium, decoupled extracts lending themselves readily to the short one- or two-reel format.[66]

As a result, by 1917 Dickens was a familiar (if not always – from the audience point of view – welcome) sight on the big screen, and adaptations of his works were already attracting character actors such as Frank Losee who were better known on the stage. *Great Expectations* was not much of a draw for screen stars, however. Jack Pickford (Vignola's Pip) was the brother of Mary Pickford, one of the period's biggest stars and most influential industry figures, but up to this point he had played mostly small roles in B movies. His break had come playing opposite Louise Huff (later to be the 'winsome' Estella) in the 1916 film version of Booth Tarkington's bestselling novel *Seventeen*, also directed by Vignola, and subsequently he was to play Tom Sawyer. But his career was not a stellar one and neither his presence nor that of the other cast members, most of whom were bit-part or contract players, indicates that big money rode on the production. Louise Huff had made her debut as an ingénue in 1910, but her career was already on the wane. Neither Zukor nor Mary Pickford mentions the film in their extant correspondence, and this suggests that it was of no particular significance. Indeed, mention of Vignola's name in Zukor's correspondence from the year 1916–17 appears solely in connection with how hard the director had to work in this period to turn out a sufficient quantity of films to meet the studio's financial targets.[67] *Great Expectations* was simply part of this production mill.

It is possible that the film's re-release in 1919 might indicate some level of popularity with audiences. But it is just as likely to indicate the reverse. After World War I, Famous Players-Lasky sensed a sea change in audience needs and moved away from Victorian morality towards the 'sexual comedy of manners'

[65]   *The Cinema, Its Present Position and Future Possibilities*, pp. xxxvii–xciii.

[66]   Petrie, 'Silent Film Adaptations Part 1', p. 9.

[67]   See, for example, letter dated 17 April 1916, in which Al Kaufman assures Zukor that Vignola's picture titled *$100* will be on schedule because he will 'work day and night on it, if necessary'. Adolph Zukor Papers, Margaret Herrick Library, Academy of Motion Picture Arts and Sciences, Los Angeles. See also Mary Pickford Papers at the Margaret Herrick Library.

centred on 'explorations of such contemporary issues as divorce, female sexuality, and the pleasures of consumerism', to which *Great Expectations*' themes were directly antithetical.[68] By this time, too, Paramount had in place a block-booking system through which film exhibitors could not cherry-pick individual films, but were forced to hire 'the entire Paramount program', the company 'selling poor films on the strength of the good'. Through this system, films which needed to recoup losses were served alongside more attractive releases. In 1917, largely as a result of having signed up to this scheme of Paramount's, Famous Players made over $1 million in profits.[69] *Great Expectations* as a film seems to have been doomed at this point in time to repeat the pattern established by the novel, earning its keep only after the application of some skilful sales tactics.

As Thomas Schatz has shown, by the late teens 'the most successful features were star vehicles', combining the attraction of big name actors and directors with 'an emphasis on spectacle and extravagance'.[70] Famous Players' production seems to have had none of these things. In fact, W.S. Gilbert's early struggles set the scene for a long-lasting disaffection between adaptors and *Great Expectations*: in 1917, directors were still struggling with the problem of exactly how new a Dickens remake needed – or dared – to be if it wanted to please the literary purists, appease the moral conservatives and simultaneously appeal to the modern ticket-buying public. After 1920, new moral classification codes governing cinema distribution in the USA further complicated these negotiations, encouraging Dickens adaptations while simultaneously ensuring their formal conservatism.

Another attempt at filming the novel came in 1922 with A.W. Sandberg's Danish version for Nordisk, *Store Forventninger*. I will discuss this more fully in Chapter 5, where it more properly belongs as part of the relationship between *Great Expectations*' non-Anglophone circulation history and the English literary canon more broadly, but suffice it to say here that despite an energetic international distribution campaign, it was a popular and critical failure and almost bankrupted Nordisk. Perhaps as a result of these two box-office failures, it was 1934, the year the USA was beginning to emerge from the Great Depression, before the story was tackled again on the screen.

Dickens experienced a revival in popularity just before and during the Depression, boosted by the work of American branches of the Dickens Fellowship which, while they began with the founding of the New York and Chicago branches in 1905, went through a significant period of expansion during the 1920s and early 1930s.[71] In 1927, according to Guerric DeBona, Dickens was voted one of 'the ten greatest men in history' by Americans of the Jazz Age, and *David Copperfield*

---

[68]   Ruth Vasey, *The World According to Hollywood 1918–39* (Exeter, 1997), p. 27.

[69]   *The American Film Industry*, ed. by Tino Balio, Revised Edition (Madison, 1985), pp. 117–18.

[70]   Thomas Schatz, *The Genius of the System: Hollywood Filmmaking in the Studio Era* (New York, 1988), p. 23.

[71]   Website of the Dickens Fellowship, http://www.dickensfellowship.org/branches [accessed 7 June 2013].

was named as their favourite novel.[72] During the period of Roosevelt's New Deal (1933–36) he seemed particularly apposite, 'a traditional yet popular British intellectual who suggested Victorian stability, and who spoke to the need for reform without revolution'.[73] Dickens's brand of democracy, exemplified in life by his self-made success as well as acted out in his fiction, had always found more favour than otherwise in the USA despite a few post-bellum dissenters, and never more so than during the 1920s and 1930s by which time, apparently, his drinking, his adultery and his Englishness had all been forgiven. Equally important, though, was his novels' moral conservatism, which played well to a populace made uneasy, perhaps, by the literary Modernists' and Realists' frank treatment of sex and by renewed anxieties about unsuitable subjects appearing on the nation's cinema screens.

It was against this backdrop that, in 1934, Universal decided to film *Great Expectations* as part of its move into 'prestige productions' and as an adjunct to its successful horror factory. The film was a reaction both to an urgent need to refill its coffers as it emerged from the Depression, and to the establishment of the Hays Code in 1930 and its entrenchment by Joseph Breen in 1934 which instituted a particular form of film censorship.[74] Thomas Schatz argues that Universal's conservative filler output of 'genre pictures, programmers, and serials' had enabled them to survive the Depression's toughest years with minimal losses compared to some other studios, and that by 1934 they were back in the black and ambitious to move into the 'first-run' market, which meant making more prestigious pictures for distribution to the more up-market cinemas. Musicals, period pieces and women's films were all likely to appeal in the first-run theatres, and it was these to which Universal's attention now turned – perhaps in response to bitter experience gained with their controversial war picture *All Quiet on the Western Front* (1930), which had suffered a box-office mauling they were not keen to repeat.[75] On paper it was a sensible move: during this period, Dickens acquired for movie makers what DeBona calls 'moral prestige', being one of the few authors able to bridge the 'divide between elite and popular'.[76] Thus, as one contemporary reviewer put it, potentially *Great Expectations* offered 'excellent entertainment for the masses as well as the critical factions'.[77]

Despite the assumption of Dickens's innate moral goodness, Universal still had to work hard to stay within the bounds of the new moral codes: some filmed scenes not in the novel were ordered to be cut by the Breen office. One in which Joe and Mrs Joe are seen in bed together and another featuring a kiss between Pip

---

[72]   Guerric DeBona, *Film Adaptation in the Hollywood Studio Era* (Urbana, 2010), p. 38.

[73]   DeBona, *Film Adaptation*, p. 40.

[74]   Douglas Gomery shows that Universal's profits were at an all-time low during 1930–33, and just barely made it into the black during 1934. See Douglas Gomery, *The Hollywood Studio System* (New York, 1986), p. 148.

[75]   Schatz, *Genius of the System*, pp. 228–9.

[76]   DeBona, *Film Adaptation*, pp. 47 and 50.

[77]   *Daily Variety*, 10 September 1934, no page number.

and Estella, along with the use of the word 'Lord', were ordered to be excised from the prints for distribution in both home and foreign markets.[78] Victorian prudishness was apparently welcome in the movie industry, if not in contemporary literature. So successful was the prudishness here, in fact, that halfway through the review process Hays wrote to congratulate Universal on 'a very good picture, and [one which] we trust will encourage more producers to turn to the classics for story material'.[79] No wonder the trade journal *Harrison's Reports* advised exhibitors that the film, being 'founded on a classic … should prove suitable for children, adolescents, and Sunday showing'.[80] One Hollywood exhibitor writing in to the *Motion Picture Herald* agreed: 'It is to be expected that the lovers of Dickens literature will want to see this picture, likewise the more intelligent patrons. The problem will be creating mass interest.' He advised fellow exhibitors: 'Exploit it with unusual means, contact libraries, schools, clubs, and seek editorial commendation.'[81] The *Motion Picture Daily* also felt that the audience would be split: 'Wherever Dickens is popular this should register, but in other spots it will need exploitation to sell.'[82]

Hays and Breen apparently thought that filming more classics – particularly British classics – would ultimately make for a morally cleaner society. But the attitude in the film industry itself was more basic: Dickens was freely available, unexceptionable, well-known, easily rendered on the screen as costume drama with entertaining caricatures and just enough social conscience without being preachy, and many of the works were therefore likely to be fairly safe bets. They were also believed to offer the potential for good sales overseas, and thus became part of Hollywood's global strategy in an era when, as Ruth Vasey expresses it: 'As the first global medium of entertainment, the movies faced the problem of how to satisfy audiences of vastly different cultural, religious and political persuasions with essentially the same diet of images and narratives.… Hollywood had to formulate a recipe for movies that could play in the North and the South, on the West Coast and in the East, from Capetown to Capri.'[83] Having already blazed much of this trail with his novels, Dickens had a head start.

---

[78]   Memo to Universal from office of Joseph L. Breen regarding Japanese distribution of *Great Expectations*, 5 December 1935, Universal Collection, Box 778, folder Z6851, Film and Television Archive, University of California, Los Angeles. Memos regarding shooting script and various subsequent prints of *Great Expectations* from Joseph L. Breen to Harry Zehner at Universal, 27 July 1934; 12 March 1935; 5 December 1935, in Folder 'Great Expectations (Universal, 1934)', Margaret Herrick Library, Academy of Motion Picture Arts and Sciences, Los Angeles.

[79]   Report from the Hon. William H. Hays, 15 October 1934. Folder 'Great Expectations (Universal 1934)', Margaret Herrick Library, Academy of Motion Picture Arts and Sciences, Los Angeles.

[80]   *Harrison's Reports*, Vol. 16, No. 34, 27 October 1934, p. 170.

[81]   'Showmen's Reviews', *Motion Picture Herald*, 20 October 1934, no page number.

[82]   *Motion Picture Daily*, 11 October 1934, no page number.

[83]   Vasey, *According to Hollywood*, p. 4.

Universal's publicists made British Dickensians a special target, arranging a premiere screening of *Great Expectations* in the study of the Dickens Museum in Doughty Street, London (where Dickens once lived), and arranging for a coach containing two Dickensian characters to parade up and down the streets picking up patrons during the film's West End run. London seems to have got into the mood willingly enough: 'When the first showing of the film was arranged at the Capitol in the Haymarket, London', the *Dickensian* reported, 'a window at Selfridge's was engaged and a fine collection of Dickens relics put on show.'[84] Critics were less enthusiastic, however. *The Times* baulked at the Hollywood treatment which rendered the story 'rich in dramatic and sentimental content' but a failure in 'the faithful reproduction of Dickensian characters', concluding: 'The cast grope about as best they may in the no-man's land between the novel of Dickens and the studios of Hollywood.' Its reference to a 'no-man's land' between book and film sums up the perennial problem of adaptation: the finding of a middle ground which does justice to both media.[85] But the war metaphor is also oddly appropriate. Dickens and Hollywood were two mutually exclusive terms as far as British critics were concerned; the more globally dominant Hollywood became, the less British and the more vulgar its films seemed among the more conservative bastions of the British press. In the nineteenth century, American enthusiasm for Dickens had been seen as testament to a genius that went beyond nationalism (even, of course, as it provided covert endorsement of notions of intrinsic British cultural superiority). But the rise of the Hollywood film industry marked the beginnings of an international culture war waged over the right – and the right way – to remediate him.

Bolter and Grusin see competition as an essential part of the way in which remediation works: 'A medium in our culture can never operate in isolation, because it must enter into relationships of respect and rivalry with other media.'[86] They do not explore the national dimension of this competition or apply their model to the adaptation of classic literature, but it is patently in operation in this interwar period in the international struggle for ownership of Dickens on film. Indeed, classic literature here becomes a key objective in the war over relative national shares in the new medium's cultural capital. British critics accepted as their due American movie makers' respect for Dickens, which continued to flatter a culturally constituted self-perception of British superiority. The British cinema-going public also embraced American cinematic innovations, the sheer volume of its production and the sophisticated distribution systems which brought its products within their reach. But a quite vocal British middlebrow faction – for which *The Times* critic clearly spoke – resisted American hegemony; a globally dominant film industry which exported American goods, stars, lifestyles and ideologies (and almost forced British products out of the market) needed to work hard to produce an adaptation of Dickens that paid sufficient homage to his roots to please this faction.

---

[84]   'When found', *Dickensian*, 31 (Spring 1935): p. 81.

[85]   Review of *Great Expectations*, *The Times*, 20 November 1934, p. 12.

[86]   Bolter and Grusin, *Remediation*, p. 98.

Walker's 1934 adaptation was caught on the horns of this dilemma. The opening scenes are certainly atmospheric and effective in their cinematography, and they are set, plausibly enough, in the environs of a village called Cooling. The presence of English actor Francis L. Sullivan as Jaggers (a role he was later to reprise for David Lean) provided some authenticity. But while the accent of Henry Hull (Magwitch) is passable, Phillips Holmes (Pip) occasionally lapses into faux Cockney and Rafaela Ottiano (Mrs Joe) struggles to disguise her Italian roots. There are also some Hollywood touches in Gladys Unger's script that might have played oddly for British audiences, and that alter the tenor of the story in significant ways. In the opening scenes between Pip and Magwitch (here called Magitch for some inexplicable reason), in line with Breen office rules about avoiding the corruption of children it is made very plain that the 'wittles' and file are borrowed, not stolen, thus setting Pip up as an inherently good character who is tragically misled by a good heart rather than easily tempted by appeals to his selfishness. The Joe/Pip plotline disappears entirely after Pip leaves the forge, wiping out all traces of Pip's cruelty to his oldest friend. There are numerous Americanisms, such as the references to Miss Havisham's 'kin' and uses of the word 'ain't'. Emphasising their divisive effects, the *Dickensian*'s reviewer noted these but decided (true to the journal's often rather proselytising spirit in this period) that since the film was aimed largely at American audiences, it was 'no drawback; rather the reverse, to the majority of audiences for whom the film is intended'.[87]

There are other changes which may have seemed anomalous to British audiences – or Dickensian purists. Florence Reed's Miss Havisham only wears her bridal gown once a year, on the anniversary of her doomed wedding day; on all other occasions she is dressed as a prudish matron and appears very much in control of her affairs (in one scene even appearing with Jaggers arranging the terms of her will). The wedding dress itself looks more like a brand new ball gown – kudos to the costume department, but nonsense in terms of her role in the plot. The film thus removes a large part of Miss Havisham's gothic weirdness and leaves Reed – an established theatre actress – little to do; she even dies conveniently off-screen of unspecified causes.

The external London scenes largely take place in the yard of a coaching inn, very obviously a cheap set, and each is announced (presumably in case American audiences had missed the reference) by the cheerful hooting of a post-horn and some rousing extra-diegetic music. This invocation of a mythical 'Jolly Olde England' was bound to set the British viewer's teeth on edge. (It is interesting that Smith finds the same device as used by Lean a decade later equally irritating, though as a contextual signal to American audiences it was clearly already an established shorthand by 1946.)[88] While Estella (Jane Wyatt) does her best with a part that requires her coldness to be an act and her love for Pip a long-hidden but unquenchable flame, the inevitable revelatory ending following an offstage

---

[87]   A.E.B.C., 'The Screen version of *Great Expectations*', *Dickensian*, 31 (Winter 1934–35): p. 102.

[88]   Smith, *Dickens and the Dream of Cinema*, p. 124.

apology by Miss Havisham is as forced, rushed and unconvincing as the same scene in Gilbert's play (from which, indeed, it appears to have drawn some of its ideas).The film was another hybrid: too British (stuffy and old-fashioned) for the Americans; too Hollywood (historically inaccurate and emotionally overblown) for the British. The important issue here is not lack of fidelity to the novel, but insufficient freedom to innovate in the new medium, coupled with overt national stereotyping that was bound to fall foul of British self-perceptions.

American reviewers, as ever, reacted differently. Both the *Los Angeles Times* and *Variety* provided an uncanny echo of Dickens's own first reviewers in their enthusiasm for the first half of the narrative and their disappointment in the second.[89] Predictably, too, some papers drew attention to the film's technical achievements; in this period Dickens still offered plenty of scope for the celebration of American technical and artistic skill. The *New York Herald Tribune* produced regular reports on the progress of filming, which took place between 1 August and 4 September 1934. It focussed one report on the special spiders and rubber cement cobwebs used in the shots of Miss Havisham's house, and – apparently in an attempt to import gravitas from the serious theatre – admired character actor Henry Hull's creation of Magwitch using makeup fit to rival his Broadway success in *Tobacco Road* the previous year.[90] In another issue, the paper described the construction of a large tank complete with a propeller for creating waves, the use of two paddle boxes with wheels and smokestacks for the 'Bordeaux' steamer [*sic*], and the use of gauze over the lights to create a spooky effect. There were some commitments to cultural authenticity: the paper also reported on the shipping in of an English stage coach and the appointment as costume advisor of a former Royal dresser to Queen Mary, who (apart from the ball gown wedding dress) duly dressed Miss Havisham in conservative dowager's clothing that renders her respectably staid rather than interestingly psychotic.[91] The *New York Times* also praised the attempts made at 'authenticity', including the casting of Francis L. Sullivan as Jaggers. While both the *Daily Variety* and the *Hollywood Reporter* praised the acting (though feeling the honours belonged to the home-grown Henry Hull, at that time a staple of Universal's popular and distinctive horror features as well as a successful character actor on the stage), both also felt the film would have benefitted from some judicious cutting. They were right: this is an unarguable flaw which was probably a result of a tight shooting schedule and an even tighter budget.[92] Biddy's scenes were cut entirely from the final print, though she appears (played by Valerie Hobson, who was to be Lean's adult Estella) in the credits, but further cuts might have helped smooth out some of the narrative's structural unevenness.

[89]   *Variety*, 29 January 1935, no page number; *Los Angeles Times*, 26 October 1934, no page number.

[90]   *New York Herald Tribune*, 26 August 1934, no page number.

[91]   *New York Herald Tribune*, 21 October 1934, no page number.

[92]   *Daily Variety*, 10 October 1934, no page number; *Hollywood Reporter*, 10 October 1934, no page number. The film was shot in just over a month, between 1 August and 4 September 1934.

Despite the much-vaunted technical wizardry, in fact, at a total cost of $178,320.47 this was a cheap production compared both with other Dickens vehicles and with the budgets for Universal's other films in this period.[93] Universal was committed to keeping its costs down to effect a post-Depression recovery, but its top feature, *Imitation of Life* (1934), cost $665,000 and even the 'low budget' *The Bride of Frankenstein* (1935) cost $397,000.[94] For comparative purposes it is worth noting that MGM's *David Copperfield* (also 1934) had a much larger budget of $1,069,254.[95]

The breakdown of actors' salaries for the Universal picture is equally revealing: whereas Claudette Colbert, star of *Imitation of Life*, was rented from Paramount for a flat fee of $90,000,[96] *Great Expectations'* highest-paid headlining star Henry Hull, on a variable rate of between $1,375 and $2,750 a day, earned a total of $13,750 on this picture.[97] The budget discrepancies indicate that *Imitation of Life* (a 'women's weepie') and *Bride of Frankenstein* (a horror picture spinning off a previous success) were deemed sure-fire sellers, and that *Great Expectations*, being generically unstable and historically unreliable in its audience appeal, was not. This tells us two interesting things about the novel's commodity status in this period.

First, we can probably read the small budget as evidence of the relatively low importance of Dickens both to Universal's post-Depression move into prestige films, and to its roughly simultaneous attempt to hold onto its share of the European market after the coming of sound. Vasey has shown that by 1920 Universal already had 175 representatives in foreign countries, and that by 1927 Great Britain was the largest foreign market for Hollywood products (representing 30.5 per cent of Hollywood's foreign income). But the coming of sound suddenly made Britain a more lucrative market still, for obvious technological and linguistic reasons as well as for less obvious reasons to do with exclusive trade agreements across Europe more broadly.[98] This film was as much an attempt to sell Dickens back to the British as to tap into the revival of Dickens's popularity in the USA. But, clearly, Universal was not counting exclusively on this as a strategy: like their risk-spreading tactics during the depression, it was merely part of a larger plan.

I have found no surviving records anywhere of the film's profits, though it seems unlikely that it did as well as MGM's *David Copperfield*, which grossed nearly $3 million and was a particular hit in Britain, an important constituent part of the 25 per cent of gross profit coming from Commonwealth countries. MGM's *Tale of Two Cities*, released a year later, was to do almost as well, grossing $2.4

[93]   Universal Collection, *Great Expectations* 1934, 'Picture Costs', Box 277/8330, Film and Television Archive, University of California, Los Angeles.

[94]   Schatz, *Genius of the System*, p. 231.

[95]   Schatz, *Genius of the System*, p. 168.

[96]   Schatz, *Genius of the System*, p. 231.

[97]   Universal Collection, *Great Expectations* 1934, 'Picture Talent', Box 277/8330, Film and Television Archive, University of California, Los Angeles.

[98]   Vasey, *According to Hollywood*, pp. 85 and 91.

million with 31 per cent Commonwealth sales.[99] By contrast, there is evidence that Walker's film was not even particularly widely distributed: John Sedgwick has shown that the film never made it to one of the most avid cinema-going centres in Britain – Bolton, located in England's industrial North – though *David Copperfield* was among the top ten favourites in the years 1934–35 in that city.[100] Annette Kuhn's findings also reflect the film's low profile: returned questionnaires from 186 British people about their memories of film-going in the 1930s reveal that while 'the largest number of films which made an impression belonged to the category of adaptations of books or plays', and that '127 such titles were offered, ranging from *A Tale of Two Cities* (1935) to *The Wizard of Oz* (1939)', *Great Expectations* warrants no mention.[101]

The second interesting thing about this film's budget is the actors' relative salaries (and the prominent place given to Hull's name in the credits): they tell us that it was the role of Magwitch that was deemed the most crucial to the film's success, and this means *Great Expectations* was still associated primarily with male character acting in this period, ignoring the undeniable mass appeal of female stars on the screen. After Hull, the next highest paid actor was Phillips Holmes (adult Pip) who earned $5,250. The female leads were paid even less: Jane Wyatt (Estella) earned $3,800 and Florence Reed (Miss Havisham) a flat fee of $2,000.[102] The time for *Great Expectations'* women was yet to come; the iniquities of male and female actors' relative salaries aside, the story was apparently not considered a suitable female star vehicle in this period.

Re-emergence on the Professional Stage 1934–39

A revival in the novel's fortunes was just around the corner. Perhaps inspired by the story's reappearance on film, in 1935 Dickens's granddaughter Ethel mounted a stage production called 'The Convict' in London, which then toured the provinces under the new name 'The Scapegoat'. Focussing on the relationships between Pip, Estella, Magwitch and Miss Havisham, the play was well-received by *The Times* which thought it 'scrappy' but 'enjoyable and fresh'.[103] This production's most important role, though, was probably as a reminder to the theatre-going public

---

[99]   Schatz, *Genius of the System*, p. 169.

[100]   John Sedgwick, 'Film "Hits" and "Misses" in Mid-1930s Britain', *Historical Journal of Film, Radio and Television*, 18 (1998): p. 343. See also Sedgwick's 'The Market for Feature Films in Britain, 1934: A Viable National Cinema', *Historical Journal of Film, Radio and Television*, 14 (1994): p. 21, which demonstrates that 'Universal had by far the poorest exhibition record of the major studios'.

[101]   Annette Kuhn, 'Cinema-Going in Britain in the 1930s: Report of a Questionnaire Survey', *Historical Journal of Film, Radio and Television*, 19 (1999): p. 538.

[102]   Universal Collection, *Great Expectations* 1934, 'Picture Talent', Box 277/8330, Film and Television Archive, University of California, Los Angeles.

[103]   'Westminster Theatre', *The Times*, Tuesday 5 February 1935, p. 12.

that *Great Expectations* existed; the first critically important twentieth-century professional stage version produced under the novel's real title happened just four years later in 1939, in the shape of an adaptation by the then little-known 25-year-old actor Alec Guinness.

Guinness's choice of *Great Expectations* and the creative approach he took to it were highly significant, personally, formally and culturally. As his biographer Piers Paul Read puts it, the 'story of an orphaned boy from a socially ambiguous background unquestionably resonated in Alec's mind. Like Alec, the hero, Pip, has a miserable home life but rises to gentility … Pip, like Alec, attaches enormous importance to wearing the right kind of clothes, and his embarrassment at the humble origins of his sister's husband, Joe Gargery, was matched by Alec's disdain for his Cuff cousins [kin to his mother, whom he described as a "whore"]'.[104] Ronald Neame, Lean's producer, wrote on Guinness's death in 2000 that he thought Guinness 'was more himself in *Great Expectations* than he was in any other film that we worked on', and it seems highly likely that the same was true of his adaptation for the stage.[105] In addition to a story of class snobbery, *Great Expectations* seems to have offered the bisexual Guinness the opportunity to explore issues of guilt and regret. It seems significant that when he was arrested for homosexual offences in 1946 while making Lean's film, he kept his real name out of the press by giving the police the false name of Herbert Pocket.[106]

Guinness himself dismissed the adaptation as the modest fruits of a fallow period when the outbreak of war had temporarily closed London's theatres and put him out of a job,[107] but in the event the play carried much more weight than this. It was chosen by a group of his theatre friends to launch their new venture, the Actors' Theatre Company, financed by small cash donations from the actors, and designed to get them all back into work with 'a mind for something better than the theatre's usual wartime fare'.[108]The chosen venue was the Rudolph Steiner Hall close to Baker Street tube station, which, according to one reviewer, was 'easy to reach in the blackout and offers good seats at low prices'.[109] The play did 'good business', running for six weeks, and garnered some good reviews.[110] The *Observer* acknowledged the perennial problem of a necessary subordination of 'richness of character' to plot but liked both Guinness's own performance as Herbert and also

---

[104] Piers Paul Read, *Alec Guinness: The Authorised Biography* (London & New York, 2003), pp. 11 and 95.

[105] Ronald Neame on Alec Guinness, 'News Review,' *The Times*, 13 August 2000, no page number.

[106] John Ezard, 'Alex Guinness's gay side revealed', http://www.theguardian.com/uk/2001/apr/16/filmnews.film [accessed 6 June 2013].

[107] Alec Guinness, *Blessings in Disguise* (London, 1997), p. 58.

[108] 'Review of Guinness's *Great Expectations*', *Observer*, 10 December 1939, no page number. Clippings file, Billy Rose Theatre Division, New York Public Library.

[109] *New Statesman and Nation*, 16 December 1939, no page number. Clippings file, Billy Rose Theatre Division, New York Public Library.

[110] Guinness, *Blessings*, p. 58.

the performances of most of the rest of the cast.[111] The *New Statesman and Nation* also praised the performances, but felt the plot would be unintelligible to those who had not read the novel.[112] Guinness had taken the landmark decisions not to cram key plot points awkwardly into the dialogue, and to cut whole themes rather than just individual characters; bold moves for a theatrical adaptor which solved the problem of textual fidelity that Gilbert had failed to negotiate successfully. The decision freed Guinness up to play around with the narrative, and it indicates the kind of audience he expected (or hoped) to attract: no longer the stalwarts of the gallery and the pit, but theatre-goers who knew their literary references and were capable of appreciating a freer-standing Dickens interpretation.

The original 1939 script does not seem to have survived, but scripts for the 1943, 1947 and 1957 revivals are extant, and according to the director of two of these (1943 and 1957), John Moody, this was the standard version for some years and we can probably therefore assume considerable structural continuity between versions.[113] Unlike later adaptations on both stage and screen, the play retains a great deal of the novel's early comedy, including much of the interplay between young Pip and Joe. This is part of a larger set of structural choices: Guinness takes the decision to foreground the male relationships (Pip/Joe; Pip/Herbert; Pip/Magwitch), using the Pip/Estella plotline purely to represent Pip's unrealistic ambitions and choosing not to bring the couple together at the end. Estella in fact remains out of reach; her last onstage lines are to Miss Havisham, as she announces that she is tired of obedience and exits to get married. She reappears later only as part of a dream sequence when Pip falls ill; in his delirium he hears her repeating her taunts to the 'coarse, common labouring boy', along with Jaggers repeating 'Great Expectations' and Magwitch intoning: 'I lived rough that he might live smooth.' There are two narrators: adult Pip in Act 1, and Biddy in Acts 2 and 3, a device which serves to make a sort of Greek chorus out of the wiser retrospective Pip and the always stalwart, good-hearted Biddy. The play thus revolves around the humbling of Pip in learning the lesson of the immutability and value of old (specifically male) friendships. The final scene takes place at the forge, with Pip being offered his old room by Biddy and Joe, knowing he has a job with Herbert when he has recovered his strength.[114] Compared to earlier versions it is a gripping piece of theatre even on the page, with distinct clarity of purpose and an innate sense not only of Dickens's own favoured plotlines, but of how to make them work dramatically. In its foregrounding of Dickensian masculinist assumptions, it also offers important scope for future feminist challenges onstage.

---

[111] The *Observer*, 10 December 1939, no page number. Clippings file, Billy Rose Theatre Division, New York Public Library.

[112] *New Statesman and Nation*, 16 December 1939, no page number. Clippings file, Billy Rose Theatre Division, New York Public Library.

[113] John Moody, foreword to Bristol Old Vic production programme, 19 February 1957, Bristol University Theatre Collection, item JM/000250.

[114] Script, cast list and prompt book for *Great Expectations*, Playhouse Theatre, Liverpool, 1943, Bristol University Theatre Collection, items JM/000046 and JM/000047.

Despite good houses and a shoestring budget, it did not recoup its investment in 1939 (due, Guinness claims, largely to the high cost of the scenery and the fact that the Shaftesbury Theatre to which it was scheduled to transfer had been bombed out[115]) and the Actors' Theatre Company folded.[116] Still, Guinness's creative decisions, motivated perhaps by his personal affinity with the story, meant it had a longer life than this in revival. In particular, Guinness's idea of introducing wise, all-knowing narrators to tie the scenes together and thus to foreground both Pip's selfishness and the novel's bitter self-reflective qualities was to mark a radical break with previous stage adaptations. It may be that his recent experience acting for radio had given him the idea of using a narrator; not precisely as Dickens did, perhaps, but as a necessary aid to dramatic continuity where excisions have had to be made. Mere months before he began writing his adaptation of *Great Expectations*, he had performed in a radio dramatization of Chekhov's *The Seagull* with Martita Hunt, who was later to play Miss Havisham.[117] Explanatory narration was a common device on radio, with a useful introspective side effect that worked equally well on the stage; Kay Walsh, Lean's wife, remembers that Guinness and his wife Marula took turns with the narration from either side of the stage, observing and commenting on as well as participating in the action.[118]

Wherever the idea came from, it was one on which David Lean was to build and proof that Lean's film owes a lot more to Guinness's production than just the reuse of Guinness and Martita Hunt as actors. Lean had been persuaded to go along to the play by Kay, who described it as 'absolutely wonderful' and her whole party, reluctant husband Lean included, as 'spellbound' within five minutes. Lean later said that without having seen this play he would never have done the film, and that it 'exerted a tremendous influence' on him.[119] I will return to this iconic film event in Chapter 4, since it helped to spark a global post-war *Great Expectations* renaissance that will carry us through to the end of this book. First, though, it is necessary to situate Lean's film as part of a broader Dickens renaissance in the contiguous medium of radio, since it is a fundamental principle of remediation that 'no medium … can … function independently and establish its own separate and purified space of cultural meaning'.[120] Just as theatre and early film shared actors, directors, technicians, stagecraft and dramatic modes as well as narratives, so theatre, radio and sound film entered into a synergistic relationship in which innovation was fuelled by a complex combination of rivalry (the need to make new adaptations ever fresher) and imitation (the need to be acutely aware of established tastes), which operated at the levels of both industry and individual artist.

---

[115] Guinness, *Blessings*, p. 58.

[116] Read, *Authorised Biography*, p. 96.

[117] This dramatization of *The Seagull* was broadcast in a 95-minute slot on Sunday 11 June 1939. *Radio Times*, Vol. 63, 9 June 1939, p. 22. © Immediate Media Company London Limited.

[118] Kevin Brownlow, *David Lean* (London, 1996), p. 206.

[119] Brownlow, *David Lean*, p. 206.

[120] Bolter and Grusin, *Remediation*, p. 55.

Over the Airwaves 1930–45

Surprisingly little has been written about Dickens adaptations in the early days of radio, let alone about *Great Expectations*' particular manifestations in this form. Paul Davis briefly examines *A Christmas Carol*'s adaptations for radio, but he is more interested in their departures from the original text than in Dickens's peculiar suitability for early radio performance and – apparently more comfortable discussing visual media – he swiftly turns his attention to the film versions.[121] Thereafter, Robert Giddings was for some years almost a lone voice in his claim for early radio's importance to the British literary heritage industry, but in situating Dickens as part of a much larger phenomenon he has usually had to content himself with listing rather than analysing the adapted works.[122] Even the most recent anthology of adaptation scholarship neglects the radio but for a brief mention in John Glavin's introduction,[123] and Holly Furneaux and Sally Ledger's useful *Dickens in Context* ignores radio altogether in its otherwise fulsome section on 'Life and Afterlife'. But the remediation of *Great Expectations* in this popular mass medium is of central importance to our current sense of its cultural ubiquity, of having 'grown up' with it. Dickens seems to have found a new natural remediation home in radio, and *Great Expectations* benefitted from the change. This too happened surprisingly slowly, but it carried with it the beginning of a significant shift in the novel's cultural and critical status.

The honour of the first Dickens-related radio broadcasts goes to the BBC, for probably the most prosaic of reasons: in the early years of British radio under the benign dictatorship of its first Director-General John Reith, the BBC set up the tradition of state-funded public service broadcasting which meant that while it had no competition, it did have a clear mission – to 'educate, inform and entertain'– to which Dickens and other classic authors were perceived to be central. American radio stations were understandably slower; they began adapting Dickens in half-hour or hour-long slots just before and during the war, usually as part of a 'masterpiece theatre' type of programme, apparently designed as an appeal to (or an attempt to construct) the tastes of more discerning listeners. But this was some time in coming. American radio in its infancy in the 1920s was somewhat chaotic, and Dickens apparently very far from its thoughts.[124] In the early days, hundreds of stations competed for a few available frequencies, and transmission quality across the continent's large distances varied greatly. The arrival of the big New York networks NBC (founded 1926) and CBS (1927) that were to dominate the airwaves

[121] Davis, *The Life and Times of Ebenezer Scrooge*, pp. 155–6. Despite its title, his fourth chapter 'The Children's Hour' has more to do with the niche marketing of the novel for children than with its adaptation for radio.

[122] Robert Giddings and Keith Selby, *The Classic Serial on Television and Radio* (Basingstoke, 2001).

[123] John Glavin, 'Introduction', *Library of Essays on Charles Dickens: Dickens Adapted*, p. xx.

[124] Susan J. Douglas, *Listening In: Radio and the American Imagination* (Minneapolis, 2004), pp. 55–82.

for some years did not help; they initially privileged sport and music, edging out the local stations which favoured other sorts of programming, including storytelling.

The question of how radio was to be financed also led to the dominance of advertising and of commercial sponsorship, both of which seem to have required a form of product placement (whether seriously or with comedic effect) in the broadcasts, and this made Dickens somewhat anachronistic until the late 1930s when – perhaps as a result of his use by the movie industry as an appeal to the intellect – he began to be associated with high-class commodities. In addition, the rise of a new and complex discourse of American masculinity during the crisis years of the Depression encouraged a style of radio programming that was intrinsically unhealthy for Dickens adaptations and might constitute another reason for their scarcity in this period. Susan J. Douglas argues that through linguistic slapstick comedy, the daring appropriation of jazz in opposition to the perceived conservatism of classical music, and the meteoric rise of sports broadcasting, the airwaves became 'a region of risk and rivalry, of conquest and victory, yet of comradeship and mutual support', in which classic period drama – particularly English classic drama – was inevitably perceived as belonging to a genteel, feminised and now passé world.[125]

Dickens did finally appear on the airwaves in the USA, particularly after key regulation by the Federal Communications Commission in 1941 prevented the big stations from monopolising the airwaves and 'increased broadcasters' freedom to choose programs for their audiences during the last years of radio's supremacy'.[126] The increased competition meant diversification and directly contributed to the rise of the dramatic play or serial adaptation. Inevitably, where Dickens was concerned, it was the early popular novels that attracted adaptation first. As far as it is currently possible to ascertain from the notoriously elusive history of this etheric medium, *Great Expectations* was not dramatized by an American radio network until 1945.

Conversely, Dickens was important from the very earliest days of the BBC, and as the station felt its way through its first experimental decade towards effective and more structured broad-appeal programming (roughly 1922–32),[127] Dickens became increasingly central to its self-defined mission as quintessentially English, informative, educative and entertaining. The first Dickens programmes, occurring in 1924–25, were not adaptations but talks, appearing as subsections of longer programmes largely aimed at children with titles such as 'Pages from Dickens' and 'Lives of Famous Men'.[128] An adaptation of *A Christmas Carol*

---

[125] Douglas, *Listening In*, p. 15.

[126] Mickie Edwardson, 'James Lawrence Fly's Report on Chain Broadcasting (1941) and the Regulation of Monopoly in America', *Historical Journal of Film, Radio and Television*, 22 (2002): p. 418.

[127] Giddings and Selby, *Classic Serial*, p. 8.

[128] Monday 30 August 1924, 8.30pm; *Children's Hour*, Wednesday 21 January 1925. Programme Records, Vol. 1, pp. 81 and 107, BBC Written Archives Centre. All material from the BBC Written Archives Centre is reproduced courtesy of the British Broadcasting Corporation. All rights reserved.

first appeared on Children's Hour in December 1925 and thereafter became an almost annual feature.[129] There were also, as a result, both regular performances of Scrooge and other characters by the Dickens actor Bransby Williams and increasing appearances of similar adaptations of the shorter works. 'Bardell v. Pickwick' was broadcast in 1927,[130] and both 'Hunted Down' and 'Dick Swiveller and the Marchioness', extracted from *The Old Curiosity Shop*, in 1928.[131]

Dramatizing a full-length play for radio was difficult in these early years when technology was still fairly rudimentary and the problem of broadcasting several speakers in turn and creating believable sound effects had not been solved satisfactorily. Some attempts at plays were made early on, particularly by the regions.[132] One of the most important of these early dramatization attempts came on 11 November 1929, when R.C. Sherriff's famous play *Journey's End* was broadcast to coincide with the 11th anniversary of the Armistice, gaining plaudits from several listeners and critics. The BBC was clearly by this point inching its way towards a schedule that reflected as well as helped to shape listeners' concerns, tastes and experiences, and it paid some attention to its audience. But there were inevitably complaints about quality. One listener (a World War I veteran) felt that while *Journey's End* was 'a masterpiece of subtle suggestion', the main character Stanhope was given some 'feeble and unreal' lines in an attempt to render his actions comprehensible in an aural medium, and he complained that 'the machine-guns sound[ed] more like motor-car engines'.[133]

In answer to a similar attack on radio plays in general by a *Daily Express* critic, a BBC programmer wrote defensively in to the *Radio Times*. The *Express* critic may have 'informed the world that radio plays are getting worse', he said, but this was surely a touch premature since 'radio drama is not yet set in any final recognisable mould. Even more than films both silent and talking, it is in a state of development and continual experiment.... Techniques, both in writing and production, must automatically improve as more and more experience is gained'.[134] In January 1930, *The Listener*'s critic, historian R.D. Charques, made an appearance in the lower-brow *Radio Times* to answer the question: 'Is There a Future for Radio Drama?' He did so with a resounding: 'Yes, if it discovers its

---

[129] *Children's Hour*, Wednesday 25 December 1925, 5.30pm. Programme Records, Vol. 1, p. 176, BBC Written Archives Centre.

[130] Monday 26 September 1927, Daventry Experimental, 8pm. Programme Records, Vol. 2, p. 75, BBC Written Archives Centre.

[131] Wednesday 5 July 1928, Daventry Experimental, 8pm; *Children's Hour*, Saturday 1 December 1928, London and Daventry 5XX, 5.15pm. Programme Records, Vol. 2, pp. 197 and 248, BBC Written Archives Centre.

[132] *Radio Times*, Vol. 25, 12 October 1929, p. 58; 29 October 1929, p. 261; 4 November 1929, p. 331. © Immediate Media Company London Limited.

[133] 'Letter page', *Radio Times*, Vol. 25, 29 November 1929, p. 659. © Immediate Media Company London Limited.

[134] 'The Broadcast Plays – are they Getting Worse?' *Radio Times*, Vol. 25, 1 November 1929, p. 314. © Immediate Media Company London Limited.

true technique', continuing: 'Artistically speaking, the trouble is, of course, that there is as yet no recognized theory or aesthetic of radio drama … we have only the vaguest ideas of what we would like it to be.'[135]

Dickens seems to have presented a particular problem in this developmental period, partly due to his entrenchment in particular forms in the minds of the influential Dickens performers whose talents were co-opted for broadcasting. There was certainly a perceived connection between radio listeners and classics readers more generally; Shakespeare was a favourite from radio's earliest days, Gaskell's *Cranford* was the featured 'Play for Schools' on 8 November 1929, and in December 1929 the BBC's Production Director included Shakespeare, Chekhov, Stevenson, Molière and Conrad (though not Dickens) in his announcement of the coming year's drama schedule.[136] Dickens does make an occasional appearance: a prospectus for the 'Charles Dickens Library in 18 volumes' plus bookcase was advertised in the *Radio Times* and offered free to readers and listeners upon presentation of a *Radio Times* coupon, proof enough that Dickens was still firmly associated in most people's minds with books, not radio drama.[137] On 8 November 1929, Cambridge academic Frank Kendon penned an avuncular article called 'Do you like being read aloud to?' and suggested readings from classics including Dickens as a way of 'reviving by wireless a simple pleasure of our fathers'.[138] In November 1929, a reader wrote in agreement with Kendon with the words: 'You cannot give us too much Dickens in any form.'[139] But the suggestion here was for a series of readings; apart from the topical shorts, the idea of dramatizing an entire Dickens novel does not yet seem to have occurred either to programmers or to listeners.

Still being critically dismissed as a popular entertainer, in the 1920s Dickens for radio programmers was thus largely a provider of raw material, useful for carving into chunks and serving up as history lessons and gobbets of light entertainment in the available spaces between longer segments of music, news and factual reporting. The view of Dickens as unsuitable for full dramatization on radio was still being articulated as late as 1931, when many other Victorian novels had been successfully dramatized. The playwright, actor and renowned Dickens reader Victor Clinton Clinton-Baddeley declared in a full-page *Radio Times* article called 'Let Radio Revive Dickens' Penny Readings' that it was Dickens's episodic nature that made him so suitable for reading aloud in segments, and that his plots were 'unimportant'. For Clinton-Baddeley, the real drama lay in the short episodes with

---

[135] 'Is there a Future for Radio Drama?' *Radio Times*, Vol. 26, 17 January 1930, p. 135. © Immediate Media Company London Limited.

[136] 'Plays in 1930 for every listener', *Radio Times*, Vol. 25, 6 December 1929, p. 699. © Immediate Media Company London Limited.

[137] *Radio Times*, Vol. 25, 25 October 1929, p. 288. © Immediate Media Company London Limited.

[138] Frank Kendon, 'Do You Like Being Read Aloud To?' *Radio Times*, Vol. 25, 8 November 1929, p. 387. © Immediate Media Company London Limited.

[139] Letter from 'A lover of Dickens, Limehouse', Letters Page, *Radio Times*, Vol. 25, 22 November 1929, p. 542. © Immediate Media Company London Limited.

their opportunities for character acting and comedy, not in the story in its entirety: '"Great Expectations"', he claimed, 'is important not for the sake of Orlick, but for the sake of Wopsle (who has precisely nothing to do with the story at all)'.[140] The fact that Wopsle is now deemed so dispensable that he seldom even makes it into contemporary adaptations for stage, radio or screen tells us a lot about the radio programmer's view of Dickens in this period; when he was not being used as a history lesson, he was an opportunity for virtuoso comedic performance rather than serious dramatic acting.

All this was to change later in the decade; as we have seen, by 1939 *Pickwick Papers* had received the full dramatization treatment, and Clinton-Baddeley himself adapted *Nicholas Nickleby* for a full ensemble cast in the same year. Despite an announcement in the *Radio Times* on 9 February 1940 that 'The Drama Department in its wisdom has decided to give Dickens a rest',[141] *David Copperfield, Edwin Drood* and *Oliver Twist* followed in fairly quick succession in serialised form during the next year.[142] Rapid programming developments in line with the development of more efficient radio technology, coupled with listener demand, seem to have swept aside Clinton-Baddeley's objections during the 1930s, and serialised drama – with Dickens playing a central role – was to become an important facet of the BBC's programming. These serialisations were part of what Asa Briggs describes as 'the last development in Drama before 1939 and one that ... pointed the way forward to the world after the war'. Central in resituating Dickens culturally, the development of the dramatic serial programme occurred 'not along American soap opera lines, but as a "middlebrow" form of popular entertainment, seldom sinking lower, sometimes rising higher.... Many listeners must have gone back to read the books after hearing the serials'.[143]

Guinness's writing of his stage version of *Great Expectations* was thus surrounded by new renderings of Dickens's earlier and more popular works on radio with which, as a radio performer himself, he was almost certainly familiar. It should therefore be seen as part of a more general revival of public interest in Dickens, as entering into a relationship with new ways of rendering Dickens's works applicable and comprehensible to modern audiences, and also perhaps as a considered response to the renewed popularity of the early works. *Great Expectations* takes on through

[140] 'Let Radio revive Dickens's Penny Readings', *Radio Times*, Vol. 33, 6 November 1931, p. 417. © Immediate Media Company London Limited.

[141] 'After Pickwick', *Radio Times*, Vol. 66, 9 February 1940, p. 9. © Immediate Media Company London Limited.

[142] *Nickleby* aired on Sunday 9 April 1939, *Pickwick* in a series of dramatized 'scenes' between Tuesday 24 October 1939 and Tuesday 30 January 1940, just months after Clinton-Baddeley had given it a solo reading treatment (on April 7 1939). *David Copperfield* aired in November 1940, *Drood* in three weekly parts beginning 2 September 1941, and *Oliver Twist* in eight weekly parts beginning 3 November 1941. *Radio Times*, 63, 7 April 1939, p. 43; 45, 20 October 1939, p. 3; 66, 15 November 1940, pp. 13 and 16; 73, 2 November 1941, p. 6. © Immediate Media Company London Limited.

[143] Asa Briggs, *The History of Broadcasting in the United Kingdom*, Vol. II: *The Golden Age of Wireless 1927–1939* (Oxford, 1995), pp. 157–8.

these relationships the mantle of a more serious, darker and potentially more artistically sophisticated Dickens, in keeping both with Guinness's own complex feelings about his social and sexual status, and with the Actors' Theatre Company's remit to offer 'something better than the theatre's usual wartime fare'. Programmers themselves recognised the advantages of tying radio to other more established and culturally respected media such as legitimate theatre, and Guinness's aspirations for his new play were made manifest in an interview with Martita Hunt in the 'Big News' section of the *Radio Times* of 24 November 1939, in which the Actors' Theatre Company's plans for the new adaptation of *Great Expectations*, to be followed by Shakespeare's *King John*, were discussed.[144]

Great Expectations' radio journey to this point had been a typically low-key affair. Its first breakthrough had come in 1930, when Clinton-Baddeley had read the novel over the national airwaves in 16 weekly instalments between 3 January and 24 April 1930, thus giving *Great Expectations* the distinction of helping to instigate the notion (if not the final form) of serialising classic novels. This was not, though, a result of some perceived inherent suitability for the task, but an accident of timing. According to F. Dubrez Fawcett, one of the first writers to acknowledge radio's importance to the twentieth-century Dickens phenomenon, and (having been invited to the studio to watch the rehearsal and recording of *David Copperfield* in 1940) a key witness to its effects, 'the first suggestion was *Bleak House*, but V.C. Clinton-Baddeley, master elocutionist and dyed-in-the-wool Dickensian, preferred *Great Expectations* for the great experiment. As he had already adapted the novel for reading purposes, and as his was the voice which was going to determine the success or failure of the enterprise, his opinion was deferred to'.[145]

The novel was broken up into 15-minute slots and aired on the London and Daventry stations at 6pm on Thursdays or Fridays. Subject both to Clinton-Baddeley's radical cuts (and his actorly focus on minor characters) and to the whims of radio programmers who did not at this period consider scheduling on set days of the week important, the readings were nonetheless greeted warmly. Several readers wrote in to the *Radio Times* to express their appreciation and ask for more, and as a result the experiment was repeated in 1930 with *Jane Eyre*, and then again in 1933 with *Dombey and Son*. But the dramatization proper of *Great Expectations* required the additional imperative of the BBC's mission to educate: it was not until 1945 that it was deemed worth dramatizing in full, and even then it was a production aimed firmly at schools.[146] Dickens and education were seen as natural companions on British radio early on; in 1937 the National Programme's regular Schools Broadcast featured a 'Book Talk' section on *Great Expectations*

---

[144] 'Big News', *Radio Times*, 45, 24 November 1939, p. 7. © Immediate Media Company London Limited.

[145] F. Dubrez Fawcett, *Dickens the Dramatist on Stage, Screen and Radio* (London, 1952), p. 213.

[146] BBC Schools: Senior English 1. Broadcast in three parts: Part 1: 1/6/1945; Part 2: 8/6/1945; Part 3: 15/6/1945. B/e1.6.45 – B/e15.6.45, BBC Written Archives Centre.

for Senior English III students.[147] But the related assumption that the novel was not suitable for general pre-war radio consumption as entertainment is explicable only if we consider the long history of its relative unpopularity with readers and its notable lack of previous success in adaptation.

The war undoubtedly had a positive effect on sales of Dickens novels; indeed, as Mazzeno has shown, 'The seminal reevaluations of Orwell and Wilson in 1940 ushered in … a reversal in Dickens's fortunes among the critics … after hostilities began again in 1939, the British public was encouraged to seek solace in the pages of a Dickens novel in times of great stress'.[148] This may be one reason for an upturn in the fortunes of *Great Expectations* afterwards, assisted by the appearance of Lean's film in 1946. But, sales being only one part of a novel's cultural affect, there is another and more interesting thread emerging here, one that potentially leads to a better understanding of the novel's iconic status in our own period. In October 1940, a BBC broadcast by Sir Hugh Walpole (one of the editors of the 1937–38 Nonesuch Dickens edition) asked: 'Can anyone read in a shelter, or can you read in your flat or your house with the guns hammering and the incendiary bombs hissing and the explosions crumping?' The answer was yes, but only a particular type of book: Walpole claims that 'there is no doubt that the Victorians are being read again', and that sales of thrillers were down. Many had 'rushed to Dickens', and he himself wanted books 'with something of nobility in them', claiming: 'What I cannot endure at this present time, whether in prose or poetry, are books that despair of or mock at mankind.' He wanted, instead, books that are 'quiet but dramatic, tragic with a lovely humorous overtone; above all … concerned with the great lasting emotions – loyalty, courage, integrity of soul'. While for this reason Aldous Huxley was 'intolerable' to him at that period, *The Portrait of a Lady*, *The Nigger of the 'Narcissus'*, *Henry Esmond* and *Great Expectations* were all named as being sufficiently noble.[149] There is surely something significant in the idea that both Guinness and Walpole seemed to recognise *Great Expectations* as a Dickens novel of a different stamp. More intellectually challenging, less straightforwardly entertaining and thus on the higher end of the middlebrow, its relative unpopularity with the general reader and the difficulties it presented in adaptation seem at this point to have begun working in its critical favour. If we follow Bourdieu's model this makes a kind of sense; for Bourdieu, cultural capital accrues at a rate directly proportionate to popular disregard.[150]

The re-emergence of new critical champions of Dickens through the late 1920s (though these, as Mazzeno points out, were 'not always fulsome in their praise'[151])

---

[147] *Book Talk*, 'Great Expectations', discussed by Desmond McCarthy. National Programme Schools Broadcast, Tuesday 11 May 1937. Programme Records, Vol. 8, p. 138, BBC Written Archives Centre.

[148] Mazzeno, *Dickens Industry*, p. 91.

[149] Sir Hugh Walpole, 'Reading in the Blitzkrieg', *The Listener*, Thursday 24 October 1940, p. 599. © Immediate Media Company London Limited.

[150] Pierre Bourdieu, *The Field of Cultural Production: Essays on Art and Literature* (Cambridge, 1993).

[151] Mazzeno, *Dickens Industry*, p. 69.

gathered speed in the 1930s and 40s, and the trend had become enough of a commonplace among middlebrow audiences to be mentioned by *The Listener*'s book reviewers after the war. Significantly, the later novels were deemed of particular importance in this reassessment. *The Listener* assigns not only distinct periods but also taste descriptors to this waxing and waning of Dickens's fortunes:

> With the nineteen-twenties, his lack of artistry, his shapelessness, his limitations of sensibility and intellect were thought too great to allow him to be regarded as more than a popular writer – at that time a serious charge. His personal character suffered, at the same time, from the fashionable 'debunking' to which all 'great Victorians' were subjected. In the last fifteen years, however, literary critics have been gradually re-establishing Dickens' reputation. As a result of this reassessment – for example in the essays by Orwell and Edmund Wilson – Dickens has re-emerged as a novelist whose intellectual powers, emotional range and control of technique increased continuously, and whose later works are masterpieces of narrative in which farcical comedy and macabre tragedy are intricately entwined, a master of symbolism, and a great influence on continental writers.[152]

There can be few higher accolades among the post-war discerning on both sides of the Atlantic than 'influence on continental writers', whose position in relation to the British Victorians was also being reassessed at that time; partly, perhaps, due to their palpable neglect by Hollywood. So marked was the distinction, in fact, that in 1949 it enabled a lucrative bit of what Bourdieu calls 'position-taking' in the shape of Vincent Minnelli's film of *Madame Bovary* which, though by no means one of the year's highest-grossing productions, cashed in sufficiently on the vogue for arty foreign authors among the intelligentsia to earn its Art Director an Academy Award nomination.[153]

By the end of World War II, Dickens – and particularly the late novels – had achieved a new status, especially in Britain. For most, this was underpinned by a sense of national identity as under siege in a period of colonial disintegration, dire economic straits and increasing global powerlessness.[154] For the middlebrow and the intelligentsia in Britain it was lent additional fuel by a nationally constituted and deeply class-based aversion to Hollywood. The BBC tapped into this complex matrix using Dickens as a tool, and both Guinness and Lean presciently recognised *Great Expectations*' potential to become one of its finest blades.

The Listener's 'Critic on the Hearth' slot is always illuminating, appealing as it does to the tastes and prejudices of middlebrow England. Philip Hope-Wallace, who made regular appearances in this column, wrote about the BBC's radio

---

[152] Review of Hesketh Pearson's *Dickens: His Characters, Comedy and Career*, in '*The Listener*'s Book Chronicle', *The Listener*, Thursday, 25 August 1949, p. 325. © Immediate Media Company London Limited.

[153] Bourdieu, *The Field of Cultural Production*, p. 30.

[154] Eric Hobsbawm, *Age of Extremes: the Short Twentieth Century 1914–1991* (London, 1995), p. 7.

adaptation of *A Tale of Two Cities* (1 January – 19 March 1947) in terms with which most of its middlebrow readers would probably sympathise:

> Getting half the nation to hang upon a Dickens story like this is going to have astonishing results in time.... Old people may moan that nobody reads Dickens anymore, and indeed the habit and pleasure of reading is not helped by the wireless; yet, in all honesty, are not serials such as the one we have just embarked upon a splendid antidote to literacy, vacancy, Hollywood and all that, and the best possible sort of bridge over the gulf that (let's face it) exists between the educated and the uneducated? ... When the author thus serialised is Dickens the occasion seems to me doubly interesting in view of the many comparative failures to put Dickens on the stage or the screen; whereas wireless adaptation has been extremely successful (let radio wear in its cap of darkness what feathers it may!)[155]

Despite anxieties about radio's cultural status and concomitant fears that it might kill off the reading habit, and despite frequent complaints from listeners about its quality or its decision to broadcast American music and comedy in the place of British fare, clearly radio could not be all bad if it could render Dickens acceptable again. David Lean's adaptation was perfectly placed to take advantage of this need for cultural bridge-building, able to appeal simultaneously to a deep-seated national need for a worthy and resoundingly British cinematic success, and to the American market's contiguous recognition of the cultural capital attached to English classics.

It is impossible to resist giving the last word to another of *The Listener*'s invited 'Critic(s) on the Hearth', one equally able to capture the acerbic voice of middle-England, and here taking the opportunity to attack official polls after their exposure as worthless in predicting the outcome of the Dewey/Truman presidential race in 1948:

> With my infernally bad sense of timing I have chosen this last week – just when polls, public opinion surveys, and all such, have received the biggest bang of their careers from Mr Truman, to indulge a private poll of my own about radio drama ... the category in my poll which (unlike many others) comes out the most important is the 'Don't know' and 'Couldn't care less' category represented by Doris and Fred ... their wireless goes all day ... like most young married couples today they have nothing to talk about, no family life, no real home, being genteel vacua through which float vague longings for cigarettes, films and cash prizes from pools ... Dickens (*Great Expectations* excepted, because they saw it as a film) bores them [as] 'old fashioned, not true to life.'[156]

If Lean's *Great Expectations* could convert Doris and Fred, the novel had entered a new phase indeed.

---

[155] Philip Hope-Wallace, 'Critic on the Hearth', *The Listener*, Thursday 9 January 1947, p. 83. © Immediate Media Company London Limited.

[156] Philip Hope-Wallace, 'Broadcast Drama: the Young Folks at Home', *The Listener*, Thursday 18 November 1948, p. 779. © Immediate Media Company London Limited.

Chapter 4
The Entrenchment of a 'Classic', 1946–2000

After World War II there was a period of energetic revivification of Dickens on the stage, on the radio and later in television in both the UK and the USA, and since for once *Great Expectations* was not left behind this had a remarkable effect on its status by mid-century. It would be impossible even in a book many times the length of this one to do full justice to all the remediations and reprints that have happened since 1946; coinciding with a general upsurge of interest in the Victorians and their legacy, this is one of the periods for which my Appendices are going to have to work the hardest and in which my narrative must of necessity become the most selective. The selection has been driven by two main principles. First, there has already been a great deal of useful critical and historical writing on many of these adaptations and on the post-war Dickens heritage industry more broadly, and I aim to avoid going over old ground unless I feel adjustments, corrections, or additions would be useful. Second, I want to fill in some historical gaps. Radio adaptations, the interrelations between transatlantic media and the sometimes significant cyclical patterns into which the remediations fall in this period have largely been ignored in previous accounts, so these will be my focal points.[1] Miles Taylor has observed that '[T]he Victorians have been made and remade throughout the twentieth century, as successive generations have used the Victorian past in order to locate themselves in the present'.[2] I want here to consider the ideological and pragmatic roles of the twentieth-century media industries in their various representations of *Great Expectations*, and the extent to which it might be viewed as an artefact from 'the Victorian past' which helps us to 'locate' ourselves in the present.

Film Adaptations 1946–65

The new lease of life post-war owes a great deal to Lean's film of 1946, and although the film was part of a momentum that was already underway, there can be little doubt that it is from this date that the tidal wave of new interest gathered speed. Lean's film has probably engendered the most extensive and detailed criticism of any adaptation of this novel. For Carol Hanbury Mackay, it 'finally remains true to more than one psychological undercurrent in both the author and the full range of his reading public', and she attributes this to Lean's 'artistic integrity' which

---

[1]   Robert Giddings and Keith Selby list, but do not discuss, half a dozen radio adaptations on the BBC, but they ignore the American versions entirely, and even in their discussion of the British context they tend to assume that radio's function was as a try-out for TV in the scheduling of classic serials. Giddings and Selby, *The Classic Serial*, pp. 49–50.

[2]   Miles Taylor, introduction to *The Victorians Since 1901: Histories, Representations and Revisions*, ed. by Miles Taylor and Michael Wolff (Manchester, 2001), p. 2.

she calls 'worthy of Dickens'.[3] This is a position with which Grahame Smith is unable to agree; for him: 'Lean and his collaborators simply do not understand the book they are attempting to adapt deeply enough.'[4] Gamely trying to break free of fidelity criticism and bridge the gulf between literature and film, Smith has coined the term 'equivalence in meaning' as a quality yardstick for adaptations, and for him Lean's version does not have the requisite amount. Giddings *et al.* go further, claiming, 'Lean simply couldn't bring himself to do it properly. It wasn't in him. What impresses viewers as "Dickensian accuracy" is really a prissy and fussy romantic historicism which is irrelevant to Dickens's intentions.'[5]

The notion of 'equivalence' is arguably more useful in discussing film than demands for 'accuracy' or 'proper' fidelity to authorial intention. But, useful as it is, even this term privileges the search for some Dickensian 'essence' or 'aura' (to borrow Walter Benjamin's term) deemed to exist in the 'original' source text to which an adaptation is expected be true.[6] The search has its uses: it keeps us cognisant of the fact that Dickens's works are not just material commodities (though crucially they are that too), but works of art which perform complex emotional, ideological and intellectual roles, and it also reminds us that they are as different from Trollope's, or Austen's, or Thackeray's works as these authors are different from each other. But it provides only one possible avenue of enquiry, and might even close off others.

What interests me here, as elsewhere in this book, is less the relative success of various adaptations in rendering or translating 'Dickensian essence', than the way in which the concept itself has been historically and culturally formed and utilised. As I have attempted to show, what we think we mean by 'Dickensian essence' has shifted a little with each new critical movement and market need. In 1985, *Great Expectations'* essence was summed up by Hanbery Mackay as the 'psychological under-current[s] in both the author and the full range of his reading public'.[7] In 2003, Smith characterised it as 'the irresolvable tensions of capitalism'.[8] These are not quite the same thing; these writers each read the novel through the lens of their own critical moment. Such differences are part of a long history of critical and cognitive fluctuation. As previous chapters have shown, during Dickens's lifetime, Dickensian 'essence' (which perhaps we might usefully characterise as what the reader anticipated getting and what they thought they eventually got from a Dickens novel) was created and perpetuated by the author, his publishers and the critical press; in raising expectations about how each new novel might measure up,

---

[3]   Carol Hanbery Mackay, 'A Novel's Journey into Film: The Case of *Great Expectations*', *Literature/Film Quarterly*, 13 (1985): p. 132.

[4]   Smith, *Dickens and the Dream of Cinema*, pp. 122–4.

[5]   Giddings *et al.*, *Screening the Novel*, p. 88.

[6]   Walter Benjamin, 'The Work of Art in the Age of Mechanical Reproduction', in *Illuminations: Essays and Reflections*, ed. by Hannah Arendt, trans. by Harry Zohn (New York, 1968), pp. 217–52.

[7]   Hanbery Mackay, 'A Novel's Journey into Film', p. 132.

[8]   Smith, *Dickens and the Dream of Cinema*, p. 73.

the concept successfully stimulated market demand. Posthumously, the notion of Dickensian essence was more complicated; it was regularly repackaged, remarketed and remediated and used in very different ways in different locations at different times. These uses include celebrating the taste of the ordinary reader, helping to create 'better' taste in new readerships, recapturing the quintessential Englishness (and implied simplicity and superiority) of a bygone era, and ameliorating tensions aroused by other more contentious productions. *Great Expectations* seems to have been rediscovered after World War II to serve all these and other needs, and notions of its 'essence' shifted – and have continued to shift – accordingly.

McFarlane highlights some of Lean's most important contributions to the novel's post-war popularity, including the film's casting. He argues that Martita Hunt's performance, in particular, was 'rendered with a flamboyance that is both riveting and affecting', and that it made her 'the definitive Miss Havisham'. There is certainly a historical shift in the emphasis placed on the female characters in Lean's film, but the claim that the complexity was put there by Dickens and that the role is 'a gift to an actress and in adaptations of varying merits the character usually emerges with the Dickensian elements of grotesquerie and pain intact'[9] is probably less accurate. Jenny Dennett may be closer to the mark when she suggests that the construction of any supposedly iconic 'gift' of a role is historically constituted. As she points out, 'writers of the 1930s seemed unconcerned either by Dickens's or the cinema's female characterisations'.[10] Certainly, in 1934 Florence Reed had been able to do little with a role that had been thoroughly tamed by the script and costume departments, despite the fact that both the writer and the costume consultant were women. And, as we have seen, previous film (and some stage) adaptations seriously downplayed Miss Havisham's role. As Regina Barreca has suggested, Lean did something new: 'it is as if he took into account the complete catalogue of possible readings of the character and then created from them a character powerfully unlike any other'.[11] Martita Hunt's performance – emerging out of decades spent as a powerful theatre and, more recently, radio actress – built effectively on that scripted potential, and one of its greatest contributions is almost certainly to later cultural expectations of the role. Post-Lean, the Miss Havisham role has demanded the casting of powerful character actors at least equal to those required to play Magwitch, and ever since adaptors (and book jacket designers) have tended to make Miss Havisham an important focal point.

Estella's pre-war characterisation as Pip's beautiful, insubstantial dream woman, a romantic heroine who does not know or dare not own up to her own feelings for him until Miss Havisham is dead, also begins to fade from this point (although, as we will see, it briefly reappears in Joseph Hardy's TV movie in 1974). In the wake of Valerie Hobson's performance, actresses taking on the role of Estella have usually been given marginally more scope to explore the

---

[9]   McFarlane, *Screen Adaptations*, p. 140.

[10]   Jenny Dennett, 'Sentimentality, Sex and Sadism: The 1935 version of Dickens's *The Old Curiosity Shop*', in *The Classic Novel from Page to Screen*, ed. by Robert Giddings and Erica Sheen (Manchester and New York, 2000), p. 58.

[11]   Regina Barreca, 'David Lean's *Great Expectations*', in *Dickens on Screen*, p. 39.

psychological damage that has been done to her. Sue Harper attributes Lean's new take on Estella to a shifting ethos in modes of production:

> All the heroines in Cineguild films were characterised by ambiguity, either in their motives or morality. Like a great painting, they were mysterious and endlessly significant … *Great Expectations* … was masterly in its recuperation of Victorian realism, and the power of its visual composition owed much to the glacial composure of Estella. The film re-interpreted the novel so as to intensify her unfathomable qualities.[12]

Harper is right to highlight both the shift and the creative team's part in it, though she rather downplays the latter. In casting the characteristically restrained Hobson, Lean proved that he was more interested in exploring the Estella role than any other director had been before, but he did not work alone; in the hands of hugely gifted cinematographer Guy Green, Estella's transformation is as much visual as scripted, directed and performed.

With the backing of J. Arthur Rank of General Film Distributors (which underwrote the film but largely left the creative team to their own devices),[13] Lean's *Great Expectations* seems to have marked not only stylistic but also production and marketing landmarks in the history of British Dickens adaptations. This is not to diminish the film's creative innovations: Lean's was undoubtedly the first adaptation of *Great Expectations* to move away from safe generic modes and develop the melodrama's more complex potential. Lean recognised the importance of the novel's theme of duality and represented it fully both in the settings (the oppositions between child/adult, country/city, working class/ gentry), and in the characters' psychology (their internal battles between duty/ desire, love/hate, happiness/aspiration). Compared with earlier versions it is thus both visually and narratively exciting. In choosing to follow Miss Havisham's influence on Estella to its logical conclusion it even, arguably, manages to produce a plausible (if conservative) resolution to the Pip/Estella plotline, something even Dickens had been unable to do. Its stylistic influence was immediate: as Kevin Brownlow notes, on its original release it profoundly affected a new generation of film-makers who saw it in their youth.[14] Elham Afnan demonstrates this influence in her analysis of Billy Wilder's *Sunset Boulevard* (1950), a film which translates Miss Havisham to the world of fading movie stardom in a relentlessly youth-obsessed culture and metes out the ultimate punishment to Pip's ambitious counterpart, wannabe scriptwriter Joe Gillis.[15] The influence on film-makers has also been long-lasting; Elizabeth Karlsen, producer of the most recent film version

---

[12]   Sue Harper, 'The representation of women in British feature film, 1945–1950', *Historical Journal of Film, Radio and Television*, 12 (1992): p. 226.

[13]   *Encyclopaedia of British Film*, ed. by Brian McFarlane and Anthony Slide (London, 2003), p. 119.

[14]   Brownlow, *David Lean*, p. 226.

[15]   Elham Afnan, 'Imaginative Transformations: *Great Expectations* and *Sunset Boulevard*', *Dickensian*, 94 (Spring 1998): 5–12.

directed by Mike Newell (UK, 2012), told me during shooting in 2011 that one of her creative team's main aims was to 'take on David Lean'.[16]

However, any reliance on the notion of Lean either as an auteur with a fidelity mission and a sense of reverence or as unequal to the task tends to elide the fact that this film was also a result of a particular set of personal, cultural and economic circumstances and the practices of a now globalised media industry. To begin with, as McFarlane notes, we should read the name Lean as a synecdoche for 'the whole extravagantly gifted team'.[17] Cineguild (founded in 1944) comprised Lean, cowriter Ronald Neame and Associate Producer Anthony Havelock-Allan, and these men contributed equally to the company's deserved reputation for 'quality' British cinema which 'discerning audiences grew to respect'.[18] Further, the script was written by Lean and Neame together, the breakthrough ending was the idea of – and written by – Lean's wife Kay Walsh, and the exaggerated sets which Lean described as 'super Cruikshank' were the brainchild of production designer John Bryan.[19] Lean's film must also be situated in relation to a general public upsurge of interest in the Victorians, as exemplified by the BBC Third Programme's 1948 series *Ideas and Beliefs of the Victorians*, comprising 57 talks and 26 readings lasting over four months, and summed up by one of its contributors, historian G.M. Trevelyan, with the words: '[T]he period of reaction is over ... the era of dispassionate historical evaluation has begun'.[20]

Re-evaluation of Victorian authors and their works was part and parcel of this movement; Humphry House had noted Dickens's modernity and contemporary relevance back in 1941, and readers were feeling it too. A March 1940 Mass Observation survey contained confirmation from several publishers that there had been a notable return to cheap reprints of the classics since the outbreak of war, and Foyle's bookstore stated that 'it is many years since we have sold so many copies of Dickens, Thackeray and Trollope and similar authors'.[21] Another Mass Observation survey in 1940 examined the reading habits of 50 seventeen-year-old schoolboys. Dickens tops the list of the boys' favourite authors, and *Pickwick*, *Copperfield* and *Chuzzlewit* are also mentioned in their list of favourite novels. Five Dickens novels including *Great Expectations* appear in answer to the question: 'Do you ever read a book more than once?' But *Great Expectations*, *Pickwick* and *A Christmas Carol* are the only Dickens works listed in answer to

---

[16] Author's interview with Elizabeth Karlsen on the set of *Great Expectations*, Hounslow, London, 27 October 2011.

[17] McFarlane, *Screen Adaptations*, p. 141.

[18] Brownlow, *David Lean*, p. 169.

[19] Brownlow, *David Lean*, pp. 208–9.

[20] Quoted in James Thompson, 'The BBC and the Victorians', in Taylor and Wolff, *The Victorians Since 1901*, pp. 151–2.

[21] 'Book reading in Wartime: report on material from publishers, book clubs, libraries and booksellers', Mass Observation File, Report No. 46, March 1940. http://www.massobservation.amdigital.co.uk/Contents/filereport.aspx?documentid=237608 [accessed 1 September 2013].

the question: 'Which books have given you the greatest satisfaction?'[22] Lean and Guinness were both part of this new-generation Dickens revival.

There can be little doubt that without Guinness's 1939 play there would have been no Lean film.[23] Guinness was an avid reader and a committed stage actor who understood how *Great Expectations* might work on the contemporary stage, bringing to it both his own complex emotional investments in Pip and Herbert, and an instinct for writing serious dramatic theatre. So dependent is Lean's film on Guinness's version, indeed, that when he heard about the planned use of a reader to link the scenes, Guinness noted in his diary that he thought it bordered on plagiarism. His biographer also finds it unlikely that he – a stage actor who seldom even went to the movies – would have taken the role in Lean's film (his first) had he not somehow wanted to protect what he saw as his property.[24]

Lean, on the other hand, was no more a reader than he was a theatre-goer, and the only Dickens he had read before he saw Guinness's play was *A Christmas Carol*. Only afterwards, with the gift of a copy of the Nonesuch Edition of *Great Expectations* for his birthday in 1940, did he become a convert.[25] The Nonesuch edition is itself a significant sign of the novel's perceived status in the publishing industry at this time. Originally published in 1937–38 in an exclusive set of 23 volumes available only on subscription for 48 guineas (around $250), the Nonesuch Edition was subject in 1939 to the UK government's crippling 'war-risks-insurance' charge on all unsold books held by British publishers. In order to rid themselves of surplus stock and avoid paying the tax, Nonesuch decided to release individual copies from the remaining 50 or so sets at a lower price. The least popular works, *American Notes* and *Reprinted Pieces*, were available for $5.75 (about £1 3s.) each. More popular works retailed for between $13.50 and $11.50. *Great Expectations*, bound with *Hard Times* in this edition, gives away its poor popularity rating by being retailed at just $9.75 – not quite $5 (about £1) per novel.[26] Lean had got hold of a bargain and – just as Guinness had done – he used the combination of its growing cultural capital with critics and its relative unfamiliarity to popular audiences in this period to create a new type of Dickens event.

The original screenplay, written by veteran novelist, playwright and screen writer 'Clemence Dane' (Winifred Ashton, 1888–1965), was too tied to the letter of Dickens for Lean. He told Brownlow in interview:

[22] 'Literary Questionnaire: 50 replies from 17 year old schoolboys on reading habits', by H.P. Elderton and G.L. Wallace, Mass Observation File, Report No. 62, March 1940. http://www.massobservation.amdigital.co.uk/Search/filereport.aspx?documentid=237623 [accessed 1 September 2013].

[23] Hanbery Mackay also acknowledges the debt, though she gets the date of the stage version wrong. 'A Novel's Journey into Film', p. 127.

[24] Read, *Alec Guinness*, pp. 203–5.

[25] Brownlow, *David Lean*, p. 206.

[26] Letter to an American subscriber from George Macy, Director of the Nonesuch Fellowship, 27 November 1939. Held in the collection of a subscriber to Librarything. Posted by Django6924, 26 July 2010, http://www.librarything.com/topic/95618 [accessed 21 September 2013].

What she wrote was so awful I cannot even begin to describe it. It had practically every incident in the book but done in shorthand so one never got to grips with any one scene. She took snippets of everything and didn't give anything real weight. If I had done it, she would have turned on me and written letters to *The Times* about the desecration of Dickens. It was hideously embarrassing.[27]

The idea that strict fidelity to Dickens does not work in a visual medium was not new, as we have seen; every previous adaptation had been forced to take liberties of some sort. But anxieties about the desecration of Dickens and Lean's solution to the problem mark an interesting development in the refashioning of Dickensian essence. 'You have to cut', Lean told Brownlow, 'and give [each chosen scene] weight and do it proud. You have to savour Dickens, you have to enjoy him. You can't just skip through in shorthand.'[28] Lean's remit was to make something that would appeal on both sides of the Atlantic without costing a fortune, and to do this he needed to create something that was capable of looking backwards sufficiently to pay homage to the revered author, and forwards sufficiently to overcome a long-term popular disregard for his thirteenth novel.[29] This could not be accomplished using the old adaptation tools.

A letter from the legendary Dickensian actor Bransby Williams (1870–1961), written to his friend and theatrical collaborator Dr Eric Jones-Evans on 22 Aug 1945, provides a marker of Lean's commitment to breaking with traditional expectations of how Dickensian essence was best rendered in performance. Indeed, Williams forms a useful demarcation point between two distinct performance styles and reception periods. Having been born the year Dickens died, started his career playing Dickens characters in music hall and theatre in the 1890s, toured the USA during 1906–7 and become a stalwart of Dickensian performance on both the stage and on BBC radio in the 1930s, for many years he was *the* actor whom programme-makers and the public alike associated with Dickens. Not so Lean. Williams's letter to Jones-Evans spells out a sea change. 'Yesterday I felt young and fit for anything', Williams writes rather plaintively, 'but it does not come and I don't know where to seek it. I was promised to be in the film *Great Expectations* – but daily I see and hear of each new engagement – so that I see now nothing left for me.'[30] Williams continued to perform his Dickens roles to great acclaim on radio, TV, stage and film for many years (indeed, he put on and acted in a performance of *Great Expectations*

[27] Brownlow, *David Lean*, p. 207.

[28] Brownlow, *David Lean*, pp. 206–8.

[29] Brownlow, *David Lean*, p. 207.

[30] Letter from Bransby Williams to Dr Eric Jones-Evans, 22 Aug 1945. Item EJE/001392, Bristol University Theatre Collection. Footage of Williams performing some of his best-known Dickensian and other roles in 1940 can be found on the Pathé News website (http://www.britishpathe.com/video/bransby-williams). Jones-Evans ran the Grand Theatre in Southampton between 1928 and 39, where he performed a number of plays from Dickens's works, some subsequently published with forewords by Williams. Most of his papers can be found at Bristol University, but some fragments are held in Southampton University Special Collections, Hartley Library.

at the King's Theatre in Hammersmith, London in July 1947, perhaps as a nose-thumb to Lean), but in general his acting and makeup styles favoured the earlier novels, and it was these to which he largely adhered. It is certainly difficult to imagine any role he could have played in Lean's film; there are Dickensian caricatures and some comedy, certainly, but they are not of the Williams stamp.

Lean's decision to make a radical change from traditional expectations for Dickens in performance proved to audiences that there was after all pleasure to be had from a text that had always tended to baffle and disappoint readers, and this flew in the face of its dominant contemporary role on both sides of the Atlantic as a dull, forbidding duty-read on school and college curricula. In introducing Dickensian essence of a different sort – more serious, more aesthetically challenging – it came closer than any previous remediation to bridging the divide between the critically acclaimed and the popular. More importantly, as a result of global post-war film industry expansion and its distribution by the American firm Universal, it won over new international audiences who knew nothing of the novel's chequered history and thus, wearing a false aura of entitlement, it took on the status of a time-served global icon.[31] This, as I will show in Chapter 5, helped to spread knowledge of the novel and its Victorian patriarchal and Anglo-centric assumptions overseas, and to set it up as a prime target for feminist and postcolonial responses.

As this history attests, the film had considerable industry support. Its producer, Ronald Neame, was sent by J. Arthur Rank to Hollywood in the early 1940s to study production methods and specifically to 'produce the kind of film he felt the Americans would enjoy', and he was convinced *Great Expectations* could be an American winner.[32] There is no way of knowing whether Neame was responsible, but there is evidence that Universal was considering a remake as early as 1941 and held off because of the war. A one-page synopsis of the novel dated 31 January 1941was written for Universal's consideration. The report on it concludes: 'Universal, I believe, made this fine, rich hunk of Dickens some five years ago. While there is an England and a memory of England [in 1941 England's actual survival was in some doubt], Dickens will always be swell stuff – there will undoubtedly again be an appropriate time to re-make this. When all the guns shall have been spiked, perhaps.' The synopsis was considered again on 12 January 1942, and while no judgement on this one's chances appears to have survived, *Great Expectations* was clearly back on the remediation agenda at this time.[33] While it might have been deemed unsuitable wartime fare by Universal, two

---

[31]   See, for example, Hiroshi Kitamura, '"Home of American Movies": The Marunouchi Subaruza and the Making of Hollywood's Audiences in Occupied Tokyo, 1946–9', in *Hollywood Abroad: Audiences and Cultural Exchange*, ed. by Melvyn Stokes and Richard Maltby (London, 2004), pp. 99–120.

[32]   Brownlow, *David Lean*, p. 207.

[33]   'Production No. F-135': synopsis of and comment on potential *Great Expectations* film plus business forecast, written and signed by Universal's Emery Kanarik, 31 January 1941, in Folder '*Great Expectations* 1917: L. Huff – J. Pickford', File 665, Margaret Herrick Library, Academy of Motion Picture Arts and Sciences, Los Angeles.

revivals of Guinness's stage production were planned during the war, one of which came to fruition in a three-week run at Liverpool Playhouse, 1–22 September 1943, directed by John Moody.[34]

One of the film's greatest successes seems to have been its commitment to as broad an international, social and generic appeal as possible, coupled with its marketing of a romanticised (and now, in 1946, victorious) brand of Englishness. As Jeffrey Sconce has noted, Dickens in this period seems to have been unique among Victorian novelists in being simultaneously considered both 'classic' literature and an everyman's favourite.[35] I would add that adaptations were largely responsible for this. While, as Guinness had recognised, *Great Expectations* was still relatively unpopular, it contained enough innate drama, comedy and mystery to make the crossover successfully when treated with the right measures of innovation and respect for tradition.

The publicity posters and the first cinema trailer for Lean's film encapsulated this position. The poster played on the title: 'Great Romance. Great Thrills. Great Suspense. Great Adventure. Great Expectations.' The trailer assured prospective audiences that Dickens had been chosen, not because he was a classic author, but because he was a 'master story-teller', that no one 'can portray more faithfully than Dickens the hopes and doubts that dwell in the heart of a boy, or hold you poised so perilously between a smile and a lump in the throat', and it affirms that the film has been painted in 'the broad colours of melodrama'. This constitutes a sensible appeal to audience tastes in this period, but the trailer also pans across the gilt spines of Dickens's novels to insinuate the classic literature connection (just as the film opens with pages of the novel being turned). For those unfamiliar with or put off by the novel, with some clever cutting it even manages to highlight the film's gothic, mystery and horror elements, complete with dark shadowy interiors and Miss Havisham's off-camera screams.[36] The poster and trailer suggest with some justification that this is Dickens as he has never been seen before: unstuffy, exciting and dramatic.

The catch-all appeal was given an extra dimension for American audiences by the addition of new material to the trailer after the film had been screened by invitation at the prestigious Radio City Music Hall, the 'Showplace of the Nation', in New York in 1947. The shooting script for this trailer tells us a lot about how Dickens – and onscreen Englishness – was being marketed in the USA in this period. The directions call for a 'very fine art background, just breathing swank'. The voiceover is done by the movie actor Fred MacMurray, famous for both chilling *film noir* and for straighter 'nice guy' roles, who lures us in with

[34] *Great Expectations* by Alec Guinness, Playhouse Theatre, Liverpool. Script, excerpts of text, annotated typescript/manuscript and prompt book. Written Documents c. 1942, items JM/000046 and JM/000047, Bristol University Theatre Collection.

[35] Sconce, 'Dickens, Selznik and Southpark', p. 174.

[36] English trailer for *Great Expectations*, 6 Feb 1947, Universal Trailer Scripts, Box 1, File 27, *Great Expectations – Gunsmoke*, Margaret Herrick Library, Academy of Motion Picture Arts and Sciences, Los Angeles. The trailer is also available to view at IMDB (http://www.imdb.com/title/tt0038574/videogallery/content_type-Trailer).

the promise of 'the high life of society [and] the low life of criminals'. The trailer also includes endorsements by the English actor Ronald Colman (famous for his cultured accent on radio and in many popular film roles, including most pertinently Sydney Carton in *A Tale of Two Cities* in 1935), and the American actor/director Robert Montgomery (a naval veteran known for horror as well as light comedy onscreen).[37] The combination emphasises both the film's appeal to general audiences and its 'class', what Sconce dubs 'a semiotic state of Britishness' aimed at attracting the middlebrow viewer.[38] As testament to its ability to build bridges between critics and popular audiences (and to help launch a new era for *Great Expectations*), the film not only achieved box-office success but also won Academy Awards for Best Art Direction and Best Cinematography.

Radio Adaptations 1946–65

Ronald Colman was a good choice for the trailer, familiar as he was to audiences on radio in addition to being an Academy Award–nominated screen presence with Dickensian credentials. In July 1946, just prior to the release of Lean's film, he had hosted one of the nationally syndicated airings of the popular NBC radio show, 'Favourite Story', featuring a half-hour version of *Great Expectations* chosen by the film and theatre character actor Walter Hampden. 'If you don't happen to be a Charles Dickens fan as I am', Colman's narration begins, 'I have a feeling you will be after you hear this Favourite Story. It isn't the best-known novel by this master storyteller, but it is one of the most intriguing'. His upper-class English accent (contrasting nicely with the regional accents of the play's working-class characters) brings with it the assumption of good taste and education, while his précis of the story focussing on 'the strange old lady on the hill', 'the brutal yet tender Abel Magwitch', and 'the unfathomable Estella' promises mystery and romance, both of which were familiar radio fare.[39]

This effective 30-minute version, airing at 9pm and thus (unlike the British radio versions of this period) probably aimed at adult listeners, uses mostly British actors or passable British accents and focusses on dramatizing the main characters' interactions through the romance and the Magwitch escape scene, with concise narration by the adult Pip filling in the blanks. Considerable license is naturally taken with both language and plot in order to render them compact and comprehensible for American listeners in a scant 30 minutes: 'My given name

---

[37]   Shooting script for *Great Expectations* Music Hall opening, 1947, Universal Trailer Scripts, Box 1, File 27, *Great Expectations – Gunsmoke*, Margaret Herrick Library, Academy of Motion Picture Arts and Sciences, Los Angeles.

[38]   Sconce, 'Dickens, Selznik and Southpark', p. 174.

[39]   'Great Expectations', 29:35 mins, episode 23 of *Favorite Story*, host and narrator Ronald Colman (usually True Boardman), announcer George Barclay, story selected by Walter Hampden, NBC (syndicated), 23 July 1946, 9pm. Lawrence and Lee Collection of broadcast recordings, Rodgers and Hammerstein Archives of Recorded Sound, New York Public Library. Reference LK–16 1, 2 sound discs, 33 1/3 rpm ; 16 in.

was Philip Pirrip, but Pip's a good deal easier on the tongue', the narrator begins, paying lip service to Victorian English but compressing Dickens's long opening paragraphs into under four seconds of airtime. The cast is pared down to Pip, Estella, the Gargerys, Miss Havisham, Magwitch, Jaggers and Molly, but the story manages to work through a focus on the most dramatic plotlines and a judicious use of atmospheric music and sound effects. It is by no stretch a faithful rendering of *Great Expectations*' 'essence' as we might now constitute it, certainly, but it is good radio.

The regular host, True Boardman, provided a different introduction for the broadcasting of this same version on the West Coast, 26 November 1946. It again emphasises the fact that *Great Expectations* has not until now been a great popular favourite and that that makes it somehow special. 'We went to the man who has published some of the greatest bestsellers of our generation: author, publisher, explorer, Mr George Palmer Putnam', Boardman begins. 'He told us that he had always liked a Dickens novel which very few people knew; its title – *Great Expectations*. So *Great Expectations*, the choice of the Dean of the world of books, is our favourite story.'[40] The extant recording of this version also preserves a key indicator of Dickens's cultural uses in this period. Between Acts 1 and 2 a well-bred English voice glides in on behalf of the show's sponsor, Bullock's Department Store, and by allying 'the great Dickens' with the 'fine furnishings' in the store's antiques department ('itself a touch of Old England'), the advertisement seamlessly conjoins literary classics and commodities, Dickens and aspirational Americans.

Since the early 1930s, the American radio industry had been working hard to understand how effective aural advertising functioned and through consumer research had refined its techniques considerably.[41] By this time the use of Englishness to promote products as 'classy' was well established (thanks largely to the precedent set by Hollywood), and literary classics including Dickens had become an integral part of the advertiser's toolkit. *Great Expectations* benefitted from radio's adoption of this strategy by ceasing to be singled out as a literary failure; here, it is simply presented as a worthwhile if relatively obscure story, chosen by men who clearly knew quality for an audience that may have been afraid it did not.

Commercial radio also enabled the rediscovery of Dickens's gifts for serial drama and *Great Expectations* was a key beneficiary in this regard too. The novel's tripartite structure was tailor-made for commercial breaks, and – as Christopher Ricks has pointed out – its loosely intertwined themes are easily detangled and the heavy symbolism trimmed without loss of dramatic interest.[42] The main relationship plotlines fall easily into the three sections, taking it in turns to raise

---

[40] 'Great Expectations', 29:35 mins, *Favorite Story* (West Coast version), sponsored by Bullock's Department Store, Los Angeles. Favorite of George Palmer Putnam. Syndicated by 'Ziv'. Author's collection.

[41] Michael Socolow, 'Psyche and Society: Radio Advertising and Social Psychology in America, 1923–1936', *Historical Journal of Film, Radio and Television*, 24 (2004): p. 524.

[42] Christopher Ricks, 'Great Expectations', in *Dickens and the Twentieth Century*, ed. by John Gross and Gabriel Pearson (London, 1962), p. 200.

dramatic peaks and resolving themselves neatly at the end through two deaths and two reconciliations. American radio adaptations such as this were responsible for subtle changes to *Great Expectations'* cultural status, and (perhaps trading on the pre-publicity) prepared the ground for Lean's film. This particular adaptation manages simultaneously to pay due deference, to make the story desirable to modern listeners by aligning it with 'classy' commodities and educated tastes, and to update it through stringent cuts and sound effects designed to foreground the drama and romance, both of which were essential in the competitive medium of commercial radio.

The novel was in desperate need of updating if it was to survive in the USA. A report by the 'Commission on Secondary School Curriculum', published a mere six years earlier in 1940, provides an insight into the ways in which the novel was being discussed and taught, what its position was relative to other nineteenth-century works and what the official plans were for its future. The English subject subcommittee declared that the classics should not become part of a student's 'intellectual baggage' but should be relevant and meet the needs 'of young people in the democratic society of America today'.[43] The report's recommendations were made based on a 'Study of Adolescents' which had gathered information on the out-of-school reading practices of 270 teenagers between 1931 and 1933. Dickens makes no appearance at all in the preferences of these students, 83.2 per cent of whom, predictably, chose to read fiction from the post-1900 period, but he does appear as a recommended author for the use of teachers in addressing this preference for the modern. His role, ironically, was rather a Gradgrindian one: to teach students about historical literary themes. *Great Expectations* itself is invoked in the sections on 'Early Childhood', 'Adulthood' and 'Convicts' (though not, interestingly enough, 'Class Prejudice'), but while it is called 'one of Dickens's best novels ... well-knit [and] notable in part for its masterly delineation of a youth's growth in character',[44] there is no sense here that it can also be enjoyable.

Radio adaptations, coinciding with the outbreak of war in Europe, seem to have helped to change that perception of Dickens, offering drama, suspense and romance alongside historical deference. The war had other effects on adaptations, too; significantly, Lean's sunlit ending is prefigured here at the end of this 30-minute NBC version when Pip says to Estella: 'A new house can rise from the old: shall we build one, my dear, high into the mist, where its towers can catch the sun?' Many critics have read Lean's ending as a metaphor (whether successful or not) for Pip's rediscovered assertiveness,[45] or for Estella's capitulation to patriarchy,[46]

---

[43]   Elbert Lenlow, *Reader's Guide to Prose Fiction: An Introductory Essay, with Bibliographies of 1500 Novels Selected, Topically Classified, and Annotated for Use in Meeting the Needs of Individuals in General Education* (London and New York, 1940), pp. v and 6.

[44]   Lenlow, *Reader's Guide*, pp. 107, 125 and 141.

[45]   Jane Baston, 'Word and Image: The Articulation and Visualization of Power in *Great Expectations*', *Literature Film Quarterly*, 3 (1996): p. 330.

[46]   Regina Barreca, 'David Lean's *Great Expectations*', in *Dickens on Screen*, p. 44.

or for 'the letting in of light on British life at large after the rigour of the war years'.[47] But the translation of Dickens's ambiguous romance-plot resolution into a wartime language of moral absolutes seems to have been part of a wider trend in broadcasting.

Post-Lean American radio adaptations are briefly relatively numerous and they undergo a subtle change, some of which might be attributable to the influence of (and competition with) Lean's film. The nine radio versions known to me which were broadcast between 1947 and 1954 continue to view Dickens as a way of accruing cultural capital, whether for their sponsors or for their sustaining stations, by forming part of 'theatre' or 'playhouse' programmes largely comprising out-of-copyright British titles.[48] But now they tend to give the novel 60 rather than 30 minutes, and thus do greater justice to its language and the web of causalities offered by its subplots. Lean had moved the goalposts, drawing together the entertaining and the educative: the emphasis is still on the drama, but the introductions now tend to emphasise the novel's historical importance as literature as well as the fond place it occupies in the hearts of a few members of the intelligentsia, and the adaptations take more care to retain Dickens's own dialogue and prose. Lean's version of Dickens is no less commodified than these radio shows, of course: the programme for its world premiere at the Gaumont Theatre, London on 16 December 1946 contains adverts for Lux soap endorsed by Valerie Hobson and advertises a Goya fragrance dedicated to her called *Great Expectations*, demonstrating an exploitation of Dickens's name and novel titles as cynical as any other in this period.[49] But by reminding viewers and listeners of its literary worth as well as its innate drama and suspense, Lean's film and its serious treatment of some of the novel's complexities (considerably more serious than previous films had managed) seems to have helped to turn an all-but-forgotten quirky 'favourite story' of the literati, taught as ancient history in schools, back into a still-relevant novel worth reading in full.

An example of the operation of this shift is provided by the 1950 NBC Theatre version which announces its middlebrow motives by opening with a bit of literary history, invoking (or inventing) the excitement in London as readers awaited the final instalment of the novel in 1861. It contains a plug for adult English Literature courses at North American universities, offers listeners the chance to win an Encyclopaedia Britannica upon enrolment, and concludes with an announcement of future broadcasts of 'the most adult dramatic fare in radio', including adaptations of D.H. Lawrence and James Joyce.[50] Post-Lean, *Great Expectations* has clearly finally joined the ranks of the exalted.

---

[47]   Brian McFarlane, *Novel to Film* (Oxford, 1996), p. 111.

[48]   A 'sustained' programme was one supported by the network, rather than a commercial sponsor.

[49]   *Great Expectations* programmes, Guy Green Papers, f. 34, Margaret Herrick Library, Academy of Motion Picture Arts and Sciences, Los Angeles.

[50]   'Great Expectations', 60 mins., episode 70 of *NBC Theater from Hollywood*, announcer Don Stanley, NBC, 1 January 1950, 2pm. Author's collection.

The influence of the film on radio adaptations is made still more explicit in other post-Lean versions: ABC's 'Theater Guild on the Air' version of 1950 features Francis L. Sullivan as Jaggers, a role he had played twice on film, most recently for Lean.[51] Lean's influence is also still very much apparent in a rerecording of this version for ABC in 1953; while between the Acts there are references to the curtain rising or falling and each is punctuated by audience applause as in live theatre, the ending is a direct replica of Lean's, complete with Pip tearing down curtains and crying: 'Estella, you must leave this house, it's a dead house! Estella – come with me out into the sunlight!'[52] Cross-media connections are also made manifest in NBC's Star Playhouse version of 1954. It is introduced by John Chapman, drama critic of the *New York Daily News*, and while it also advertises forthcoming operas its main attraction is the presence of popular Hollywood screen stars such as Roddy McDowall (who played Pip in this version) and Joan Fontaine (who had starred as Estella for ABC in 1950 alongside Francis. L. Sullivan).[53]

As far as I have been able to ascertain, American radio adaptations of this type petered out in the 1950s, probably due to competition with television: indeed, McDowall was to star in the first TV version of *Great Expectations* on NBC's 'Robert Montgomery Presents' in June of 1954, three months after this radio appearance.[54] But for a brief period the novel made a stronger showing on radio than most other Dickens works, coming in a close third behind *A Tale of Two Cities* and *A Christmas Carol*.[55] Given the timings, this is almost certainly a direct result of the success of Lean's film, just as *A Tale of Two Cities* on radio seems to have benefitted from the 1935 Ronald Colman film. The intimate relationship between popular mass media in this period, between them reaching almost every American home, provides an important context for a revival of the novel in book form. By 1968, when George Ford surveyed the American circulation of Dickens's works, he found that *Great Expectations* came second only to *A Tale of Two Cities* in terms of sales, with 238,670 copies sold in that year.[56] Not a massive sales

[51]   'Great Expectations', 60 mins, episode 191 of *Theater Guild on the Air*, ABC, 16 April 1950, 7.30pm. Jerry Haendiges Vintage Radio Logs. Also in Martin Grams, Jr., *Radio Drama: A Comprehensive Chronicle of American Network Programs 1932–1962*, Vol. 2 (Jefferson, 2008) p. 511.

[52]   'Great Expectations', 60 mins, episode 306 of *Theater Guild on the Air*, ABC, 5 April 1953, 7.30pm. Author's collection.

[53]   'Great Expectations', 60 mins, episode 25 of *NBC Star Playhouse*, adapted by Ernest Kinoy, host John Chapman, NBC (sustaining), 21 March 1954, 8pm Author's ollection.

[54]   Copy available to view by appointment at UCLA, ref. 'Great Expectations (Television program: 1954)'.

[55]   Other Dickens works adapted for broadcasting during the period 1938–54, according to all the hard copy and online catalogues I have consulted, include: *A Tale of Two Cities* (15 times), *A Christmas Carol* (10), *Oliver Twist* (5), *Pickwick* (5), *David Copperfield* (3), *The Signalman* (2).

[56]   George Ford, 'Dickens in the 1960s', *Dickensian*, 66 (May 1970): pp. 170–71.

figure by modern standards, but not bad for a 100-year-old novel that had never previously been a hit with Americans.

Great Expectations had a rather leaner decade on radio in Britain, and when the adaptations did happen they differed in interesting ways. *David Copperfield*, *Edwin Drood* and *Oliver Twist* all did well during the war, but *Great Expectations* was still being discussed on the BBC purely as a school text: even the first full-length adaptation (in three weekly parts 1–15 June 1945) was produced for Senior English Level 1 students. The first serialisation for general listeners, adapted by Mabel Constanduros and Howard Agg, was broadcast on the BBC Home Service on Sunday evenings, 8:30–9:00pm, in 12 weekly episodes between 19 September and 5 December 1948. The extant script indicates that it works hard to keep the humour, the suspense and the pathos, but as well as keeping some of the characters often excised (Wopsle, Startop and Trabb's Boy) and excising others (Orlick), it adds some interesting twists of its own.

Unusually on radio, the scene in Trabb's shop in which Pip is mocked while trying on new clothes is rendered in full, emphasizing the moral vacuity of luxury goods. This might well have struck a chord with a post-war, rationing-hit British audience. Its episode breaks also emphasise significant themes, particularly Pip's manipulation by powerful unseen forces outside his control and his sad self-reflections on the conflict between fate and self-determination. These are not always emphasised in the same way by Dickens. For example, while Episode 2 ends like Ch. 9 in the novel, with Pip's musings on 'the formation of the first link on one memorable day', Episode 3 ends on a fade-out of Jaggers reading out the list of conditions attached to Pip's good fortune and picks up the list again with a fade-in at the beginning of Episode 4. This structural device serves to inflect the good news of Pip's impending fortune with an ominous note of manipulation going on over his head which is not present in any other version I have found. More significantly still, this version ignores both the no-Estella ending chosen by Guinness and still dominant on the stage in this period, and the cathartic ending chosen by Lean. Here, Pip determines to pay Joe back, agrees to go to Cairo with Herbert in order to earn the money to do so and then, encountering Estella in the ruins of Satis House before he goes, *without* the novel's break of 11 years, gets together with her instead. There are two possible implications here: either he will abandon his plans to travel, get married, and use Estella's remaining money from the sale of Satis House to pay Joe, or they will travel to Egypt together, putting behind them the ruins of their old life and seeking their fortunes abroad. Pip's choices are thus between exploiting Estella, or exploiting Egypt. We are never told the outcome, and in a twentieth-century context the removal of Pip's 11-year sojourn abroad creates a new, unresolved tension around the story's denouement. [57] In the 1840s–1860s Cairo was a rapidly modernising international city full of opportunities for Western investment and exploitation (no problem for

---

[57] *Great Expectations*, 12 × 30-min. instalments, adapted by Mabel Constanduros and Howard Agg, BBC Home Service Sunday, 19 September – 5 December 1948, 8.30pm. Play Library GR-GZ, BBC Written Archives Centre.

a Victorian), but by 1948 it was constantly in the news as part of a troubled former British colony struggling for autonomy and still occupied by British troops.

The differences are significant in the context of post-war Britain. Between 1946 and 1949, as Thomas Hajkowski has shown, the BBC pursued a programming strategy that was oddly ambivalent about the dissolution of the empire, on the one hand working to 'promote the new, multiracial Commonwealth in talks and news programs', while on the other 'its entertainment programs reproduced the "romantic" empire of adventure, exoticism, power and racism'. During these years the BBC dramatized a number of Victorian and Edwardian imperial novels by Rider Haggard, Edgar Wallace and Cutcliffe Hyne, the heroes of which 'represent the opportunities provided by the empire and reveal different aspects of the national character'.[58] Constanduros and Agg's ending – repeated nowhere else that I have found – seems to enact a new, specifically mid-twentieth-century British problem. Surrounded by these popular dramatizations of empire adventure novels, it can be seen to add to Dickens's ending, inflected as it is with social and emotional disillusionment, a reactionary imperial nostalgia implicitly underpinned by postcolonial anxiety.

Nonetheless, perhaps because it still had one eye on the schools market (each episode aired at 8.30pm and lasted only 30 minutes), and certainly because it had the luxury of a total of six hours of airtime, this version makes textual fidelity a paramount consideration compared to American versions. As the BBC's Director of the Spoken Word Harman Grisewood put it in 1955, the function of the BBC as he saw it was to be 'the interpreter of British genius'.[59] Due partly to the long-lasting paternalistic Reithian mission to make the BBC morally and intellectually responsible for the general population's leisure listening, and partly to the lack of airtime competition which enabled it to treat literary adaptations far more fully than most of its American counterparts, the BBC made serialised classic novels a speciality.[60] This respectful approach, along with the paternal eye kept on school-age listeners, largely sums up *Great Expectations'* life on British radio until the1970s. Most adaptations in this period were broadcast for schools, many of them carved into chunks for use as reading and comprehension lessons, such as 'Young Pip' (2 May 1951), 'Pip and the Convict' (5 Dec 1960), and 'The Pale Young Gentleman' (1 July 1965).[61] But the BBC also clearly saw classic serials including Dickens as an important part of its commonwealth mission in the face of crumbling colonial control. In addition to the imperial nostalgia written into

---

[58]   Thomas Hajkowski, *Studies in Popular Culture: The BBC and National Identity in Britain, 1922–53* (Manchester, 2010), pp. 72–3.

[59]   Quoted in Hajkowski, *Studies in Popular Culture*, p. 234.

[60]   I have found only one Dickens serial adaptation on American radio in this period: a four-part 'Tale of Two Cities', broadcast in 30-minute sections on Fridays, 11.30 to midnight, on *The World's Greatest Novels* series on NBC (sustaining) between 21 November and 26 December 1947.

[61]   *Great Expectations* Script files BC/HS 2.5.51, BC/HS 5.12.60 and BC/HS 1.7.65, BBC Written Archives Centre.

the ending in 1948, it broadcast a new serialisation of *Great Expectations* on its 'Calling West Africa' programme between 9 October and 18 December 1951, the year in which Libya was granted independence by Italy and Egypt renounced control of the Sudan, provoking Britain to do likewise not long afterwards.[62] Dickens seemed to stand in this period for unassailable Britishness; useful, no doubt, at a time when national confidence abroad was being shaken.

One of the most prolific literary adaptors for BBC radio in the 1950s and 1960s was H. Oldfield Box, who adapted several Dickens novels as well as a number of Trollopes, Austens and others.[63] His *Great Expectations* adaptations were broadcast in 1958 (*Children's Hour*, seven 40-minute episodes) and 1961 (twelve 45-minute episodes for family listening, aired in the serial drama slot early on Sunday evenings). Both abide by the fidelity principle to an extent: Oldfield Box keeps Pip as narrator and is true to much of Dickens's dialogue, though only insofar as it furthers the action. But the prose (particularly in the narration) is modernised, the children's version beginning: 'My name is Philip Pirrip – Pip for short.' This version's early instalments focus on the comedy between Pip, Joe, Wopsle and Pumblechook and on the horror of the meeting with Magwitch, and it has us feeling rather more sympathy with Pip than we do in any nineteenth-century version of the novel by beginning with an expression of gratitude to Joe: 'Wretched indeed would those years of my childhood have been but for the gentle kindness of her husband, Joe Gargery. Dear old Joe!' To the same end it also excises Pip's callousness to Biddy, emphasises Estella's cruelty to Pip through the administration of two slaps instead of one, and has him admit to feeling sorry for Miss Havisham. This version thus makes a soft-hearted Pip the centre of a series of abuses by various characters rather than a temporary miscreant; its rather paternalistic lesson seems to be simply that greed, cruelty and lying are bad. Oldfield Box clearly knew his audiences: the longer family version is more dialogue heavy and it emphasizes the romance theme more, choosing to include scenes featuring Drummle as competition for Estella and Orlick as competition for Biddy, and providing a more obviously happy (and less platonic) ending for Pip and Estella.

These are among the loosest rewritings for British radio, but it seems significant that Hodder & Stoughton deemed them successful and relevant enough for modern audiences to bring one of them – based on the second, family version – out as an abridged book in their Fiction Classics series. *Great Expectations* was published in this series in 1955, sporting a front cover that advertises the book as a teen romance through an image of young Pip gazing longingly at Estella as she glides haughtily up the stairs (see Fig. 4.1).

---

[62] BC/Reg. West Africa 9.10.51–18.12.51, BBC Written Archives Centre.

[63] See the Appendix of Radio Versions, in *Jane Austen and Co.: Remaking the Past in Contemporary Culture*, ed. by Suzanne Rodin Pucci and James Thompson (Albany, 2003), pp. 264–6.

Fig. 4.1   Detail from the front cover of *Great Expectations*, abridged by H.
              Oldfield Box (London: Hodder & Stoughton, 1955), artist unknown.
              Author's collection.

This is a touch misleading: the story here is faithful in almost all particulars to
Dickens, including his ambiguous and largely unromantic ending. It begins much
as the children's radio version does, but omits the reference to gratitude for Joe:
'I Philip Pirrip (Pip for short) never consciously saw my father or mother. And
never, consciously or unconsciously, did I see my five elder brothers who died
in babyhood. I was brought up by my only sister, and her husband, Joe Gargery,
the blacksmith.'[64] It gives full weight to all the characters and episodes in
exactly the order Dickens chose for them, cutting only unnecessary dialogue and
condensing the prose. Even Trabb's boy (so often a victim of cuts) is here, though
his comedic contribution, like all other comic episodes, is condensed: 'Trabb's
boy, seeing me approaching, prostrated himself before me in mock humiliation,

---

[64]   Charles Dickens, *Great Expectations*, abridged by H. Oldfield Box (London, 1955),
p. 9.

which other passers-by found more amusing than I did.'[65] Hodder & Stoughton, clearly targeting young people, thus provided a new generation of readers with truncated Dickens that was nonetheless still dubbed a 'classic', and was on this occasion also sanctioned by Box's association with the BBC as signalled on the book jacket. If unfamiliar with the original, these new readers may never have known the difference; but for them, the 'essence' of *Great Expectations* would be something rather more serious than funny.

The shifting definition of 'Dickensian essence' in the immediate post-war period was grounded in, formed and informed by these discrete and distinct national histories of radio and cinema and their links with contemporary publishing. Like the early Hollywood movie directors, post-war American radio adaptors felt free to take liberties and played up the English/Britishness (the terms are often used interchangeably in this period) *in lieu of* fidelity to the text; the novel's provenance, the accents of the cast and a few direct quotes were deemed 'Dickensian essence' enough. By contrast, the publicly funded British radio versions foreground textual fidelity in the adaptation of classics as part of a commitment to endorsing and inculcating an idealised version of British national identity comprised equally of history, taste and intellect – a 'mission of middle-class enlightenment'.[66] Although Reith left the BBC in 1938, his famous claim that 'few people know what they want and even fewer what they need'[67] informed programming at least until the late 1950s, and while the regular adaptation of favourite early works such as *A Christmas Carol* may have given audiences what they wanted, the late novels were clearly part of what it was thought they needed.

With this in mind, the timings and treatment of the first full British radio dramatizations of *Great Expectations* for general listeners, after years of appearances only in serial 'readings', might be significant. They suggest that these adaptations might have been conceived, at least partly, as a corrective to Lean's interpretation, presumably because it was feared in some quarters that ill-educated listeners might wrongly take it to be accurate and even definitive. The film's reviewers tended to encourage this view. *Variety* called it 'honest, highly effective filming'. The *Hollywood Reporter* deemed the treatment of this 'lesser-known' work 'superb'. 'When the English really want to do one of their own classics', it concluded, 'no-one can beat them at it on the screen.' [68] But Philip Hope-Wallace's characterisation (discussed in Chapter 3) of the typical young British couple as bored by Dickens except for Lean's *Great Expectations* suggests considerable cultural anxiety about the effect of movie versions of classics on the average British intellect. The implication here is that if Lean's film could interest 'Doris and Fred', it couldn't be remotely faithful to Dickens or edifying to the

---

[65]   Oldfield Box edition of *Great Expectations*, p. 117.

[66]   Quoted in Lez Cooke, *British Television Drama: A History* (London, 2003), p. 10.

[67]   Quoted in Cooke, *British Television*, p. 29.

[68]   *Variety*, 26 March 1947, no page number; and The *Hollywood Reporter*, 26 March 1947, no page number. '*Great Expectations* (Eagle Lion, 1945)' clippings file, Margaret Herrick Library, Academy of Motion Picture Arts and Sciences, Los Angeles.

viewer. The BBC seems to have made it an ambition to redress the balance, and the fidelity mission – mediated through emergent new dramatic forms – informed much of what it did for several years to come.

Television Adaptations 1954–2000

The period from the mid-1950s to the late-1990s represents the rise of TV as a major Dickens remediator, and although within this period there were notable disappearances as well as a continued life on British radio (see Appendix C), the TV format certainly helped to keep the novel before the public. The timings of these adaptations (1954, 1959, 1967, 1975, 1981, 1989 and 1999) suggest a possible responsiveness to cycles of economic boom and bust. In 1969, Raymond Williams took another tack, suggesting that this sort of TV programming was simply reflecting a recent critical sea change: 'The shift of critical opinion which has made *Dombey*, *Little Dorrit*, *Great Expectations* and *Our Mutual Friend* the major novels is now at last coming through.'[69] I would add to William's reliance on the influence of critical opinion an acknowledgement among the international TV industries themselves – reinforced by *Great Expectations'* success on radio and film – that it had something to offer to modern audiences. The opinions of powerful literary critics were important to the TV industry, but so were viewing figures and the sometimes complex tensions between these two things have an important bearing on the history of *Great Expectations* on TV.

Sarah Cardwell has offered a persuasive reading of television as different from other adaptation media such as theatre and particularly film. In addition to a historically sensitive approach that sees adaptation as part of a culturally constructed (rather than author-sanctioned) 'ur-text' – something I have likewise tried to do in this book – she suggests that the classic novel adaptation on television is 'sited in a unique and contradictory position'. As she argues: 'On the one hand, it is clear that the programmes' emotive representations of the past and distinctive, filmic, slow-paced style are part of their continuing appeal; on the other, the televisual context in which they are situated is characterised by its emphasis on its contemporaneity, presentness and performativity.'[70] The classic serial is thus defined as much by its juxtaposition with other types of programming as by its internal semiotics. As Cardwell shows through her analysis of *Brideshead Revisited* (UK, Granada, 1981–82), serialisation enables TV to reproduce the languorous feeling associated with reading, something that came to be particularly important to classic novel adaptation and formed a key part of its cultural capital in a context in which TV was still being viewed with suspicion in relation to books.[71] For Cardwell, these serials'

---

[69]   Raymond Williams, 'Television', *The Listener*, Thursday 4 September 1969, p. 322. © Immediate Media Company London Limited.

[70]   Sarah Cardwell, *Adaptation Revisited: Adaptation and the Classic Novel* (Manchester, 2002), pp. 4 and 26.

[71]   Cardwell, *Adaptation Revisited*, p. 112.

'measured pace is defined negatively against youth culture and consumer culture, both of which value speed; classic-novel adaptations thus implicitly reject the new, the young, emphasising their connections with the durable, the old, the past'.[72]

But we also need to see TV as interacting and competing with other media forms besides literature (and itself). A 'text' is constructed in culture to a greater or lesser degree by and through its paratexts, including adaptations, which in *Great Expectations'* case were proliferating once more and engendering a whole new set of meanings for a whole new set of audiences. By the 1950s and 1960s, the text known as 'Charles Dickens's *Great Expectations*' was no longer the serialised unillustrated version its British readers had first been offered, or the comically illustrated serial the first American readers had encountered. Nor was it the teaspoonfuls appearing unannounced in a newspaper, or the illustrated first-volume edition. It was just as likely to be intellectually and emotionally constructed through the memory of David Lean's film, an edition with an explanatory introduction or a preface, the H. Oldfield Box truncated version sanctioned by association with the BBC, a school textbook mediated through classroom guidance, a dramatic short radio performance with adverts, a more textually faithful radio serial, or the cartoons in a newspaper. McFarlane notes the contribution to the novel (the 'hypotext') of the hypertext of Lean's film,[73] but new hypertexts were constantly being provided by all of these other things too.[74] A hundred years after its first publication, for most Anglophone cultures *Great Expectations* was more than just a book; the event created by Dickens in 1860 had garnered hypertextual modifications the moment it was published and it has continued to accrue them ever since.

Elsewhere, Cardwell sets off promisingly down this road when she acknowledges that adaptation is capable of helping to *construct* as well as *reproduce* the 'source' novel's cultural position. She somewhat undermines the potential of this approach, though, by seeing *Brideshead Revisited* as anomalous compared to '*Emma*, *Pride and Prejudice*, *Great Expectations*, and so on', which are, she claims, part of a 'now-established genre', a group of acknowledged screen classics whose exalted ranks *Brideshead*'s serialisation belatedly enabled it to join.[75] The history of *Great Expectations* adaptations we have examined thus far suggests that any claims about their generic stability are unlikely to be accurate. But the claim that hypertexts are more constructive than reflexive of cultural status is an important one; TV adaptations appear to have added several new dimensions to the *Great Expectations* hypertext.

---

[72]   Cardwell, *Adaptation Revisited*, p. 113.

[73]   Gérard Genette defines 'hypotext' as the earlier occurring text in the relationship between Text A ('hypotext') and Text B ('hypertext') through which one informs, but does not necessarily comment on, the other. In this model, translations, adaptations, spoofs and spin-offs are all hypertexts. Genette, *Palimpsests: Literature in the Second Degree* (Lincoln, 1997), p. 5. The important addition subsequent scholarship has made to Genette's model is to see the hypotext as a culturally constructed but unstable demagogue, subject to changes in critical fashion.

[74]   McFarlane, *Screen Adaptations*, p. 73.

[75]   Cardwell, *Adaptation Revisited*, p. 109.

As Robert Giddings and Keith Selby have pointed out, early television drama drew much of its audience and its stars, as well as its proven successful scheduling slots, from experience gained in radio and film. In Britain the Sunday teatime serial, established on radio in the 1930s, continued to be a staple of family viewing on TV.[76] In the USA, cross-media cooperation is equally apparent. The first TV adaptation of *Great Expectations*, a black-and-white version in two parts, starred Roddy McDowall as the adult Pip and appeared on 'Robert Montgomery Presents' (NBC, June 1954). As a child McDowall had become a star and garnered critical acclaim through his performances in sentimental films such as *How Green Was My Valley* (1941), *My Friend Flicka* (1943) and *Lassie Come Home* (1943), but in the 1950s he temporarily retired from films to concentrate on the theatre and TV. His stint with Robert Montgomery, beginning in 1951, marked his TV debut and a transition from child to adult roles onscreen. The Pip role was thus a good choice: the 26-year-old McDowall combines wistful English boyishness with Broadway credentials as a serious adult actor, giving an effective performance of adolescent angst moving through confused ambition to mature self-awareness. Like Lean's film, this version opens with a shot of the book to remind us of the story's provenance and, like Lean, director Norman Felton chooses to end it with Pip tearing down the curtains to let the sunlight in on Estella sitting alone in 'Havisham House'. But there are crucial differences, most obviously the focus on Pip's motivations as admirable rather than misguided. In this version, he visits 'Havisham House' after he meets Magwitch but *before* he takes the stolen food to him on the marsh, and his harsh treatment by his prejudiced social betters in the Havisham House scene is heavily emphasised. Estella haughtily questions Miss Havisham's instructions to offer food to this common labouring boy, for example, but Miss Havisham insists with the explanation, 'You would feed a dog, wouldn't you?' That night Pip has a protracted conversation with the convict in which he admits his desire to be educated for a gentleman, a sentiment with which we can wholeheartedly sympathise having witnessed how the lower orders are treated, while for his part Magwitch warns him to stay out of prison and admits that a woman caused his own downfall. There is thus a strong bond forged early on between a kindly child and a fallible man, both mistreated by a cruel social system underpinned by emotional exploitation, particularly by women. Pip is even comfortable enough with the convict to offer to help file off his shackles.

The overriding theme in this version, reflecting a prevailing mood in booming, anti-European post-war America, is one of the squandering of talent by a stagnant class system which equates criminality with the lower orders while sanctioning it in the élite. Pip is a clear victim of this system: his intelligence and his affectionate, honourable qualities are innate, rather than learned. In examining Pip's handwriting, for example, Joe soliloquises that he has seen worse writing done by gentlemen, and wonders aloud whether someone who can write so fine a hand could ever be happy being a blacksmith. Likewise, Miss Havisham's 'Love her!' speech is also done as a soliloquy, ending softly with a reflection on Pip's

---

[76]   Robert Giddings and Keith Selby, *The Classic Serial*, p. 11.

unselfish nature: 'Love her, Pip; even you, who never asked for anything.' Pip is briefly shocked that he has abandoned his family to satisfy 'the crazed ambitions of a convict', yet his compassion for Magwitch – forged in that second meeting – is genuine and quickly reasserted; on the convict's deathbed he murmurs, 'Be merciful to him.' Then, after a pause, he adds, 'A sinner?' and shakes his head emphatically in the negative. In this version, Pip's pride is only skin-deep and soon overcome. The final scene is conventionally romantic; Pip and Estella get together over her assurance: 'Love, Pip, is greater than great expectations.' But it is underpinned by two hours of TV in which ambition has been thwarted but not condemned: in this version Estella's love is figured as Pip's just reward for harbouring honest ambition when European social mores were against him.

The adaptation history of *Great Expectations* in some ways demonstrates in microcosm the variety and particularity of individual media responses to twentieth-century sexual politics. The role of Miss Havisham has become, arguably since Martita Hunt's performance on stage and afterwards on screen, a powerful and challenging professional attraction for female performers which, while it was to achieve its apotheosis on the twentieth-century stage, also informed TV and film casting. The 71-year-old Estelle Winwood's gaunt, scarecrow-like Miss Havisham in the 1954 version is as powerful in its way as Martita Hunt's, bringing with it the memory of her many TV 'character' roles since the 1940s and her reputation as a theatre star. Her regret is genuinely moving as she weeps on Pip's sympathetic shoulder following Estella's abandonment, the image of aristocratic dissipation having come to a sticky end. She was one among several memorable Miss Havishams in this post-Lean period, part of a new commitment to the centrality to this story of female performances which have subtly – and sometimes radically – altered its politics.

Similarly, while Magwitch had always been a draw for theatre and film performers, the other male 'character' roles of Jaggers and Joe have experienced upturns of fortune onscreen since the appearance of Francis L. Sullivan, and these newly spotlit characters draw renewed attention to the novel's often previously neglected theme of official versus unofficial forms of justice. The part of Estella, however, seems to have proved harder to cast and handle effectively. In this 1954 NBC version the part went to Nina Reader, a young unknown. She does a passable job given the limitations of a script which requires her to be little more than a romantic prize for Pip and to realise his value (and her own feelings) when she learns in the nick of time during her elopement with Drummle that he has revealed Magwitch's whereabouts to the police. But the role did not launch Reader in other classic leads. Her TV roles after this were supporting ones in soap operas.

This was not unusual. In the hands of scriptwriters in the often still-conservative medium of the classic TV serial (traditionally 'family' viewing), the romantic heroine's role has often tended to be written as a retrogressive one. Producers have seemed happy enough to give an older woman free histrionic reign and allow her body to show the ravages of pain and time (indeed, the role of Miss Havisham is one of the few good ones available for older actresses outside of Shakespeare).

But they have been afraid to tamper with the conservative function of young, white, middle-class females in the mainstream media, which is to be attractive, compliant, and thus deserving of a fairy-tale heterosexual ending. Few Estellas in TV and film *appear* 'bent and broken … into a better shape'. The capitulation to patriarchy is seldom written on Estella's body; it is usually just signalled through her clothes, as she swaps ball gowns for widow's weeds. Through this physical coding we understand why Pip has always loved her, and why he is happy to take her back: she is still beautiful.

There is, though, one notable exception: Hugh Leonard's 1967 BBC version chooses Dickens's original 'unhappy' ending, and has Estella (Francesca Annis) bump into Pip (Gary Bond) and Young Pip in a London museum after a separation of several years. The camera gives us a long close-up of Estella's pale, drawn, aged (that is, unmade-up) face and the dark shadows under her eyes, while she tells Pip of her second marriage to the Shropshire doctor. But this 'faithfulness' to the first Dickens ending is largely in the service of emotional closure for Pip. After Estella kisses Young Pip on the cheek and they all go their separate ways, the director departs from Dickens and has her gazing wistfully after the two Pips as they walk away.[77] Estella has been humbled, but Pip – his expression thoughtful and a touch smug rather than regretful – has become a 'catch'; the closure is his victory, not his punishment. A particularly unpleasant and arrogant Pip in Bond's hands, he seems to have learned nothing by the final episode except that those who are cruel to him will end badly.

On the whole, despite Lean's innovations, it has taken far longer for film and TV adaptations to depart from Dickens's monochromatic Estella than it has taken their counterparts on the stage and in literature. This might seem natural to us now; in the twenty-first century, literary novels and serious plays are considered middle to highbrow media in which readers and audiences accept, expect and even demand more innovative and politically challenging aesthetics. But this position in some ways represents a reversal of the novel's and the theatre's cultural status for much of the nineteenth century, when both often struggled for respectability. The arrival of new contenders helps to consecrate the older forms and this is true even within a particular medium, as the arrival of commercial television was to prove for the BBC in Britain. It is also true in terms of international competition: in the 1950s and 1960s the BBC explicitly styled itself in terms of its opposition to the 'vulgarity' of American commercial radio and TV, as well as to the 'vulgar' commercial channels available in the UK. Dickens – coded quintessentially English, morally unobjectionable and intellectually beneficial on both sides of the Atlantic, largely through his appropriation for purposes of self-consecration by film directors and radio programmers – played a key part in these battles.

The BBC first adapted *Great Expectations* for TV in 1959.[78] It is described by Giddings and Selby as 'one of the best early BBC television serials', and they

---

[77]	Interestingly, this lingering look is not in the script. TV Drama Scripts: Great Expectations 1967, Films 147–8 (Gi – He), BBC Written Archives Centre.

[78]	Available to view by appointment at the British Film Institute, London.

quote adaptor P.D. Cummins defending her creative decisions in terms of keeping the serial 'faithful to the spirit of Dickens'.[79] The spirit, perhaps (whatever that means), but not quite the letter; there are some interesting creative departures in this version. But it is equally interesting that these engendered no complaints about lack of fidelity. *The Listener*'s Irving Wardle, for example, wrote that the repetition of the series after its first run was 'amply justified; Colin Jeavins's rueful, bouncing Herbert Pocket, in particular, is one of the best Dickens performances television has had'.[80] The *Dickensian* also thought it 'the most satisfactory adaptation of Dickens we have had in any theatrical or film medium', and was pleased to report that – true to Dickens's long-established role as an ambassador for Englishness – 'it may get a showing in other countries'.[81] I have found no proof that it was ever screened overseas, but it does seem to have been a successful adaptation at home. It attracted a ten per cent national audience share, equal to ITV's in this period, and the first episode gained a positive 'Reaction Index' of 75 per cent (well above the 67 per cent average for most Children's TV) in the BBC's Audience Research Report based on its regular survey of listening and viewing.[82] The series maintained this good rating, too, achieving a 74 per cent average overall.[83]

This is unsurprising: the drama is striking and effective even now. Colin Spaull is a cutely awkward and unselfconscious young Pip in his confused responses to the story's repeated injustices, and Jerold Wells is a touching as well as menacing Magwitch. Strong parallels are drawn between the two characters; in the first episode we cut back and forth between Pip tossing restlessly in his little bed with Magwitch's threats ringing in his ears, and Magwitch plaintively protesting his innocence as he tries to sleep on the frozen churchyard ground. The doubling appears again later with different results in Episode 3, as Pip tosses in his bed hearing Estella's voice alternately taunting and flirting with him; here we begin to recognise the parallels between Pip's two tormentors which will later be revealed as blood-ties. This version foregrounds Miss Havisham's cruel manipulation of both Pip and Estella, lingering on a shot of her wizened hand deliberately knocking over one of Pip's abandoned chess pieces after he's been sent home, while Estella laughs cruelly off-screen. It also makes a great deal more of Orlick than most others, making him older and more threatening towards Mrs Joe and thus providing both a suitable dark double for Pip and a ramping up of the general villainy. Biddy and Joe marry early on, united as the perfect happy couple whose

---

[79]　Giddings and Selby, *The Classic Serial*, p. 20. These authors claim Cummins is male, but a closer contemporary, 'J.G.,' writing in the *Dickensian* in 1959, calls the adaptor 'Miss P.D. Cummins'.

[80]　Irving Wardle, 'Critic on the Hearth', *The Listener*, Thursday 19 May 1960, p. 899. © Immediate Media Company London Limited.

[81]　J.G., '*Great Expectations* realised', *Dickensian*, 60 (September 1959): p. 139.

[82]　Audience Research Report for *Great Expectations* 1959, Episode 1, 23 April 1959, BBC Written Archives Centre.

[83]　Audience Research Report for *Great Expectations* 1967, Episode 1, 20 February 1967, BBC Written Archives Centre.

function, rather than to disappoint Pip, is to represent unflinching love, truth and goodness. After Pip's downfall and promise to pay Joe back, Biddy muses: 'He has learned his lesson – and is a real gentleman now.'

Overall, this version focusses most closely on the abuse and manipulation of a child and its psychological consequences. To this end, the denouement departs from all previous versions in its treatment of Dickens's ambiguous ending. It reveals that Pip has been telling his story retrospectively to his godson, Young Pip, outside Satis House, and when he gets to the final parting from Estella the child asks: 'Can't you make it a happier ending?' Older Pip hugs him and then obligingly goes into the overgrown garden – and there finds Estella. They are romantically reunited in a scene which could easily be either fantasy or reality, but which signals above all the unreliability of the narrator of these traumatic events. The adaptation's disconcerting qualities seem to have worked: some younger audience members allegedly had to 'hide their eyes at some parts', but most of the adults and children surveyed responded enthusiastically nonetheless – fear, of course, being part of the pleasure of a good mystery.[84]

Alan Bridges's 1967 adaptation, which also aired in the Sunday classic serial slot, took a different approach. Bryan McFarlane remembers that the opening 'closely mirrored Lean's',[85] and *The Listener* also compared it to Lean and liked it a lot less as a result:

> *Great Expectations*, the BBC 1 Sunday Serial, suffers because of our lively memory of the David Lean film. It is slow, there is too much walking from A to B, there is an irrelevant tone of menace which the music gladly, and exclusively, exploits. But the accents are right, and the eye for detail is very sharp (some of us do look for this).[86]

The emphasis on period accuracy is significant in terms of the history of Dickens adaptations on TV, but equally important are the references here to the pace and tone.

According to Cooke, the production of television period drama had lagged behind in the UK in the 1940s, but after 1950 it became an important part of the BBC's new-look programming in response to an increase in the number of TV owners, a new Head of Drama, a new spirit of innovation which sought to move televised drama away from the 'filmed theatre' look of earlier dramatic productions, and a new spirit of competition, spurred on by the advent of commercial TV in 1955.[87] As a result, while early TV had emulated radio's proven formats and successes, by the late 1950s and early 1960s there was a new zeitgeist altogether

---

[84]   Audience Research Report for Great Expectations 1959, Episode 1, 23 April 1959, BBC Written Archives Centre.

[85]   McFarlane, *Screen Adaptations*, p. 65.

[86]   Anthony Burgess, 'Television', *The Listener*, Thursday 9 February 1967, p. 207. © Immediate Media Company London Limited.

[87]   Cooke, *British Television*, pp. 17–29.

at the BBC; the 1959 version was probably part of a general expectation that TV could – and should – translate classics differently from radio. It is certainly in marked contrast to the dutiful audio versions in this period.

By 1967, the innovations were burgeoning. Alan Bridges's version was surrounded on TV by realist drama such as the BBC's acclaimed *Cathy Come Home* (1966), and by gritty crime shows and science fiction and fantasy programmes (some now in colour). The preproduction promotion material explicitly references *Great Expectations*' relevance both to modern audiences and to modern realist dramatic modes, particularly theatrical ones:

> It is a study in human weakness and human surrender. It describes how easily a
> free lad of fresh and decent instincts can be made to care more for rank and pride
> and degrees of our own stratified society than for old affection and honours. It
> is thus remarkably fresh and modern, and shows how little human instincts,
> ambitions and society have changed. Such modern plays as Osborne's 'Epitaph
> for George Dillon', Wesker's 'Poots' and Joe Orton's 'Loot' are all plays on the
> same theme as Great Expectations.[88]

By these measures – and in Sarah Cardwell's model – this slow-paced, darkly serious realist treatment should have been a winner. But there was a new type of adaptation in town, exemplified by the BBC's lavish serialisation of John Galsworthy's *The Forsyte Saga* (BBC2, Saturday evenings, 26 episodes between 7 January and 1 July 1967, repeated Sunday evenings on BBC1 in 1968). This series was the BBC's most successful yet, costing £250,000 to make and gaining an audience of over 165 million in 45 countries.[89] Despite its period fidelity, Bridges's 1967 *Great Expectations* with its modest budget of just under £28,000 could not compete.[90] The episodes ran concurrently with those of *The Forsyte Saga* for some weeks, and the differences between them must have been palpable; a *Great Expectations* taking realism to these lengths is tame stuff compared to Galsworthy's family saga filled with allusions to illicit sex, and with much more dramatic representations of ostentatious new wealth and sudden bankruptcy.

Bridges's version consists of unnecessarily long takes, pervasive moody music, the injudicious use of a corpse on a gibbet (which engendered outraged letters from several viewers who claimed their children had been terrified by the sight[91]), and gloomy chiaroscuro lighting which makes no dramatic distinctions between the marshes, the forge, Satis House and London. It starred some known names including, as we have seen, the theatre actor Gary Bond who also had an onscreen

---

[88]   Promotion material, 'Great Expectations 1967: general' file, T5/1, 448/1, BBC Written Archives Centre.

[89]   Cooke, *British Television*, pp. 83–4.

[90]   Total budget sheet, 'Great Expectations 1967: general' file, T5/1, 448/1, BBC Written Archives Centre.

[91]   Correspondence between viewers and BBC producer Campbell Logan, 'Great Expectations 1967: general' file, T5/1, 448/1, BBC Written Archives Centre.

period pedigree, having recently appeared in Granada TV's 1963 adaptation of *War and Peace* and the successful 1964 film *Zulu*. Maxine Audley, who played Miss Havisham, was also (true to now traditional screen-Havisham history) an established theatre actress. In light of the rise of Miss Havisham as a dramatic icon, it is significant also that she was the production's most highly paid artist, in contrast to the salary and billing hierarchy prevalent in the 1930s which privileged the role of Magwitch.[92]

But the script took an irredeemably dark view of the novel. Pip is deeply unlikeable as both child and adult (he is, for example, contemptuous of Joe's ignorance even before he visits Satis House), the pervasive menacing tone is narratively meaningless, and the final resolution – the use of broken Estella to salvage Pip's ego as previously discussed – borders on misogyny. That may have been the point, though the idea that this adaptation works as a critique of Victorian patriarchy would be hard to prove. Overall, through its deliberate and cinematically self-indulgent realism, this version presents Victorian Britain as relentlessly dark, cold, cruel and hopeless; it is kitchen-sink Dickens. Audiences were less enthusiastic than they had been in 1959; several reviewers including the *Western Daily Press* felt that it was 'slow-moving',[93] a number of viewers wrote in to complain about the downbeat ending (which, interestingly, they all failed to recognise as based on Dickens's original) as well as the frightening gibbet,[94] and while the first episode attracted 14.7 per cent of the national audience (compared to ITV's average of 15.8 per cent), this had dropped slightly by the final episode to 9.8 per cent. The average 'Reaction Index' for all 10 episodes was 69, 5 per cent down on the 1959 version's score.[95]

Why film the novel like this? If competition for viewers was not its motive (and why should the BBC compete with itself?), we must look elsewhere for an explanation. The attempt to emulate a previous Dickens success was the initial motive for a new dramatization, the publicity material for this version using this as its main selling point: 'Great Expectations ranks equally in popularity with David Copperfield, which was viewed last year on Sundays at 5.30pm by an average of nearly 11 million each week.'[96] We should note here in passing the change in the novel's perceived popularity status by this period. But a comparison with contemporaneous radio versions provides clues about the possible reasoning behind the dramatic mode selected for this particular TV version. On radio, *Great*

---

[92]   Artists' contracted and actual per-episode fees appear in the weekly episode files for 'Great Expectations 1967.'

[93]   TV Weekly Programme Review Meeting, 29 Mar 1967, BBC Written Archives Centre.

[94]   Correspondence between viewers and BBC producer Campbell Logan, 'Great Expectations 1967: general' file, T5/1, 448/1, BBC Written Archives Centre.

[95]   Audience Research Report, 2 May 1967, T5/1, 453/1, BBC Written Archives Centre.

[96]   Promotion material, 'Great Expectations 1967: general' file, T5/1, 448/1, BBC Written Archives Centre.

Expectations was still being featured in the old fidelity format for schools and on programmes like *Storytime* and *Book at Bedtime* (1965, 1966, 1972 and 1975). Donald Bancroft's 1966 adaptation for the latter is a case in point. The script reveals that this was a solemn, faithful version, complete with (understandably somewhat trimmed) Dickensian prose, plenty of Dickens's own dialogue (with only the occasional modernisation), and Dickens's own revised 'happy' ending.[97] Subsequent repeats of sections of this version were broadcast for schools in 'Listening and Writing' slots over the next two years; evidently the dual education/ entertainment mission was still an important part of the classic serial remit on radio. The emphasis on this as a 'story' or a 'book' and radio as the best medium for its faithful translation may have been intended to counter the perceived evils of the new challenger – television – for those who deplored its advent and worried about its long-term effects. But the competition for cultural capital clearly existed *within* particular media forms as well as *between* them: Dickens seems to have fulfilled a need for 'morally improving' and socially aware television in the 1960s as a countermeasure to the more racy fare such as *Forsyte* demanded by TV audiences. If, as Cardwell suggests, classic serials generally present themselves as intrinsically worthy through their opposition to fast-paced youth culture and their languorous emulation of the act of reading, Dickens shot like a gritty documentary has worthiness in spades.

The difference between TV, stage and film treatments of Dickens was brought home in 1968 by the transference to film of the 1960 Lionel Bart musical *Oliver!*, which ushered in a whole new era of Dickens in adaptation. *Great Expectations* almost made it into musical film in this period. Throughout 1967–69, songwriting duo André and Dory Previn were in discussion with National General Productions (and later with Boardwalk Productions) about a musical version to be written by the TV playwright Tad Mosel (a veteran writer for PBS TV), directed by Robert Mulligan and produced by Alan J. Pakula, the team that had directed and produced the Oscar-winning *To Kill A Mockingbird* in 1962. Sums of money changed hands, various agreements were signed, the script and the songs were written, but in the end the project fell through for undisclosed reasons, possibly to do with National General Productions pulling out.[98] The history of Dickens in adaptation might have been very different.

Joseph Hardy's 1974 made-for-TV movie, the first adaptation in colour, arrived in this changing field. Perhaps aiming to fill the gap left by the ill-fated Previn film, it was originally made as a musical, though it is less clear why the songs were removed at the last minute. It was not a critical success, despite an all-star cast of established transatlantic film stars including James Mason, Anthony

---

[97] Radio Talks Scripts Pre-1970, Gray-Greet, T188, BBC Written Archives Centre.

[98] *Great Expectations* script, 25 April 1929, f. 927. Also miscellaneous letters between various law firms, National General Productions and William Morris Agency, April–May 1967, and agreement between NGP and WMA, 14 Feb 1968, Alan J. Pakula Papers, f.928 and f. 929, Margaret Herrick Library, Academy of Motion Picture Arts and Sciences, Los Angeles.

Quayle and Robert Morley and the useful addition of a score by Maurice Jarre, who had previously worked for Lean. It was nominated for (though failed to win) a Golden Prize at the Moscow International Film Festival of 1975, and it seems significant that the eventual winner was *The Promised Land* directed by Andrzej Wajda (Film Polsky/Zespól Filmowy X, 1975), a Polish film about the struggles of three men – a Pole, a German and a Jew – to build a factory in the cut-throat world of nineteenth-century capitalism. This film explicitly referred to the civil unrest that exploded in Poland during the 1970s; Hardy's *Great Expectations* clearly did not have the requisite anti-capitalist message for Soviet-era Moscow. As Chapter 5 will demonstrate, this was neither the first nor the last time that the novel missed the mark with Communist audiences.

The lukewarm reception extended to Hardy's film in the West might have other causes, however. There is something deeply conservative about this production given the turbulent political and media worlds into which it emerged. Michael York, like Gary Bond, seems to have been chosen for his looks as much as his onscreen pedigree (he had acted in Shakespeare in the 1960s and 1970s, as well as playing the role of Jolly Forsyte in the hit TV series *The Forsyte Saga* in 1967), but his trademark androgyny and educated accent make him far more convincing as a gentleman than as a blacksmith. The 33-year-old Sarah Miles's casting as both the young and the older Estella is even less explicable. She had a reputation for raw onscreen sexuality, but the script permits none of it; the scene at the end in which she reveals her long-hidden love to Pip is even more unconvincing here than it had been in 1871 and 1934.

The Listener's critic, seeing the film at the cinema (where it was screened in the UK), was thoroughly unconvinced:

> *Great Expectations* (Odeon, Marble Arch) is a misnomer on a giant scale. Everything is wrong about it, with a sort of inspired, dedicated attention to wrongness that in itself is breathtaking. Infected by the incompetence all round, even veteran ace cameraman Freddie Young goes over the top, lighting the inside of every jug and bottle, and throwing pups up every nostril. Miss Havisham's eerie sepulchre is as bright as a ballroom. Great swathes have been carved out of the plot, and what remains lacks flavour, suspense, accuracy and, most important of all, the gravity that makes this one of Dickens's most serious treatments of class, crime and moral culpability. Only Anthony Quayle catches anything of Dickens in his Jaggers.[99]

The charge that the film lacks 'gravity' as a result of its neglect of the novel's 'serious treatments of class, crime and moral culpability' is indicative of the shift in cultural and critical perceptions about Dickens's intentions which was simultaneously producing (or perhaps had been at least partially produced by) its gritty realist treatment on TV. But it also draws attention to the prevailing climate in mid-1970s Britain in which, as Lez Cooke has expressed it, 'the social

---

[99]   Gavin Millar, 'Gags and Knickers', *The Listener*, Thursday 22 January 1976, p. 88. © Immediate Media Company London Limited.

consensus and economic stability of the post-war period began to break down' and period drama provided 'opportunities to draw historical parallels between past and present'.[100] Hardy's adaptation, cast for sex appeal which the script refuses to fulfil and treated with a sort of cinematic insouciance, fails miserably on this score. But then, this version had been charged with the difficult task of appealing to what we now know were, historically speaking, two very different audiences for Dickens (American and British) in two quite distinct media (TV and film), and it had also ended up changing genres in the cutting room. The compromises did it no favours.

Julian Aymes's 1981 serialisation of *Great Expectations* struggled to make creative headway against the trend for more cheerful Dickens on film and sexier classics adaptations on TV, while trying to hang onto the self-constructed 'worthy Dickens' badge.[101] It is described by McFarlane as 'a leisurely, well-crafted version', and he rightly draws attention to the stellar performances and the small but significant innovations, including 'a strong emphasis on the concept of what may shape the futures of young men in different circumstances'.[102] Deferential fidelity was, however, its overriding principle; the pathos and the comedy are there, but the dialogue is so ponderously faithful to the novel that it becomes tedious onscreen and, viewed from the other side of the ground breaking Andrew Davies adaptations of the 1990s and 2000s – *Middlemarch* (1994), *Pride and Prejudice* (1995), *Moll Flanders* (1996), *Vanity Fair* (1998), *Bleak House* (2005) and *Little Dorrit* (2008) – the deference seems pointless, and is only explicable if we place it in the context of what Dickens represented for British programme makers in this period. Aymes's version was competing directly with ITV's equally leisurely but much more decadent and sumptuous (and multiple award-winning) adaptation of *Brideshead Revisited*, which premiered in the UK on 12 Oct 1981, just a week after the first episode of *Great Expectations*. There seems to have been an enduring assumption in the BBC at this time that while sex, intrigue, glamorous international locations and vicarious conspicuous consumption had their place, British audiences needed a regular dose of historically grounded 'English' literary realism to keep them rooted, and Dickens was the man for the job. The Weekly Programme Review reports consistently praise the adaptation's 'sense of period' and fidelity to the novel, one even commenting that the Director 'had been taking on David Lean and winning'.[103] The subtext here is that beating Lean was more about textual authenticity than audience figures; it was intended to be a cultural as much as a financial victory.

The 1989/91 mini-series directed by Kevin Connor might be significant not only for its locations in Kent, but also for being the second adaptation to appear in this famously economically challenging decade. As Robert Douglas-Fairhurst

---

[100]   Cooke, *British Television*, pp. 90–91.

[101]   On the back of successes *Oliver!* (1968) and *The Stingiest Man in Town* (1978), this decade created both *Mickey's Christmas Carol* (1983) and *Scrooged* (1988).

[102]   McFarlane, *Screen Adaptations*, pp. 65–8.

[103]   Programme Review Reports, 'Great Expectations 1981', 21 October 1981 – 23 December 1981, BBC Written Archives Centre.

put it: 'In the 1980s this story of class mobility and get-rich-quick ambition resonated with all the force of a modern parable.'[104] The decade certainly produced a rash of stage productions. This version is, however, probably more significant still when considered relationally. Being a well-funded UK/USA (HTV/Disney) coproduction aimed at family audiences, it sticks closely to the plot but deviates considerably from the BBC's darkly solemn renditions to the extent of adding pirates, chase scenes, Christmas carols, rosy-cheeked village children, callous redcoats, jolly locals, bucolic scenery and pathetic fallacy aplenty. The only things missing here are the hum-along songs; this sets out to be an entertaining rather than educative view of Dickens, more reminiscent of *Oliver!* than the BBC.

But the more serious additions are interesting. Pip and Herbert go to India, not Egypt. Perhaps to American producers, India – a safely historically distant, ex-British colony – seemed an innocuous option compared to Egypt, which was at this time an uneasy American ally following the rise to power of Mubarak, the Iran-Iraq war, and a long history of Palestinian sympathies. Or perhaps it was simply felt that India had a less ambiguous and more easily recognisable link with Britain's imperial past. The moral 'message' is very clear in this version: Pip is angry that Joe has paid his debts and continues to call him 'Sir', raging to Biddy: 'How could he put me in this position?' Biddy – pretty, intelligent, loyal and a genuine romantic contender in this version – demands of him in return: 'Is there no end to your self-pity?' Later, a slow-motion shot of Pip's face under falling confetti as he discovers he has lost Biddy to Joe hammers home the 'count your blessings' and 'bird in the hand' themes. When he bumps into Estella in the churchyard where the story began, they walk away together as self-declared 'friends' with no confirmation that they will ever be anything more. The sense of the dashing of aspirational middle-class hopes is palpable in this version. But alongside this warning, the happy nuptials of Joe, Biddy, Wemmick and Miss Skiffins and the Disney jollity of its minor characters provide an undeniable feel-good factor.

The 1999 TV-movie adaptation by Tony Marchant sums up the rapid changes that took place during this decade, largely spearheaded by Andrew Davies and the BBC. It has tremendous creative energy, constructed largely through the creator's decision to play with Dickens's sequence of events.[105] Ioan Gruffudd brings with him the resonance of his then ongoing heroic role as Horatio in *Hornblower* (1998–2003), while Justine Waddell (Estella) was already an established adaptation star, having recently appeared in *Tess of the D'Urbervilles* (1997) and *Anna Karenina* (1998). The ending sees them playing cards together as friends: Pip has not only lost out romantically, but also socially. As McFarlane notes, 'There is no sense that the old confining class barriers have been torn down ... What angered Dickens, seemed hopeful to Lean in 1946, now seems to be a matter of atrophy to Jarrold and Marchant in 1999.'[106] Nonetheless, through a combination of script,

---

[104] Robert Douglas-Fairhurst, 'Among the Greats', *Guardian Review*, 29 September 2011, p. 6.

[105] See McFarlane's astute analysis of this version in *Screen Adaptations*, pp. 72–81.

[106] McFarlane, *Screen Adaptations*, p. 81.

cinematography and performance styles, and following hard on the heels of Alfonso Cuarón's star-studded, sexy and playful 1998 recasting of the story in contemporary Florida, this version helps to jettison 30 years of worthy British televisual reverence.

Stage Adaptations Since 1946

By comparison with even the most recent TV adaptations, most professional stage versions have been energetic in their creative reconstruction of 'Dickensian essence', drawing very different things out of the novel; ever since Guinness, *Great Expectations* for playwrights has meant the opportunity to take liberties. As a result, not only were revivals of Guinness's version steady between 1943 and 1980, but new adaptations emerged on a regular basis, particularly after the radical transformation of British theatre in the 1950s and 1960s. This is generally acknowledged to have begun with the Royal Court's season of new plays by Beckett, Osborne and others under director George Devine in the 1950s, but it gathered speed when a Royal charter was granted to the Shakespeare Memorial Theatre in 1961, a National Theatre was established in 1963, and the stifling powers of censorship that had been granted to the Lord Chamberlain in the eighteenth century were finally abolished in 1968. Yet *Great Expectations* has never, to my knowledge, been performed at the National Theatre and has only recently been performed by the Royal Shakespeare Company, despite the resounding success of the RSC's 10-hour West End production of *Nicholas Nickleby* in 1980. *Great Expectations* continues to occupy a curious place in the history of theatre, still often dependent on the enthusiasm of individuals. Overall, its life onstage has overwhelmingly been a story of regional, touring, and bold but relatively short-lived one-off productions, and it has been considerably more popular in Britain than the USA (see Appendix C).

Like most other Dickens novels apart from *Oliver Twist*, *Great Expectations* has proved resistant to adaptation of the big, popular (and particularly filmed) musical variety. A few musical versions have been staged with some success – notably Margaret Hoorneman's (1980, reprised 2008 and 2011) in the USA[107], and in Britain, Hal Shaper and Trevor Preston's 1975 version starring a 70-year-old John Mills, which won an Ivor Novello Award for Best British Musical. Mike Read's (1993) and Tim Baker's (2009) were also moderate successes in Britain, but none have had the impact of *Oliver!*, and *Great Expectations* has never appeared on Broadway. Professional stage adaptations in the USA were generally rare until the 1970s when an operatic version, 'Miss Havisham's Fire', appeared. [108] Rewritten as 'Miss Havisham's Wedding Night' and relaunched in 1981, they

---

[107] Reviews for the LA production are available at http://www.greatexpectationsmusical. com/press.html.

[108] No entries for *Great Expectations* appear in the *Encyclopaedia of the American Stage*, ed. Samuel L. Leiter and Holly Hill (Westport, CT and London, 1985) in the period 1940–60.

are both described by David Haldane-Lawrence as unsuccessful.[109] The financial crisis of the 1980s seemed the ideal moment for a renaissance; Barbara Field's 'straight' 1982 version was reprised and toured several times during this decade. In this period, too, the producer of another planned (though unrealised) American musical version, David Singer, explained his interest in the novel explicitly in terms of its cultural relevance: 'It's about a man who becomes happy after he loses his fortune. If this isn't a story for the 1980s, I don't know what is.'[110] However topical the story and however stellar the proposed creative team (Peter Coe, director of the original *Oliver!*, was set to direct, and Jane Seymour had been offered the lead), ironically enough it seems to have been a victim of the financial crisis. This was the third time a big musical version was planned and failed to find favour; this musical, adapted by Margaret Hoorneman, had been staged by the Pennsylvania Theatre Company in 1980 (where Singer had seen it), but it did not find critical favour: *Variety* called it a 'disappointment',[111] and in the end Singer's attempt to raise the necessary $1.5 million to take the show to Broadway failed.[112]

The archives give no clue as to a reason, but one plausible explanation might be the novel's uneven history in the popularity stakes, reinforced by its Lean-inflected cultural position in this period as straight realism from Dickens's 'darker' period. The comparative gloominess is insufficient explanation in itself: *Les Misérables*, Victor Hugo's far darker novel (1862), was a musical stage hit in this same period, premiering in 1980, and it continues to attract enthusiastic audiences to this day. (Interestingly, its original adaptor, Alain Boublil, had had the idea while watching *Oliver!*[113]) But *Great Expectations'* less-than epic scale, its interiority, its down-beat conclusion and its uncomfortable relevance to modern problems probably militated against easy conversion into big-stage musical form. The accepted view of it – thanks to Lean and all the respectful radio and TV versions since – was unlikely to encourage a light musical touch of the *Oliver!* kind. As a press release for the 2011 revival of Hoorneman's musical in Utah puts it: 'Despite the novel's elaborate detail, in the course of trial and adaptation, artistic collaborators found *Great Expectations* to be introspective, personal, and really very intimate. They decided "a sprawling, grand production would not serve the story as much as an intimate production."'[114]

The perception that *Great Expectations* was different seems to have been well established by this time. In reviewing *Oliver!* in 1960, critics had worried about it inspiring spin-off musical productions of other Dickens novels. As S.A. Weltman

[109] David Haldane-Lawrence, 'Charles Dickens and the World of Opera', *Dickensian*, 107 (Spring 2011): pp. 17–18.

[110] Carol Lawson, 'News of the Theatre', *New York Times*, 22 April 1981, p. 19.

[111] *Variety*, 24 December 1980, p. 66.

[112] *Women's Wear Daily*, Monday 15 June, 1981, p. 20.

[113] Edward Behr, *The Complete Book of Les Misérables* (New York, 1989), p. 50.

[114] Heidi Masden, 'Adaptation Still Seems Strangely Misunderstood', Utah Shakespeare Festival website (http://www.bard.org/education/studyguides/greatexpect/greatadapt.html).

has noted, the *Evening Standard*'s influential critic, Milton Shuman, 'imagined being called upon to review "The Pickwick Capers" or "Miss Havisham Misses a Wedding" while Kenneth Tynan of the *Observer* predicted *David! Great!* and *Bleak!*'[115] While the sniffiness over a mere musical might be typical of these British critics (though he claimed to speak for the 'common man', Shulman was notoriously anti-Hollywood and exclusively West End, and Tynan was a devotee of realism and was in this period enthusiastically championing Angry Young Man theatre), it seems significant that both used *Great Expectations* as an example of the pale beyond which Dickens musicals should not go. He was a valuable heritage commodity and his late novels, in particular, had been instrumental in rescuing his critical reputation. Musical versions threatened that hard-won status. As Weltman has pointed out: 'There is a sense in which – particularly for a twentieth- or twenty-first-century American – Victorian simply means Dickensian, and Dickensian means *Oliver!*'[116] This was not intended as a compliment.

But Weltman also explains *Oliver!*'s success in terms of its cross-class appeal, related to its generic modes: 'Although the genre of Broadway or West End musical theatre is both middle class and middlebrow, both the novel and this musical are associated with melodrama, which is of course a working-class genre.'[117] As we saw through the struggles (and failures) of nineteenth-century adaptors to make *Great Expectations* fit the requirements of both 'respectable' theatre and crowd-pleasing melodrama, it is not a novel which lends itself easily to generic hybridity onstage. Hence, possibly, the overwhelming emphasis in modern theatrical adaptations on innovations that foreground serious contemporary concerns: the gothic, the psychological, the politics of gender and generation. To this end, ever since Martita Hunt's performance, Miss Havisham has gradually become the dominant role in stage versions, feeding her influence via theatre-actress performances even into film and TV adaptations, where costume and setting (and the disintegration of older women's bodies) can also be given full imaginative rein.

In the UK there seem to have been many more adaptations than in the USA, including revivals of the Guinness version in the period between 1943 and 1999, which peaked in the 1970s and 1980s, and we have evidence of others besides Singer's that fell by the wayside in the planning stages.[118] The Dickens Fellowship and Dickens Festival productions account for some of these, but by no means all. Probably thanks to Guinness and Lean, *Great Expectations* seems to have hit a national chord with playwrights and theatre-goers in Britain. These adaptations

---

[115] Sharon Aronofsky Weltman, '"Can a Fellow Be a Villain All His Life?": *Oliver!*, Fagin and Performing Jewishness', *Nineteenth-Century Contexts*, 33 (2011): p. 372.

[116] Weltman, 'Can a Fellow', p. 373.

[117] Weltman, 'Can a Fellow', p. 374.

[118] See, for example, Correspondence of Anthony Page, Artistic Director of the Royal Court Theatre, London (1964–65, 1969–72), relating to playwright Henry Livings's proposed adaptation of Great Expectations, June–July 1964, in folder THM/273/4/11/3, Dept. of Theatre Performance, Victoria & Albert Museum. I have found no evidence that this was ever staged.

are notably less concerned with fidelity than the television versions, and this bold playfulness increases as time goes on. It is possible to see this development as occurring alongside, and perhaps in opposition to, the 'official' reverent versions appearing on radio and the small screen; despite the many adaptations performed for children, theatre is one of the places where *Great Expectations* has most often been remediated for grown-ups. But this took time. The reprisals of Guinness's version were discussed in Chapter 3, but we can further note here that while the addition of the narrators, the removal of Estella early on and the emphasis on male friendships were bold moves, the extant scripts and set designs show few other innovations.[119]

The Mermaid Theatre's version in 1960 also seems to have been fairly staid. It chose Dickens's original unhappy ending in keeping with contemporary perceptions of *Great Expectations* as representative of serious, darker Dickens, the programme even calling Dickens's second and more romantic ending 'ludicrous'. Throughout this programme, the sense of appeal to those who know their Dickens (and know how they want their Dickens) is palpable: the cast list is called 'Our Mutual Friends', the technical acknowledgements are 'Household Words', and the cast biographies are called the 'Curiosity Shop'.[120] The reviews of this production illuminate the odd position the novel occupied in stage history at this time. On the one hand there is disappointment at its conservatism, perhaps indicating a certain irritation with the prevailing reverent approach on radio and the small screen along with expectations that in 1960 the stage had licence to be bolder. But on the other there is palpable frustration at its inability to recreate the whole novel faithfully enough – a hangover, perhaps, from anxieties about the irreverent *Oliver!* approach. Milton Shulman in the *Evening Standard* was one who found it staid, calling it 'a kind of cardboard cut-out' and prophesying: 'This précis of *Great Expectations* might do for those taking their school certificate. Others, I suspect, will be disappointed by this capsularised, dehydrated and anaesthetised Dickens.'[121] But the *Morning Telegraph*'s reviewer wanted more fidelity, not less: 'It cannot be said that [Sally] Miles [the director] scores … whatever we do get, we

---

[119] The set designs and lighting plans for several wartime productions of the Alec Guinness text are in the Bristol University Theatre Collection, items JM/000046 (script, cast list and excerpts of text, Playhouse Theatre, Liverpool,1942); JM000047 (prompt book, 1942); OVP/7/5/4-3-2 (programmes for touring production, 1942–43); BOV/P/000014/1-17 (publicity photos, Bristol Old Vic, 1947); JM/000250 (programme, Bristol Old Vic,1957); JM/000251 (prompt book 1957); JM/000252 (stage plans 1957); JM/000253 (lighting notes 1957); JM/000254 (set notes, 1957); BOV/P/000121/001/7 (photo of set of Miss Havisham's house, 1957); BOV/LTP/000033 (publicity photos, Little Theatre Bristol, 1965); OVP/PG/000703 (programmes for Old Vic, London production, 1984).

[120] Programme for Mermaid Theatre, London production, 5 June 1960. Author's collection.

[121] *Evening Standard*, Thursday 14 April 1960, no page number. Clippings file, Billy Rose Theatre Division, New York Public Library.

don't get Dickens.'[122] The *Illustrated London News* felt that the compromise was the best that could be hoped for; the play 'put more of the Dickens narrative on the stage than we are ever likely to see again in a single night. It has been done, I think, extraordinarily well', and the reviewer felt sure the production would increase demand for the book.[123] *Great Expectations* was apparently a slippery thing for playwrights at this time; caught between realist homage, theatrical innovation and the popular success of early Dickens in musical form, adaptors seem to have found its 'essence' hard to pin down (or create anew).

Beyond this period, though, the theatrical revolution that took place in Britain and the USA in the 1950s and 1960s gradually fed into *Great Expectations* adaptations; these proliferated in the 1970s and afterwards, and became increasingly concerned both with the story's relevance to feminist and postcolonial discourse, and with its potential for foregrounding the gothic motifs that serve to disrupt and disfigure societal norms. So widespread has this expectation become, indeed, that by 2005 when the Royal Shakespeare Company mounted a production, the *Observer*'s reviewer felt there was: 'Not enough mist, not enough fear, and not enough sulphurous strangeness … it's got too much good taste for Dickens.'[124]

Jo Clifford's 1988 production, part play, part dance, was among the most ground breaking. Following a triumphant tour of Scotland with an international tour that took in Baghdad, Cairo, Alexandria, Madras, Bombay, Delhi, Calcutta and Dhaka, Clifford claims that the experience impressed her indelibly with Dickens's relevance to non-Western societies:

> It impressed me particularly deeply in Bangladesh. Dhaka is a cruel city. Its population is swollen by the hordes of the landless: people cut off from their earth, from their family, and from their roots. People on the edge. People holding onto life with their fingernails. Side by side with [the] cruel ostentation of the rich. Dickens must have known this, I thought. This is what he saw. This is what his London must have been like…. Ours too, I suspect, as life gets harder for everybody. Perhaps his world is not so far away as we may wish to imagine.[125]

In its 2012/13 revival at the Vaudeville Theatre in London's West End (*Great Expectations*' first performance in this famed theatre district), Miss Havisham embodied this figure of 'cruel ostentation' whose misuse of power affects everyone in her world. She was never offstage, but melted eerily into the upholstery whenever the scene shifted away from Satis House, and every character's costume carried a subtle cobweb motif. Bathsheba Doran's version for children at the Lucille Lortel

[122] *Morning Telegraph*, 26 April 1960, no page number. Clippings file, Billy Rose Theatre Division, New York Public Library.

[123] *Illustrated London News*, 30 April 1960, no page number. Clippings file, Billy Rose Theatre Division, New York Public Library.

[124] Susannah Clapp, *Observer*, 11 December 2005, p. 11.

[125] Jo Clifford, 'Adapting a Classic', in programme for *Great Expectations* revival at the Vaudeville Theatre, 1 February 2013. Author's collection.

Theater, New York (2006) also made Miss Havisham central; she draped the set with huge dust sheets, indicative of social as well as personal atrophy, which were only flung off at the start of the performance.[126] It is powerful evidence of the centrality of Miss Havisham to audience's expectations of the play that one reviewer felt Kathleen Chalfont's performance in this production 'will probably disappoint any adult who is psyched to see Chalfont in a role that promises to be a tour-de-force'.[127]

Overall, the novel has provided fertile material for cultural criticism onstage, in direct opposition to the conservatism of most small-screen productions which continue to celebrate Dickens's central role in the Western canon. In 1996, in a Pennsylvania Stage Company production, Estella was played for the first time by an African American actress, Jeanine T. Abraham. Recognising the potential for a disruption of what Anika Mukherjee has called 'the social discourse informing memorable acts of literature',[128] in 2011 Tanika Gupta transposed the whole story to nineteenth-century Calcutta, drawing attention simultaneously to Victorian colonial assumptions, and to the ways in which the canonisation of this novel has often served to entrench them. Literary recastings, as we will see in the final chapter, go even further to critique the uses to which *Great Expectations* has been put in Western culture.

---

[126] Betsy Winchester, review of Bathsheba Doran's adaptation, *Curtain Up*, 31 August 2008, no page number. Clippings file, Billy Rose Theatre Division, New York Public Library.

[127] Online review by Stan Richardson, 14 November 2006, for mytheatre.com.

[128] Mukherjee, 'Missed Encounters', p. 109.

Chapter 5
Translating *Great Expectations*, 1860–2012

My preceding chapters focussed on revealing the industrial, cultural and sociopolitical processes through which a widely disseminated novel by a famous Victorian survived a protracted period of unpopularity to re-emerge as a popular classic, and ended up as a cornerstone of the process through which twenty-first-century Western (and particularly English) readers constitute their own cultural DNA. As Philip Womack puts it, '[Dickens] … more than any other author, stands firmly entrenched in the lineage of English writing.… He is part of the genetic coding of the way we think about books'.[1] My final chapter extends this examination beyond the Anglophone world and the realm of straight dramatic adaptation, exploring how *Great Expectations* has operated in some very different national, linguistic and generic contexts both during and after Dickens's lifetime.

Ankhi Mukherjee has offered a related exploration of what she calls the 'constructedness of the literary artefact' using Freudian and Lacanian psychoanalysis. By these means she explores the work of several examples of postcolonial literature and film that use *Great Expectations* as their framework, creating a 'remembering and reinterpretation of the literary canon, in acts of generative citation that bring the (Eurocentric) literary past to recurring life'.[2] Mukherjee is acutely alert to the novel's transmutability and its availability for 'opportunistic symbolic appropriations' such as those which this book has attempted to investigate. But a reconstruction of the 'habitual coherence of cultural experience'[3] focused solely on the Eurocentric can only ever be partial – and partisan. While *Great Expectations* was born in England, its symbolic appropriation has not been confined to, or ever been controllable solely by, either European Victorians (including Dickens), or post-Victorian nostalgics bent on commemorating an idealised past (his canonisers). Equally, the attraction to addressing the novel's ideological assumptions and prejudices has not been the preserve solely of the postmodern postcolonials (Kathy Acker, Sue Roe, Alfonso Cuarón and Peter Carey) on whom Mukherjee focusses; political engagement with Dickens is not new. *Great Expectations* was certainly born into a powerful, extensive and influential family: both Dickens's popular fame and his entrenchment in the Western canon have fed into the novel's remediation in other languages and locations almost since the moment of its first publication. But the remediations

---

[1]   Philip Womack, 'Why Charles Dickens Speaks to Us Now', *Daily Telegraph*, 7 February 2012. Online edition, http://www.telegraph.co.uk/culture/books/9066463/Why-Charles-Dickens-speaks-to-us-now.html, posted 7 February 2012 [accessed 2 April 2014].

[2]   Mukherjee, 'Missed Encounters,' p. 109.

[3]   Mukherjee, 'Missed Encounters,' p. 131.

themselves have served very different political and ideological agendas, by no means all of them capitulations to the Euro- or Anglo-centric world view.

The first sections of my final chapter aim to examine some of these other locations. Here I build on Professor Nisbet's unfinished work of the 1960s–80s,[4] tracing some of the paths taken by *Great Expectations* in both non-Anglophone and non-European reception contexts and seeking to reveal some of the uses to which the novel has been put in locations far beyond Dickens's original plans for it. The contributors to Michael Hollington's two-volume *The Reception of Charles Dickens in Europe* (2013) have furnished me with additional information for the European contexts, though at times my findings have been different. I have, for example, come across earlier translations in some instances than Hollington and Cummins's timeline in these volumes suggests, usually because I have included translations for periodical publication which often predated the first translations into volume form.[5] I have also sometimes come across translations not mentioned by Hollington's contributors, and I have included these wherever I have been able to verify their existence beyond reasonable doubt.

Global Journeys 1860–2012

At the end of the 1990s, Franco Moretti offered the notion of 'literary geography' as a way of trying to understand literature's influence beyond its own linguistic borders, tracking the translation histories of a 'sample of popular [mostly nineteenth-century] British novels' in order to 'measure the internal variation of the European system' of publication, translation, import and export. His sample includes seven Dickens works – two early works, two Christmas stories, and three 'late works' (unspecified) – as representative of the trans-European movements of 'Dickens' between the 1790s and about 1920. Perhaps predictably given his methodology he found '[a]ll of Europe unified by a desire, not for "realism" … but for what Peter Brooks has called "the melodramatic imagination"'; the works, that is, that aimed to engender strong feeling rather than appeal to the intellect.[6] This may well be a fair claim – broadly speaking. But it elides some important discrepancies. Attempting to track multiple authors and genres over nine European countries and 100-plus years means limited space for detail; Moretti was forced to base his analysis solely on the presence of translations in library and publisher catalogues, inferring reading tastes and literary influences from these alone. He does not consider translation for serial publication or international copyright

---

    [4]   Unless otherwise stated, all data in this chapter is extracted from and reproduced with the kind permission of John O. Jordan, Dickens Project Director, Ada B. Nisbet Archive, The Dickens Project, University of California, Santa Cruz.

    [5]   Michael Hollington and Anthony Cummins, 'Timeline of the European Reception of Charles Dickens, 1833–2013', in *The Reception of Charles Dickens in Europe*, ed. Michael Hollington, Vol. 1 (London and New York: Bloomsbury, 2013), pp. xxv–xliii.

    [6]   Franco Moretti, *Atlas of the European Novel 1800–1900* (London and New York, 1998), pp. 174–7.

agreements (or their absence) or piracies or private authorial arrangements which might skew or particularise the results. Nor does he consider the significance of patterns of retranslation or failure to retranslate, instead counting a single translation instance as sufficient evidence of a novel's influence in a particular cultural context over a long period. And he does not have the room to consider (or at least not fully enough) communities with access to and facility in multiple languages, in which some were favoured over others in different vernacular or official (governmental and educative) contexts, and in which a translation might therefore indicate something other than popularity or preference.

Moretti's notion of literary geography has rightly been influential; a whole field of enquiry based on 'geographies of the book' has subsequently sprung up. But this later work has shown that publication (or translation) of a book is no guarantee that it found favour with – or even reached – large numbers of readers, or that it meant very much even to those who did buy or borrow it. Library catalogues tell us only what was stocked and occasionally what was borrowed, not what was actually read (let alone what its readers thought of it or whether they ever finished it). Publishers' advertisements about the numbers and sizes of editions say nothing about unsold stock mouldering in warehouses. Publishers themselves take fewer risks than we would like; in publishing terms, 'the canon' is probably based less often on deserving literary genius than on financial precedent, coalescing most enthusiastically around the titles representing the lowest per-unit costs and the lowest risk. Not all these details are recoverable in every instance, of course. But we need to bear them in mind whenever we can. In mapping as many of this one canonical novel's movements across Europe and beyond as possible and in offering tentative explanations for its presence or absence, I hope here to add some nuances to Moretti's broad conclusions about the homogeneity of non-Anglophone literary tastes in the nineteenth century and afterwards.

In Dickens's lifetime, *Great Expectations* travelled far beyond the USA and the UK, first reaching Europe via Tauchnitz who published a two-volume European English-language edition in his 'Collection of British Authors' series in 1861.[7] English language copies had also reached even the remoter parts of Australia by October 1861, the bookseller Robertson of Melbourne regularly appearing in the Chapman and Hall accounts as a purchaser of small quantities, and records of the novel's popularity there abounding in contemporary Australian journals.[8] These were the official migrants, but there were unofficial ones too. The New York *Sun*'s pirated serialisation was discussed in Chapter 1. A better-known English-language piracy was by the editor of the *Eastern Province Herald* in Port Elizabeth, South Africa, who began serialising the novel on 5 March 1861 before being forestalled

---

[7]   *Great Expectations* was published as vols. 547 and 548 in the series.

[8]   Patten, *Dickens and His Publishers*, 385. See also Tim Dolin, 'First Steps Towards a History of the Mid-Victorian Novel in Colonial Australia', *Australian Literary Studies*, 22 (2006): pp. 273–93; Coral Lansbury, 'Charles Dickens and His Australia', *Journal of the Royal Australian Historical Society* (June 1966): pp. 115–27; and Coral Lansbury, 'Terra Australis Dickensia', *Modern Language Studies*, 1 (Summer 1971): pp. 12–21.

by Dickens taking legal action.[9] The editor of the *Herald* seemed surprised that Dickens had prevented the circulation of the novel instead of being flattered by it: 'Postal facilities in this country are none of the best,' he explained in an apologetic letter to the author following the Supreme Court's ruling against him, 'and I know that … in the columns of the *Eastern Province Herald* your tale would find its way to many a farmhouse where *All the Year Round* … would never enter. I had even thought that you might be gratified by such a result, but it appears I was mistaken'.[10] Anyone more familiar with Dickens's media profile would have known better than to try to cheat him; the British newspapers frequently (and not always approvingly) reported the prices he was paid for American copyrights and other foreign rights, often tacitly equating Dickens's active and legally informed pursuit of a fair price for his works with poor taste. In this case, though, they took his side: the piracy was a newsworthy item countrywide and all these reports expressed outrage at the bare faced theft of an author's work, many taking the opportunity to comment on the widespread practice of piracy at home. 'To rifle an author's brain', opined the *Cheltenham Chronicle*, 'is, to our mind, quite as indefensible in South Africa as in Great Britain, and we are glad to see that "the arm of the law" … can stretch over hundreds of leagues to seize the guilty'.[11] The *Falkirk Herald* agreed. 'It is only right that the product of a man's brain should be protected',[12] it nodded, lifting the phrase directly out of *Lloyd's Weekly's* report on dramatic piracy more broadly. This paper had taken heart from Dickens's success, and concluded: 'The Secretary of the Dramatic Author's Club ought to be apprised that the law here is powerful enough to enforce justice in such cases.'[13] Such reports helped to construct the world beyond Britain's borders as a dangerous 'Other' space into which Dickens's works (however critically denigrated at home) shone the light of British culture. He was ambassador as well as author. But there was another useful side effect to his international transportability: the illegal exploitation abroad of high-profile aesthetic exports such as Dickens was able to condemn, by association, related criminal practices at home.

In addition to the widespread circulation (both authorised and unauthorised) of English-language versions, there were several non-English language versions in this early period. There were almost immediate translations into French, Dutch, Danish, German, Polish and Swedish, for example. Even these early translations are worth pausing on since they tell very varied stories, but some of the posthumous translation histories are more remarkable still, demonstrating a late period of interest in the novel which sometimes occurs in tandem with Western trends but, equally, occasionally works in opposition to them.

---

[9]   K.J. Fielding, 'The Piracy of "Great Expectations"', *Notes and Queries* (November 1955): pp. 495–6.

[10]   Quoted in Fielding, 'Piracy', p. 495.

[11]   *Cheltenham Chronicle*, Tuesday 8 October 1861, p. 6.

[12]   *Falkirk Herald*, 17 October 1861, no page number.

[13]   *Lloyd's Weekly Newspaper*, Sunday 6 October 1861, p. 8.

In the immediate post-publication period, L. Moltke produced a Danish translation of *Great Expectations* in his collected works series ('Samtlige Vaerker', 2nd ed., 1861–70);[14] in Russia two anonymous translations appeared: *Bol'šie ožidanija* in the *Russian Herald*, Feb–Aug 1861, and *Bol'šie nadeždy* in *Records of the Fatherland*, Apr–Aug 1861;[15] and there was a Dutch translation (*Groote Verwachtingen: Een Verhaal*) by C.M. Mensing in 1862.[16] Also in 1862 a French translation by Charles Bernard Derosne (called rather wordily *Les Grandes Espérances du nommé Philip Pirrip, vulgairement appelé Pip*) was published in daily instalments – apparently with Dickens's blessing – in the Paris Journal *Le Temps*, beginning on 20 February. While several British newspapers reported the event, this was an odd choice of journal in some ways: *Le Temps* had only been launched in 1861 and its circulation was a mere 3000 in that year and grew but slowly.[17] Perhaps its liberal Protestant leanings appealed to Dickens; we cannot be certain since his surviving correspondence is silent on this point.[18]

In the first couple of years after its initial UK and American publication, *Great Expectations* was thus already a seasoned traveller and had become known (or notorious) quite far afield. Dickens's international reputation was a matter of some pride to British newspapers: on 5 April 1862, for example, the *Yorkshire Gazette* reported that 'the Australians want the author of that tale [*Great Expectations*] to go and give his readings amongst them. He is offered a large sum of money, all the expenses of his sea and land travelling, a house, servants, carriage, and a liberal table. I wonder whether he will go'.[19] (He didn't.) This was just the start of the novel's journeys, though; the early foreign serialisations quickly gave way to more volume editions.

In 1864, a French book-length version (also translated by Derosne, the title now shortened to *Les Grandes Espérances*) was published by Hachette.[20] Derosne's translation, authorised by Dickens, was unchallenged for decades, and despite a new contender finally arriving in the shape of Six Adamson's French translation for the Belgian publisher Le Carrefour in 1947, Derosne's was still being reprinted

---

[14]   Jørgen Erik Nielsen, 'Danish Translations', Ada B. Nisbet Archive.

[15]   Igor Katarskij, 'Dickens in the USSR', trans. by Rodney L. Patterson, Ada B. Nisbet Archive.

[16]   Oscar Wellens, 'The Earliest Dutch Translations of Dickens (1837–1870): An All-inclusive List', *Dickensian*, 97 (Summer 1997): p. 129. Also Willem van Maanen, 'Dickens in Holland', Ada B. Nisbet Archive.

[17]   See, for example, *The Salopian Journal*, Tuesday 18 March 1862, p. 8; the *Yorkshire Gazette*, Saturday 5 April 1862, p. 8.

[18]   Sylvère Monod, 'Dickens in France', Ada B. Nisbet Archive. Also see notice in the *Salopian Journal*, Tuesday 8 March 1862, p. 8. The serialisation began on 20 February 1862 in *Le Temps*, No. 316. For all issues of this serialisation, see *Le Temps* digital archive at Gallica Bibliothèque Numérique http://gallica.bnf.fr/ark:/12148/cb34431794k/date1862.

[19]   *Yorkshire Gazette*, Saturday 5 April 1862, p. 8.

[20]   Hollington gives this as the first translation. Hollington, *The Reception of Charles Dickens in Europe*.

in the 1960s, perhaps due to a certain amount of reverence towards an edition sanctioned by the author; the 'Charles Dickens' edition of 1867–68, the last over which Dickens exercised authorial control, has garnered a similar critical fan base. In the French case, however, the reverence did not survive outside academia; as Anny Sadrin has pointed out: 'Dickens is no longer (if he ever was) a "popular" author in this country … one whose name, books and characters are familiar to all or a large majority of people.'[21] Sylvère Monod puts some finer detail on this: 'A French reader can probably find a more or less decent *David Copperfield* or *Oliver Twist*', he informs us, 'but a *Pickwick Papers* or even a *Great Expectations* is more unlikely to crop up, and a *Bleak House* is out of the question.'[22] In France (perhaps, as Moretti suggests, because of the proliferation of more sophisticated French novels during this period[23]), Dickens was a peripheral phenomenon known largely through his early works. The popular and critical dismissal of the late works certainly extended to *Great Expectations*, as the gap of almost a century between translations amply testifies. However, French translations – and pirated versions of them – circulated widely in Belgium and Switzerland, where Dickens had a friendlier reception.[24]

In other languages the novel's life and influence reached even further. In 1862 it was translated into German in several different versions by Julius Seybt (Leipzig: Wiedemann and Weissenburg), Marie Scott (Leipzig: J.J. Weber), Heinrich von Hammer (Vol. 1, Leipzig: Voigt and Gunther; Vol. 2, Vienna: Margraf) and H. Roberts (Leipzig: Weber).[25] These translations were also deemed worthy of note by British newspapers, but more importantly they have had an active afterlife.[26] During the first half of Dickens's career he was almost as popular in Germany as he was in the UK and USA, but after the 1848 revolution, as Antje Anderson has remarked, 'the famous "turn" inward in the 1850s … led to a decreasing interest in British social fiction and a yearning for idyllic idealizing literature just at the time when Dickens was beginning to produce darker, less idyllic works'.[27] *Great Expectations* was in some respects a casualty of this shift; while translations continued throughout the 1860s, Anderson notes that the novel was 'rarely

---

[21] Anny Sadrin, 'French Studies on Dickens since 1970', *Dickens Quarterly*, 12 (1995): p. 188.

[22] Sylvère Monod, 'Translating Dickens into French', in *Dickens, Europe and the New Worlds*, ed. by Anny Sadrin (London and New York, 1999), p. 230.

[23] Moretti, *Atlas*, p. 184.

[24] See Carlene A. Adamson, 'Boz as Tutor: The Reception of Dickens in Francophone Belgium', in Hollington, *The Reception of Charles Dickens in Europe*, pp. 259–71; also Neil Forsyth and Martine Hennard Dutheil de la Rochère, 'Dickens in Francophone Switzerland', in Hollington, *The Reception of Charles Dickens in Europe*, pp. 272–80.

[25] Heinz Reinhold, 'Dickens in German,' Ada B. Nisbet Archive.

[26] See, for example, *Belfast News Letter*, Thursday 5 December 1861, p. 4.

[27] Antje Anderson, 'Dickens in Germany: The Nineteenth Century', in Hollington, *The Reception of Charles Dickens in Europe*, p. 29.

reviewed', and the translations had dried up by 1864.[28] A couple reappeared in 1895 and 1908, but after the Richard Zoozman translation in 1910 the novel seems to have lapsed until after World War II. Heinz Reinhold suggests that this post-war revivification might have been because 'the novel's true significance has only recently been grasped',[29] but we might add to this the suggestion not only that Lean's film began to circulate in some German-speaking countries after the war, engendering, as we will see, a ripple of new European interest, but also that the 30-year gap between new translations in the nineteenth century and the 40-year gap between those in the twentieth were publishing hiatuses, not necessarily lapses in reader engagement. Other evidence demonstrates that the German translations not only continued to circulate quite widely, but also continued to exercise a certain amount of influence. They were, for example, among the most likely reasons that the first translation into Czech (part of the Austro-Hungarian Empire and thus also part – however uneasily – of a German-speaking linguistic community until 1918) did not occur until 1900. Zdeněk Beran confirms that most Czechs knew of early Dickens through German translations, 'which were more readily available in Prague than the English originals'. The later Dickens novels had a different audience, but it was often still reading in German for reasons to do with political control: Dickens became 'an unwelcome, subversive voice in the 1850s and 1860s. Intellectuals read him in German, but access for a wider reading public was thought undesirable'.[30]

Translation into Hungarian was even slower (1924), possibly for similar reasons. Dickens had been popular with the literati in Hungary since the 1830s, and while this popularity had ebbed by the early twentieth century as elite readers turned to French Symbolism and Naturalism,[31] he continued to appeal to ordinary readers. During World War I a national poll placed him fifth in popularity with the reading public behind two Hungarian poets, Shakespeare, and Goethe.[32] The 1924 translation of *Great Expectations* into Hungarian was quite late, but it occurred after the dissolution of the Austro-Hungarian Empire in 1918 and the devastating Treaty of Trianon in 1920, which stripped Hungary of almost two-thirds of its lands and over half of its population. It was in fact part of a rash of Dickens translations in the 1920s that may well have been a kind of vernacular publishing backlash; that Dickens was being used for revolutionary purposes is evidenced by the example of a Hungarian Communist who in 1921 'promoted his views in a novella that he claimed was written by Dickens'.[33]

---

[28]   Anderson, 'Dickens in Germany', p. 31.

[29]   Heinz Reinhold, 'Dickens in Germany', Ada B. Nisbet Archive.

[30]   Zdeněk Beran, 'An Uninterrupted Journey: Seventeen Decades of Dickens Reception in the Czech Lands', in Hollington, *The Reception of Charles Dickens in Europe*, p. 450.

[31]   Géza Maráczi, 'Dickens in Hungary', in Hollington, *The Reception of Charles Dickens in Europe*, p. 566.

[32]   Anna Katona, 'Dickens in Hungary', Ada B. Nisbet Archive.

[33]   Maráczi quoting Katona, in 'Dickens in Hungary', p. 567.

Further intriguing evidence, both of the possible spread of German translations of Dickens generally and of the influence of *Great Expectations* in particular, appears in more recent scholarship, which has delved even further beyond the lists of editions. Nehama Aschkenasy demonstrates that despite the total absence of references to reading Dickens in the letters and other records of Hebrew author S.Y. Agnon, there are unmistakable traces of *Great Expectations* in his 1939 story 'Baya'ar uva'ir'. *Great Expectations* was not translated into Yiddish until 1939 and Hebrew until 1955, but having been born in Galicia in the Austro-Hungarian Empire and tutored in German, Agnon was an avid reader of fiction in – and translations of classics into – German during the 1910s and 1920s. In addition, Aschkenasy suggests, 'it is possible that parts of the novel appeared earlier in serialized form in one of the Yiddish periodicals'.[34] Similarly, Marika Odzeli draws attention to *Great Expectations'* demonstrable impact on the Georgian poet Galaktion Tabidze in the late 1920s; Tabidze not only wrote to his mother of the powerful emotions he had experienced after he had stayed up all night reading *Great Expectations*, but he gave the novel's name to the diary in which he described this reaction and he went on to express Dickens's influence through much of his published work.[35]

The 'hidden' distribution of *Great Expectations* encompasses other linguistic border crossings, too. Krzysztof Gluchowski argues that Polish readers admired Dickens and could always avail themselves of English originals and French translations; they may well have done so alongside the first Polish translations of the novel in serial form in 1863, and prior to the first edition in volume form in 1918.[36] The first Swedish translation, *Lysande utsigter eller Pip Pirrips Märkvärdiga lefnadsöden* (Stockholm: J.L. Brudins förlag, 1861) was also available in Finland; indeed, as we have seen, there was no translation into Finnish until 1934.[37] Equally, many of the first translations of Dickens into Spanish were from the French, not the English versions.[38] A detailed analysis of how the text and thus potentially the reception of *Great Expectations* might have been affected by these circumstances is beyond my language skills, but it seems important to acknowledge that there are likely to be immense differences between English and American reception contexts and the experiences of Finnish readers reading a translation in Swedish, or Spanish readers encountering the novel doubly remediated via French.

It is impossible to be certain how much Dickens earned even from his legitimate translations and thus how popular they really were. But he was

---

[34] Nehama Aschkenasy, 'Agon's Dickensian Moment: "Baya'ar uva'ir"', *Journal of Modern Jewish Studies*, 2 (2003), pp. 174–90. Reprinted in Jordan and Perera, *Global Dickens*, p. 96.

[35] Marika Odzeli, 'The Reception of Dickens in Georgia', in Hollington, *The Reception of Charles Dickens in Europe*, pp. 585–6.

[36] Krzysztof Gluchowski, 'Dickens and Poland', *Dickensian*, 98 (Spring 2003): p. 44.

[37] Irma Rantavaara, 'Dickens in Finland'; and Ishrat Lindblad, 'Dickens in Sweden', Ada B. Nisbet Archive.

[38] Paul Smith, 'Dickens in Spain', Ada B. Nisbet Archive.

obviously very familiar to many nineteenth-century European readers; the name 'Charles Dickens' was clearly sufficient to command the attention of foreign editors and, as Patten has demonstrated, he was certainly one of the first authors to understand how to work foreign markets.[39] In fact, in light of his long experience with translation arrangements it seems surprising that he entrusted Baron von Tauchnitz to name his own terms for the first English-language foreign edition of *Great Expectations*.[40] Perhaps Dickens's poor health and his mental and emotional states while he was writing it prevented any enthusiastic investment in its long-term future beyond the pressing necessity to rescue AYR: the polite but short note to the Baron was penned when he still had most of the writing ahead of him. We do not even know how well the Tauchnitz edition did in Europe, since the Chapman and Hall ledgers do not specify profits from this edition.[41] We do know that he was paid £40 upfront,[42] less than for *A Tale of Two Cities* (£44 19s. 6d.)[43] or *Our Mutual Friend* (£75), and only a little more than he was paid for 'Hunted Down' and 'The Uncommercial Traveller' (£35).[44]

We can speculate, however, that while Tauchnitz seemed keen to include the novel in his series and therefore evidently felt it had an assured market (albeit a smaller one than for other works), and while Australians also clearly welcomed it, in other contexts and for a variety of reasons its reception was probably a more qualified success, and this is where we might suggest some further amendments to Moretti's findings. *Les Grandes Espérances du Philip Pirrip* was apparently of insufficient interest to Parisians to prevent *Le Temps*'s owner from having to borrow money from friends to rescue the magazine in the face of poor circulation during its run.[45] And in 'many a farmhouse'[46] containing the South African readers of the *Eastern Province Herald*, there may have been some frustration over the sudden curtailment of the story by legal action. We do not know when – or if – those readers ever got to find out what happened to Pip and Magwitch.

We often have little information beyond such snippets glued together with guesswork. But, fragmentary as the evidence is about both English-language and translated versions of this novel, the available publication data demonstrates some potentially intriguing patterns beyond notions of homogeneity of taste. One of the most striking of these is just how slow the novel seems to have been in

---

[39]   Patten, *Dickens and His Publishers*, p. 274.

[40]   Letter to Tauchnitz, 22 Dec 1860, *Letters*, Vol. 9, p. 351.

[41]   See Patten, Dickens and His Publishers, Appendix A, 'Sales and Profits of Dickens's Works: *Great Expectations*'; pp. 385–6.

[42]   Letter to Tauchnitz, 14 Jan 1861, *Letters*, Vol. 9, p. 368.

[43]   Letter to Tauchnitz, 10 May 1859, *Letters*, Vol. 9, p. 63. A final payment of £30 for *A Tale of Two Cities* was acknowledged by Dickens on 2 Dec 1859, *Letters*, Vol. 9, p. 174.

[44]   Letter to Tauchnitz, 21 Nov 1861, *Letters*, Vol. 9, p. 341.

[45]   http://gallica.bnf.fr/ark:/12148/cb34431794k/ [accessed 3 March 2013]. *Le Temps* had also serialised Collins's *The Woman in White*.

[46]   Letter to Dickens from the Editor of the *Eastern Province Herald* explaining the piracy. Quoted in Fielding, 'Piracy', p. 495.

making it into translation in a number of languages, sometimes even as compared to other Dickens novels. Not only were Hungarian, Finnish and Czech translations relatively late (and potentially explicable by the availability of other foreign-language editions, especially in German), but there were also slow translations into Japanese (1924), Spanish (1930), several Russian languages (1935–50s), Bulgarian (1938), Portuguese (1942), Romanian (1947), Norwegian (1948), Arabic (1950), Chinese (1954) and Bengali (1955). In some of these locations we can detect the same preference for early Dickens as we have found in the UK and USA; *Great Expectations* seems to have been a casualty of mid-nineteenth-century tastes well beyond the Anglophone world. But in others, *Great Expectations'* slow arrival and the uses to which it was put when it did arrive were probably the result either of long-lasting preferences for indigenous literature, or the same sorts of complex cultural and political forces that were behind the Austro-Hungarian cases.

One such possible example is the novel's reception in China. Indeed, Eva Hung suggests that 'Dickens, as one of the first major English writers to be introduced into China [from around 1906], is a good example in the study of ways in which an author and his works are understood and interpreted in the changing social and literary climates of a different culture'.[47] Dickens's reception closely reflects the changing political scene. As Hung explains:

> [D]uring the initial stages of the introduction of western literature into China, Chinese scholars and readers fitted western literary works into their own established modes of perception.... With the growing popularity of Socialist ideas in China from the late 1930s on, some Chinese critics began to look at Dickens' social criticism from a new angle ... an obvious turn of the tide came in the mid-1940s. Dong Qiuisi, one of Dickens' Chinese translators during the 1940s, considered Dickens' vision of society inadequate because he failed to pinpoint the cause of social evil, i.e. an exploiting class empowered by Capitalism.... This is the point of view espoused by all mainland Chinese critics after the Communist government of the People's Republic of China was established, in 1949.[48]

Great Expectations' role in the appropriation of literature for political and ideological purposes in this context is an intriguing one. Perhaps it lacked the kind of 'social conscience' of Dickens's earlier works and was driven by what could easily be seen as capitalist motivations; at any rate, it did not get translated into Chinese until 1954. Perhaps equally unsurprisingly, Dickens's revolution novel, *A Tale of*

---

[47]   Eva Hung, 'The Introduction of Dickens into China: A Case Study in Target Culture Reception', *Perspectives: Studies in Translatology – Special issue: Chinese Translation Studies*, 4 (1996): pp. 29–41; reprinted in Jordan and Perera, *Global Dickens*, pp. 31–44. Page numbers cited are to this edition (p. 31). See also Klaudia Lee, 'Cross-Cultural Adaptation of Dickensian Spatiality: The Case of *Little Dorrit*', *English*, 62 (Spring 2013): pp. 6–21, for a reading of Dickens's reception in late nineteenth and early twentieth-century China.

[48]   Hung, 'Introduction of Dickens into China', pp. 33–5.

Two Cities, tops the Chinese popularity charts between 1949 and 1960.[49] Yet *Great Expectations* has been translated numerous times since; in fact Chinese translations after the Sino-Soviet split constitute one of the longest entries in Appendix B. It might not be unreasonable to suggest that the novel's exploration of the tension between aspiration and tradition began in this period to speak particularly clearly to a Chinese readership becoming increasingly aware of its own internal divisions between rural poverty and urban wealth, and between traditional ways of life and a burgeoning desire to embrace Western-style modernity.

In Soviet-era Poland, as Ewa Kujawska-Lis has demonstrated, *Great Expectations* initially suffered a similar fate, and for similar reasons. Dickens had always been popular in Poland, but after World War II:

> New socialist leaders strove to create a new mass culture subordinated to the dominant ideology. In their activities they had to confront Dickens who could not have been ignored, given his great popularity. He was an established writer in the public awareness. New editions of his works could have been banned, as was the fate of many other writers such as George Orwell.... Yet that would have been counterproductive – Dickensian descriptions of capitalist realities were valuable for propaganda purposes. His fiction could be easily used to guide a mass readership into the belief that capitalism was destructive to the human element.[50]

Guidance is the operative term here. As Kujawska-Lis goes on to explain, 'There was a problem with Dickens.... The commentators realized that his novels criticised the capitalist system by showing its negative facets, such as workers' exploitation or child labour, yet the writer never suggested its overthrow'.[51] The answer was for translators or editors to provide prefaces and notes which guided the reader's interpretation of the text, and were largely designed to shift attention away from Dickens the humourist to Dickens the social reformer. Even *A Tale of Two Cities* and *Hard Times* required some critical acrobatics in order to convince readers that Dickens believed in revolution and championed workers' rights. An interpretation of British history emphasising its reluctance to embrace revolutionary change provided the necessary excuses for his shortcomings.[52] Most of the early novels were treatable in this way. But the later ones were more problematic. For one Marxist critic in Poland, *Great Expectations* and *Our Mutual Friend* were works which demonstrated that Dickens had given up on political and social issues. For others, nonetheless:

> [H]e remained a good source of information concerning capitalism, as proven by *Great Expectations*. Critics stressed that in this novel Dickens showed that a human being was the result of the social system.... The entire novel was

---

[49]   Hung, 'Introduction of Dickens into China', p. 40.

[50]   Ewa Kujawska-Lis, 'The Transformations of Charles Dickens in Early Socialist Poland', *Literature Compass*, 10 (April 2013): p. 397.

[51]   Kujawska-Lis, 'Transformations', p. 397.

[52]   Kujawska-Lis, 'Transformations', pp. 399–400.

interpreted along the class axis – the class difference between Pip and Miss Havisham. Pip's tragedy lies in his being lured by the magic of the privileged classes when he was still a child.[53]

Prefaces and notes are not, of course, the only means through which translations remediate and thus guide reader interpretation of novels: the act of translation is in itself a form of adaptation.[54] The very different meanings which become available (or indeed are of necessity offered) to non-Anglophone readers of Dickens are outlined by Toru Sasaki in his lively account of the difficulties of translating *Great Expectations* into Japanese (first translation 1923; Sasaki's 2-volume edition 2011). 'In Japan', Sasaki explains, the novel 'has always been called *Ooinaru Isan* … which signifies "great legacy." It is not possible in Japanese to express the meanings of "great hope" and "expected great fortune" in one phrase: the very title is already a problem!'[55] The cultural significance and influence of Dickens's title is thus entirely different in this context; not only does it not have a phrasal tradition on which to draw as it did in English prior to 1860, but it cannot itself become a comparable cultural reference point afterwards.

The difficulties continue: Sasaki outlines several further ways in which the nuances of Dickens's text have to be handled differently in translation, among them the problem of rendering into Japanese the Dickensian puns and idiosyncratic (and often comedic) dialogue such as that used by Joe. More difficult still is the accurate translation into Japanese of the shifting modes of formality of address which a novel about social climbing requires; Japanese is a language in which the proper second person pronoun is of vital import in rendering social and generational relationships, and there is no scope for evolution in those roles.[56] Small wonder that for years Dickens was largely only used in schools in Japan: as Masaie Matsumura puts it: 'English novels were too difficult for most of the young literary men of Japan; and the morality and social consciousness so characteristic of them were not qualities that provoked envy.'[57]

In other locations, while Dickens was generally available and sometimes even popular, *Great Expectations* translations lagged behind those of the earlier novels for reasons that are less easily explicable. In Spain, for example, Dickens was even more popular than Scott, but it was the early works – particularly *Oliver Twist*, *David Copperfield* (around 20 translations apiece in the nineteenth century) and *A Christmas Carol*, *Hard Times*, *The Old Curiosity Shop* and *Pickwick Papers* (ten times each) – that dominated for several decades. *Great Expectations* was not

---

[53]   Kujawska-Lis, 'Transformations', p. 402.

[54]   I am grateful to Klaudia Lee for a fruitful email discussion on 2 July 2012 on the subject of translation as a form of adaptation.

[55]   Toru Sasaki, 'Translating *Great Expectations* into Japanese', *Dickensian*, 107 (Winter 2011): p. 197.

[56]   Sasaki, 'Translating', pp. 198–200.

[57]   Masaie Matsumura, 'Dickens in Japan', in Jordan and Perera, *Global Dickens*, p. 60.

translated into Spanish until 1930.[58] In Russia, too, while Dickens was generally greeted enthusiastically and *Great Expectations* was serialised anonymously in 1861, over the next half-century it only reappeared in shortened versions: 'The Criminal's Daughter', retold by Lankas Karlis and published in the *Dzimtenes Balss (Motherland's Voice) Literary Supplement* in 1898, and another anonymous shortened version published in Liepaia (Latvia) in 1902. It was not translated into Russian in full book form until 1935. (In the same year it was also translated into Azerbaijan.) The Russian version, however, was closely followed by a more influential one: a short edition for children, 'Pip', published in 1937 as a booklet by the Detskaja Literature publishing house, which provided the template for all the first translations into several other Russian languages: Udmurt (1938), Chuvash (1939) and Belorussian (1940).[59]

The relative slowness of a full translation for adults into Russian could well be a result of the novel's complex – and perhaps quite culturally specific – themes, structure and language, just as they were in Poland. By the time *Great Expectations* made it into book form in Polish in 1918, Dickens's works had for some time been out of fashion to the extent that only six of the early ones survived in print, and those only in school book form.[60] It took a Communist revolution to reintroduce Dickens to Poland, and even then, as we have seen, he needed to be remediated through the language of radical politics. Similarly, although in nineteenth-century Russia 'Dickens's books made part of even half-educated Russians' literary knowledge', in the early days of his popularity, as Nina Diakonova explains, 'it was as a satirist and as an enemy of the Establishment, as a man who exposed the hideousness of capitalist exploitation, that he was valued by Soviet historians and teachers'.[61] During the 1980s, however, critics and scholars 'only too obviously do not concentrate on social and political contexts as Soviet scholars were expected to … the main tendency is to get away from established Soviet clichés and to define the unique, individual, moral and aesthetic value of Dickens's books'.[62] *Great Expectations* had a new lease of life – five new translations in this single decade – as a result.

There are equally interesting cycles of popularity in India. Dickens in English was essential classroom reading from the end of the nineteenth century,[63] and also very popular in public libraries (though less popular than G.M.W. Reynolds), but – unlike Reynolds, Scott and Defoe (all of whom were translated into more than four Indian languages) and Collins and even Bulwer-Lytton (translated into at least

---

[58]   Paul Smith, 'Dickens in Spain', Ada B. Nisbet Archive.

[59]   Rodney L. Patterson, 'Dickens in Russia', trans. by Igor Katarskij, Ada B. Nisbet Archive.

[60]   Maria Lyźwińska, 'Dickens in Poland', Ada B. Nisbet Archive.

[61]   Nina Diakonova, 'Russian Dickens Studies, 1970–1995', *Dickens Quarterly*, 12 (1995): pp. 181–2.

[62]   Diakonova, 'Russian Dickens', p. 185.

[63]   H.K. Trivedi, 'Dickens in India', Ada B. Nisbet Archive.

one apiece) – he was not translated into any Indian language prior to the twentieth century.[64] 'In the nineteenth-century cottage industry of translation', Priya Joshi tells us, 'with its paltry remuneration, a translator had to be notably enthusiastic about a book, or the book had to promise success before it was worth the expense and exercise of translating it.'[65] *Great Expectations* did not make the grade until much later – after independence, in fact – and the translations did not oust English even then; there are a number of English language versions produced by Indian publishers between 1957 and the 1990s which existed alongside translations of *Great Expectations* into Indian languages, including Bengali (1955) and Gujerati (1964). The front cover of the 1964 Gujerati version (see Figure 5.1) places Estella and Miss Havisham centre stage, as many English-language versions did during this period, and while the racial identity of the two figures is largely indeterminate, Miss Havisham's wedding dress is unmistakably Western. There is, however, an undeniably comic quality to the illustration which, while it was probably designed to appeal to younger readers, cannot help but undermine any sense of solemn cultural reverence.

The endurance of English-language books might seem altogether incongruous in the period after independence, and perhaps particularly after India ceased to be a Crown dominion in 1950. But it was likely to be a result of necessity; this was a linguistically heterogeneous nation in which English was the only common language, and (as the jokey Gujerati cover suggests) its semantic and ideological range had long been appropriated for other ends quite independent from colonial officialdom. In 1959 an expert on Indian writing in English, Professor K.R.S Iyengar of Andhra University, claimed during a lecture at the University of Leeds that by this time 'Indian English had changed. It had ceased to be British; it had liberated itself from the tastes, opinions, morals, and intellect of its shadow motherland. It had come of age, creating its own nation and its own literature'. But, as Priya Joshi reminds us: 'Although the desire for national sovereignty was indeed one of the major catalysts for the new [Indian] literature [in English], it was not enough to create and sustain it.' For that, she maintains, we must look at the work of Indian novelists 'whose literary concerns were not exclusively defined by nationalism'.[66] From the language of oppression through the language of expediency to a new language that had nothing to do with either; *Great Expectations* in translation in India seems to have been at first a casualty, and then latterly a brief beneficiary, of this shifting paradigm.

Political and pragmatic imperatives such as those I have discussed are, though, only two of several possible forces behind foreign translations and the enduring – or revivified, or indeed short-lived – demand for Dickens in non-Anglophone

---

[64]   Table 2.2, 'Novelists in Indian Library Catalogues I', and Table 2.3, 'Works Translated or Adapted into Indian Languages', in Priya Joshi, *In Another Country: Colonialism, Culture and the English Novel in India* (New York, 2002), pp. 64–5 and pp. 70–71.

[65]   Joshi, *In Another Country*, p. 68.

[66]   Joshi, *In Another Country*, pp. 205–6.

Fig. 5.1   Front cover of *Great Expectations*, translated into Gujerati by Jayanti Dalāla (Ahmedabad: Viśvasāhitya, 1964), artist unknown. Reproduced by kind permission of John O. Jordan, Director, the Dickens Project, Ada B. Nisbet Archive, University of California, Santa Cruz.

and non-European contexts which is apparent after World War II. One of the
most powerful of these additional driving forces seems to have been the global
distribution policies of twentieth-century media industries.

Remediation as Translation 1900–1986

In this section I take the notion of 'translation' in its broader sense, to mean not
only 'removal or conveyance from one person, place, or condition to another', but
also the 'expression or rendering of something in another medium or form'.[67] This
adds to the term 'remediation' an explicit acknowledgement of its operations in
different cultural and linguistic contexts.

The first such non-Anglophone remediation of *Great Expectations* was Danish
director A.W. Sandberg's silent film version, *Store Forventninger*, written for the
Nordisk film company by Laurids Skands and premiered in Denmark on 8 August
1922 (probably not 1920 or 1921 as many film historians claim).[68] Sandberg was
a prolific director who tackled several Dickens novels during this period: *Great
Expectations*, *David Copperfield*, *Little Dorrit* and *Our Mutual Friend*. These were
not, as Petrie remarks, 'always the most obvious choice of titles in terms of popular
taste, which still tended to prefer the earlier, largely comic novels to the darker,
later ones',[69] and while they seem to have been popular in Denmark they were
aimed predominantly at foreign markets where they were much less successful.
Over the next two years *Store Forventninger* was also distributed in Norway,
Sweden, Finland, Germany, Austria, Hungary, the Netherlands, Belgium, Poland,
the Balkan Countries, the UK, France, Spain, Portugal, North America, Argentina,
Australia, New Zealand, Russia, Chile, Peru, Bolivia and Czechoslovakia.[70]
Petrie's useful examination of the extant footage demonstrates that it focussed far
more on the Pip/Estella than the Pip/Magwitch plotline and that this makes Pip a
far more sympathetic character than in the novel,[71] but both audience and reviewers
were apparently unimpressed with the alterations Sandberg had made to the plot,
and probably also with what Pointer calls 'excessively wordy intertitles';[72] the

---

[67]   OED online, s.v. 'translation', accessed 23 Aug 2013, http://www.oed.com/view/En
try/204844?redirectedFrom=translation#eid.

[68]   Michael Pointer, for example, lists the Danish premiere as having taken place in
1920, and dates the general release in Denmark to 28 Aug 1922. Pointer, *Charles Dickens
on the Screen: The Film, Television, and Video Adaptations* (Lanham, 1996), p. 128. IMDB
lists the premiere as Denmark 28 February 1922. However, the Danish Film Institute's
archive confirms the later date – August 8 1922 – for the premiere. http://www.dfi.dk/
faktaomfilm/film/da/16030.aspx?id=16030 [accessed 24 April 2013].

[69]   Graham Petrie, 'Silent Film Adaptations of Dickens Part III: 1920–1927',
Dickensian, 97 (Winter 2001): p. 203.

[70]   I am grateful to Birgit Granhøj, Research Librarian at the Danish Film Institute
(DFI), who kindly translated and interpreted the DFI's records on this film for me.

[71]   Petrie, 'Silent Film Adaptations Part III', p. 205.

[72]   Pointer, *Dickens on the Screen*, p. 43.

film's gross income of 1,230,000 Danish Kroner was insufficient to prevent the company from almost going bankrupt.[73] Nordisk was already in financial trouble in this period, and the European banking crisis of the early 1920s which severely devalued the Danish Kroner and closed many Danish banks may also have had something to do with the shortfall. Independently of these external factors, though, an examination of Appendix B bears out the film's lack of international success, demonstrating that it probably had little impact on publishing and translation patterns. Czech and Hungarian re-translations in 1924 and a possible Swedish translation in 1925 might have been connected to the film's release, but since no film stills were included there is no proof of this.[74] In any case, by all accounts the foreign reviews were not favourable.[75]

David Lean's sound film was a far more successful global event. Pointer suggests that 'by 1946, the techniques of sound motion pictures had been developed so well that the happy conjunction of film and Dickens novel reached what may well remain its peak in *Great Expectations*'.[76] There is a certain truth in this; as we have seen, the film's success owed at least as much to twentieth-century technology and creative teamwork as it did to the innate qualities of Dickens's story. But the confluence may have more contributory factors than Pointer acknowledges; while the 'happy conjunction of film and Dickens' may have had specific effects in the case of *Great Expectations*, perhaps because Lean drew attention to latent and relevant themes ignored in previous remediations, it was almost certainly the addition of mid-twentieth century film distribution and publishing practices and the increasing sophistication of projection facilities and movie theatres far beyond Britain and the USA that enabled a maximisation of the film's potential to reach diverse markets.

The distributors for Cineguild Productions (GFD in the UK and Universal in the USA) ensured that the film brought *Great Expectations* to countries that had never previously heard of the novel, and revivified interest in some places where it had died out. It was released on 26 December 1946 in the UK, and then overseas in a staggered series: the USA in April/May 1947; Sweden, Austria, Finland, Denmark and France between August and December 1947; Turkey, Italy, Hong Kong and Portugal in 1948; Japan in 1949; and Spain in 1950. It did not reach East Germany until 1960 and West Germany until 1971.[77] An examination of translation patterns alongside these dates is revealing, suggesting both that the film's distribution may have sparked new interest and also, perhaps, that non-Anglophone publishers prepared for it with new pre-release translations. The 1950s saw several new

---

[73]   Danish Film Institute records.

[74]   Film 'tie-in' books as a publishing strategy were in their infancy in this period, but they were already available in the UK and USA and there is evidence that they were emerging in Europe too. See Mary Hammond, 'The Multimedia Afterlives of Victorian Novels: The Readers Library Photoplay Editions in the 1920s', *Nineteenth Century Theatre and Film*, 37 (December 2010): pp. 28–44.

[75]   Danish Film Institute records.

[76]   Pointer, *Dickens on the Screen*, p. 68.

[77]   See 'Great Expectations (1946) release info' in IMDB http://www.imdb.com/title/tt0038574/releaseinfo?ref_=tt_dt_dt#akas

German translations which would have been available in Austria where the film was shown. In France there were new editions of translations in 1948 and 1949. In Italy there were two in 1947 and two more in the 1950s. In Japan the translation patterns are still more remarkable: there were new ones in 1948, 1949, 1951 and 1952. As Matsumura notes, in Japan *Great Expectations* was actually better known through Lean's film than through translations of the novel, for reasons which he fleshes out more fully in his article in *Global Dickens*.[78] There are equally interesting correlations in Portugal (1947), Romania (1947), Greece (1949) and Spain (1945, 1946, 1949 and three in the 1950s).[79] In Norway, too, the film's popularity clearly created new demand (and benefitted from the now widespread practice of tying film distribution to book rerelease): the first translation into Norwegian was in 1948 in an edition that contained 16 stills from the film, and in this period *Great Expectations* outsold *David Copperfield* in Norway at 9,700 and 5,200 copies respectively.[80] In Hong Kong, English translations were probably readily available, but it seems significant that in 1946 there was also a translation into Chinese of the 'book of the film'.

In some contexts, the likelihood is that the adaptations were used to supplement English-language and literature teaching in schools, as they had long done in the USA,[81] but in others there seem to have been less official forces at work. Irma Rantavaara even suggests that the impact on Finnish readers of film and television versions of Dickens was as profound as the magazine culture of the 1840s and 1850s in Britain which brought Dickens to a wider audience; two new translations of *Great Expectations* appeared in Finnish in 1969 and a further one appeared in 1976, all in reaction to versions which had been shown on Finnish television.[82]

Not all the adaptations were imports. *Grote Verwachtingen* was produced in three parts for Dutch radio by David Koning in 1963.[83] A French television film version (*Les Grandes Espérances*) appeared on Christmas Day in 1968. There was a 35-minute Swiss film version directed by Leopold H. Ginner in 1971. A 50-minute Spanish version (*Grandes Esperanzas*) appeared as Episode 213 of the long-running Spanish serial drama 'Novela' on 3 July 1978. The South African English Service adapted the novel for radio in 26 half-hour episodes aired between 19 July and 21 Oct 1975, and another adaptation in 35 instalments was done by Springbok radio for their *Bestsellers* programme, airing between 25 Feb and 12 April 1985.[84] This was an interesting time for canonical British fiction to have

---

[78]   Matsumura, 'Dickens in Japan', Ada B. Nisbet Archive.

[79]   Alexandru Duțu, 'Dickens in Romania', Ada B. Nisbet Archive.

[80]   James Wesley Brown, 'Dickens in Norway', Ada B. Nisbet Archive.

[81]   See Steve J. Wutzler, '*David Copperfield* (1935) and the US Curriculum', in *Dickens on Screen*, pp. 155–70.

[82]   Irma Rantavaara, 'Dickens in Finland', Ada B. Nisbet Archive.

[83]   Willem van Maanen, 'Dickens in Holland', Ada B. Nisbet Archive.

[84]   I am grateful to Retha Buys, Senior Archivist, Springbok Radio, South African Broadcasting Corporation, for this information. SABC Catalogue references: E 93/412–437 and ES/362–378.

appeared on South African radio. Both programmes were aimed at white, middle-class, suburban and largely English-speaking South Africans, particularly women. The first (broadcast by the state-owned English Service, which was for decades the organ of the ruling Afrikaans party) appeared at the height of apartheid, during the forcible relocation of three million black South Africans into 'homelands' and a year before protest against the policy erupted in the Soweto riots. It was also broadcast in Namibia, then under South African control but already agitating for liberation. The second version appeared during ongoing township riots and in the middle of a national state of emergency, a matter of months before Springbok radio was closed down. The remediation of *Great Expectations* in these contexts might have been part of an oppositional broadcasting policy, but they might just as easily have served (or at least failed to disturb) right-wing political agendas that were very far removed from those which prevailed in communist countries during this period.

A better known (because more readily available) English-language non-UK/USA version is Tim Burstall's spin-off for Australian TV, *Great Expectations: The Untold Story*, broadcast in 1986.[85] 'The concept was good', Pointer explains, 'but seems not to have been too successfully accomplished, to judge from the reviews available.' Quoting *Variety*, he draws attention to a perennial complaint: 'This will irritate purists, though one suspects that Dickens – or any of the classic writers in the English language – is so little read and respected in these days of encroaching sub-literacy that few will know enough to complain.'[86] By this time Dickens had served as a yardstick for cultural literacy – and Dickens on TV and film as the most common way of raising it as an issue – for over 50 years.

But, as McFarlane's interview with Burstall reveals, the original idea was not to trip up the culturally uninformed but, on the contrary, to reflect 'the convict basis of some of Australia's egalitarian values'. *Great Expectations* serves here as an exemplar of erroneous official histories, and for such a redress to work to the full, knowledge of the original is almost essential. As McFarlane notes, 'there are always aspects of novels which, for whatever reason, the author has not developed…. [This one] picks up Dickens's vague sense of how a new life might be forged away from centuries-ingrained patterns of social division and expectation … true gentlemanliness … comes to be equated, perhaps chauvinistically, with Australia, which is represented as a crucible in which a man's real virtues, regardless of his birth-class, might have a chance to emerge'.[87] John O. Jordan goes further, arguing

---

[85]   McFarlane conducted an interview with Burstall in Melbourne in 2005. McFarlane, *Screen Adaptations*, p. 52. Records of the production are available at the National Film and Sound Archive, Australia. Title No: 656251 (draft scripts, cast listings, synopsis; also includes correspondence relating to casting, locations, film stock, discussions with the Australian Taxation Office, papers relating to copyrights, a medical report for Tim Burstall and other papers); Title No: 656818 (screenplay for two-hour feature film); Title No: 656213 (stills and publicity material, and some scripts for the same story penned by Jason Drummond and shorter than Tim Burstall's versions).

[86]   Pointer, *Dickens on the Screen*, p. 109.

[87]   McFarlane, *Screen Adaptations*, p. 54.

that Burstall's rewriting resituates 'Dickens's novel more firmly in a global context ... forcing it to speak ... in a different accent. Or, to put it more directly in [Homi] Bhabha's terms, *Great Expectations: The Untold Story* confirms the inaugural power of the English book while at the same time enacting its cultural displacement'.[88]

Although for obvious reasons 'the shadow' of this novel has certainly fallen particularly heavily 'across Australian literary and cultural production',[89] the cultural displacement of *Great Expectations* is not, as we have seen, solely an Australian phenomenon. Nor do all remediations in non-English contexts necessarily 'confirm the inaugural power of the English book'; on the contrary, some at least tend rather to support Robert Fraser's claim, based on his intricate analysis of the complex and often intrinsically transnational histories of print culture in Africa and South Asia, that a 'recognition of ... divergent histories ... embarrasses attempts such as Bhabha's to bring book history into line with fashionable theories of colonial interaction'.[90] Not every instance of cross-cultural remediation, even in once-colonised locations, fits the postcolonial critical model. Not every mention of Dickens's name is a point scored for his home team. The translation and migration histories of *Great Expectations* demonstrate that it seems to have been used for a range of purposes other than to affirm 'the inaugural power of the English book'. Though that may well have been a factor in some market contexts, readers are nothing if not rebellious, and their reading is undertaken for all sorts of reasons, by no means all of them respectful or naively absorptive of ideology. Katherine Mansfield, growing up in New Zealand in the 1900s, read extracts from Dickens aloud to make her sewing class cry in order to beat her elocution competition rival Jinne Moore.[91] En route home from South Africa via Lisbon in 1884, Lady Charlotte Schreiber read Dickens to her husband Charles to send him to sleep.[92]

Burstall's was not, in any case, the first Anglophone 'cultural displacement' of *Great Expectations* for foreign television that went further than straight adaptation; the novel had made itself readily available for that purpose more than 25 years earlier, appearing almost incognito as an episode of the popular American TV show *Wagon Train*, which ran between 1957 and 1965 in the USA. The episode based on Dickens's novel was called 'The Tom Tuckett Story' (Season Three, Episode 21). It was written by Jean Holloway and directed by Herschel Daugherty,

---

[88]   John O. Jordan, 'Great Expectations on Australian Television,' in Glavin, *Dickens on Screen*, p. 52.

[89]   Jordan, 'Great Expectations on Australian Television', p. 46.

[90]   Robert Fraser, *Book History through Postcolonial Eyes: Rewriting the Script* (Abingdon and New York, 2008), p. 21.

[91]   Katherine Mansfield, *Journal of Katherine Mansfield*, ed. by J. Middleton Murry (Hamburg, Paris and Bologna, 1935), p. 77. http://www.open.ac.uk/Arts/reading/UK/record_details.php?id=3831 [accessed 29 October 2013].

[92]   Lady Charlotte Schreiber, *Lady Charlotte Schreiber: Extracts from Her Journal 1853–1891*, ed. by the Earl of Bessborough (London, 1952), p. 180. http://www.open.ac.uk/Arts/reading/UK/record_details.php?id=27775 [accessed 29 October 2013].

and aired on 2 March 1960 during a period when the show topped viewer ratings in both the USA and the UK. Tautly scripted and well-acted in line with the show's customary high production values, there is no doubt that it claimed the American West as another 'crucible in which a man's real virtues, regardless of his birth-class, might have a chance to emerge', and equally forced the novel to 'speak with a different accent'. This remediation is seldom discussed, but it is worth pausing on; it is evidence of a cultural use for Dickens situated tangentially to the usual axis which critical histories have tended to draw between homage (as exemplified by Lean's *Great Expectations* and the BBC) and 'writing back' (as exemplified by Burstall's *The Untold Story*).

As the title suggests, the names of the major characters have been changed. Tom Tuckett ('Tuck') is the Pip character; Nat Burkett (played by Robert Middleton) is the name given to Magwitch; Miss Havisham (Josephine Hutchinson) becomes Miss Stevenson, and Estella (Louise Fletcher) becomes Elizabeth. The story opens on a misty night by the banks of the Kaw River in Kansas in 1854 (almost certainly chosen because it was the year in which US Congress opened the area for white settlement). Burkett is an army lieutenant on the run from a fanatical unit leader, whose mission was to 'teach the Indian once and for all who rules in this country' by wiping out a Kaw village filled with women, children and the elderly. Burkett warns the villagers that a raid is coming and they escape in the nick of time, an action that results in Burkett's court martial for treason and the enduring friendship of five Native American nations who thereafter pledge to hide and protect him from US law. Tuck, a poor Kansas country boy, encounters the exhausted Burkett on the banks of the river after he has escaped from the prison wagon, and provides him with a file and some food.

Fifteen years pass and we next encounter the grown-up Tuck (Ben Cooper) dressed as a gentleman after an expensive education in a New York law school, and joining a wagon train bound for San Francisco where his mysterious benefactor has secured a partnership for him in a prestigious law firm. Confident, arrogant, and frustrated by wagon leader Major Seth Adams (Ward Bond)'s continued refusal to tell him who has paid for his education and his passage, on the wagon train Tuck encounters two acquaintances from his Kansas days: the eccentric recluse Miss Stevenson and her niece Elizabeth, with whom he has always been in love.

Part of the function of the Western as a genre is to offer a corrective to the problems of over-civilization; as Jane Tompkins has put it, '[the Western] seems to offer escape from the conditions of life in modern industrial society: from a mechanized existence, economic dead ends, social entanglements, unhappy personal relations, political injustice. The desire to change places also signals a powerful need for self-transformation'.[93] The transposition of *Great Expectations*' famous wealthy recluse to the rough living associated with a westbound wagon train means the impending transformation can be clearly signalled at once, through simple material juxtaposition. Ridiculously, Miss Stevenson has brought

---

[93]   Jane Tompkins, *West of Everything: The Inner Life of Westerns* (Oxford, 1993), p. 4.

her decaying house full of painful memories with her in her wagon, in the shape of once-precious but now useless items such as an old clock which, she tells Tuck, 'I used to watch when I was young, stopped at the moment when my heart was broken', a disused candelabra which 'used to light the face that was turned toward mine', and a battered pillow 'on which I used to dream'. As a result, Miss Stevenson comes across as emotionally weak and morally decayed by her spoiled and delusional life in the city, and her quavering exhortations to Tuck to 'love her, love her!' appear in this scene as the unambiguous ravings of a lunatic; eventually they drive the young couple out of the wagon in embarrassment. Of course, Elizabeth still warns Tuck that she has been taught well and that, 'The man who loves me will pay for the man who did not love her.' The West has not yet begun to work its magic on any of them.

More disappointments are in store for Tuck when Burkett pays him a surprise visit and reveals himself as the source of Tuck's good fortune following several years spent making a lucrative living by trading furs in Canada. Tuck, with all his 'book learning', is convinced he knows the definition of a good man, and that Burkett is not it. Forced to spend a few days on the trail with the older man, though, he learns that he is a martyr and not a traitor, and when the commander of the wagon train's cavalry guard recognises Burkett, Tuck agrees to see him safely back to Canada to escape the clutches of the law. Native drums sounding on the night of their escape warn Burkett that the cavalry pursuing the two of them are riding into an ambush and he returns to rescue them, risking rearrest – and his neck – in the process. After a truce is agreed during which the chiefs of five Native American nations demand a promise from the Major that 'the white man with so much goodness in him will not be punished for that goodness', the Major agrees to let him go. The episode ends with Tuck acknowledging Burkett as his surrogate father, a man of 'wisdom, courage and loyalty' and the finest 'gentleman he has ever known', and returning to Elizabeth who has (predictably, since she has been on the trail for a few days now) finally discovered that she loves him. Meanwhile, the wagon master sternly tells a repentant Miss Stevenson: 'You can't tell people how to live their lives.' In failing to ruin the couple's romantic prospects thanks to the regenerative crucible of the Western frontier, she (like the army's xenophobes) has learned a valuable lesson about human rights.

The credits acknowledge that the story is based on the novel by Dickens. But while the narrative takes as its core Dickens's theme of innate, simple moral goodness versus corrupt high-society values, the transposition of the story into the American West successfully enacts a particularly American historical poetics, a vision of effete (Europeanised) Easterners learning about masculinity, and the socially powerful (whether governments or guardians) learning the importance of individual freedom. In the context of the Cold War and the simultaneous problems attendant on the US Government's policy of the relocation of Native Americans from reservations to cities in this period, the episode is an effective example of the way in which the novel has been used to speak to contemporary issues. Crucially, though, through the name, plot and thematic changes which render the original pretty much immaterial, it does so without necessarily 'confirming the inaugural power of the English book'. The episode would – and probably did – work equally well for an American viewer who had no idea who Dickens was, while for one who did the nod to classic literature may have been a marker of quality (or, conversely, given *Wagon Train*'s clearly defined generic boundaries, a sign that this particular episode would be a welcome relief from the usual stuffy modes of classic adaptation). In Britain it might well have had a different appeal, one more inflected with national pride in the source text's origins. But in Britain, too, the Western as a genre had an audience that may well have cared more about fantasies of escape than cultural flattery. Many of those who watched *Wagon Train* in the 1960s and 1970s (and I was one) did not give Dickens a thought.

The point this example brings home is that *Great Expectations*' global survival and the range of meanings it has offered to readers and audiences have by no means depended on an accurate rendering of 'authentic' Dickensian essence, or on Bhabha's notion of 'the inaugural power of the English book' (which are often taken to mean the same thing). On the contrary, they have sometimes – perhaps just as often in fact – required a wilful debunking or complete jettisoning of notions of authenticity. They have, in fact, been the result of several different motives at various historical moments, such as a general demand for Anglophone products as part of a global trade in cultural and linguistic capital (to which Dickensian authenticity is often immaterial), or of a desire to address deified Victorian institutions such as imperialism or industrial capitalism for purposes of criticism or self-definition (which may depend on authenticity, but only insofar as it aids in the deconstruction or reconstruction process). Equally, more pragmatically, they have also often been the result of a basic need for easily decoupled dramatic scenarios with powerful moral themes and, wherever possible, an established success rating which works in a number of different publishing contexts. This is something at which Victorian novelists were generally very good and Dickens in particular excelled, and which the post-Victorian media has enduringly valued. If Dickens is able in any sense to define our literary 'genetic coding', it probably has as much to do with the birth of multiplatform publishing as with national identity; we may be closer to the nineteenth-century's media practices than its ideologies. The important thing to note here is that 'Dickensian essence' in all the cases I have outlined above was indisputably radically altered through linguistic, generic or political remediation; sometimes through all three at once. As Anny Sadrin has remarked, 'undeniably, the readers of different translations all read the same stories, but they do not read the same books'.[94] The same is undoubtedly also true of 'translations' in their broader sense; 'Charles Dickens's *Great Expectations*' has adopted many different shapes in its lifetime. The common post-Victorian construction of such adaptability as a problem and those who take advantage of

---

[94] Anny Sadrin, '"The Tyranny of Words": Reading Dickens in Translation,' in *Dickens: The Craft of Fiction and the Challenges of Reading: Proceedings of the Milan Symposium*, ed. by Rossana Bonadai, Clotilda de Stasio, Carlo Pagetti and Alessandro Vescovi (Milan, 2000), p. 275.

it as tampering disrespectfully with the Master should surely properly be seen as another historically constituted part of the novel's still-proliferating hypertexts. On one level, 'Authentic Dickens' is just another marketable commodity.

Cultural Translation: 'writing back' and 'mucking around' 1986–2012

Remediations such as the 1960 *Wagon Train* episode offer a useful corrective to the ways in which dramatic adaptation and 'writing back' have tended to be characterised in culture and criticism. Pointer claims in his fairly exhaustive survey of Dickens in adaptation (which includes – though it does not discuss – 'The Story of Tom Tuckett') that 'Dickens has not been treated like any mere writer of fiction whose books can be distorted and altered beyond measure.... On the contrary, Dickens's works form part of that corpus of literature that is so well known and loved that film makers and dramatists tamper with it at their peril. In a way they have become sacrosanct, and indeed are sometimes treated with a veneration unsuited to their real literary worth'.[95] Notions of literary worth aside, this might be true of academic criticism, but it was not true of the remediators themselves even in the late 1990s when Pointer was writing. Some dramatists (notably those working for the BBC) have certainly, like Lloyd Jones's complex, tragic fictional schoolteacher, Mr Watts, felt that one should not 'muck around with Dickens.... [It] would be an act of vandalism, like smashing the window in a chapel',[96] and have accordingly treated Dickens with cautious veneration. But others (often, though not always, working in different national contexts) have been driven by different motives. Many have realised, as Mr Watts eventually does, that in some contexts it is necessary to pull 'the embroidery out of Dickens' or otherwise rework him if he is to remain relevant to modern audiences and a continued publishing success.

Examining some of the most radical results of this process, Jay Clayton argues that '[t]here is a logic in this afterlife ... a logic not entirely alien to the patterns in Dickens's own stories.... Another way of putting this point is to say that Dickens anticipates some of the characteristic features of postmodern life ... tracing the misshapen forms of his survival in today's world will tell readers something about themselves – and about Dickens too'.[97] In previous chapters I have been somewhat more interested than Clayton in understanding the different shapes (and indeed misshapes, though that term too is ideologically loaded) which those forms have taken over time, since it has seemed to me that if we are positing a relationship between 'the patterns in Dickens's stories' and 'the characteristic features of postmodern life', then we need to examine some of the links in the chain that binds them. The claim for Dickens's modernity in his apparent anticipation of

---

[95]   Pointer, *Dickens on the Screen*, p. vi.

[96]   Lloyd Jones, *Mister Pip* (London, 2008), p. 196.

[97]   Jay Clayton, *Charles Dickens in Cyberspace: The Afterlife of the Nineteenth Century in Postmodern Culture* (Oxford, 2003), p. 147.

future media needs has also, of course, been echoed in many other critical works, some of which have informed previous chapters. What Clayton adds to these generally more historically focussed approaches (including mine thus far) is the attention he pays to the more radical 'misshapings' of Dickens that have dominated the late twentieth and early twenty-first centuries, from theme parks that permit interactions with facsimiles of his characters, to internet dating sites that have appropriated his thirteenth novel's title. Since *Great Expectations* has been a favourite target for such misshapings of every stamp from the playful to the furious, it seems appropriate to finish this chapter on translation with a discussion of their variety and significance, and to situate them in relation to the continued production of straighter and often still quite reverent adaptations.

Some of these re-workings or appropriations have, like 'Pip', Season 4, episode 14 of the cult television show *South Park* (2000), savaged or satirised the plot and the characters. Some have read them through the lens of feminism (Kathy Acker, *Great Expectations*, 1983; Sue Roe, *Estella: Her Expectations*, 1982); through postcolonialism, metafiction and postmodern pastiche (Lloyd Jones, *Mister Pip*, 2006; Peter Carey, *Jack Maggs*,1997); some have soberly, angrily or comically reflected on their dangerous, mistaken, or simply silly assumptions and prejudices (Tim Burstall, *Great Expectations: The Untold Story*, 1986; Mark Evans, *Bleak Expectations*, BBC Radio 4, 2007–12); or built on and exposed their techniques (Alfonso Cuarón, *Great Expectations*, 1998). Some (often the least successful) have simply exploited the bits left over or left out (Michael Noonan, *Magwitch*, 1982; Tony Lester, *The Magwitch Trilogy*, 2010–12). There are, in addition, numbers of playful appropriations that redeploy Dickens in new generic fields such as supernatural fiction.

I am more interested here in the dissemination and reception of these works than in their formal mechanics, and interested most of all in the remediations which have attracted the least attention. There has already been considerable critical response to the serious literary and filmic 'writings-back'; Beverly Taylor, for example, reads Peter Carey's darkly satirical novel *Jack Maggs* as driven by the twin themes of abortion and theft which 'emblematize the relationship of colonial Australia to its parent England'.[98] Hermione Lee takes a different view, suggesting that 'Carey reads Dickens in order to produce a late twentieth-century story of equally pitiable isolation, of trauma, wounds, secrets and confessions.… More than an imitation, this is an exploration … of how writing works as a form of trickery and mesmerism'.[99] Brian McFarlane, however, reads the novel as

---

[98]   Beverly Taylor, 'Discovering New Pasts: Victorian Legacies in the Postcolonial Worlds of *Jack Maggs* and *Mister Pip*', *Victorian Studies*, 52, Special Issue: Papers and Responses from the Seventh Annual Conference of the North American Victorian Studies Association, held jointly with the British Association for Victorian Studies (Autumn 2009): p. 96.

[99]   'Great Extrapolations: Hermione Lee Reviews *Jack Maggs* by Peter Carey', *Observer*, Sunday 28 September 1997. http://www.theguardian.com/books/1997/sep/28/fiction.petercarey [accessed 2 April 2014].

'an elliptic, idiosyncratic narrative of a post-modern take on a story of poverty, hardships, expectations, risings in society and the utter collapse of hopes'.[100] Carey's novel gets off relatively lightly as 'writings back' go. This may well be a result of the fact that, in addition to being a fine novelist, in this particular work he is as respectful as he is critical of his subject, and he demonstrates above all that he has taken it seriously by engaging with it at the deepest level. Much of the sorts of criticism which other remediators have attracted, though, has tended to coalesce around the old fault lines, using a highly politicised language that pits tradition (fidelity) against innovation (radical transformation). This critical language can tell us a great deal about *Great Expectations'* current role in Western culture.

Film adaptation seems to have engendered the most suspicion from Dickensian critics. Even those who are willing to accept film adaptation as permissible disagree on the level of 'mucking about' they expect or are willing to tolerate. For Mukherjee, Cuarón's self-reflexive 1998 film is not radical enough: it 'seems to have no motive beyond the fact that it takes advantage of technology to cinematically rethink Dickens's powerful narrative in MTV format ... Cuarón does not look awry at literary and cinematic tradition: he simple-mindedly sees through it'.[101] Shari Hodges Holt likes the film better, seeing its structural and largely industry-motivated conservatism as useful in that the melding of transformation and fidelity is able to demonstrate 'the particular relevance of Dickens's Victorian narrative for postmodern generations'.[102] McFarlane also likes Cuarón's film; for him too it updates yet manages to preserve something of Dickens's original, being 'a genuinely sexy take on that tale of romantic obsession and lives being wrenched out of predictable courses'.[103] He is far less comfortable with Sue Roe's novel, partly (revealingly) because it has 'only tangential connections with Dickens', partly because it is 'ostensibly a feminist text', proof of which for him, rather bizarrely, lies in the fact that the Miss Havisham character calls off her wedding rather than being jilted at the altar. The novel, he tells us, reads 'as if Gertrude Stein were having a go at writing a romantic novel – and failing'.[104] The twin charges he levels at this novel – of its overly loose relation to the original, and its unsuccessful (or, to McFarlane, simply baffling) feminist poetics comprising Modernism, pulp fiction and the refusal of societal and literary norms – serve as illuminating examples of the conservative standards to which Western critical culture often adheres when anyone attempts to remediate Dickens in a way that upsets the post-Victorian requirement of due respect.

---

[100] McFarlane, *Screen Adaptations*, p. 46.

[101] Mukherjee, 'Missed Encounters', p. 111.

[102] Shari Hodges Holt, 'Dickens from a Postmodern Perspective: Alfonso Cuarón's *Great Expectations* for Generation X,' *Dickens Studies Annual*, 38 (2007): p. 70.

[103] McFarlane, *Screen Adaptations*, p. 126. See also Pamela Katz's interesting interview with Cuarón about the making of this film, the creative and pragmatic decisions that he made, and the freedom that growing up in Mexico where Dickens was not required reading gave him. Katz, 'Directing Dickens: Alfonso Cuarón's 1998 *Great Expectations*', in Glavin, *Dickens on Screen*, pp. 95–103.

[104] McFarlane, *Screen Adaptations*, p. 50.

There are similar disagreements about Kathy Acker's *Great Expectations*. For Mukherjee, the novel is successful at radical transformation, using Dickens as a tool through which to deconstruct and even partially explain the instability of the postmodern self:

> The novel is a neurotic shape-shifter which cannibalizes older, mostly canonical texts … the temporal unification of past and future with one's present – an unmistakable symptom of (Acker's purchase on) the postmodern condition – leads to a breakdown of personal identity … the hysterical protagonist of Acker's novel is dissatisfied, dis-gusted, and sick with desire: he or she ambivalently negotiates a cultural wasteland, where even language has been defeated by that which it could not speak for or of.[105]

There is a sense here, for Mukherjee, of a breaking out and breaking away from icons and the certainties of history they represent – with inevitable but rather dire results for the postmodern subject. For Kathryn Hume, however, the novel is not about breakdown (except of the demagogues of the literary past) but about freedom, of a kind which constitutes rather than breaks down individual identity: 'Freedom is defined against oppressive familial and social expectations and is experienced when narrators violate those social norms because they wish to…. [L]ike the Romantics, the Acker [novels'] voices value madness over bourgeois sanity'.[106] Dickens, of course, is part of the 'bourgeois sanity' which Acker aims to attack; it is the canon, as much as this individual novel, which is her target, as it is so often the target of writers writing back. For Hume, Acker's novel is a fantasy of escape: she has recognised that the canon is a post-Romantic construction in which we are largely still trapped.

These examples usefully demonstrate how difficult we often still find it to speak or write about misshapen Dickens using anything but the old lexical binaries of fidelity and iconoclasm. This is surely a result of the fact that most of this criticism adheres to middlebrow remediations which depend on a familiarity with the original: in 'writing back' to *Great Expectations*, these authors almost always assume – must assume, if their critiques are to work – that we have read it, that we recognise its cultural prejudices, though the kindest criticism is usually reserved for remediations which on some level prove that they also, on some level, admire it. One final example underlines this point. Beverly Taylor, while acknowledging in her article on *Mister Pip* that 'contemporary novelists "muck around with Dickens" to address contemporary concerns', still ends with a warning that if we set too much store by the results, we might miss something crucial in the original. She couches the overcoming of this tendency in terms of a process of maturation of both fictional character and real reader:

> Matilda's maturation culminates in her finding a way to talk back by penning her own narrative of herself, Mr. Watts, and her mother; in this regard, she resembles

---

[105] Mukherjee, 'Missed Encounters', pp. 112–5.

[106] Kathryn Hume, 'Voice in Kathy Acker's Fiction', *Contemporary Literature*, 42 (Autumn, 2001): pp. 495 and 508.

Lloyd Jones and Peter Carey, who also talk back to Dickens. Like Matilda, we
must be attentive to how we read texts, both Victorian and neo-Victorian. Like her,
we should consider how we "magg" to suit our own ends, taking what we need
at the moment while neglecting other patterns or overlooking other treasures. [107]

For Taylor, the strength of Lloyd Jones's novel lies in its demonstration of what she
takes to be a truism: that while 'magging' is fine and even important in its place,
'maturity' comes when we learn to read holistically, understanding the novel in its
entirety and learning to appreciate all its 'treasures' even if we eventually jettison
them.

Questions of maturity aside, in a real sense the social stratification of taste and
understanding implicitly carried by Taylor's formulation may well be accurate:
academics (whose number, significantly, Matilda joins at the end of Jones's novel)
and the professional literati might be the only readers with sufficient specialist
competence now to care about or fully comprehend *Great Expectations*. As
Glavin has pointed out, everyone else in the twenty-first century probably needs
the adaptations and the misshapes because they 'generate whatever possibilities
remain for reading the fiction'.[108] On one level, of course, 'writings back' (and
the criticism that addresses them) are also part – a fairly high-profile part – of
the perpetuation of the Dickens hypertexts. But there are many other less radical
(but no less interesting) contemporaneous examples of this ongoing process of
proliferation which get little attention. As publishers who continue to issue his
novels in significant numbers well know, if they are to be successful, new editions
must also contain explanatory introductions by scholars or respected members
of the media, and those for sale outside education institutions must also sport
photographs of the latest stars to play the leading roles on film or television. All these
editions add new layers to the *Great Expectations* hypertexts. The 2011 Random
House edition of *Great Expectations* is a case in point; published to accompany
the 2011 BBC series, it carries a cover picture of handsome Douglas Booth as
Pip, rising theatre and TV star Vanessa Kirby as Estella, and in the background
Gillian Anderson, star of the long-running TV science fiction show *The X-Files*,
here setting out to prove that she can be an equally eccentric Miss Havisham and
that Dickens can be spooky too. The book is also provided with an introduction
by the series adaptor Sarah Phelps, well-known to British audiences for modern
screenplays such as the long-running soap *EastEnders*, and here assuring readers
that *Great Expectations* is 'a savage novel that's part rite of passage, part revenge
tragedy, part mystery thriller and part furious interrogation of the inequities of the
law'.[109] This should sound familiar; it is in effect 'Great Romance! Great Thrills!
Great Suspense! Great Adventure!' with a twenty-first century edge.

Juliet John quite rightly sees nothing new or problematic in the postmodern
symbiosis between hypo- and hypertext, arguing that 'the "real meaning" of

---

[107]   Taylor, 'Discovering New Pasts', pp. 95 and 103.

[108]   Glavin, *Dickens on Screen*, p. 6.

[109]   Sarah Phelps, 'Introduction,' in *Great Expectations* (London, 2011), p. vii.

Dickens has always compounded the perceived message of the novels with the cultural idea of Dickens'.[110] And the 'cultural idea of Dickens', as we have seen, is a moveable feast. The question that remains to us now is: has there been a change in this interdependent relationship across the millennium, and if so, what can that tell us about how we are currently using, not using, understanding or wilfully misunderstanding *Great Expectations*? Does the novel have a life outside the canon of middlebrow literature and mainstream film on which most critics focus?

Notwithstanding the 2013 survey which claimed that a third of British people questioned had no idea who had written *Great Expectations*, there are many signs of the novel living an active life in various other generic dimensions, some of them digital, but many of them literary.[111] One of the least technically accomplished of these spin-offs is *The Magwitch Trilogy* (2010–12), self-published through FeedARead by Tony Lester. It is certainly amateurish. But it is significant as an example of something akin to fan-fiction, attempting, like Michael Noonan's *Magwitch* (1982), to perform the same work as Burstall's *Untold Story* but without the big budget, the publicity, or the official endorsement of a TV station or a mainstream publisher. Spin-off fiction, like non-professional online reviewing and fan blogging, is an important development in the history of Dickens remediation.

Mukherjee suggests that 'We can read literary rewriting as an intentional act of wish fulfilment that emphasizes the retroactivity of meaning.... The forms and content literary rewritings seek to find, or refind, are often phantasmic in nature. They look back in anger or longing for objects always already lost'.[112] She is writing specifically about postmodern and postcolonial 'writings back', but the claim works equally well for spin-off and cult-genre fiction in which there is certainly a consciousness of the phantasmic nature of the object, and through which longing for and fear of the objects 'always already lost' are often enacted through the literalising of metaphors placed there by Dickens himself. Two prime examples are *Pip and the Zombies* by Louis Skipper (Houston: Rock Island Press, 2010) and *Grave Expectations* by Sherri Browning Erwin (2011), both part of the 'monster classic' or 'mashup' trend which also offers paranormal takes on Jane Austen, Mark Twain and others. Both invoke nostalgia for a past time when the existence of non-humans might just – with only a small stretch of the Dickensian imagination – have had some foundation in fact. Readers reviewing *Pip and the Zombies* are generally enthusiastic about the synergy: 'The writing is amazing. It's hard to tell what was written by Charles Dickens and what was written by Louis Skipper', blogged one on the *Goodreads* site in August 2013. *Grave Expectations* performs a similar feat of cross-fertilisation. Browning Erwin layers over Dickens's prose a playful ghoulish narrative of a world in which the non-human secretly abounds despite human attempts to repress it. Pip, the half-

---

[110] John, *Dickens and Mass Culture*, p. 285.

[111] Andrew Levy, *Mail Online*, 25 September 2013, http://www.dailymail.co.uk/news/article-2431259/Now-Dickens-wrote-er-Great-Expectations-Third-adults-idea-wrote-classic-novel.html [accessed 1 November 2013].

[112] Mukherjee, 'Missed Encounters', p. 122.

human, half-werewolf pup (patently embodying the socially unacceptable face of desire), meets an older full-blooded convict werewolf in silver shackles in a graveyard under a full moon. The story adheres remarkably closely to Dickens's for purposes both of historical colour and of comedy – too close for some readers, one of whom blogged on *Goodreads*: '[T]here was way too much of Dickens' writing left in it, so that I felt I was wading through the story instead of enjoying it' (2 March 2012). Another reader, however, felt that '[w]hile the werewolves, vampires, and zombies play clear roles in the story, Dickens' original purpose in writing the novel shines through should readers bother to think about it' (31 August 2011). [113] Given Dickens's own description of Pip as a 'young dog' in this scene (*Great Expectations*, ed. Rosenberg, p. 10), repeated in his first dealings with Estella (*Great Expectations*, ed. Rosenberg, p. 53), and of Magwitch's repeated dehumanisation by the narrative, it is no real stretch to imagine them as werewolves. Likewise the transformations of the other characters: Miss Havisham appears as a vampire, and Estella is revealed as a slayer from whom Pip must hide his real form or risk getting a silver stake through the heart. The only things not put here by Dickens are the metaphors' literal embodiments. The themes of prejudice, aspiration, irony, cruelty, self-delusion, forbidden desire, a search for origins and unrequited love are all intact; mashups serve to update these themes in perhaps the only way young readers find tolerable; by returning them to a version of the past which resides in an exciting but safely distant world of the imagination.

An interesting – and in some ways related – development has come with the recent appearance of graphic novel versions. Drawing on the combined popularity of Japanese manga and Western comics, they are expressly designed, as one publisher's website puts it, as 'a lively and fascinating way to introduce Dickens to a new generation'.[114] Among the best of the *Great Expectations* graphic novels in terms of production values are those by Rick Geary and William B. Jones (New York: Papercutz, 2007) and Brigit Viney (Andover: Heinle Cengage Learning, 2009). They add an attractive new dimension to the story, forcing the reader unfamiliar with comics to traverse the page differently, using the vertical as well as the horizontal axis, and to consider the relationship between image and text in a way we have probably not experienced since the novel's first appearance in illustrated form in the mid-nineteenth century. Certainly, for this reader (who has read, viewed and listened to more versions of this text than most), the graphic novels were among the most effective in rendering it anew.

They do not, however, necessarily work so well for readers more familiar with graphic novels and manga. The *Goodreads* review blogs generated by the *Great Expectations* graphic novel are illuminating. 'Since I was forced to read this (the real version) in high school and hardly remember a word of it', one young reader

---

[113] http://www.goodreads.com/book/show/10578373-pip-and-the-zombies; and http://www.goodreads.com/book/show/9814690-grave-expectations [accessed 1 November 2013].

[114] The Book House, a division of the Salariya Book Company. http://www.book-house.co.uk/Graphic/Graffex/Pages/gtexpectations.html [accessed 1 November 2013].

blogged on 5 December 2009, 'I thought it might be nice to try again, this time with pictures. I have to say, adding pictures to classic novels makes a whole lot of sense. This time around, I could actually follow the plot.' But the simplification clearly did not help to fix the problem of the story's age or its intrinsic flaws, since she adds the significant caveat, '[A] lot of the characters' motivations were baffling to me'. On 21 April 2013, another blogger agreed: 'Nice pictures, but I just couldn't handle the writing. I pretty much only understood what was going on from the pictures alone.' A third wrote on 10 May 2013: 'I didn't expect this book to take me this long to finish since I usually finish graphic novels pretty quickly. But I found myself bored at times and I even started questioning why this book is a classic and that really slowed me down.' For these readers, Dickens – or perhaps his cultural weight – gets in the way of their enjoyment. The reviews are not all bad; one blogger enthused: 'I now understand why this book is considered one of the greatest books of all time' (15 November 2012). Another worried that some crucial bits were being left out: 'While I believe this adaptation is well done considering the depth of the original text, I finished the graphic novel feeling as though I really didn't get a thorough enough exposure to the quality and complexity of Dickens' writing,' (1 January 2013) – a response which inevitably makes one wonder why they did not simply read the 1861 version.[115] Offering too much Dickens or not enough, the graphic novels are fairly numerous at present but they are not overwhelmingly endorsed by readers, who tend to be suspicious of their motives.

One illuminating positive review comes (perhaps unsurprisingly) from an English teacher working in Oman. It indicates both the extent to which teachers need help in teaching *Great Expectations* in the twenty-first century and the extent of its continued presence in non-Anglophone cultures. Its author, Neil McBeath, begins with the *Guardian Weekly*'s 4 September 2009 report on graphic novels having earned nearly $16 million in 2008, and he claims that English as a Foreign Language curriculum planners have been slow to recognise their potential as teaching tools. McBeath argues for a change to that position:

> It is easy for teachers of EFL, particularly native speakers with a background in English literature, to forget how completely foreign (in every sense) Dickens' world must be to a young Chinese, Gulf Arab or South American student. The graphic element of this story, therefore, helps to reduce that distance. There is no chance that the students' suspension of disbelief will conjure up false images. When Miss Havisham retorts "I am yellow skin and bone", we see that she is telling the truth.[116]

Teachers might welcome them, but Charles Hatfield captures the ambivalence with which this particular type of Dickens remediation is often greeted by young readers.

---

[115] http://www.goodreads.com/book/show/16134303-classical-comics-great-expectations [accessed 1 November 2013].

[116] Neil McBeath, online review of *Great Expectations: The Graphic Novel*, adapted by Brigit Viney (Andover, 2010), www.hltmag.co.uk/aug10/pubs02.rtf [accessed 1 November 2013].

He suggests that the form offers exciting flexibility, an enticing breakdown of traditional generic boundaries: '[A] graphic novel can be almost anything: a novel, a collection of interrelated or thematically similar stories, a memoir, a travelogue or journal, a history, a series of vignettes or lyrical observations, an episode from a longer work – you name it. Perhaps this very plasticity helps explain the currency of the term'. But the sting lies in the second half of the designation, the word 'novel'. 'Ironically, the novel – once a disreputable, bastard thing, radical in its formal instability – is here being invoked as the very byword of literary merit and respectability.'[117] *Great Expectations* in graphic novel form, remediated largely to help teachers to fulfil the requirements of a curriculum that increasingly seems to alienate students, weighs heavy on the 'literary merit and respectability' side. It seems to fool very few by wearing the mantle of a contemporary cult form. Perhaps the adaptors are still caught between making Dickens comprehensible and keeping him 'authentic'; Dickens's own dialogue is often still here in these adaptations along with the story's flaws, implausibilities and creaky coincidences, and young people seem to notice. The crucial thing seems to be, not just that all these young readers know about Dickens, but that they know how they are supposed to react to him; they know he is being taught to them, and unless they are concerned with their grades, they seem to react as generations of schoolchildren have no doubt reacted when something smacks of proselytising: they switch off.

Screen Adaptations 2011–12

Alongside the playful misshapes, the educational remediations and the extravagant Gothicism of Jo Clifford's recent West End theatrical version, the serious dramatic adaptations for the screen keep going too, though for a different set of reasons and largely for different audiences. Their aims and construction can tell us something about the current state of play in the novel's long and varied cultural life, and something about the diversity of its contemporary appeal.

Debates about the respective merits and weaknesses of the 2011 serialised version (BBC three-part serial, 27, 28 and 29 December 2011) and the 2012 film occupied many columns of newsprint during the bicentenary celebrations, and they often centred on discussions of the very different performances of Gillian Anderson and Helena Bonham Carter as Miss Havisham. This icon of deranged femininity has recently undergone another historical shift as older actresses once known for their beauty take her on as a way of extending their careers into early middle age. The shift seems indicative of an attempt to make the novel relevant to modern audiences by highlighting its theme of thwarted sexual, as well as social, desire. I asked both the film's producer Elizabeth Karlsen and the BBC serial's producers, George Ormond, Hilary Salmon and Anne Pivcevic, whether they had chosen *Great Expectations* for the Dickens bicentenary because it seemed

---

[117] Charles Hatfield, *Alternative Comics: An Emerging Literature* (Jackson, 2005), pp. 5–6.

particularly apposite – more so than other Dickens novels – in the middle of a new economic recession, with an ageing population, and at a moment when the sexualising of classic literature has reached new heights with Andrew Davis's trademark adaptations and the success of neo-Victorian texts such as Sarah Waters's *Tipping the Velvet* (novel 1998; BBC TV series 2002).

The BBC team told me in an email exchange that the idea had come from screenwriter Sarah Phelps, who loved the book, felt strongly that it was due for a remake, and pushed hard for the chance to do it on television. The producers denied that they agreed because they thought the novel spoke to contemporary concerns; they felt that while the novel's reference to the personal cost of economic recession was bound to strike a chord with some viewers, to make topicality a central motivation would be to risk patronising their audience.[118] In a separate interview in 2012, however, Sarah Phelps made her own views on topicality more explicit, admitting that she would love to do a remake of *Nicholas Nickleby* just as the British education cuts started to bite,[119] and publicity interviews with the cast indicate that they too were thinking about their performances in terms of how to make them relevant.

The renewed emphasis on female performance, in particular, has had useful side effects in foregrounding the role of Estella in new ways as well as extending our understanding of Miss Havisham. Vanessa Kirby, for example, recognised during her preparation for the role of Estella in the TV version that since the girl's story is told solely from the point of view of Pip, her frigidity and coldness are probably blown completely out of proportion by him as a result of his obsessive infatuation. She therefore deliberately played the part as a young woman manipulated by patriarchal and generational abuses of power and by the conventions of the male-centred Victorian canon. She also angled her performance towards a younger audience, as the series rode the coat-tails of other successful TV period dramas such as *Downton Abbey* (UK, directed by Julian Fellowes, first aired 2010), with which critics often bracketed it. As Kirby described the Pip/Estella plotline: 'It's just a case of first love which, as everyone who's experienced it knows, just takes over your life, it's so intense.'[120]

The film, too, was designed with a contemporary audience and contemporary issues in mind, though its focus was slightly different. Jeremy Irvine (Pip), fresh from his role in Steven Spielberg's *War Horse* (Dreamworks, 2011), described how he sees his character as dangerously flawed due to his upbringing: 'This isn't some little game he's playing. He's been seriously abused as a child and in

---

[118] Author's email interview with BBC Drama producers George Ormond, Hilary Salmon and Anne Pivcevic, 30 November 2011.

[119] Sarah Phelps, onstage interview at 'Adapting Dickens for Television' event, BFI Southbank, London, 28 January 2012.

[120] Caroline Frost, 'Great Expectations: Star Vanessa Kirby Defends "Young Estella in First Love –We've All Been There"', *Huffington Post*, 26 December 2011, http://www.huffingtonpost.co.uk/2011/12/26/great-expectations-vanessa-kirby-estella_n_1169892.html [accessed 4 November 2013].

this version, it's real domestic abuse at its most violent.'[121] The additional power derived from Irvine's recent portrayal of a boy and his horse caught up in the destructive forces of history (for which in 2011 he was nominated for a London Critics' Circle Film Award for Young British Performer of the Year and an Empire Award for Best Male Newcomer) surely resonated with the casting director, if not always with audiences. Viewer reviews are mixed: some called it a 'masterpiece' and commended the acting and the sets, while others found the pace disappointing and the casting unconvincing.[122] Critics were similarly divided: Joe Walsh of Cinevue (USA) recognised the themes which the writer, director and actors had intended to draw out, but felt they were unsuccessful in the execution: 'Brought to the forefront this time around is the psychological development of the once-lowly Pip as a product of his abusive upbringing and environment. The result is that Pip's motivation to be a gentleman is, above all, to escape the horrors of his childhood. But this modern twist on the tale loses the essence of a story that is essentially about love.'[123] Few other critics I have come across consider love to be the story's 'essence', but this reference to the perennial search for one is telling in itself. Operating on a similar principle, *Empire* felt this version struggled to find something new to say (and reiterated the Anderson/Bonham Carter rivalry): '[T]here's nothing it does well that hasn't at least been equalled, and in similar fashion, by a previous attempt. Its brooding, murky atmospherics still stand in the long shadows of Lean's film, while Alfonso Cuarón's 1998 modern-dress version betters it for youthful sexual frisson. And you'd think the reliably dotty Helena Bonham Carter would be the Miss Havisham to end all Miss Havishams, but Gillian Anderson brought more tragic mystique to the role on telly last year'.[124] Philip French of the British Sunday broadsheet the *Observer* was more impressed and pronounced on the story's contemporary relevance: '[T]his handsomely designed, unobtrusively edited and thoughtfully acted film moves at quite a clip, reminding us what a fantastic, morally complex, eternally relevant story the book tells us of good and evil, decency and generosity, snobbery and love, of dealing with forces beyond our control, of accepting life and understanding the world'.[125]

Unlike the BBC, Karlsen was upfront about the creative team's conviction that the novel had something to say to modern audiences, and that this something

---

[121] John Preston, 'Behind the scenes on "Great Expectations,"' *Telegraph*, 30 October 2012, http://www.telegraph.co.uk/culture/9632836/Behind-the-scenes-on-Great-Expectations.html [accessed 4 November 2013].

[122] Reviews on IMDB, http://www.imdb.com/title/tt1836808/reviews?ref_=tt_ov_rt [accessed 9 November 2012].

[123] Joe Walsh, 'Film Review: "Great Expectations"', *Cinevue*, http://www.cine-vue.com/2012/11/film-review-great-expectations.html [accessed 9 November 2013].

[124] Guy Lodge, 'Great Expectations Pipped to the Post', *Empireonline*, http://www.empireonline.com/reviews/reviewcomplete.asp?FID=137427 [accessed 9 November 2013].

[125] Philip French, '*Great Expectations* review', *Observer*, Sunday 2 December 2012, http://www.theguardian.com/film/2012/dec/02/great-expectations-review [accessed 9 April 2014].

had global potential: 'People reinvent[ing] themselves across the social divide … aspiration, the question of origins, bad parenting … social exclusion, striving for material worth depriving you of a moral code … there are so many themes that are relevant today', she told me. 'And there's such a sense of hope by the end; it's very American actually.'[126] International audiences were in fact a key part of the marketing strategy. On the strength of its assembled talent, the film was bought immediately by the following countries for release during 2012–14 (first in theatres and then on DVD): Australia, Belgium, Brazil, Canada, the Czech Republic, Estonia, Germany, Greece, Hungary, Ireland, Israel, Italy, Kuwait, Lithuania, the Netherlands, New Zealand, Poland, Portugal, Russia, Singapore, Spain, Taiwan, Turkey and the USA. Its remediation here, like the translated novels, often carried an extra dimension: in each location, decisions were made independently of the film's producers about whether the film should be dubbed or subtitled. Karlsen told me: 'The film will be released dubbed or sub-titled depending on what is standard in the territory. For example, in Italy films are always dubbed, in France they tend to sub-title and dub.'[127] These localised decisions will have had additional effects in terms of viewers' experiences of the text.

Interestingly, the bicentenary was not part of the decision to film this particular novel again, but adaptation cycles were; backers were persuaded by the fact that *Great Expectations* had not been made as a straightforward period adaptation on film for 67 years. Equally, its readily adaptable shape attracted the creative team. As Karlsen put it, 'It's the most filmable [Dickens novel] in a way. His texts are big, but it's easier to find a line through [this one] … there's less of those Dickensian elements that are wonderful … but a bit cartoony.'[128] Perhaps as a combined result of its filmability, its apparent topicality and the personal preferences of powerful individuals, the film attracted top acting, writing and directing talent. Mike Newell (Director), famous for the hit British film *Four Weddings and a Funeral* (UK, 1994) and *Harry Potter and the Goblet of Fire* (UK, 2005) and David Nicholls (Screenwriter), famous for the hit novel *One Day* (2009), bonded over their love for what both claim is their favourite novel. David Nicholls said:

> Read a book at the right age and it will stay with you for life. For some people it's *Pride and Prejudice*, *Jane Eyre* or *Wuthering Heights*, but for me it is *Great Expectations*. I first read it at age 14 or so and … it has remained my favourite novel ever since. By some miracle, a story written in the mid- 1850s [*sic*] had captured much of how I felt in a small provincial town at the end of the 1970s…. It is the supreme coming-of-age novel, the best account of those years when we flee our childhood selves without any clear notion of where we're heading.[129]

---

[126] Author's interview with Elizabeth Karlsen on the set of *Great Expectations*, Hounslow, London, 27 October 2011.

[127] Author's email interview with Elizabeth Karlsen, 21 August 2013.

[128] On-set interview with Karlsen.

[129] David Nicholls, 'Degrees of Fidelity,' *Guardian* [review section], 17 November 2012, p. 2.

In an interview for the *Telegraph* he was still more specific: '[I]t strikes a chord with all of us – especially men – when we look at our younger selves: at our foolish aspirations and our desire to be something that we're not'.[130]

Mike Newell likewise had 'always loved the novels and ... this one in particular'.[131] Newell had another motive, too. 'I wanted it to be about money', he said, 'and about how money screws things up, how it deludes people. That's very much in our times right now. It's about abused children as well, and the way that these children get abused is that the adults have in their turn been horribly damaged and they have passed that damage on.... That was something very contemporary as well. I was trying to make a contemporary film in sheep's clothing'.[132] In a *Telegraph* interview he added: 'It's as if Dickens was really coming clean about himself. About his relations with his family and about being prepared to do anything to get ahead.'[133]

The contemporary 'wolfish' edge that Newell intended to give the film potentially sits quite comfortably alongside the mashup werewolf and zombie versions which its audiences might well be reading at the same time. In theory it is a short step between the two gothic worlds. In practice, however, the producers had a different audience in mind. Karlsen told me after the film had been released that their main target had been older women, the kind who liked period drama, who had enjoyed *Pride and Prejudice* (UK, directed by Joe Wright, 2005), *The Queen* (UK, directed by Stephen Frears, 2006) and *The King's Speech* (UK, directed by Tom Hooper, 2010).[134] Helena Bonham Carter, who played the Queen consort to Colin Firth's King George VI in the latter, provides a crucial link between Newell's *Great Expectations* and these sumptuous nostalgic productions, all of them trading on an internationally marketable version of Britain's past.

It seems significant that while the 2012 film failed to win any awards and received mixed reviews, the 2011 BBC TV version garnered four Emmy awards and was generally reviewed more enthusiastically by ordinary viewers who, while they sometimes objected to the casting, generally found themselves gripped and moved by the plot. There were, ironically given the difference in airtime, few complaints about slow pacing or a boring script. Serialisation seems to be the key, perhaps because it enables private indulgence at home in a media event which is not necessarily very appealing in a more public and demographically diverse space. Watching heritage drama in the twenty-first century seems to be something of a guilty pleasure.

---

[130] John Preston, 'Behind the scenes on "Great Expectations"'.

[131] Zara Miller, 'Mike Newell,' *Little White Lies*, 29 Nov 2012, http://www.littlewhitelies.co.uk/features/articles/mike-newell-2–22583 [accessed 4 November 2013].

[132] Sam Wigley, 'Mike Newell: "This is Dickens's *Jekyll and Hyde*"', BFI Film Forever Tuesday, 27 November 2012, http://www.bfi.org.uk/news/mike-newell-dickens-s-jekyll-hyde [accessed 4 November 2013].

[133] John Preston, 'Behind the scenes on "Great Expectations"'.

[134] Author's email interview with Elizabeth Karlsen.

Critically, too, the adaptation seemed to fare better on TV, and this might be a result of formal difference; since serialisations generally allow more airtime they seem to permit indulgence in a fantasy of completeness which brings us closer to the original. Yet, as David Nicholls admitted, while there is a sense in the industry itself that TV drama has an advantage over film, this does not necessarily mean a more faithful version: 'There is no such thing as a completely faithful adaptation.... In an adaptation, the clock is always ticking. Dramatists who've been given the task of cramming immense works into a few hours often find themselves looking longingly at the TV version of *Brideshead Revisited*, 11 hours of screen-time for a novel that could be read in eight. Yet even *Brideshead* isn't a neutral or "invisible" adaptation'.[135] All adaptations, that is, are fantasies which 'oscillate between immediacy and hypermediacy, between transparency and opacity', variously scratching or failing to scratch the critical itch for a past – represented by iconic Dickens in pure, whole, unadulterated form – that may never have existed.[136]

These two recent adaptations demonstrate above all that Dickens's main value now seems to be as a heritage commodity, a status gained through a fortuitous combination of inbuilt remediation potential, transferable and easily visualised character stereotypes, and the development of modern international publishing and distribution infrastructures whose early years Dickens witnessed firsthand, and which he quickly learned to exploit. Like the Tower of London, his novels may have outlived their original function, but they remain alive as income-generating landmarks. Most crucially of all, as this book has attempted to show, the ways in which they are kept alive are as dependent on diverse and adaptable media outlets now as they were in Dickens's own lifetime.

---

[135] David Nicholls, 'Adapting Great Expectations for the screen', *Guardian*, Friday 16 November 2012. http://www.theguardian.com/books/2012/nov/16/adapting-great-expectations-david-nicholls [accessed 9 April 2014].

[136] Bolter and Grusin, *Remediation*, pp. 19–20.

Coda

In the City Archives of the English south-coast port of Southampton are a few fragmentary records of what was once a thriving nineteenth-century printing trade. Most of the history of this local trade has been lost due to decay, company dissolutions, or the effects of the bombs and incendiary devices which destroyed around 45,000 of the city's buildings between November 1940 and May 1941, including most of the High Street around which the printing trade was centred. The surviving fragments are rare, but they include some of the records of a now-defunct book binding firm, George Cawte and Co. (later Cox and Cawte), whose operations were central to the life of a busy steamship port which, fed by the railways, saw the daily arrival and departure of thousands of tons of goods and mail and hundreds of steamship passengers going to or returning from other British ports, Continental Europe, Egypt, India, South Africa, the East and West Indies, South America and the east coast of the United States. These fragments provide a small but tantalising glimpse of part of *Great Expectations*'s fortunes during a period that saw major changes not only in British lifestyles, but also in the publishing and printing industries and the reading practices that drove or responded to them.

Most pertinent for our purposes are a series of 'Day Books' containing binding orders for large parts of the period 1858–1921.[1] This period saw the rise of Southampton as a significant international transport hub second in the UK only to London (it became known in the early twentieth century as the 'Gateway to the Empire'), and a concomitant increase in both skilled labour and a middle-class population with money to spend on books or subscription libraries. It was a period which encompassed the boom years of the luxury steam liners. The *Titanic* departed from Southampton, and its loss seriously depleted the city's resident population of stewards, stokers and engineers and also claimed the lives of many transitory Irish and East European migrants (as well as a few visiting millionaires). This period also witnessed World War I which taught Britons (perhaps especially Southamptonians, whose docks sent off many of the departing troops and landed almost all the returning wounded) some even harder lessons about hubris. The surviving records tell their own small but significant story of the period before David Lean had filmed *Great Expectations* to entertain a population tired of war, and helped turn the novel into an international icon. They give us a glimpse of a part of the novel's – and Dickens's – past that is now beyond living memory, and provide one additional fragment of *Great Expectations*'s lesser known publishing and reception history.

---

[1]   Cox and Cawte Bindery Day Books 1858–63, 1879, 1880–82, 1887–90, 1909–10 and 1915–21, D/Cox G1/1 – 6, Southampton City Council Archives.

Cox and Cawte handled both stationary and letterpress binding. Thus, among the thousands of entries logging the binding of books of tickets, manifests, captain's reports, nautical charts, baggage books and ticket books for the shipping companies, are thousands more logging the binding of more personal types of reading matter including novels. Usefully enough for us, these books are often listed by title in order to help the company's binders and record keepers differentiate between sometimes very specific types of instructions, and thus different prices, for individual books. Three genres heavily dominate the lists of non-stationary items, particularly in the earlier period: religious books, periodicals and the works of Charles Dickens. The customers are often official or institutional ones; many booksellers are mentioned by name, as are several libraries including the Hartley Institute (a precursor to the University of Southampton), the Southampton Athenaeum library and the library of the Royal Engineers. But there are almost as many private individuals as companies ordering the binding or repair of books or periodicals, and the dominance of Dickens in these entries tells us not only that he was an author who was being read again and again until the books fell to pieces, but that he was also an author whose novels many British people treasured enough to spend money on preserving: most of the entries request binding in half-calf or sheep or other durable binding, at prices ranging from 1s. 2d. for a half-calf *Christmas Carol*[2] to 2s. 6d. for a half-calf gilt *Little Dorrit*.[3] In the nineteenth century, Dickens was clearly an author whom British readers liked to personalise as well as to treasure. Sometimes these books and periodicals were clearly intended for local homes, but on occasion – particularly in the later part of the period – there are additional details in the entries such as instructions which tell us the books were to be delivered to the 'outward baggage' office for loading onto a particular shipping line, or lists of books repaired or rebound for the library of a named ship. These details remind us of something else: that readers liked to take books (including Dickens) with them when they travelled and read them en route or treasure them at their destinations, whether the journey was a short one or marked the start of a new life abroad.[4]

The prevalence of Dickens's name in these lists is not remarkable in itself: we know he was more popular than any other author in at least the first part of this period. The prevalence of religious reading and periodicals (often the same thing) is not surprising either. But if we look more closely at the data, these fragments of

---

2   Entry for 20 December 1860, Cox and Cawte Daybook 1858–62, D/Cox G. 1/1.

3   Entry for 26 July 1858, Cox and Cawte Daybook 1858–62, D/Cox G. 1/1.

4   There are entries for the repairing of novels for the libraries of the 'SS Lydia' (17 March 1910), the 'SS Adriatic' (9 August 1910), the 'SS Majestic' (30 August 1910) and the 'SS Oceanic' (20 September 1910), Cox and Cawte Daybook 1909–10, D/Cox G.1/5. The listed titles include *Germinal, Lorna Doone, Richard Feveral, Don Quixote, Plain Tales from the Hills, In Japan, Innocents Abroad* and *Round the World in 80 Days*, an eclectic mix which almost certainly included Dickens (as witness Lady Schreiber reading him aloud to help her husband get to sleep en route from South Africa), though he was apparently no longer being read to pieces.

a binding company's operations give us some clues about the waxing and waning of Dickens's popularity and the different patterns of his use over time which both supplement the available sales figures and reviews on which I largely focussed in Chapters 1 and 2, and point to the changes in the ways he was being distributed and read which I attempted to trace in subsequent chapters. One thing stands out immediately: while most of Dickens's novels are mentioned several (sometimes many) times in relation to binding or repair, *Great Expectations* is mentioned by name only once, in an entry on a repair carried out for the Hartley Institute on 1 August 1888.[5] It might, of course, have been part of the many other entries which do not list titles such as 'binding of 3 volumes Dickens's works'[6] and '6 vols. Dickens's works'.[7] But, even allowing for the unknowable, its showing as a named title is a poor one compared with that of other novels (except for *Hard Times* and *Edwin Drood*, which come joint last) and tends to support the evidence presented elsewhere in this book of a comparative lack of reader interest in treasuring it. Nowhere here is there evidence of individual readers rebinding or repairing *Great Expectations*.

But there is another layer of evidence in these ledgers which a focus on the volumes of novels alone elides. Two of the most frequent entries in the five-year period beginning in 1858, apart from the binding of religious periodicals, are for the binding of volumes of HW and, beginning on 30 September 1859, AYR. Dozens of individuals, libraries, printers and clubs send volumes of these two titles for binding, a practice which indicates either considerable reader demand or considerable library and bookseller faith in Dickens's name as a draw. The binding patterns strongly suggest the former. Initially, HW is the front runner, but after 6 December 1860 (a date that is of some significance to us, since it marks the week of the first instalment of *Great Expectations)* AYR outnumbers all other single periodical bindings, including religious periodicals and Thackeray's *Cornhill*.[8] The relative numbers are striking during *Great Expectations*'s run. In 1858 there were 8 bindings of volumes of HW. In 1859 (AYR's first) there were 12 bindings of HW and 2 of AYR. *A Tale of Two Cities* apparently failed to win Southampton's favour in serial form. In 1860 there were 5 bindings of HW (after the magazine was discontinued) and 18 of AYR. Evidently Lever's *A Day's Ride* found better favour with (or at least failed to put off) Southampton's readers. In 1861 there were 30 bindings of volumes of AYR, and it is significant that 22 of them take place between January and August, the period of *Great Expectations*'s run. The journal is bound for individuals and printers as well as libraries, including the

---

[5] Entry for 10 January 1888, Cox and Cawte Daybook for 1887–88, D/Cox G. 1/4.

[6] Entry for 9 January 1879, Cox and Cawte Daybook for 1879, D/Cox G. 1/2.

[7] Entry for 7 June 1879, Cox and Cawte Daybook for 1879, D/Cox G. 1/2.

[8] As Laurel Brake has shown, AYR sold three times the number of HW. 'Second Life: All the Year Round and the New Generation of British Periodicals in the 1860s', *Charles Dickens and the mid-Victorian Press, 1850–1870*, ed. by Hazel Mackenzie and Ben Winyard (Buckingham, 2013), p. 11.

Royal Engineers.[9] In 1862 the binding number is back down to 11, at which it remains during 1863, the last year for which we have records during Dickens's lifetime. What these numbers suggest is that in nineteenth-century Southampton, at least, *Great Expectations* was initially read most often in instalments, that it beat *A Tale of Two Cities* in that form, and that thereafter interest in preserving copies of it all but disappeared.

Fragments such as this have underpinned and guided the arguments in this book. They have in fact been central to my analysis of *Great Expectations*'s cultural life, an analysis which would otherwise have had to rely upon a set of assumptions based on an unavoidably subjective close analysis of textual 'meaning' supported by an at best partial list of publishing statistics. From this process of sifting through and piecing together such fragments it has emerged that this now-iconic novel probably did not always possess its current power and influence, contrary to the assurance provided by twenty-first century marketing blurbs which almost inevitably contain the phrases 'universal favourite' or 'timeless classic'.[10] In fact quite the opposite is true, judging by the absence from Cox and Cawte's records of evidence to suggest that readers had it bound individually as they did for *Pickwick* and other novels. Further proof is provided by its lack of popularity among nineteenth-century patrons of the mid-western town of Muncie, by its slow appearance or rapid disappearance in non-Anglophone contexts where Dickens was generally enjoyed, and by the relative dearth of references to people reading it in the work of recent scholars who have scrutinised nineteenth-century letters and diaries. It was not just that, like all Dickens's 'darker, late works', it initially fell short of most readers' tastes and expectations. Despite the mixed reviews it seems to have worked well in serial form, and in volume form to have been widely purchased by libraries. But the scarcity of records of subsequent sales, borrowings, bindings, rebindings and reader testimonies suggests that on some level it disappointed nineteenth-century readers in volume form, and that it was more misunderstood, and for longer, than almost any other Dickens work apart from *Hard Times*. The public's lack of interest (aside from loyal members of the International Dickens Fellowship, of course) continued well into the early twentieth century. A general upturn of public interest in Dickens during World War I does not seem to have helped its fortunes: few extant records of Commonwealth soldiers' reading mention it. The Cox and Cawte records contain no references to it being rebound during this period, which is dominated by the binding of copies of *The Great War* and *The War Illustrated* punctuated only by the occasional *Pickwick*. The New York Public Library's only copy of the Peterson's Uniform Edition of 1861 was not purchased for the library until 1914 and was taken out

---

[9]   Entry for 23 June 1861, Cox and Cawte binders Daybook 1858–62, D/Cox G.1/1.

[10]   It is glibly described as a 'timeless classic' on numerous publishing websites and in countless reviews, and the phrase has even been enshrined in the title of a series run by Saddleback Educational Publishing which published *Timeless Classics: Great Expectations* in 2010.

only three times in the next four years, and never more than once in any one year. There were no professional twentieth-century stage adaptations prior to 1939, and the film adaptations generally showed poor profits. Only with the outbreak of World War II and a concomitant surge of renewed interest in the later novels, boosted by the release of Lean's globally circulated film in 1946, did the novel begin to generate the kind of interest and the kinds of sales and circulation patterns with which we have come to associate it, and which we have so often carelessly de-historicised as given and constant.

It has been one of this book's findings that the extended life of this novel has to a great extent depended on modern mass-media technologies, including a series of new adaptation media which had little use or need for faithful rendition; the novel has easily lent itself to being co-opted for a range of different uses over time, and it has appeared in myriad different guises. It would be reductive to put this remediation history down to post-Victorian misinterpretation or exploitation by cynical media industries. After all, even in the 1860s, the novel's 'capsular' form led immediately to its reprinting, repackaging and remediation for different and often highly individualistic uses. As we have seen, for newspaper and magazine editors and apparently some pirates, the novel worked just as well carved into chunks or served up in teaspoons; for Dickens himself it was a small matter to write Estella out of the public reading version, while for W.S. Gilbert Miss Havisham worked just as well if she was kept offstage. The facts of its appropriation and reshaping – either then or now – should not trouble us. It is probably more significant that while the teaspoons and chunks circulated easily enough and were initially relatively successful, once the initial flurry of interest had subsided, the novel as a whole largely failed to find its mark with readers. The personal relationships Dickens was used to forging with his readers simply did not seem to come this time: *Great Expectations* felt too different, perhaps; too dark, too messy, too unresolved. As Mike Newell puts it, 'I'm sure in a way that this is Dickens's *Jekyll and Hyde* … I think this novel – in a funny sort of way – is Dickens tiptoeing into this great unknown'.[11] Given R.L. Stevenson's own struggles (and failure) to get sufficient grip on the novel in 1883 to put it on the stage, this is an apt analogy. It is indeed a novel with surprises up its sleeve, most of them uncomfortable ones. But the great 'unknown' sensed and cautiously entered into by its troubled author in the dark days of December 1860 seems to have become monstrously knowable in the post-World War 2 years when, perhaps, the novel's nostalgia for an innocent agrarian past, its exposé of the vacuity of ambition, and the cost of the single-minded pursuit of exclusionary ideals may have lent it particular force.

There is no doubt that, thematically and structurally, *Great Expectations* was tailor-made to take full advantage of its re-emergence into the mid-twentieth-century limelight. Its linguistic and thematic modernity has been noted by

---

[11]   Sam Wigley, 'Mike Newell: "This is Dickens's Jekyll and Hyde"', *BFI Film Forever,* Tuesday 27 November 2012, http://www.bfi.org.uk/news/mike-newell-dickens-s-jekyll-hyde [accessed 4 November 2013].

critics from the Leavises onwards,[12] and if its 'capsularity' by means of which elements can be easily decoupled for recycling in new forms had not done the job, its 'quadripartite scheme of plots', half of which are unresolved by the author and demand creative resolution, certainly began to appeal in all sorts of new ways during that period. It has remained in the spotlight for several decades since, for very good and sometimes quite complex reasons. Ever since Freudian psychoanalysis became an established theoretical tool in academia in the 1960s there has been enduring interest in its characters' psychology, while its proto-feminist villainess and heroine have been of increasing importance in terms both of gender studies generally and of the history of female performance in particular. The themes of prejudice and social dislocation, and of a highly personal conflict which is also profoundly political, seemed equally significant during the 1960s.

It was in this period when I was growing up in Yorkshire and had reached the age of about nine that a friend's much older sister (a trainee teacher) collared me at their tea-table and charged me to name my favourite Dickens novel, and when I confessed that I had never read any Dickens, there was an awful silence and an exchange of disapproving glances around the table. They were a Welsh mining family who had moved to England after World War II. Theoretically Marxist but in practice extremely socially aspirational, they somehow felt that Dickens spoke to and for that contradictory position like no other author. Not to appreciate – not to *love* – Dickens was both to betray one's working-class roots and, bizarrely, simultaneously to prove oneself uncultured. (I was clearly guilty on both counts.) TV adaptations of Dickens thus – in theory at least – got right to the heart of a post-war social dilemma in a period of transformation: Sunday-night Dickens rendered one's ostentatious new colour TV set morally acceptable, even if one was a Marxist. In this period he often appeared to be some kind of secular saint, a Victorian prophet who somehow anticipated and understood post-war social complexities.

The emphasis in Britain on Dickens as an integral part of who we are and why it's ok for us to be going where we're going was a recurring theme throughout the 1970s, 1980s and even 1990s. It may, arguably, have continued into the first decades of the twenty-first century. But it may also be on the wane. Despite the popularity of the annual Dickens Universe conference held in Santa Cruz (which in 2011 made *Great Expectations* its theme), evidence may be mounting of 'the Victorians' as existing in most young Westerners' minds now only in playful, sexy, postmodern variants such as *Tipping the Velvet* (novel 1998; BBC TV series 2002) and *Sherlock* (BBC TV series from 2010), and of Dickens's fading relevance to anyone but academics, policy-makers anxious about twenty first-century

---

[12] In 1970 Q.D. Leavis suggested that 'The sense in which Great Expectations is a novel at all is certainly not to be arrived at by applying to it the ordinary conventions and assumptions derived from Victorian novels in general.' Leavis, p. 288. A year later, Ann Dobie goes so far as to call it an early stream-of-consciousness novel. 'Early Stream-of-Consciousness Writing: Great Expectations', *Nineteenth-Century Fiction*, Vol. 25, March 1971, pp. 405–416.

schoolchildren's literacy skills, and the middle-aged middle classes who fondly remember a time when he mattered. Since in my introduction I darkly hinted that this book might just as easily end up being part of *Great Expectations*' obituary as its healthily-proliferating hypertexts, it seems appropriate to finish with a look at the current state of play.

In 2003 the BBC conducted a nationwide poll called 'The Big Read', aiming to find 'The nation's best-loved novel'. Out of three quarters of a million votes collected, *Great Expectations* was No. 17 on the list, ahead of any other Dickens novel. (*David Copperfield* was No. 34, *A Christmas Carol* No. 47; *A Tale of Two Cities* No. 63.)[13] The poll seemed encouraging, but it probably shows us nothing beyond the already well-known fact that BBC viewers who are also readers and have enough leisure time to answer surveys are also those most likely to set a certain store by the canon. The more recent survey reported by the *Mail Online* demonstrating that a third of British people 'have no idea who wrote *Great Expectations*'[14] covers a wider demographic, and is thus probably more accurate; the survey was carried out by Opinion Research Services, 'an independent social research practice' that works across the UK on behalf of the public, voluntary and private sectors, and this suggests a less partial result.[15] The fact that it was reported by the *Daily Mail* (a right-leaning tabloid with a 53 per cent female readership) is, however, just as revealing as the BBC's in terms of the ideologies currently circulating around the teaching of the canon. The report called the survey results 'worrying', and added that Dickens was not alone: '28 per cent of adults admitted never having read one of the classics', including Shakespeare, a result that for this journalist appears to indicate an inexorable erosion of British national identity.

This is, of course, something of a myth; in many other contexts Dickens is alive and well and *Great Expectations* doing better than most, as witness Project Gutenberg which provides a daily list of the relative popularity of its downloadable books. In 2008, according to Juliet John, Dickens was the second most downloaded author, ahead of Shakespeare but behind Mark Twain.[16] By October 2012 he had slipped down to fourth place in the international list behind Sir Arthur Conan Doyle (a new favourite, no doubt due to the success of the TV show *Sherlock*), Mark Twain and Jane Austen,[17] and by November 2013 he was back up to second behind Twain, with Doyle and Austen snapping at his heels but Shakespeare nowhere to be seen.[18] This is a reasonable performance over five years. In the international title list *Great Expectations* hovers around the second or third most downloaded Dickens novel mark, sharing the medals with *A Tale of Two Cities* and *A Christmas Carol*. The fact that these placings shift around seasonally between the 'Yesterday's Top 100' and the '30 Days Ago Top 100' lists,

13   http://www.bbc.co.uk/arts/bigread/top100.shtml [accessed 10 November 2013].

14   Andrew Levy, *Mail Online*, 25 September 2013.

15   http://www.ors.org.uk/ [accessed 12 November 2013].

16   John, *Mass Culture*, p. 14.

17   http://www.gutenberg.org/browse/scores/top [accessed 9 October 2012].

18   http://www.gutenberg.org/browse/scores/top [accessed 12 November 2013].

that they number in the hundreds of readers rather than the thousands, and that they are flanked by the kinds of books written by the Brontës, Joyce, Melville, Ibsen, Whitman and Frederick Douglass, suggests that they are being downloaded by students. This seems unlikely to change any time soon; as long as we think the novel worth teaching, it will be read.[19]

Different sites give different but equally interesting results. At the time of writing, *Great Expectations* is No. 95 on Amazon's hourly-updated top-100 free fiction downloads list. *The Great Gatsby* appears at No. 15 (probably as a result of the recent film) and *The War of the Worlds* appears at No. 29.[20] Some old favourites (and the sources for some successful adaptations) are also there: *Pride and Prejudice* is at No. 39, *Les Misérables* No. 49, *Alice's Adventures in Wonderland* No. 51, *A Tale of Two Cities* No. 59, *A Christmas Carol* No. 61, *Dracula* No. 73, *Jane Eyre* No. 78 and *Wuthering Heights* No. 84. *Great Expectations's* showing is a respectable one given this company; evidence, perhaps, not only that adaptations do encourage some viewers to read the source book, but that, just as Dickens may have intended, it has enough romance, gothic horror, mystery and enticing indeterminacy to appeal to and sit outside of contemporary fashions.

But the phenomenon known as '*Great Expectations*' is also as plural, and as much a shape-shifter, now as it has ever been. Its showing on top-100 book lists is one thing, but its name and its cultural 'meanings' have continued to be utilised in other ways too, and these may even be proliferating. For example, it has furnished titles for many pop songs and albums (at least a dozen of these between 1992 and 2010). It gave Carol Ann Duffy some excellent material for a haunting poem, 'Havisham', in 1993. It appears either by association or as a meaningful prop in numerous movies and TV shows such as Season 1, Episode 8 of the California-based comedy *Modern Family* (USA, 2009), in which inappropriate gift-giving and learning to count one's blessings are the themes; or Season 3, Episode 9 of the thriller *Homeland* (USA, 2012), in which a CIA agent is investigated by his colleagues for suspected double-dealing and turns out to own only one book, a Penguin edition of *Great Expectations*, in which is concealed the clue to his real identity.

These are a fraction of the available examples, all trading on a kind of cultural consensus about what *Great Expectations* means, what it stands for; an in-joke that keeps on playing in indefinite new contexts. They prove that in some ways it is clearly still now what it has always been: a rich and clever book not only thematically, but also structurally. Tailor-made to fit a wide range of different media contexts in 1860, it continues to do so in 2014. This means that while for the literary critic it is able to illuminate complex Victorian cultural mores and

---

[19]   The latest literary version to have come to my attention is The Pigeonhole.com's student-friendly online reissue of the serial instalments, each accompanied by contextual material. https://thepigeonhole.com/books/greatexpectations.

[20]   http://www.amazon.co.uk/Best-Sellers-Kindle-Store-Fiction/zgbs/digital-text/362270031/ref=zg_bs_fvp_p_f_362270031?_encoding=UTF8&tf=1#2 [accessed 12 November 2013].

gesture towards their interactions with social change, for the book historian it is able to operate something like a cultural radioisotope, illuminating the internal machinations of the dynamic industries it has successfully negotiated for so long. In the end, this innate responsiveness to historical needs may be *Great Expectations*' most lasting legacy, as well as the root of a large part of its author's gift.

Appendix A
Select List of British and American Volume Editions of *Great Expectations*, 1861–1939

Sources

Archive: British Library; Charles Dickens Museum; Huntington Library; Library of Congress; New York Public Library

Print: Robert L. Patten, *Charles Dickens and his Publishers* (Oxford: Oxford University Press, 1978); Paul Schlicke, ed., *The Oxford Companion to Dickens* (Oxford: Oxford University Press, 2000); Walter E. Smith, *Charles Dickens: A Bibliography of His First American Editions 1836–1870* (New Castle, DE: Oak Knoll, 2012).

Online: Victorian Web (http://www.victorianweb.org/); Worldcat (https://www.worldcat.org/).

3 Vols. London: Chapman and Hall, 1861.

Peterson's Uniform Edition, with engraved portrait of author by Bobbett-Hooper. Philadelphia: T.B. Peterson Bros., 1861

2 Vols, with frontispiece photogravure drawing by Felix O. Darley. New York: James G. Gregory, 1861.

Library Edition, with 8 plates by Marcus Stone. London: Chapman and Hall, 1862.

With 4 engravings by F.O. Freeman. Boston: G.A. Fuller, 1862.

Cheap Edition. London: Chapman and Hall, 1863.

Confederate Edition. Mobile, AL: S. H Goetzel & Co., J. Y. Thompson, Printer, 1863.

Peterson's cheap edition for the million. Philadelphia: T.B. Peterson & Bros., 1865.

People's Edition. London: Chapman and Hall, 1867.

The works of Charles Dickens with twenty illustrations. New York: P. F. Collier, 1868.

With *A Tale of Two Cities*. The Diamond Edition, with 8 illustrations by Sol Eytinge. Boston: Ticknor & Fields, 1867.

Charles Dickens Edition, reprinting Marcus Stone plates. Chapman and Hall, 1868.

Cambridge, MA: Riverside Press, 1868.

With *Pictures from Italy* and *American Notes*. New York: American News Co., 1870

With *A Tale of Two Cities*. Boston: James R. Osgood and Company, late Ticknor & Fields, and Fields, Osgood, & Co., 1873.

With *Sketches*. New York: Appleton, 1874.

Household Edition, with 28 plates by F.A. Fraser. London: Chapman and Hall, 1875.

New Illustrated Library Edition, intro by E.P. Whipple. Boston: Houghton Mifflin, 1877.

With *Oliver Twist, David Copperfield* and *Our Mutual Friend*. The works of Charles Dickens, with 40 illustrations, Vol. 1. New York: P.F. Collier, 1879.

With *Pictures from Italy*, *Master Humphrey's Clock* and *No Thoroughfare*. Boston: Estes and Lauriat, 1881.

With *Pictures from Italy* and *American Notes*, with illustrations by Marcus Stone. Carleton's New Illustrated Edition. New York: G.W. Carleton & Co., 1883.

With 20 plates plus frontispiece by F.W. Pailthorpe, keyed to the 1861 edition's pages. London: Robson & Kerslake, 1885.

With *Christmas Stories*. Chicago and New York: Belford Clarke and Co., 1885.

With *Pictures from Italy* and *American Notes*. New York, G.W. Carleton. Reissued in 1885 as Carleton's New Illustrated Edition, 1885.

With *Christmas Stories*. New York and London: White, Stokes & Allen, 1885.

With *A Tale of Two Cities*, Philadelphia: Porter and Coates, 1888.

With *Oliver Twist*. Works of Charles Dickens: Unchanged and unabridged. New York: F.M. Lupton, 1889.

With *American Notes*. New York: Hurst & Co., 1889.

Macmillan Edition. Reprint of 1861 edition, with introductions by Charles Dickens Jr., including collection of letters edited by Georgina Hogarth and Kate Perugini. London: Macmillan, 1892.

The Complete Works of Charles Dickens, illustrated by Frederick Barnard. Philadelphia: Gebbie & Co., 1892–94.

The Writings of Charles Dickens, with critical and bibliographical introductions and notes by Edwin Percy Whipple and others. Boston and New York: Houghton, Mifflin and Co., 1894.

Gadshill Edition, with 10 plates by Charles Green, reprinted from Dickens's corrected edition of 1867–68, edited and introduced by Andrew Lang. London: Chapman and Hall and New York: Scribners, 1897.

Nelson's New Century Library Edition, with illustrations by John A. Bacon. London: Nelson, 1899.

Rochester Edition, with introduction by George Gissing and notes by F. G. Kitton. London: Methuen, 1899–1901.

Edition de Grande Luxe of the Works of Charles Dickens, with more than one thousand illustrations, including all the usual & very many unusual plates, edited by Richard Garnett. London: Merrill and Baker, 1900.

With *Master Humphrey's Clock*. London: J.M. Dent, 1900.

With *Martin Chuzzlewit*. The Complete Works. New York: P.F. Collier & Son, 1900.

The Imperial Edition, illustrated with 8 plates by H.M. Brock. London: Gresham, 1901–3.

Oxford India Paper Edition. London: Chapman and Hall, 1902.

With the *Uncommercial Traveller*. London: Caxton, 1902.

With *Master Humphrey's Clock*. Temple Edition, illustrated by John A. Bacon, introduced by W. Jerrold. London: J.M. Dent, 1903.

With the *Uncommercial Traveller*. Biographical Edition, with original illustrations, introduced by Arthur Waugh. London: Chapman and Hall, 1903.

Edition de Luxe, reissue of the Gadshill Edition. London: Chapman and Hall, 1903.

Authentic Edition with coloured frontispiece. London: Chapman and Hall, 1905.

Fireside Edition, illustrated by Charles Green (reissue of the Oxford India Paper edition). London: Chapman and Hall and New York: Oxford University Press, 1903–7.

Everyman's Library Edition, with introduction by G. K. Chesterton and Walter Jerrold. London: J.M. Dent, 1907.

National Edition (limited edition of 750 sets). London: Chapman and Hall, 1907.

Imperial Edition of the Works of Charles Dickens, with 8 plates by H.M. Brock, introduction by George Gissing. London: Gresham, 1908.

Lloyd's Sixpenny Dickens Edition, London: Edward Lloyd, 1909–11.

Popular Edition, London: Chapman and Hall, 1907.

Eighteen Penny Illustrated Edition (reissue of the Fireside Edition). London: Chapman and Hall, 1908.

Charles Dickens Library Edition, with 27 plates by Harry Furniss. London: Chapman and Hall, 1910.

Waverley Edition of the Works of Charles Dickens, with 4 plates by Charles Pears, introduction by John Oxenham. London: Waverley, 1910.

With *Master Humphrey's Clock*. The works of Charles Dickens with introduction, critical comments, and notes. New York: Collier, 1911.

Centenary Edition (reissue of the Gadshill De Luxe Edition). London: Chapman and Hall, 1911.

With 'Other stories', The Works of Charles Dickens: Standard Edition. London: Heinemann, 1912.

Universal Edition. London: Chapman and Hall, 1912.

With *Christmas Books*. New York: Scribner's, 1924.

With *Oliver Twist*. London: Hazell, Watson and Viney, 1933.

Limited Editions Club edition, with introduction by George Bernard Shaw, illustrations by Gordon Ross. Edinburgh: R. and R. Clark, 1937.

With *Hard Times*. The Nonesuch Dickens. London: The Nonesuch Press, 1937.

Heritage Edition, with 64 Plates by Edward Ardizzone. New York: Heritage Press, 1939.

Appendix B
List of Translations, 1861–2012

Sources

Archive: Ada Nisbet Archive, University of California, Santa Cruz; Charles Dickens Museum; British Library; New York Public Library.
Print: Michael Hollington, ed., *The Reception of Charles Dickens in Europe*, 2 vols. (London and New York: Bloomsbury, 2013).
Online: Worldcat (https://www.worldcat.org) Note: This source can be unreliable. In order to minimise the risk of imported cataloguing errors, I have included entries drawn from Worldcat only when I have been able to verify their details from at least one other source.

Organisation

Listings are in alphabetical order by language. Names of translators, editors, preface writers and/or illustrators appear after the title, though in some cases it has not been possible to identify these separately. Variant spellings used by the Ada Nisbet Archive scholars have been retained as part of the historical record.

Arabic

Al-Amal al-kabirah. Trans. Mahmud Massud. Cairo: Al-Mostaqbal al-Kazhim, 1950.
Amal Kibar. Trans. Isma'il Kamel. Cairo: n.p., 1951.
Al-Amal al-kabirah. Trans. Fayeq Entabawi. Damascus: n.p., 1956.
Al-Amal al-kabirah. Abridged and trans. Gayyath Jajjar. Beirut: n.p., 1963.
Al-Amāl al-kabīrah. Simplified translation. Bayrūt, Lubnān: Manshūrāt Dār Maktabat al-Ḥayāh, 1985, reprinted 2005.
Al-Āmāl al-kabīrah. Dimashq: Dār Usāmah, 1991.
Al-Amal al-kabirah. Bayrut: Dar al-Bahar, 1993.
Great Expectations. Beirut: DarSea, 1993.
Al-Āmāl al-kabīrah. Bi-lingual English-Arabic edition. Bayrūt: Dār al-Biḥār; Bayrūt, Lubnān: Dār wa-Maktabat al-Hilāl, 1999; 2003.
Amal 'azeemah. Maha Fakhri Qanbar. Aleppo: Sha'a' Lil-Nashr wa al-'Aloom, 2007.

Armenian

Mets huyser. Erevan: Sovetakan Grogh, 1983.

Azerbaijan

Pip [fragment]. Trans. A. Zeinalov. Baku: n.p., 1935.

Bengali

Anek asha. Trans. and adapted by Mahindra Datta. Calcutta: Turiksham, 1955.
Baṛa āśā kare. Kabir Chowdhury. Ḍhākā: Sāhitya, 2002.
Greṭa eksapekaṭeśanasa. Ḍhākā: Pāñjerī, 2009.

Bulgarian

Pip: Roman za detsa i junoshi. Trans S. Barov. Sofia: Chipev, 1938.
Istorijata Pip. Sofia: Chipev, 1947.
Golemite nadezhdi. Trans. Nevyana Rozeva. Sofia: Narodna mladezh, 1960.

Catalan

Grans esperances de Pip. Trans. Josep Carner. Biblioteca a Tot Vent. Barcelona:
    Proa, 1934; reprinted 1985,1995 and 2005.

Chinese

Gu xing xie lei. Trans. Qian-li Ying, for juvenile readers. Tai bei shi: Ming hua,
    1954.
Gu xing xie lei. Trans. Qianli Ying. International government publication. Tai bei
    shi: Ming hua, 1959.
Gu xing xue lei. Trans. Qian-li Ying and Pa Jie. Tai bei shi: Ming hua, 1960.
Gu xing xue lei. Abridged. Trans. Ying Ch'ien Li. Taipei: n.p., 1960.
Gu xing xue lei. Abridged. Trans. Jin-hui Lu: Tai bei shi: Wu zhou, 1963.
Gu xing xue lei. Trans. Qian-li Ying. Tai bei shi: Ming hua, 1964.
Gu xing xue lei. Trans. Josephine Page, Qianli Ying. Taiwan: Er you shu ju,
    Minguo, 1964.
Ku-hsing hsieh-lei. Pirated edition, intro. Edward Wagenknecht. Taipei: Hsin-lu
    shu-chu, 1966.
Gu xing xue lei. Abridged bilingual edition, trans. Lee Mu Hwa. Taipei: Hua-mei
    ch'u-pan-she, 1968.
Gu xing xue lei. Xianggang: Ying yu chu ban she, 1968.
Gu xing xue lei. Trans. Qiunan Li. Tai bei shi: Zheng wen shu ju yin xing, 1971;
    1973.
Yuan da qian cheng [A Future Full of Promise]. Trans. Keyi Wang. Shanghai:
    Shanghai yi wen chu ban she, 1979.

Gu xing xue lei. Trans. Chen tai xian. Juvenile title. Chang sha: Hu nan ren min chu ban she, 1981.

Gu xing xue lei. Trans. Zhiye Luo. Nanjing: Yi lin chu ban she, 1990.

Gu xing xie lei: yuan da qian cheng. Keyi Wang. Shanghai: Shanghai yi wen, 1990.

Gu xing xue lei. Trans. Ming An. Tai bei shi: Kai jin wen hua chu ban Zhi dao zong jing xiao, 1995.

Gu xing xue lei. Illustrated edition. People's Literature Publishing House, 2000.

Gu xing xue lei. Bejing: Foreign Language Teaching and Research Press, 2011.

Chuvash

Pip [fragment]. Trans. S. Udvorter. Cheboksari: n.p., 1935.

Croatian

Velike nade. Trans. Zlatko Gorjan. Zagreb: Matica Hrvatska, 1951.

Czech

Velké naděje. 2 Vols., trans. Pavla Moudrá. Prague: Radikální listy, 1900–1.

Veliké naděje. 2 Vols., trans. P. Moudrá. Praha: Melantrich, 1924.

Nadějné vyhlídky. Trans. Emanuel Tilsch and Emanuela Tilschová, afterword by Jaroslav Hornát. Prague: SNKLHU, 1960.

Nadějné vyhlídky. Trans. E. Tilsch and E. Tilschová, afterword by J. Hornát, illus. Miroslav Váša. Prague: Mladá fronta, 1965.

Nadějné vyhlídky. Trans. E. Tilsch and E. Tilschová, essay and notes J. Hornát, in Knihovna Klasiků: Spisy Charlese Dickense 14 [The Works of Charles Dickens]. Prague: Odeon 1972.

Nadějné vyhlídky. Trans. Emanuel Tilsch and Emanuela Tilschová, afterword by Bohuslav Mánek. Prague: Ikar, 1997.

Nadějné vyhlídky. Trans. Emanuel Tilsch and Emanuela Tilschová, afterword by Jaroslav Hornát. Frýdek-Místek: Alpress, 2009.

Danish

Store forventninge. Trans. L. Moltke. *Fædrelandet*, serialised 18 Feb–6 Aug 1861.

Store forventninge. Trans. L. Moltke. Vol. 26 of *Samtlige Værker* 3, 2nd ed., Copenhagen: Eibe, 1861.

Store forventninger. Trans. L. Moltke. Kbh: Eibe og Erslev, 1894.

Store forventninger. Trans. Julie Meyn, Folkets bogsamling 1. Copenhagen: Hagerup,1896.

Store Forventninger. Trans. L. Moltke, illus. Marcus Stone. Copenhagan: Steen Hasselbalch, 1919.

Store Forventninger. Trans. L. Moltke, intro. by Ove Jørgensen, Gyldendals bibliotek 37. Copenhagen: Gyldendal, 1930.

Store Forventninger. Trans. L. Moltke, intro. by Elsa Gress, Illus. F.W. Pailthorpe, 2 vols. Copenhagen: Spectators Girafbøger, 1964.

Store Forventninger. Geneva: Edito, 1972.

Store Forventninger. 1976. Braille Book. Copenhagen: Danmarks Blindebibliotek, 2004.

Store Forventninger. Trans. Eva Hemmer Hansen, illus. F.W. Pailthorpe. Copenhagen: Hernov, 1982.

Store Forventninger. Trans. Niels Brunse, illus. F.W. Pailthorpe. Copenhagen: Gyldendal, 1999.

Store Forventninger. Copenhagen: Gyldendal, 2003.

Dutch

Groote verwachtingen: een verhaal. Trans. C.M. Mensing. Amsterdam: Van Kampen, 1862; 1867.

Groote verwachtingen, in *Collected Works*. Trans. C.M. Mensing, Mrs van Westhreene, Mark Prager Lindo, illus.by F.A. Fraser. Schiedam: Roelants; 1868–83.

Groote verwachtingen. Nijmegen: Cohen, 1887.

Groote verwachtingen. In Complete Works, ed. A.G. van Kranendonk; J.W.F. Werumeus Buning. Utrecht and Antwerp: Spectrum, 1952.

Great expectations. Trans. Vincent Laarhoven; Jan van Holsteyn; Eugène de Smet. Utrecht: Stichting Teleac, cop., 1986.

Pip: naar Charles Dickens' "Great expectations." Trans. Ivo de Wijs. Arnhem: Toneelgroep Theater, cop., 1986.

Hoge verwachtingen. Trans. Rein Akkermans. Alkmaar: Toneeluitgeverij Vink, cop., 2001.

Grote verwachtingen. Trans. Hein de Bruin. Leeuwarden: Brilliant Books, cop., 2005.

Grote Verwachtingen. Trans. Eugene Dabekaussen and Maarten Hart. Amsterdam: Athenaeum-Polak and Van Gennep, 2006; 2010.

Finnish

Suuria Odotuksia. 2 Vols., trans Alpo Kupiainen. Hämeenlinna: Karisto, 1934; reprinted 1969; 1976; 1989.

Loistava tulevaisuus. 2 Vols., trans. Maini Palosuo. Helsinki: Otava, 1960; reprinted 1969; 1970.

French

Les Grandes Espérances du nommé Philip Pirrip, vulgairement appelé Pip. Serialised daily in *Le Temps* (Paris), beginning 20 February 1862 in *Le Temps* No. 316. Trans. Charles Bernard Derosne.

Les Grandes espérances, traduit de l'anglais par Charles Bernard-Derosne, avec l'autorisation de l'auteur. Charles Bernard Derosne. Paris: Hachette, 1864.

Les Grandes Espérance: Préface de Guy Mazeline. Roman traduit de l'anglais, avec l'autorisation de l'auteur, par C. B. Derosne. 2 Vols., trans. Charles Bernard-Derosne; Guy Mazeline. Lagny: impr. Emmanuel Grevin et fils; Paris: Gallimard, 1936; reprinted 1949; 1967.

Les Grandes espérances. Trans. Six Adamson. Bruxelles: le Carrefour, 1947.

Les Grandes espérances. Trans. Pierre Leyris; Philippe Jullian. Paris: Grasset, impr. de J. Crès, 1936; reprinted 1945; 1948 ; 1954.

Les Grandes espérances. Trans. Renée Swinney. Illustrations de Suzanne Jung. Paris: Gründ, 1948.

Les Grandes espérances. Trans. C.B. Derosne; preface Guy Mazeline. Paris: Gallimard Lagny: impr. de E. Grevin et fils, 1949.

De grandes espérances. Trans. Léon Lemonnier; Pierre Leyris; André Parreaux; Madeleine Rossel; Lucien Guitard; Francis Ledoux. Paris: Gallimard Pléiade, 1954; reprinted 1956.

Les Grandes espérances. Trans. Charles Derosne. Verviers: Gérard et Cie, impr. de Gérard et Cie, 1958.

Les grandes espérances. Trans. Sylvère Monod. Paris: Garnier frères, 1959; 1968.

Oeuvres complétes, Vol. 13: *Great expectations.* Londres: Oxford University Press, 1968–69.

Les grandes espérances; Le mystère d'Edwin Drood; Récits pour Noël. Trans. Charles-Bernard Derosne; Amédée Pichot; Jean Gattégno; et al. Paris: R. Laffont, 1981 ; reprinted 1991.

De grandes espérances. Trans. Pierre Leyris. Paris: B. Grasset, 1991.

Les grandes espérances. Trans. René Belletto. Paris: POL, 1994.

Les Grandes espérances; Les Aventures de M. Pickwick. Trans. Stefan Zweig. Paris: Omnibus, 1997.

Great Expectations. Trans. Jean-Pierre Naugrette. Paris: Ellipses, 1999.

Great Expectations. Trans. Laurent Le Paludier. Paris: Ed. Messene, 1999.

German

Grosse Erwartungen. Trans. Julius Seybt. Leipzig and Weissenburg: Meyer, 1862.

Grosse Erwartungen. Trans. Marie Scott. Leipzig: Weber-Lorck, 1862.

Grosse Erwartungen. Trans. Heinrich von Hammer. Vol. 1, Leipzig: Voigt and Gunther; Vol. 2, Vienna: Margraf, 1862.

Sämmtliche Werke. Grosse Erwartungen, Vols. 1–6. Illus. Hablot Knight Browne; H Roberts. Leipzig: Weber, 1862.

Grosse Erwartungen. Trans. L. Dubois. Stuttgart: Hoffman, 1864.

Grosse Erwartungen. Trans. Paul Heichen. Naumburg: A.S. Schirmer, 1895.

Grosse Erwartungen. Trans. Kurt Wilding. n.p., 1908.

Grosse Erwartungen. From series Romane der Welt Literatur, trans. Richard Zoozman. Leipzig: Hesse and Becker, 1910 reprinted 1950.

Die grossen Erwartungen: Roman. Hans Kühl. Weimar: Kiepenheuer, 1953.

Grosse Erwartungen: Roman. Trans. Josef Thanner. München: Winkler, 1956; reprinted 1972.

Grosse Erwartungen. Illus. Gerhard Gossmann. Berlin: Verlag Neues Leben, 1958.

Große Erwartungen: Roman. Trans. Josef Thanner. München: Dt. Taschenbuch Verl., 1972.

Große Erwartungen. Trans. Ruth Gerull-Kardas. Berlin: Verl. Neues Leben, 1979.

Große Erwartungen. Illus. F.W. Pailthorpe; Josef Thanner. München: Franklin Bibl,1980.

Grosse Erwartungen. Trans. Margit Meyer. Frankfurt: Insel-Verl., 1988.

Greek

Megales prosdokies. Ikaros: n.p., 1949.

Megales prosdokies. Vlesas: n.p., 1950.

Megales prosdokies. Romantso: n.p., 1956.

Megales prosdokies. [The following published editions in 1980: Bergadi, Pehlivanindis, Minoas, Pangosmia, Logotehnia, Astir. No place of publication provided.]

Megales prosdokies. [The following published editions in 1997: Zaharapoulis, Polis. No place of publication provided.]

Megales prosdokies. [The following published editions in 1998: Papadopoulos, Kedros, Kastaniotis, Livanis, Vlesas, Romantzo, Modern Times, Deagostini, Patakis. No place of publication provided.]

Megales prosdokies. Trans. Paulina Pampoudē. Athēna: Ekdoseis Patakē, 1998.

Megales prosdokies. [The following published editions in 2006: Nea Sinora. Eleftherotypia. No place of publication provided.]

Gujerati

Ane āśā bahu lāṃbī. Trans. Jayanti Dalal. 3 Vols. Ahmedabad: Viśvasāhitya, 1964.

Hebrew

Tiḵyot gedolot. Ḳ Katsenelson. Tel Aviv: Yosef Shim'oni, 1955.

Tiḵyot gedolot [High Hopes]. Ester Kaspi. Tel Aviv: Sifriyat po'alim, 1983.

Tiḵyt gedolot. Le'ah Leyin. Kefar Monash: Ofarim, 2000.

Hindi

Baṛī icchāeṃ. Trans. Arajuna Sharamā. Chandigarh: Lokgeet parkashan, 2011.

Hungarian

Nagy várakozásc. Trans. Lajos Mikes and Bèla Telekes. Budapest, 1924.
Nagy várakozásc. Trans. Andor Halasi, Kázmér Pogány, Oszkar Fekete; intro Tivadar Landor; illus. by Semjén. n.p: 1928.
Szép remények; regény. Trans. Tibor Bartos. Budapest: Európa Könyvkiadó 1959.
Szép remények. Trans. Tibor Bartos. Budapest: Magvető, 2004).

Icelandic

Glæstar vonir. Adapted by Stella Houghton Alico; illus. Angel Trinidad, trans. Sigriður Magnúsdóttir. Reykjavík: Græna gáttin, 1995.

Italian

Grandi speranze:Romanzo. Trans. Verdinois. Milano: Treves 1907; reprinted 1949.
Grandi speranze. Trans. C.F. Savici. Milano: Aurora, 1936.
Grandi Speranze. Trans. Carlo Linati. Milano: Martello, 1945; reprinted 1947.
Grandi Speranze. Trans. Bruno Maffi. Milano: Biblioteca Universale Rizzoli, 1955.
Grandi Speranze. Trans. Maria Luisa Giartosio De Courten, intro. Carlo Fruttero, illus. P. Plescau. Turin: Einaudi, 1959.
Grandi Speranze. Abridged and trans. Virginia Galante Garrone; ed. Paoline Vicenza. Rome: Paulist Press, 1962.
Grandi Speranze. Trans. Caesara Mazzola; Giorgio Manganelli. Rome: Casini, 1967.
Grandi Speranze. Trans. Maria Luisa Giartosio De Courten; intro Carlo Fruttero; illus. Peter Plescan; Valerio Fissore. Turin: Einaudi, 1975.
Grandi Speranze. Trans. Michela Conti. Milan: Peruzzo, 1986.
Grandi Speranze. Trans. Bruno Maffi; Guido Almansi. Milano: Biblioteca Universale Rizzoli, 1987.
Grandi Speranze. Trans. Caesara Mazzola; Alessandro Monti; Giuseppe Tomasi di Lampedusa. Rome: Gherardo Casini, 1991.
Grandi speranze. Trans. Caesara Mazzola. Milano: Oscar Mondadori, 1991.
Grandi Speranze. Trans. Marisa Sestito. Milano: Garzanti, 1994.
Grandi Speranze. Trans. Maria Luisa Giartosio De Courten; G.K. Chesteron. Turin: Einaudi, 1998.
Grandi Speranze. Trans. Maria Felicita Melchiorri; Mario Martino. Roma: Newton Compton, 1998.

Grandi speranze. Torino: Einaudi, 1998.
Great expectations: nel laboratorio di Charles Dickens. Trans. Francesco Marroni. Roma: Aracne, 2006.

Japanese

Great expectations and Little Dorrit. The Kobunsha series for higher schools, Shelf 2, No. 23, 1923.
Nazo-no onkeisha (The Mysterious Benefactor). Vol. 3 of *Tales from Dickens*, Yasushi and Keiko Matsumoto. Tōkyō: Chūō Kōronsha, 1936.
Ōinaru isan. Yasuo Okubo. n.p., 1948.
Ōinaru isan. Eiichi Yamanishi. n.p., 1948.
Ōinaru isan. Abridged guide to David Lean film, trans. Motori Kojima. Tōkyō: Eikoku Eiga Bunko [English Film Library], 1949.
Ōinaru isan. 2 Vols. Trans. Eiichi Yamanishi, with new postscript. Tōkyō: Shinchōsha, 1951; 1966.
Ōinaru isan. 3 Vols. Trans. Masayoshi Yamamoto. n.p., 1952–55.
Ōinaru isan. Trans. Hachiro Hidaka. Tōkyō: Chuo-Koronsha Treasury of World Literature, 1967.
Ōinaru isan. Trans. Yōko Tanabe. Hiroshima: Keisuisha, 2011.
Ooinaru isan. 2 Vols. Trans. Toru Sasaki. Graphic Novel. Tōkyō: Kawade Shobo Shinsha, 2011.

Korean

Widaehan yusan. Trans. Sŏul T'ŭkpyŏlsi: Hyewŏn Ch'ulp'ansa, 1987; 1999.

Latvian

Lielās cerības. Trans. Anna Bauga, illus. Gunārs Kļava. Riga: Liesma, 1972.

Malay

Memuncaknya harapan. Vol. 4 of Siri cerita popular. Kuala Lumpur: Whereever Distributors, 1983.

Norwegian

Store forventninger. With 16 stills from Lean film, trans. Eljert Bjerke. Oslo: Dreyers Forlag 1948; reprinted in 1951 and then again in 1968 without stills.
Store forventninger. Trans. Ragnhild Eikli, 'De Store Romana.' Oslo: Aschehoug, 1997.

Store forventninger. Trans. Ragnhild Eikli, 'En Maxi-klassiker fra Aschehoug.' Oslo: Aschehoug, 2001.

Store forventninger. Trans. Ragnhild Eikli, 'Verdensbiblioteket.' Oslo: Den Norske Bokklubben 2002.

Store forventninger. Trans. Ragnhild Eikli, 'Aschehoug klassiker.' Oslo: Aschehoug, 2008.

Store forventninger. Trans. Ragnhild Eikli, 'Aschehoug bibliotek.' Oslo: Aschehoug, 2008.

Store forventninger. Oslo: Egmont serieforl, 2010.

Oriya

Aneka āśā. Baṃsīdhara Dāśa. Kaṭaka: Grantha Mandira, 1971.

Persian

Ārizū'hā-i buzurg. Trans. Ibrāhīm Yūnisī. Tehran: Nashr-i Nil, 1961.

Ārizū'hā-yi buzurg. Tehran: Kitāb-i Maryam, 1994.

Ārizū'hā-i buzurg. Tihrān: Intishārāt-i Majīd, 1998.

Polish

[Translated for serial publication in Poland in 1863 and 1881, according to Maria Lyźwińska, 'Dickens in Poland', MS in Ada Nisbet Archive, but no further details are given]

Wielkie nadzieje. Vols. 8–9 of Wybordziel (Selected Works, 9 Vols.), ed. Antoni Mazański. Poznán: Printing and Books św.Wojciecha, 1918.

Wielkie nadzieje. Trans. Wanda Piątkiewicz. Warsaw, 1951.

Wielkie nadzieje. Pref. Halina Brodowska-Suwała. Warsaw: Książka i Wiedza, 1953.

Wielkie nadzieje. Trans. Karolina Beylin. Warszawa: Prószyński i S-ka, 2009.

Portuguese

Grandes esperanças. Trans. and illus. Alceu Masson. Porto Alegro: Globo, 1942; reprinted 1947.

Grandes esperanças. Trans. and illus. Alceu Masson. Rio de Janeiro: Globe, 1960.

Grandes esperanças. Trans. Armondo de Morais. Lisbon: Portugália Editora, 1969.

Grandes esperanças. Trans. Carmen Gonzalez. Mem Martins: Publicações Europa-America, 1975.

Grandes esperanças. Trans. José Eduardo Ribeiro Moretzsohn. Rio de Janeiro: Francisco Alves, 1982.

Punjabi

Waḍḍiāṃ āsāṃ. Trans. Accharū Siṅgha. Caṇḍīgaṛha: Lokagīta Prakāshana, 2007.

Romanian

Marile Sperante. Trans. Vera Călin. Bucharest: Editura de stat, 1947; reprinted 1949.
Marile Sperante. Trans. Vera Călin, pref. Dan Grigorescu, 2 vols. Bucarest: Editura pentru literatură, Biblioteca pentru toţi [Everyman's Library]115–16, Editura albatross, Lyceum collection. Bucharest: Universul familei,1969; reprinted 1973; 1992.
Marile Sperante. Trans. Cornelia Niţulescu, pref. Adrian Niţulescu. Craiova: Editura Oltenia, 1992.
Marile Sperante. Trans. Veronica Focşeneanu, pref. Dan Grigorescu. Bucharest: Leda, Adevărul Holding, 1998; reprinted 2004; 2008.

Russian

Bol'šie oẑidanija. Translator unknown. Serialised in the *Russian Herald*, Feb-Aug 1861.
Bol'šie nadeẑdy. Translator unknown. Serialised in *Records of the Fatherland*, Apr-Aug 1861.
Bol'shie Ozhidaniya. Illus. E. Budovskiy. Moskva: Gosudarstvennoe Izdatelstvo Detskoy Literatury, 1935.
Bol'shie Ozhidaniya. Trans. and intro by B.M. Engelgardt. n.p., 1941.
Pip: Otr. iz romana "Bol'sie ozidanija!". Trans. G. Titmarevoj. Moskva: Goz. Izd. detskoj Lit., 1952.
Bol'šie nadeẑdy. Trans. M Lorie. Moskva: Gosudarstvennoe izdatel'stvo hudoẑestvennoj literatury, 1952; incl, as Vol. 23 in Collected Works in 1960.
Bol'šie nadeẑdy. Moskva: Gosudarstvennoe izdatel'stvo detskoj literatury Ministerstva prosveščenija RSFSR, 1957.
Bolshie Nadezhdy. Vol. 20 of 30. Moskva: Gosudarstvennoe Izdatelstvo Khudozhestvennaya Lite, 1960.
Bol'shie nadezhdy. Leningrad: 'Khudozhestvennaiā̄literature,' Leningr. otd-nie, 1970.
Bolshie Nadezhdy. With *Christmas Books* and *Hard Times*, Vol. 8 of 10. Moskva: Gosudarstvennoe Izdatelstvo Khudozhestvennaya Lite, 1986.
Bolshie Nadezhdy. Makhachkala: Dagestanskoe Knizhnoe izdatelstvo, 1986.
Bol'shie nadezhdy: roman. Moskva: 'Khudozh. lit-ra,' 1986.
Bolshie Nadezhdy. St. Petersburg: Khudozhestvennaya Literatura, 1987.
Bolshie Nadezhdy. Moscow: Moskovskiy Rabochiy, 1987.

Serbian

Prevod dela. Trans. Živojin V Simić. Beograd: Prosveta, 1950.

Slovak

Vel̓ké nádeje: roman. Trans. Jožo Dubeň. Bratislava: Slovenský spisovatel̓, 1951.

Spanish

(Los) Grandes esperanzas (de Pip). Trans. Manuel Vallvé. Barcelona: Editorial Juventud, 1930.
Grandes esperanzas. 2 Vols., trans., prologue and notes José Méndez Herrera. Madrid: Aguilos, 1945; reprinted 1949; 1957; 1964.
Grandes esperanzas. Trans. R. Berenguer. Barcelona: Reguera, 1946.
Great Expectations. Trans. Latif Doss. Harlow: Longman, 1952.
Grandes ilusiones. Trans. Juan B. Riera García. Barcelona: Miguel Arimany, 1955(?)
Grandes esperanzas. 2 Vols., trans. J.de Zengoita. Barcelona: M. Arimany, 1956.
Grandes esperanzas. Trans. María Dolores García-Lomas. Barcelona: Editorial Mateu, 1958.
Grandes esperanzas. Trans. Manuel Vallvé. Barcelona: Juventud, cop. 1973.
Grandes esperanzas. Trans. Deborah Chiel; Mitch Glazer. Barcelona: Plaza & Janés, 1998.
Grandes esperanzas. Trans. María Engracia Pujals. Madrid: Valdemar, 2001.
Grandes esperanzas. Trans. Miguel Angel Perez. Alianza Editorial Sa, 2011.

Swedish

Lysande utsigter, eller, Pip Pirrips märkvärdiga lefnadsöden. Trans. Carl Johan Backmann. Ångbåts och Jernvägslitteratur 24, 2 vols. Stockholm: J.L. Brudins förlag, 1861.
Lysande utsigter Trans. 'M. B-e', 2 vols. Stockholm: Häggström, 1885.
Lysande förhoppningar. Trans. Th. Wallbeck-Hallgren, 2 vols. Stockholm: Nordiska, 1914.
Lysande utsikter, eller Pip Pirrips märkvärdiga levnadsöden. Trans. Tom Wilson. Berömda böcker 91. Stockholm: Björk & Börjesson, 1922.
Lysande förhoppningar. Trans. Erik Björkbro. Selected copies of original illus., 2 vols. Malmö: Scandinavia, 1925–26.
Lysande utsikter. Trans. Margareta Ångström. Stockholm: Bonnier, 1950.
Lysande utsikter. Trans. Margareta Ångström, new ed. Stockholm: Forum, 1977.
Lysande utsikter. Trans. Margareta Ångström, new ed. Stockholm: Forum, Manadens bök, 1986.
Lysande utsikter. Lund: Btj, 2006.

Thai

Rǣngčhai lǣ fai fan. Trans. Rangsimā Dīsawat. Krung Thēp: Frīfǫm, 2011.

Tibetan

Dun-pa chen-po. Dharamsala: Education Development and Resource Centre, 1993.

Turkish

Büyük ümitler. Trans. A Bekir Sıtkı. İstanbul: Ak, 1961.
Büyük umutlar. Trans. Hüseyin Yavuz Yıldırım. İstanbul: Karınca, 1999.
Büyük umutlar: roman. Trans. Nihal Yeğinobalı. İstanbul: Can yayınları, 2001.

Udmurt

Pip [fragment]. Trans. A. Luzhanin. Azhevsk, 1938.

Ukranian

Velyki spodivanniā: roman. Kharkiv: Folio, 2003.

Vietnamese

Uớc vọng lớn lao cuộc đời của Pip (Great Desire: Pip's Life). Juvenile title. Nhất Ly. Hà Nội: NXB Văn Hóa-Thông Tin, 2006.

Welsh

Myfi Pip. Abridged by Beti Hughes. Llandybie, Sir Gaerfyrddin: Llyfrau'r Dryw, 1969.

Yakut

Pip [fragment]. Trans. P. Ellyaev. Yakutsk: n.p., 1970.

Yiddish

Groyse oyszikhṭn. Trans. Binyamin Marshaḳ. Ḳiev: Melukhe-farlag far di natsyonale minderhayṭn in USSR, 1939.

Appendix C
Adaptations for Stage, Radio, Film and Television, 1861–2012

Sources

Archive

BBC Sound Archives;
BBC Written Archives Centre;
Billy Rose Theatre Division, New York Public Library;
British Film Institute;
British Library;
Cinema Arts Library, University of Southern California;
Film and Television Archive, University of California, Los Angeles;
Garrick Club Library, London;
The Lawrence and Lee Collection, Rodgers and Hammerstein Archives of Recorded Sound, New York Public Library Centre for the Performing Arts.

Print [see bibliography for full publishing information]

Adair Fitz-Gerald, *Dickens and the Drama*;
Allardyce Nicoll, *A History of English Drama 1660–1900*;
Bolton, *Dickens Dramatized*;
The Dickensian;
Dickens Studies Newsletter;
Dickens Quarterly;
The Era;
Giddings and Selby, *The Classic Serial on Television and Radio*;
Glavin, *Dickens on Screen*;
Grams, *Radio Drama*;
Marill, *More Theatre*;
McFarlane, *Screen Adaptations*;
Morley, 'Stages of *Great Expectations*';
Win Faxon, ed., *Dramatic Index*;
Wearing, *The London Stage*.

Online

IMDB (www.imdb.com/)
Digital Deli Too American Radio Catalogue (http://www.digitaldeliftp.com/DigitalDeliToo/dd2home.html)

Jerry Haendiges Vintage Radio Logs (http://www.otrsite.com/radiolog/)
National Film and Sound Archive, Australia (www.nfsa.gov.au/)
Scottish Theatre Archive (http://special.lib.gla.ac.uk/)
South African Broadcasting Corporation archives (www.sabc.co.za/)

Stage adaptations

Note: I have provided dates for complete runs of performances where possible, but where a single date is given it corresponds to the date of the first known performance.

Australia

Great Expectations, play, directed by Simon Phillips. Western Australia Theatre Company, Perth, 1986.

Great Expectations, musical, directed by Eric Taylor. York Theatre, Chippendale, NSW, 28 September 1991. Lyricist: Hal Shaper. Composer: Cyril Ornadel. Cast: Gabriel Andrews, Vincent Ball, Zoe Bertram, Raymond Duparc, Philip Gould, Lester Morris, Jackie Rees, Doug Scroope, Dinah Shearing, Bruce Venables, Tom Wealer, David Webb, Megan Williams.

Great Expectations, play, directed by Simon Phillips. Melbourne Theatre Company, 16 September – 18 October 2002. Cast: Simon Aylott, Stephen Costan, Julie Forsyth, Jan Friedl, Linal Haft, Jonathan Hardy, Sam Healy, Huw Higginson, Bob Hornery, Asher Keddie, Angus King, Monica Maughan, Colin Moody, Richard Piper, Angela Punch McGregor, Benjamin Winspear.

Great Expectations, play, adapted by John Clifford, directed by Julie Redlich. Hunters Hill Theatre, Hunters Hill, NSW, 7–22 March 2003.

Great Expectations, play, adapted and directed by Tania Lieman. Frog Hollow Centre for the Arts, Darwin, NT, 17–27 September 2003.

Great Expectations, play, directed by John Harrison. Australian Theatre for Young People, Bakehouse Theatre, Walsh Bay, 31 October 2012. Cast: Shannon Ashlyn, Jarrod Crellin, Alan Dearth, Cheyne FInn, Kieran Foster, Sophie Haylen, Stephen Lloyd-Coombs, Richard Hilliar, Daniel Hunter, Jim McCrudden, Callum McManis, Jacki Mison, Jessica Paterson, Rebecca Saffir, Patrick Sherwood.

Canada

Great Expectations, play, directed by Michael Shamata. Soulpepper Theatre, Toronto, 6 July – 17 August 2013. Cast: Naomi Agard (Young Estella/Young Biddy), Oliver Becker (Magwitch/Londoner), Oliver Dennis (Joe/Wemmick), Leah Doz (Estella/Biddy), Deborah Drakeford (Mrs. Joe/Molly/Londoner), Jesse Aaron Dwyre (Soldier/Bentley/Sarah Pocket/Lieutenant/Londoner), John Jarvis (Uncle Pumblechook/Compeyson/Raymond Pocket/Aged Parent/Londoner), C. David Johnson (Jaggers/Sergeant/Londoner), Jeff Lillico (Pip), Paolo Santalucia (Herbert/Orlick/Camilla Pocket/Londoner), Kate Trotter (Miss Havisham).

UK

Great Expectations, play, adapted and directed by W.S. Gilbert. (Royal) Court
Theatre, London, 29 May 1871. Cast: Edward Righton (Joe), J.C. Cowper
(Magwitch), John Clayton (Jaggers), Eleanor Bufton (Estella), Kate Bishop
(Biddy), Jessie Powell (Young Pip), Maggie Brennan (Adult Pip). Revived
at Aquarium Theatre on 19 March 1877 with same cast except for Blanche
Marian Henri (Estella), James Fawn (Joe) and Fred Dewar (Jaggers).
Pip's Patron, play, adapted by William J. Rix. Town Hall, Beccles, 26 January 1871.
Great Expectations, play, adapted by Percival Steed. Athenaeum, Glasgow, 22–27
February 1918. A Dickens Fellowship Production.
Great Expectations, play, adapted by Mrs Laurence Raithby. Edinburgh, 7
February 1920. A Dickens Fellowship production.
Scenes from Great Expectations, play, adaptor/director unknown. Woodville and
District, autumn season, 1925. A Dickens Fellowship production.
Scenes from Great Expectations, play, adaptor/director unknown, Bath, October
1925.
Great Expectations, play, adapted by Mrs G.W. Panzetta. Whitefields, London,
December 1925. A Dickens Festival production. Cast: Percy Gayler (Herbert),
Harry Dunlop (Wemmick), Harry Charles (Pumblechook), Mrs Gertrude
Heaton (Mrs Joe), Miss Ethel Bagley (Miss Havisham).
Great Expectations, sketch, adaptator/director unknown [Bolton lists several
possibilities including Hodges, Holroyd, Openshaw and E. Dickens, but I have
been unable to verify any of these from any other source]. 1931; one of a
medley of Dickens sketches performed for charity in about 12 performances.
The Convict, play, adapted by Ethel Dickens and Charles E. Openshaw. Westminster
Theatre, London, 4 February; 4 and 7 November 1935. Cast: Sir J. Martin-
Harvey (Magwitch), Wilfred Walter (Joe), John Garside (Jaggers), Hubert
Gregg (Adult Pip), Dick Curnock (Young Pip), Jean Cadell (Miss Havisham),
Thea Holme (Estella), Mary Casson (Biddy), Robert Ginns (Herbert), Mary
Mayfern (Mrs Joe). [Morley claims Martin-Harvey took the play, re-named
'The Scapegoat', on tour the following August; Bolton has it at the Theatre
Royal, Birmingham, 4–10 Nov 1935.]
Great Expectations, play, adapted by Frances Jolly, 1935.
Great Expectations, play, adapted by Alec Guinness. Actors' Theatre Company,
Rudolph Steiner Hall, London, 7 December 1939. Cast: Guinness (Herbert),
Roy Emerton (Magwitch), Marius Goring (Pip), Martita Hunt (Miss Havisham),
Richard George (Joe), Wilfred Caithness (Jaggers), Beryl Measor (Mrs Joe),
Yvonne Mitchell (Young Estella), Vera Lindsay (Adult Estella), Frank Tickle
(Pumblechook). Revivals at Liverpool Playhouse (1943–44, Dir. Jon Moody);
Toynbee Hall, London (1946); Oxford (1947); Bristol Old Vic (19 February
1957); Citizen's Theatre Co., Glasgow (20 March – 1 April 1961); the Grand
Theatre, Swansea (26 June 1973); Ipswich Arts (28 November 1973); Torch
Theatre, Milford Haven (10 September 1980, Dir. Graham Watkins); Theatr
Clwyd, Mold (30 September 1980, Dir. Graham Watkins); Theatr y Werin,

Aberystwyth (14 October 1980, Dir. Graham Watkins); Thetr Gwynedd, Bangor (28 October 1980, Dir. Graham Watkins).

Great Expectations, play, adapted by William Deneen, Michael Sherwin and Bransby Williams. The King's Theatre, Hammersmith, 7 July 1947. Cast: Bransby Williams (Magwitch).

Great Expectations, play, adapted by Alice Chadwicke. 1948.

Great Expectations, play, adapted by Ross Barrington. George Inn, Southwark, 1950.

Great Expectations, play, adapted by Gerald Frow, directed by Sally Miles. Mermaid Theatre, London, April – June 1960. Revived at the Mermaid Theatre, Nottingham in December 1961 and at Margate, Christmas 1961. Cast: John Hall (Young Pip), Gary Watson (Adult Pip), Dan Meaden (Joe), Jocelyn Page (Mrs Joe), Josephine Wilson (Miss Havisham), Gillian Gale (Young Estella), Suzanne Fuller (Adult Estella), Michael Logan (Jaggers), Paul Curran (Magwitch), Brian Hewlett (Young Herbert), Richard Coe (Adult Herbert), Mairhi Russell (Biddy), Colin Ellis (Wemmick), Blake Butler (Aged P) .

Great Expectations, play, adapted by John Maxwell. Dundee Repertory Company, 13–26 March1961. Cast: Kate Binchy, Edward Fox, William Marlowe, Trevor Martin, Lillias Walker, Ann Way, Nicol Williamson.

Great Expectations, play, adapted by Jane Bacon. Portland Hall, London, 5 May 1961.

Great Expectations, play, adapted by John Maxwell. Marlowe, Canterbury, 8 December 1964.

Great Expectations, play, adapted by Bruce Walker. Golders Green Hippodrome, London, 2 May 1966.

My Gentleman Pip, musical, writer/director unknown. The Opera House, Harrogate, December 1968.

Great Expectations, play, directed by Steve Gooch. Liverpool Playhouse, 1970.

Great Expectations, play, adapted by Joan Taylor and Gladys Waterer. Broadstairs, Kent, June 1970. A Dickens Festival Production.

Miss Havisham's Revenge, play, directed by Michael and Mollie Hardwick. 1970.

Great Expectations, play, adapted by James Lovell. Dundee, 12–30 January 1971. Cast: László Antal, Ron Bain, Alan Carnegie, Steve Gardner, Drew Griffiths, Martyn James, David Jarrett, James Kennedy, Robin Lefevre, Glen Park, Tricia Scott, Jennifer Stevenson, Hamish Wilson, Jan Wilson.

Pip and the Convict, play, adapted by Guy R. Williams. 1971.

Great Expectations, play, adapted by John Maxwell. Harrogate, 21 November 1973.

Great Expectations, play, adapted by Joan Knight. Perth, 27 November – 14 December 1974.

Great Expectations, musical, adapted by Hal Shaper and Trevor Preston. Musical Director Cyril Ornadel. Yvonne Arnaud Theatre, Guildford, 24 December – 31 January 1975/6. Also at Theatre Royal, Brighton (2 Feb 1976); Richmond (16 Feb 1976); Bath (1 Mar 1976). Cast: John Mills (Joe), Moira Lister (Miss Havisham), Martin Connor (Herbert), Leonard Whiting (Pip).

Great Expectations, play, adapted and directed by Joan Taylor. Ramsgate, 17 November 1977. A Broadstairs Dickens Players Production.

Great Expectations, play, adapted by Priscilla Donald, directed by John Knox. Hilderstone Theatre, Broadstairs, June 1980. A Dickens Festival production.

Great Expectations, play, adaptor/director unknown. Everyman Theatre, Liverpool, 19 May 1983.

Great Expectations, play, adapted by George Curry. Netherbow, Edinburgh, August – September 1983. A Festival Fringe production.

Great Expectations, play, directed by Michael Napier Brown. Royal Theatre, Northampton, 3 May 1984.

Great Expectations, play, adapted by Greg Hersov, James Maxwell, Braham Murray and Caspar Wrede. Royal Exchange, Manchester, 30 October – 8 December 1984. Cast: Nick Stringer (Magwitch), Art Malik (Herbert), Amanda Donohoe (Estella), Michael Mueller (Pip).

Great Expectations, play, directed by Peter Coe. Old Vic, London and thereafter on UK tour, 26 December – 2 February 1984/5. Cast: Roy Dotrice (Magwitch), Sheila Burrell (Miss Havisham), Leon Greene (Joe), Tony Jay (Jaggers), Charles Lawsen (Wemmick), Lynn Clayton (Estella), Collin Johnson (Herbert), Ian McCurrach (Pip).

Great Expectations, play, adapted by John (later Jo) Clifford, directed by Ian Brown. Tag Theatre Company tour of Scotland, 10 May – 10 October 1988.

Great Expectations, musical, adapted by Christopher G. Sandford, music/lyrics by Mike Read. Theatr Clwd, Mold, Wales, 3 October 1993 – 22 January 1994 and thereafter on UK tour. Cast: Darren Day (Pip), Steven Osborne (Magwitch), Christopher Corcoran (Joe), Victoria Pritchard (Mrs Joe/Molly), John Summerfield (Orlick/Drummle), Melanie Stace (Clara/Mrs Hubble), Michael Vaughan (Wemmick/Pumblechook), Nick Cavaliere (Mr Hubble/ Startop), Mark Faith (Woplse/Mr Pocket), Alistair Petrie (Herbert/Sergeant), Elizabeth Renihan (Estella), Tamara Ustinov (Miss Havisham), Nigel Williams (Jaggers), Caroline Fitzgerald (Biddy).

Great Expectations, play, directed by Declan Donnellan and Nick Ormerod. Royal Shakespeare Company at the RST, Stratford, 25 November 2005 – 4 February 2006. Cast: Sian Phillips (Miss Havisham), Brian Doherty (Joe), Harry Davies and Samuel Roukin (Pip), Robert Hastie (Herbert), Jo Woodcock and Neve McIntosh (Estella), Tobias Beer (Orlick), Roger Sloman (Magwitch).

Great Expectations, play, adapted by Neil Bartlett, directed by Roger Haines. Library Theatre, Manchester, 5–17 January 2009. Cast: Leon Williams (Pip), Helen Ryan (Miss Havisham), Richard Heap (Magwitch).

Great Expectations, musical, directed by Tim Baker, music by Dyfan Jones. Everyman Playhouse, Liverpool, 24 – 28 March 2009 and thereafter a month-long UK tour. A Clwyd Theatr Cymru production. Cast: Steven Meo (Pip), Vivian Parry (Miss Havisham), Eleanor Howell (Estella), Steffan Rhodri (Joe), Robert Perkins (Jaggers), Simon Watts (Herbert).

Great Expectations, play, adapted by Tanika Gupta, directed by Nicolai Foster. English Touring Theatre, UK tour 17 February – 11 May 2011. Cast: Jude Akuwudike (Magwitch), Rob Compton (Compeyson), Giles Cooper (Herbert), Russell Dixon (Jaggers/soldier), Lynn Farleigh (Miss Havisham), Pooja Ghai

(Mrs Joe/Molly), Shiv Grewal (Pumblechook), Simone James (Estella), Tony Jayawardena (Joe), Tariq Jordan (Pip), Darren Kuppan (Wemmick), Kiran Landa (Biddy).

Great Expectations, play, adaptor/director unknown. Watermill Theatre, Berkshire, 2011.

Great Expectations, play, adapted by Jo Clifford, directed by Graham McLaren. Vaudeville Theatre, London, 7 February – 30 March 2013. Revival following international tour in the 1980s (see above). Premiere screened live in cinemas worldwide on Dickens's 200th birthday, 7 Feb 2013. Cast: Jack Ellis (Jaggers), Chris Ellison (Magwitch), Paula Wilcox (Miss Havisham), Paul Nivison (Adult Pip), Grace Rowe (Estella), Taylor Jay-Davies (Young Pip).

USA

Great Expectations, play, adapted and directed by Julie de Marguerittes. Walnut Street Theater, Philadelphia, 16 September 1861. Cast: Edwin Adams (Magwitch), S. Hemple (Joe), Alice Grey (Miss Havisham), Miss C. Jefferson (Young Pip), Mr Bascomb (Adult Pip).

Great Expectations, play, adapted by George L. Aiken, scenery by Hielge. Barnum's Museum, NY, eight performances from 7 October 1861. Cast: T.H. Hadaway (Joe), W.L. Jamison (Orlick), Addie Le Brun (Young Pip), Mrs J.J. Prior (Adult Pip), J.E. Nagle (Magwitch), Mrs R. France (Miss Havisham), C. Alford (Estella), E. Haviland (Jaggers), John Bridgeman (Pumblechook), George Brooks (Wopsle), H. Cunningham (Compeyson), H.E. Chapman (Brownlow), George H. Clark (Herbert Pocket), Addie Le Brun (Sarah Pocket), Jennie Walters (Mrs Joe), Mr Anderson (Mr Camilla), W.L. Jamieson (Orlick), Mr Ryley (Cousin Josh), Mr Hughes (Herbert) [*sic*], Miss Thomas (Mrs Hubble), Miss R. Moreland (Mrs Camilla), Miss McCormick (Georgiana).

Great Expectations, play, directed by Benjamin J. Woolf. Boston Museum, 7–19 October 1861. Cast: Oriana Marshall (Young Pip), J. Wilson (Adult Pip), William Whalley (Magwitch), Frank Hardenberg (Orlick), Josephine Orton (Miss Havisham), Emil Maystayer (Mrs Joe), William Warren (Joe).

Great Expectations, play, adapted by Adah Isaacs Menken. Louisville, Kentucky, 28 March 1862. Also produced by Menken's friend William Tayleure at the Holliday Street Theatre, Baltimore, 1862, and the Howard Athenaeum, Boston, 9 July 1862. Cast: Menken (Young and Adult Pip).

Great Expectations, play, adapted by W.S. Gilbert. Boston Museum, 16 October 1871.

My Unknown Friend, play, directed by Charles Augustus (Shafto) Scott. Wallack's Theater, NY, 1872. Cast: Miss Lewis (Young Pip), Mr Edwin (Sergeant), John Parselle (Magwitch), Mr Arnott (Orlick), Jon Clarke (Joe), Mrs Sefton (Mrs Joe), Mr. H.J. Montague (Adult Pip), Mr Gilbert (Jaggers), Mr Stevenson (Herbert Pocket), Miss Burke (Estella), Ada Dyas (Biddy).

Botany Bay, an original melodrama founded in part on Great Expectations, play, directed by Levin C. Tees. 15 July 1893.

Great Expectations, play, adapted and read by Mr Phidelah Rice. Brook Theatre, Cleveland, 1936.

Great Expectations, play, adapted by Paul Lee, directed by Jonathan Bolt. Cleveland Playhouse, Ohio, 25 November 1977 – 7 April 1978.

Miss Havisham's Fire, opera, adapted by Dominick Argento, directed by H. Wesley Balk, libretto by John Olon-Scrymgeour. New York City Opera, 22 March 1979. Revived 1996 and 2001. Cast: Rita Shane (Miss Aurelia Havisham), Alan Titus (Pip), Suzanne Morsee/Gianna Rolandi (Estella), Lorna Wallach (Young Estella), John Lankston (Drummle), Paul Ikena (Magwitch).

Great Expectations, musical, adapted by Margaret Hoorneman and Drew Kalter, directed by Gregory S. Hurst, music and lyrics by Jeremiah Murray. J.I. Rodale Theatre, Allentown, PA, Pennsylvania Stage Company, 3 December 2010. Revived 1 July – 28 August 2010 at Randall L. Jones Theatre, Cedar City, Utah, directed by Jules Aaron. Cast: Gian-Carlo Vellutino (Young Pip), Richard White (Adult Pip), James Fleetwood (Magwitch), Whitney Webster (Young Estella), Catherine Gaines (Adult Estella), Victoria Boothby (Miss Havisham), Jack Davison (Joe), Sara Woods (Mrs Joe), Ric Stoneback (Compeyson/Mr Misfit), J.R. Horne (Jaggers), Robert Hayman (Young Herbert), Dennis Warning (Adult Herbert), Scott Severance (Pumblechook/Wemmick/Butler), Barbara Marineau (Hannah), Michael Goldberg (Sergeant/Newgate guard/Policeman/anxious man), Tricia O'Connell (Biddy), Trace Paterson (Mrs Misfit), Stanton Cunningham (Drummle/Sailor), Beth Leavel (Whore/Molly), Stephen Hope (Sharkie), Alice Morgan (Poll).

Miss Havisham's Wedding Night, opera, a 1-Act rewriting of *Miss Havisham's Fire*, adapted by Dominick Argento, directed by H. Wesley Balk, libretto by John Olon-Scrymgeour. Tyrone Guthrie Theater, Minneapolis, MN, 1 May 1981. Revived at Fashion Institute, New York, 31 March 1983.

Great Expectations, play, adapted by Barbara Field, directed by Eric Samuelsen. Pardoe Theater, Brigham Young University, UT, 1982. Cast: Doug Kaufman (Pip), Conrad Pack (Joe), Robert J. Gibbs (Magwitch), Nola Smith (Miss Havisham), Amanda Scheffer (Estella).

Great Expectations, play, adapted by Barbara Field, directed by Richard Edwards. Poncho Theater, Seattle, WA, 30 September 1983. Cast: Jonathan Bridgman and Isaac Benjamin Sterling (Young Pip), Robert I. Lee (Magwitch), John Prebyl (Joe), Katherine Kramer (Estella), Barbara McKean (Miss Havisham), Breet Keogh (Pip). Revived, directed by Stephen Kanee, Guthrie Theater, Minneapolis touring branch, 7 June 1985. Cast: Mitchell Lichtenstein (Pip), Kathryn Dowling (Estella), Allen Hamilton (Magwitch).

Great Expectations, play, adapted and directed by Robert Johanson. Papermill Playhouse, NJ, 1985. Revived at the Papermill in 1995 and at Brundage Park Playhouse, NJ, 9 October 2009. Cast: Michael James Reed (Adult Pip), Darren Edward Higgins (Young Pip), Elizabeth Franz (Miss Havisham), Jennifer Holmes (Young Estella).

Great Expectations, play, adapted by Barbara Field, directed by Jeff Frank. Pennsylvania Stage Co., PA, 12–14 April 1996. Cast: Jeanine T. Abraham (Estella), Charlie Schroeder (Pip).

Great Expectations, musical play, adapted by John Jakes. Elizabeth Wallace Theater, Hilton Head Island, SC, 21 April 1999. Revived 2 – 26 Aug 2001.

Great Expectations, musical, adapted by Margaret Hoorneman. Utah Shakespearean Festival, Cedar City, UT, 1 July – 28 August 2010. Previewed at a workshop in Hollywood, CA, May 2001 with Cloris Leachman, Hugh Panara, Anastasia Barzee, and at the Odyssey Theater in Los Angeles, CA, 2009. Cast: Jack Noseworthy (Pip), Max Robinson (Magwitch), L.J. Benet (Young Pip), Lillian Castillo (Mrs. Joe), Dave Barrus (Joe Gargery), Jeff Steitzer (Pumblechook, Wemick), Summer Sloan (Young Estella), Ellen Crawford (Miss Havisham), Marshall Hunt (Young Herbert), J. Michael Bailey (Jaggers), Alexandra Fisher (Young Biddy), Melinda Pfundstein (Biddy), Jason Michael Spelbring (Herbert), Jennifer Whipple (Young Miss Havisham), Emily Trask (Estella/Molly), Will Mobley (Startop), Jesse Easley (Compeyson), Jennifer Whipple (Clara).

Great Expectations, play, directed by Mark Clements. Walnut Street Theatre, PA, 2001.

Great Expectations, musical, adapted by John Jakes, directed by Kent Thompson, music by Mel Marvin, choreography by Janet Watson. Norma Terris Theatre, Chester, CT, 2 – 26 August 2001. Cast: Rita Gardener (Miss Havisham), Terence Goodman (Joe), William Ryall (Jaggers), Rachael Warren (Estella), Michael Winther (Pip), Robert Aronson (Magwitch), Elizabeth Arnold (Mrs Joe).

Great Expectations, play, adapted by Bathsheba Doran, directed by Will Pomerantz. Lucille Lortel Theater, NY, 8 November – 3 December 2006. Cast: Kathleen Chalfont (Miss Havisham), Emily Donahoe (Estella).

Great Expectations, ballet, adapted and choreographed by Margaret Wingrove. San Jose Stage Theatre, CA, January 2010.

Great Expectations, play, directed by Neil Bartlett. A Noise Within Theatre, Glendale, CA, December 2010. Cast: Jason Dechert (Pip), Daniel Reichert (Magwitch), Deborah Strang (Miss Havisham), Jaimi Paige (Estella).

Great Expectations, play, directed by Jared Reed. Curio Theatre Company, PA, 3 February – 5 March 2011. Cast: Eric Scotolati (Pip), Paul Kuhn (Magwitch/ Pumblechook/Wemmick), Liam Castellan (Compeyson/Jaggers/Orlick/ Bentley/Biddy/Soldier), and Ken Opdenaker (Joe/Herbert/Mike/Aged Parent/ Arthur).

Radio Adaptations

Note: programme, running time, date and station details are given inconsistently both between and within individual radio archives. I have standardised as far as possible, but in some cases full details were unavailable.

Australia

'Great Expectations', episode 15 of *Radio Station Drama* series (broadcast 1935–1975), 2GB, Sydney. No date.

'Great Expectations', adapted for Radio in 10 episodes by Richard Hamilton Lane. No date but probably 1950s.

'Great Expectations', 60 mins., *Lux Radio Theatre* (based on American show of same name). Cast: Thelma Scott, Peter Finch, Harvey Adams. No date.

'Great Expectations', episode 6 of *Playhouse of World Famous Authors*, Artransa Studios, Sydney. c. 1960.

'Great Expectations', docudrama about origins of Miss Havisham, directed and produced by C.T. Parkinson, NSW. No date.

South Africa

'Great Expectations', 26 x 31-min. episodes, adapted by Michael McCabe, produced by Roger Spence. Springbok Radio English Service, 19 July – 21 October 1975. Cast: Nigel Daily, Dennis Smith, Billy Matthews, Sue Trower, Judy Goldman.

'Great Expectations', 34 x 25-min. episodes of *Bestsellers* series, produced by Kenneth Hendel. Springbok Radio, 25 Feb – 12 April 1985. Cast: Bruce Millar, Patricia Saunders, Richard Cox, Brian O'Shaughnessy, Julian Bailer, Robin Smith, Valerie Dunlop, Angus Neill, Justin Hambloch, Lilian Randall, Lynda Stuart, Therese Iglich, John Carson, Trish Swart, David Sherwood, Arthur Hall, Keith Galloway.

UK

'Great Expectations', 16 x 15-min. weekly instalments, adapted and read by V.C. Clinton Baddeley, BBC London and Daventry Programme, 3 January – 24 April 1930, 6pm.

'Great Expectations', *Book Talk* with Desmond McCarthy, BBC Schools (Senior English III), National Programme, 11 May 1937.

'Pip's early life', *Book Talk* with Morna Stuart, BBC Schools (Senior English), Home Service, 7 December 1943, 2.35pm.

'Great Expectations', 3 × weekly parts, BBC Schools (Senior English 1), 1 – 15 June 1945.

'Great Expectations', 12 × 30-min. instalments, adapted by Mabel Constanduras and Howard Agg, BBC Home Service Sunday, 19 September – 5 December 1948, 8.30pm. Episodes 1–3 repeated Thursdays 3.30–4pm; episodes 3–12 repeated Thursdays 4.30–5pm. Cast: Michael Lister (Young Pip), Cyril Cusack (Adult Pip), William Devlin (Magwitch), Laidman Browne (Joe), Natalie Kent (Mrs Joe), Hermione Hannen (Estella), Norman Shelley (Uncle Pumblechook), Lawrence Bascomb (Mr Wopsle), Cyril Gardiner (Mr Hubble), Susan Richards (Mrs Hubble), Alastair Duncan (Compeyson), Catherine Campbell

(Clara Barley), David Enders (Startop), Franklin Dyall (Jaggers), Ernest Sefton (Trabb), D. Bryer (Trabb's Boy), Gladys Young (Miss Havisham), Charles Leno (Wemmick), Donald Eccles (Herbert), Franklyn Bellamy (Aged P). Ep. 1: 'The Fearful Man', 19 September; Ep. 2: 'One memorable Day', 26 September; Ep. 3: 'The Lawyer from London', 3 October; Ep. 4: 'Bright Fortunes', 10 October; Ep. 5: 'Barnard's Inn', 17 October; Ep. 6: 'The Princess with no Heart', 24 October; Ep. 7: 'The Benefactor', 31 October; Ep. 8: 'The Dreaded Visitor', 7 November; Ep. 9: 'A Dream is Broken', 14 November; Ep. 10: 'Mill Pond Bank', 21 November; Ep. 11: 'Down the River', 28 November; Ep. 12: 'An End and a Beginning', 5 December.

'Great Expectations', interlude reading by V.C. Clinton-Baddeley, BBC, 23 May 1950, 6.37pm.

'Young Pip', adapted by Sylvia Goodall, BBC Schools (Junior English), 2 May 1951.

'Great Expectations', 12 episodes, BBC Calling West Africa, 2 October – 12 December 1951. Ep. 1: 'Pip Meets the Convict', 2 October; Ep. 2: 'The Convict is Recaptured', 9 October; Ep. 3: ''Pip Meets Miss Havisham', 16 October; Ep. 4: [Script/title missing], 23 October; Ep. 5: 'Pip has Great Expectations', 30 October; Ep. 6: 'Pip Arrives in London', 6 November; Ep. 7: 'Estella Sends for Pip', 13 November; Ep. 8: 'Pip Comes of Age', 20 November; Ep. 9: 'Pip Meets his Benefactor', 27 November; Ep. 10: 'Magwitch tells his Story', 4 December; Ep. 11: 'Pip Makes Two Discoveries', 11 December; Ep. 12: 'The Reunion', 18 December.

'Pip and the Convict', BBC Schools (Prose and Verse Readings), 12 January 1953.

'Great Expectations', 6 parts, adapted by Antony Brown, BBC Home Service for Schools (Senior English II), 17 February – 24 March 1953, 2.40pm.

'Great Expectations', adapted by Ian E. Ball, for *May We Recommend* ... BBC Home Service, 15 October 1953, 5.25pm. Repeated in 1959.

'Great Expectations', interlude readings selected by V.C. Clinton-Baddeley, BBC Home Service, 15 October 1953, 5.25pm.

'Pip and the Convict', adapted by H. Oldfield Box, read by Carlton Hobbs, BBC Home Service for Schools, 17 January 1955. Repeated 27 May 1957.

'Great Expectations', 7 episodes, adapted by H. Oldfield Box, BBC Children's Hour, 12 January – 23 February 1958. Cast: Jean England (Young Pip), Timothy Bateson (Adult Pip), John Sharp (Magwitch), Preston Lockwood (Joe), Patience Collier (Mrs Joe), Oliver Burt (Uncle Pumblechook), Alexander Archdale (Wopsle), Alan Reid (Startop), Pauline Letts (Miss Havisham), Denise Bryer (Estella), Simon Lack (Herbert), Charles Leno (Wemmick), Barry Letts (Orlick), Leslie French (Aged P), Joan Ireland (Sarah Pocket/ Jaggers' Housekeeper), Peter Bull (Jaggers), Rosamond Barnes (Biddy). Ep. 1: 'Pip Has a Memorable Christmas', 12 January; Ep. 2: 'Pip Visits a Strange House', 19 January; Ep. 3: 'Pip Has an Astonishing Change of Fortune', 26 January; Ep. 4: 'Pip Starts Educating for a Gentleman', 2 February; Ep. 5. 'Pip Has an Unexpected Midnight Visitor', 9 February; Ep. 6: 'Pip's Patron Goes into Hiding', 16 February; Ep. 7: 'An End and a New Beginning', 23 February. Last episode repeated on Children's Hour Request Week, 20 April 1958.

'The Pale Young Gentleman', BBC Schools (Prose and Verse Readings), 21 April 1958.

'Great Expectations', episode 20 of *Beyond Our Ken* Season 2, BBC Light Programme, 30 July 1959, 7pm. Cast: Kenneth Horne, Kenneth Williams, Hugh Paddick, Betty Marsden, Bill Pertwee.

'Great Expectations', adapted by Ian Ball, BBC Children's Hour, 20 October 1959.

'Young Pip', adapted by Sylvia Goodall, BBC Schools (Adventures in English), 31 June 1960.

'Pip and the Convict', BBC Schools (Prose and Verse Readings), 5 December 1960.

'Great Expectations', 12 × 30-min. episodes, adapted by H. Oldfield Box, BBC Home Service, 16 April – 4 July 1961, 5.15pm. Cast: Hugh Dickson (Adult Pip/ Narrator), Terry Raven (Young Pip), Jason Hayter (Joe), Patricia Routledge (Mrs Joe), Julian Somers (Uncle Pumblechook), John Saunders (Mr Wopsle), Prunella Scales (Estella), Barbara Couper (Miss Havisham), Gladys Spencer (Camilla Pocket), Rosamund Greenwell (Sarah Pocket), Roderick Cook (Raymond Pocket), Peter Pratt (The Stranger), Norman Shelley (Jaggers), David Robinson (Young Herbert), Aubrey Woods (Adult Herbert), Peter Claughton (Orlick), Kenneth McClellan (Byers), Peggy Butt (Biddy), Wilfred Babbage (Wemmick), Keith Williams (Aged P), Nigel Anthony (Drummle). Ep. 1: 16 April (Repeated 18 April); Ep. 2: 23 April (R. 25 April); Ep. 3: 30 April (R. 2 May); Ep. 4: 7 May (R. 9 May); Ep. 5: 14 May (R. 16 May); Ep. 6: 21 May (R. 23 May); Ep. 7: 28 May (R. 30 May); Ep. 8: 4 June (R. 6 June); Ep. 9: 11 June (R. 13 June); Ep. 10: 18 June (R. 20 June); Ep. 11: 25 June (R. 27 June); Ep. 12: 2 July (R. 4 July).

'Pip and the Convict', adapted by Sylvia Goodall, BBC Schools (Listening and Writing), 26 January 1962.

'Christmas at the Forge', read by Michael Deacon, BBC Morning Serial, 23–27 December 1963.

'The Pale Young Gentleman', BBC Schools (Prose and Verse Readings), 1 July 1965.

'Great Expectations', 3 parts, abridged by Donald Bancroft, read by Gary Watson. *Book at Bedtime*, BBC Home Service, 1 March – 3 June 1966, 11.02–11.15pm. Part 1: 'Pip's Early Years', 1–18 March; Part 2: 'Pip's London Life', 11–29 April; Part 3: 'Pip's Homecoming', 16 May – 3 June. Excerpts repeated in BBC for Schools (Listening and Writing), 26 January 1967, 24 October 1969 and 31 October 1969.

'Pip and the Convict', BBC for Schools (Listening and Writing), 29 January 1969.

'Miss Havisham', dir. by Barry Campbell, *Story Time*, BBC Radio 4, 25 October 1970.

'Great Expectations', 10 × 30-min. instalments on consecutive weekday afternoons, abridged by Howard Jones, read by David Buck, produced by Trevor Hill, *Story Time*, BBC Radio 4, 20 November – 1 December 1972, 4.30pm. Ep. 1: 'The Convict'; Ep. 2: 'Satis House'; Ep. 3: A Change of Fortune'; Ep. 4: 'Pip in London'; Ep. 5: 'Again Estella'; Ep. 6: 'Getting on Badly'; Ep. 7: The Blow is Struck'; Ep. 8: 'The Plan of Escape'; Ep. 9: 'In Hiding'; Ep. 10: Parting and Reunion'.

'Great Expectations', 10 × 60-min. instalments, adapted by Charles Lefeux, produced by Ian Cotterell. *Sunday Serial*, Radio 4, 21 September – 9 November 1975, 9am. Repeated the following Tuesdays, *Afternoon Theatre*, 3pm.

'Miss Havisham's Wedding Day', adapted by Carolyn Sally Jones, directed by Ronald Mason, BBC Radio 4, 4 and 11 February 1980.

'Great Expectations', 12 × 30-min. episodes, adapted by Ray Jenkins, produced by Sally Evens, BBC Radio 5, 4 October – 22 December 1991. Cast: Timothy Bateson, Jim Carter, Emma Gregory, Douglas Hodge, Robert Lang, Amanda Redman, John Shrapnel, James Simmons, Michael Turner.

'Great Expectations', 60-min. musical play, adapted by Christopher G. Sanford, lyrics by Mike Read, produced by John Taylor, BBC Radio 4, 27 February 1994. Cast: Adan Gillett (Narrator), Darren Day (Pip), Elizabeth Renehan (Estella).

'Great Expectations', 3 × 60-min. episodes, adapted by Martin Wade, produced by Marilyn Imrie, BBC Radio 4, 30 July, 6 August and 13 August 2006. Ep. 1: 'Common Boy'; Ep. 2: 'The Gentleman'; Ep. 3: 'The Truth'. Cast: Roger Allam (Jaggers), Ken Campbell (Magwitch), Jim Carter (Joe), Stephen Critchlow (Wemmick), Ben Crowe (Watchman), Maggie McCarthy (Molly), Anna Maxwell Martin (Estella), Oliver Milburn (Pip), Harry Myers (Compeyson), Adrian Scarborough (Herbert), Janet Suzman (Miss Havisham), Robin Weaver (Biddy).

USA

'Great Expectations', 29:35 mins., episode 23 of *Favorite Story*, host and narrator Ronald Colman (usually True Boardman), announcer George Barclay, story selected by Walter Hampden, NBC (syndicated), 23 July 1946, 9pm. Also broadcast on 26 November 1946 (West Coast) and 21 February 1948 (East Coast). Cast: Eddie Baker, Joel Davis, Peggy Webber, Thomas Aimes, Gloria Gordon, Edwin MacDonald, Virginia Gregg, Eric Snowden.

'Great Expectations', 29:35 mins., episode 6 of *Favorite Story*, host True Boardman, story selected by George Palmer Putnam, KFI (syndicated), 23 July 1946, 9pm. Cast: as above.

'Great Expectations', 30 mins., episode 71 of *Romance*, CBS (sustaining), 14 July 1947, 10pm.

'Great Expectations', 60 mins., episode 587 of *Lux Radio Theatre*, CBS from Hollywood, 13 October 1947, 9pm. Cast: Ann Blyth, Robert Cummings, Howard Da Silva.

'Great Expectations', 30 mins., episode 62 of *Tell it Again*, adapted and directed by Ralph Rose, host/narrator Marvin Miller, CBS (sustaining), 21 May 1949, 10am. Cast: unspecified, but likely to include regulars David Ellis, Marvin Miller, Ken Harvey, Ramsey Hill, Helen Jerrold, Don Morrison, Jeff Chandler.

'Great Expectations', 60 mins., episode 70 of *NBC Theater from Hollywood*, announcer Don Stanley, NBC, 1 January 1950, 2pm. Cast: Terry Kilburn (Pip), Donald Morrison (Magwitch), John Ramsay Hill (Young Pip), George Pembroke (Joe), Phyllis Morris (Mrs Joe), Alec Harford (Pumblechook), Raymond Lawrence (Compeyson), Constance Cavendish (Estella), Norma

Varden (Miss Havisham), Ramsay Hill (Jaggers), Ben Wright (Wemmick), Hugh Thomas (Herbert).

'Great Expectations', 60 mins., episode 191 of *Theater Guild on the Air*, ABC, 16 April 1950, 7.30pm. Cast: Joan Fontaine, Richard Todd, Francis L. Sullivan.

'Great Expectations', 30 mins., episode 99 of *Hallmark Playhouse*, host James Hilton, announcer Frank Goss, CBS, 9 November 1950, 9pm. Cast: contains Richard Todd. Casts for this show normally contained a large number of 'big-name' stars, but the full cast for this particular broadcast is unclear.

'Great Expectations', 60 mins., episode 114 of *NBC University Theater of the Air*, NBC, 9 November 1950, 10pm.

'Great Expectations', 60 mins., episode 306 of *Theater Guild on the Air*, ABC, 5 April 1953, 7.30pm. Cast: Rex Compton (Young Pip), Boris Karloff (Magwitch), Melville Cooper (Jaggers), Margaret Phillips (Estella), Tom Helmore (Pip), Estelle Winwood (Miss Havisham), Carl Harvard (Joe), Anthony Kemble Cooper (Herbert), Sarah Burton (Mrs Joe), Veronica Cole (Young Estella).

'Great Expectations', 60 mins., episode 25 of *NBC Star Playhouse*, adapted by Ernest Kinoy, host John Chapman, NBC (sustaining), 21 March 1954, 8pm. Cast: Cyril Ritchard (Jaggers/Pumblechook), Roddy McDowall (Pip); Evelyn Varden (Miss Havisham); with Joan Lorring, Joe Huntley Wright, John Stanley, Ivor Francis, Susan Douglas, Chester Stratton, William Griffiths, Everett Sloane, Burford Hampden, Lester Fletcher.

'Great Expectations', 60 mins., episode 893 of *Lux Radio Theatre*, CBS from Hollywood, 12 October 1954. Cast: Rock Hudson, Barbara Rush, William Conrad, Jeanette Nolan, Alan Reed, Peter Votrian, Susan Seaforth, Christopher Cook, Parley Baer, Vivi Janiss, James McCallion, Lillian Buyeff, Norman Field, Howard McNear, Leo Britt, Edward Marr.

Film adaptations

Denmark

Store Forventninger, B&W silent, dir. by A.W. Sandberg, adapted by Laurids Skands (Nordisk, 1922). Cast: Gerhard Jessen (Joe Gargery), Ellen Rovsing (Mrs Gargery), Martin Herzberg (Young Pip), Harry Komdrup (Adult Pip), Peter Nielsen Smedesvenden (Orlick), Emil Helsengreen (Magwitch), Marie Dinesen (Miss Havisham), Olga d'Org (Estella), Esther Kjær Hansen (Young Estella), Egill Rostrup (Jaggers), Ellen Lillien (Biddy), Alfred Meyer (Pumblechook), Hjalmar Bendtsen (Herbert).

Switzerland

Great Expectations, colour, 35 mins., dir. by Leopold H. Ginner (Unknown distributor, 1971). With Petra von der Linde, Volker Vogeler, Gerard Vandenberg. Shown at San Remo Festival 1971.

UK

The Boy and the Convict, B&W silent, 12 mins., dir. by Dave Aylott. Williamson (Kinematograph Company, 1909).

Great Expectations, B&W, 118 mins., directed by David Lean, adapted by David Lean, Ronald Neame, Kay Walsh, Anthony Havelock-Allan, Cecil McGivern (Universal/Cineguild, 1946). Cast: John Mills (Adult Pip), Anthony Wager (Young Pip), Valerie Hobson (Adult Estella), Bernard Miles (Joe), Francis L. Sullivan (Jaggers), Finlay Currie (Magwitch), Martita Hunt (Miss Havisham), Jean Simmons (Young Estella), Alec Guinness (Herbert), Ivor Bernard (Wemmick), Freda Jackson (Mrs Joe), Torin Thatcher (Drummle), Eileen Erskine (Biddy), Hay Petrie (Pumblechook), George Jayes (Compeyson), O.B. Clarence (Aged P), Everly Gregg (Sarah Pocket), John Burch (Mr Wopsle), Grace Denbigh-Russell (Mrs Wopsle), John Forrest (Pale Young Gentleman).

Great Expectations, colour, 124 mins., dir. by Joseph Hardy, screenplay by Sherman Yellen (Transcontinental/ITC, 1974/5). Screened in UK in cinemas, and in USA on NBC TV, 22 November 1974. Cast: Michael York (Pip); Sarah Miles (Estella); James Mason (Magwich [sic]); Margaret Leighton (Miss Havisham); Robert Morley (Pumblechook), Anthony Quayle (Jaggers), Joss Ackland (Joe), Rachel Roberts (Mrs. Joe), Andrew Ray (Herbert), Heather Sears (Biddy), Simon Gipps-Kent (Young Pip), James Faulkner (Drummle), Peter Bull (Wemmick), Sam Kydd (Compeyson), Maria Charles (Sarah Pocket), John Clive (Wopsle), Celia Hewitt (Molly), Noel Trevarthen (Sergeant).

Great Expectations, colour, 128 mins., dir. by Mike Newell, screenplay by David Nicholls (BBC/Lipsync/Number 9 Films, 2012). Cast: Helena Bonham Carter (Miss Havisham), Ralph Fiennes (Magwitch), Jeremy Irvine (Pip), Robbie Coltrane (Jaggers), Jason Flemyng (Joe), Ewen Bremner (Wemmick), Holliday Grainger (Estella), Sally Hawkins (Mrs. Joe), David Walliams (Pumblechook), Sophie Rundle (Clara), Tamzin Outhwaite (Molly), Jessie Cave (Biddy).

USA

Great Expectations, B&W silent, 50 mins., dir. by Robert G. Vignola and Joseph Kaufman, screenplay by Paul West and Doty Hobart (Paramount, 1917). Cast: Jack Pickford (Pip), Louise Huff (Estella), Frank Losee (Magwitch), William Black (Joe), Marcia Harris (Mrs Joe), Grace Barton (Miss Havisham), Herbert Prior (Jaggers).

Great Expectations, B&W, 100 mins., dir. by Stuart Walker, screenplay by Gladys Unger (Universal, 1934). Cast: Phillips Holmes (Adult Pip), Georgie Breakston (Young Pip), Anne Howard (Young Estella), Jane Wyatt (Adult Estella), Florence Reed (Miss Havisham), Henry Hull (Magwitch), Alan Hale (Joe), Rafaela Ottiano (Mrs Joe), Francis L. Sullivan (Jaggers), Walter Armitage (Herbert), Jackie Searle (Young Herbert), Harry Cording (Orlick),

Douglas Wood (Wopsle), Forrester Harvey (Pumblechook), George Barraud (Compeyson), Philip Dakin (Drummle), Eily Malyon (Sarah Pocket), Virginia Hammond (Molly).

Great Expectations, colour, 111 mins., dir. by Alfonso Cuarón, screenplay by Mitch Glazer (Twentieth-Century Fox, 1998). Cast: Ethan Hawke (Adult Finnegan Bell), Gwyneth Paltrow (Estella), Anne Bancroft (Ms. Dinsmoor), Robert De Niro (Prisoner/Lustig), Hank Azaria (Walter Plane), Chris Cooper (Joe), Josh Mostel (Jerry Ragno), Kim Dickens (Maggie), Nell Campbell (Erica Thrall), Gabriel Mann (Owen), Jeremy James Kissner (Young Finnegan), Raquel Beaudene (Young Estella), Stephen Spinella (Carter Macleish), Marla Sucharetza (Ruth Shepard), Isabelle Anderson (Lois Pope).

Television Adaptations

Australia

Great Expectations, animation, colour, 69 mins., animated by Warwick Gilbert, script by Alex Buzo, Burbank Films Classics Series, 1983. Cast (voices): Bill Kerr, Phillip Hinton, Robin Stewart, Barbara Frawley, Marcus Hale, Moya O'Sullivan.

Great Expectations: The Untold Story, 6-part mini-series, colour, dir. by Tim Burstall, Australian Broadcasting Corporation, 1987. Cast: John Stanton (Magwitch), Noel Ferrier (Jaggers), Todd Boyce (Pip), Anne Louise Lambert (Estella), Jill Forster (Miss Havisham), Bruce Spence (Joe), Annie Byron (Mrs Joe), Brian Moll (Pumblechook), Danny Simmonds (Young Pip), Leah Richardson (Young Estella), Leigh Biolis (Drummle), David Sandford (Herbert), Jennifer Hagan (Molly), Nell Schofield (Biddy), Alan Tobin (Wemmick), Tony Taylor (Wopsle), John Linton (Startop), Anthony Wager (Sergeant), Ron Hackett (Trabb), Philomena Lonergan (Sarah Pocket).

Canada

Great Expectations, animation, 72 mins., director/animator unknown, WBTV Productions, 1978.

France

Les Grandes Espérances, TV Movie, B&W, 120 mins., dir. by Marcel Cravenne, 1ère chaîne ORTF, Société Française de Production (SFP), 1968. Cast: Charles Vanel (Magwitch), Madeleine Renaud (Miss Havisham), Jean-Roger Caussimon (Jaggers), Stéphane Di Napoli (Young Pip), Paul Le Person (Joe), Danielle Chinsky (Miss Gargery), Jean Antolinos (Coupeyson [*sic*]), Clément Harari (Plumblechook [*sic*], Bernard Musson (Wopsle), Paul Rieger (Hubble),

Jacqueline Rouillard (Miss Hubble), Marie-Pierre de Gérando (Le sergent), Pascale Christophe (Young Estella), Gérald Denizeau (L'inconnu), Martine Ferrière (Sarah Pocket), Michel Dacquin (Raymond), Thierry Bourdon (Young Herbert), Jacques Hilling (Le guide de Londres), Teddy Bilis (Wemmick), Jean-Claude Dauphin (Adult Pip), Laurent Wesman (Adult Herbert), Marika Green (Adult Estella), Tony Mallet (Pepper), Jacques Brunet (Drummle).

Spain

Grandes Esperanzas, 50 mins., dir. unknown, episode 213 of serial drama *Novela*, distributor unknown, 3 July 1978. Cast: Valeriano Andrés (Wemmick), Carmen Bernardos (Miss Havisham), Mercedes Borqué (Mrs Joe), Enriqueta Carballeira (Biddy), Pablo del Hoyo (Young Pip), José Franco (Pumblechook), Manuel García (Manuel Garco), Carlos Mendy (Magwitch), Pedro Osinaga (Herbert), Jesús Puente (Jaggers), Manuel Torremocha (Joe), Silvia Tortosa (Estella), Luis Varela (Pip).

UK

Great Expectations, B&W, 13 × 30-min episodes, adapted by P.D. Cummings, BBC London Programme, 5 April – 28 June 1959, 5.40pm. Repeated 30 June – 22 July 1960. Cast: Dinsdale Landen (Adult Pip), Colin Jeavons (Herbert), Michael Gwynn (Joe), Ronald Ibbs (Wemmick), Kenneth Thornett (Jaggers), Marjory Hawtrey (Miss Havisham), Robert Mooney (Compeyson), Richard Warner (Orlick), Jerold Wells (Magwitch), Margot van der Burgh (Mrs Joe), Gabrielle Hamilton (Biddy), Roger Kemp (Startop), Colin Spaull (Young Pip), Jack Chissick (Page), Nigel Davenport (Bentley Drummle), Lionel Marson (Judge), Sandra Michaels (Young Estella), Brian Moorehead (Soldier), Edward Palmer (Porter), Raymond Rollett (Pumblechook), Elsie Wagstaff (Sarah Pocket).
'Excerpts from Great Expectations', writer unknown, but probably sections of above, *Lifeline*, BBC, 4 June 1959.
'Miss Havisham', 25 mins., written by Peter Holiday, dir. by Robert Lynn, *Tales from Dickens*, UK/ABC, 1959. Repeated 1966 and 1969. Cast: Jon Skinner (Pip), Jill Haworth (Estella), Florence Eldridge (Miss Havisham), Michael Aldridge (Joe), Joan Hickson (Mrs Joe), Fiona Duncan (Biddy), Phyllis Morris (Sarah Pocket), Betty Turner (Camilla), Karl Lanchbury (Herbert).
Great Expectations, colour, 10 × 30-min. episodes, dir. by Alan Bridges, screenplay by Hugh Leonard, produced by Campbell Logan, BBC, 22 January – 26 March 1967. Cast: Gary Bond (Pip), Christopher Guard (Pip as a Boy), Douglas Mann (Pip as a Youth), John Tait (Magwitch), Francesca Annis (Estella), Maxine Audley (Miss Havisham), Elsie Wagstaff (Sarah Pocket), Marjorie Wilde (Georgina), Joan Geary (Camilla), Christopher Steele (Raymond), Neil McCarthy (Joe), Richard O'Sullivan (Herbert), Derek Landen (Young Herbert), Peter Vaughan (Jaggers), Bernard Hepton (Wemmick), Norman Scase (Pumblechook), Hannah Gordon (Biddy), Shirley Cain (Mrs Joe), Ronald Lacey (Orlick), Frederick Piper

(Aged P), John Tate (Magwitch), Kevin Stoney (Compeyson), Sidney Vivian (Mr Hubble), Ursula Hirst (Mrs Hubble), John Gill (Wopsle), John Caesar (Sargeant), Redmond Phillips (Trabb), Hazel Bainbridge (Miss Skiffins).

Great Expectations, TV Movie, colour, 124 mins., dir. by Joseph Hardy, Transcontinental/ITC, 1974/5. For cast information see *Film Adaptations* (above).

Great Expectations, colour, 12 × 30-min. episodes, adapted by James Andrew Hall, dir. by Julian Aymes, produced by Barry Letts. BBC, 4 October – 20 December 1981. Repeated in 6 weekly episodes, August 1983. Cast: Stratford Johns (Magwitch), Graham McGrath (Pip aged 9), Paul Davies-Prowles (Pip aged 12), Gerry Sundquist (Adult Pip), Joan Hickson (Miss Havisham), Patsy Kensit (Young Estella), Phillip Joseph (Joe), Marjorie Yates (Mrs Joe), Jason Smart (Young Herbert), Tim Munroe (Adult Herbert), Peter Whitbread (Compeyson), Sarah-Jane Varley (Adult Estella), Derek Francis (Jaggers), John Stratton (Pumblechook), Mollie Maureen (Sarah Pocket), Peter Benson (Wopsle), Walter Sparrow (Hubble), Christine Ozanne (Mrs Hubble), Lionel Haft (Orlick), Christine Absalom (Biddy), Colin Jeavons (Wemmick), James Belchamber (Trabb), Colin Mayes (Trabb's Boy),Timothy Bateson (Mr Pocket), Elizabeth Morgan (Mrs Pocket), Iain Ormsby-Knox (Drummle), Kevin Hart (Startop), Tony Sympson (Aged P), Charlotte West-Orm (Miss Skiffins), Melanie Hughes (Clara Barley), Roger Bizley (Bill Barley), Judith Buckingham (Molly).

Great Expectations, colour, 2 × 90 min. episodes, screenplay by Tony Marchant, dir. by Julian Jarrold, BBC, 12 and 13 April 1999. Repeated in a full-length omnibus version, 17 April. Cast: Ioan Gruffudd (Pip), Justine Waddell (Estella), Charlotte Rampling (Miss Havisham), Daniel Evans (Herbert), Gemma Gregory (Young Estella), Bernard Hill (Magwitch), Ian McDiarmid (Jaggers), Gabriel Thomson (Young Pip), Clive Russell (Joe).

Great Expectations, 3-part serial, screenplay by Sarah Phelps, dir. by Brian Kirk, BBC, 27, 28 and 29 December 2011. Broadcast on PBS in the USA, April 2012. Cast: Ray Winstone (Magwitch), Gillian Anderson (Miss Havisham), David Suchet (Jaggers), Douglas Booth (Adult Pip), Mark Addy (Pumblechook), Frances Barber (Mrs Brandley), Tom Burke (Bentley Drummle), Shaun Dooley (Joe), Oscar Kennedy (Young Pip), Vanessa Kirby (Estella), Harry Lloyd (Herbert Pocket), Susan Lynch (Molly), Izzy Meikle-Small (Young Estella), Paul Rhys (Compeyson/Denby), Paul Ritter (Wemmick), Jack Roth (Orlick), Claire Rushbrook (Mrs Joe), Perdita Weeks (Clara), Eros Vlahos (Young Herbert).

USA

Great Expectations, 2-part serial, B&W, written by Dora Folliott, dir. by Norman Felton, host Claude Rains, *Robert Montgomery Presents* ... NBC, 14 June and 21 June 1954. Part 1: 'The Promise'; Part 2: 'The Reality'. Cast: Rex Thompson (Young Pip), Roddy McDowall (Adult Pip), Estelle Winwood (Miss Havisham), Jacques Aubuchon (Magwitch), Malcolm Lee Beggs (Jaggers), Scott Forbes (Joe), Lucie Lancaster (Mrs Joe), Nina Reader (Estella).

Great Expectations, 6 × 60-min. serial, colour, screenplay by John Goldsmith, dir. by Kevin Connor, HTV/Walt Disney, USA release 24–6 July 1989, UK release 21- 25 August July 1991. Cast: Jean Simmons (Miss Havisham), John Rhys Davies (Joe), Ray McAnally (Jaggers), Anthony Calf (Pip), Kim Thomson (Estella), Adam Blackwood (Herbert), Anthony Hopkins (Magwitch), Sean Arnold (Compeyson), Niven Boyd (Orlick), Susan Franklyn (Biddy), Martin Harvey (Young Pip), Charles Lewsen (Wemmick), Rosemary McHale (Mrs Joe), Frank Middlemass (Pumblechook), John Quentin (Wopsle), Owen Teale (Drummle), Frank Thornton (Trabb), Preston Lockwood (Hoddle), Eve Pearce (Mrs Hoddle), P.J. Davidson (Sargeant), Maria Charles (Sarah Pocket), Madeleine Moffatt (Georgina Pocket), Gerald Campion (Mr Raymond), Hilary Mason (Mrs Pegge), Shirley Stelfox (Camilla), Henry Power (Young Herbert), Simon Warwick (Startop), Carolyn Jones (Molly), Angela Ellis (Mrs Pocket), Arthur Hewlett (Aged P), Jonathan Newth (Matthew Pocket), Paul Reynolds (the Avenger), Sarah Crowden (Miss Skiffins), Stephanie Schonfeld (Clara).

Appendix D
Contemporary British and American Reviews

British Reviews

Examiner, Saturday 1 December 1860, p. 5.
One of the pleasantest events of the week has been the promising commencement of 'Great Expectations,' a new story by Mr Dickens in *All the Year Round*, which is to entertain the country for the next eight months, and may live to be read, perhaps, by the next eight generations.

'Artistic and Literary', *Derby Mercury*, Wednesday 5 December 1860, p. 6.
Our two great novelists are beginning to bestir in themselves. Mr. Dickens's new story "Great Expectations," has now commenced in *Household Words* [*sic*], and has all the elements of one of the author's most characteristic tales. An oppressed boy, an escaped convict, a termagant materfamilias, and a good-natured bullied husband, are unequivocal properties of Mr. Dickens's, and bid fair to renew for us all the old types of his imagination. The hero is called Philip Pirrip, commonly called Pip, and we shall watch his career with great expectations of our own. Mr. Thackeray also has his "Adventures of Philip," and they are to begin in the *Cornhill Magazine* next month.

Hereford Journal, Wednesday 5 December 1860, p. 8.
Whether apprehensive of a dangerous rival or not, Mr. Charles Dickens has last week given a "fillip" to *All the Year Round*, by commencing in it his new story entitled "Great Expectations." It is exceedingly droll, with the usual admixture of quaint observation and shrewd remark peculiar to that eminent writer: the absorbing terror inflicted on the mind of a young boy by an escaped convict, is at once most ludicrous, and yet touching; there is, however, too little of the story in each weekly issue, to carry it on with interest, and, in my opinion, it would have been more likely to prove successful, had it been brought out in the old monthly green numbers. But, I suppose, Mr. Dickens ought to know best, though I cannot forget that his last story, produced in the same form as the present, "Hunted Down," proved a sad failure – for him.

'Epitome of News', *Kentish Chronicle*, Saturday 8 December 1860, p. 3.
Mr Charles Dickens has commenced a new and very amusing story in *All the Year Round* entitled "Great Expectations."

'Metropolitan Gossip from our London Correspondent', *Leamington Spa Courier*, Saturday 8 December 1860, p. 2.
Dickens's new tale in All the Year Round, "Great Expectations," which opened in the last week's number, promises well. So far as it goes, it has all the freshness of his early writings, and calls back to the memory "Oliver Twist" – decidedly the best book he ever wrote.

'Literary Memoranda', *Northampton Mercury*, Saturday 8 December 1860, p. 7.
Mr. Dickens has commenced in "All the Year Round" his new tale entitled "Great Expectations." It has all the vivid originality of his writings, and promises to be a great attraction. The mingled yarn of comic and tragic incident of which the web of his tales is constituted, is manifest in the earliest instalments. The hero of the tale is an orphan boy with the peculiar name of Philip Pirrip, abridged by his own lisping tongue into Pip. The comedy is in the hands of "Pip's" sister (greatly his senior, and by whom he has been brought up), and her husband, a blacksmith, with the capital name of Joe Gargery. Both these personages are admirably sketched: even in these few opening passages their individuality is as marked as a couple of photographs. "Mrs Joe" is a wonderful bit of nature; her real kindness for the boy, and her own very unpleasant manner of shewing it, are contradictions only too much in accordance with common experience.

Lincolnshire Chronicle, Friday 14 December 1860, p. 1.
Mr Dickens's first instalment of "Great Expectations" in *All the Year Round* contains a wonderful bit of child's autobiography – enough to make us wish for more.

'Our London Letter', *Bath Chronicle and Weekly Gazette*, Thursday 27 December 1860, p. 5.
Mr Charles Dickens opens his new tale "Great Expectations," and although every character that has yet been introduced is eminently disagreeable, the effect is far from unpleasant.

Bradford Observer, Thursday 10 January 1861, p. 7.
All the Year Round for December is an unusually full and interesting number. Mr. Dickens's new tale, "Great Expectations," itself makes the miscellany worth its price.

'Literature', *Taunton Courier and Western Advertiser*, Wednesday 6 February 1861, p. 2.
All the Year Round. – Whether the "great expectations" which the readers of this publication have formed are to be realised remains to be seen, for the tale has not yet progressed sufficiently to pronounce an opinion on it. It appears, however,

to differ widely from any of Mr. Dickens's previous works, and as far as it has proceeded affords little to excite the curiosity, arouse the interest, or call forth the sympathy of the reader. The whole volume, however, affords a variety of reading and entertainment. "A Day's Ride – A Life's Romance" is a humorous and laughter-stirring tale, and there are miscellaneous articles on such subjects and treated with such talent that is sure to retain for All the Year Round that popularity and welcome among all classes that it has so deservingly obtained.

'All the Year Round – London: Chapman and Hall', *Chester Chronicle*, Saturday 9 February 1861, p. 5.
The principal tale in the January part of this work is "Great Expectations", by Charles Dickens, in which "Pip" and "Joe" figure conspicuously. The whole of the characters are depicted in the clever, truthful, easy, and happy manner for which Mr Dickens is so justly celebrated, and the materials are thrown together in such an interesting form that no-one can help reading "Great Expectations" with avidity.

Bradford Observer, Thursday 14 February 1861, p. 7.
All the Year Round continues to maintain its position in the very first rank, we may say at the head, of miscellanies of its particular class. The leading tales "Great Expectations", by Mr. Charles Dickens, and "A Day's Ride", grow in interest.

Hereford Journal, Wednesday 13 March 1861, p. 5.
Mr Dickens's "Great expectations" have decidedly disappointed the *great expectations* raised by themselves; the work does not improve with succeeding numbers. The humour is more forced and exaggerated than ever, and it labours under a manifest difficulty in depicting the feelings and observations of a youth in an inferior position, from his mouth when he is a man, and in a higher station of life. In this instance the difficulty is *not* overcome.

The Literary Examiner, Saturday 20 July 1861, pp. 4–5.
All who have read this story from week to week, as it appeared in the vigorous and entertaining pages of Mr. Charles Dickens's popular journal, should join those who now read it for the first time as a finished work. It is a finished work in the best sense. There are, we believe, some readers whose taste goes no further than enjoyment of the wit and animal spirit of Pickwick, and who prefer the simply joyous humour of that book to the maturest and best work of the mind that produced it. Such readers may and do cling as they will to their own pleasures of the past. Let it not be forgotten that to the sober middle-aged man who believes only in Pickwick and Nickleby, those books were among the choicest delights of twenty years ago, when he read only for enjoyment, delighted openly and heartily in all that he enjoyed, and had a mind that he could deliver alive into the hands of his entertainer. Such power of enjoyment may be blunted now, but very sure we are that in the author of Pickwick the power of giving a true and high pleasure has been sharpened and refined. Mr Dickens is at this day not only a writer of rare

and original genius – when at his best, we say it most deliberately, the greatest master of the whimsical and the pathetic yet to be found in any age among the prose writers of Europe – but he has wrought himself into a novelist who is a master of his art. In place of old sketch books of adventure lengthened at will, and the pathetic or humorous personifications of life that were the spontaneous outpouring of an earnest mind and a swift fancy, we have now the same wit that has so vividly represented detached scenes, concentrated with its whole strength upon the construction of a plot that shall knit every fragment of its detail into one round and perfect whole. We dwelt upon the singular success with which this result had been achieved in *A Tale of Two Cities*. In the story of *Great Expectations* the same thing is equally remarkable. And the new story has this advantage over its predecessor, that its scene is in England, and that its contrivance allows scope for a fuller display of the author's comic power. There is not a character that does not fit into the plot as a stone into an arch. Every dialogue is necessary to the outline or the proper colour of the one thing told. The opening pages could not have been written until the contents of the last pages were known. Chance phrases in the very first chapter bear so directly – though at the time imperceptibly – upon events to come, that after they have served their purpose in giving the sense of a perfect continuity and harmony to the whole work, it is worth any man's while, and the better the man the more it is worth his while, to read the tale twice – for the second time critically, in order to observe the exquisite art of passages that at the first reading influence, at the author's will with unsuspected subtlety, alike the cunning and the simple.

Everything in art, good or bad, should have, and usually has, a central thought to which its parts bear some harmonious relation. In *Great Expectations* the thought is one often enforced by Mr Dickens: that far greater than great expectations from without is the worth of an honest man's own wholesome labour. Joe Gargery lies at the core of the tale, an illiterate blacksmith living by his own large arm and loving with his own large heart, strong as a man, simple as a child, but like a good woman gentle and true, and unconsciously self-denying. About him revolves Pip, the orphan child he has reared and loved; a good fellow enough and bright fellow enough, but not greater than the vanity of youth, he is unwilling to be seen with his simple friend of the forge when a mysterious provision of money as to the source of which he has made a wrong guess, and the assurance of great expectations from the same unknown source, transform him suddenly into a gentleman. His great expectations are the fairy gold that turns to dead leaves in the morning. There is gold enough, but his benefactor is only a convict who has amassed fortune in Australia, and whose craze it has been to make a gentleman of the boy who fed him upon one occasion of his greatest misery and need. He escapes from Australia to see and rejoice in the gentleman of his own making, and thus becomes a sort of upside down and altogether human Frankenstein monster to the youth, who is threatened with a life-long companionship, not of the monster that he made, but of the poor monster that made him. The monster, a born "warmint" and jail-bird, is sketched with a generous and wise humour. That he is a humiliating patron from whom great expectations cannot rationally be allowed to flow, Pip sees and feels. But the wealth he would not take from such hands becomes forfeit when the man is condemned as an escaped convict to the gallows; and from the deathbed that only anticipates the sentence of the law, Pip turns to his neglected foster-father Joe Gargery, the blacksmith; Joe, who had in these late years found the fallen Pip in his distress, tenderly nursed him in sickness, quietly bought out the execution for an extravagant jeweller's bill with the coin earned by his own daily sweat, and vanished when his work of patient love was done. Pip turns to the true-souled labourer at his forge with the old childish love again before he goes abroad to begin life anew dependent on his own day-labour.

One with this story is that of Miss Havisham and *her* foster child, Estella, who becomes the object of Pip's love, and by a network of incidents in no point violating probability is shown to be his convict benefactor's daughter. Wealthy Miss Havisham, courted in fraud by a villain and by the deceit, made manifest on her wedding morning, turned so far mad that she shuts out the light of day, stops the clock at the hour fatal to her great expectations, and cherishes the wedding garments yellow with time and the mouldy marriage feast, is only unnatural inasmuch as she is insane. Yet the unwholesome cherishing and the perversion of her passion are so true in art that, as it has usually happened with the most singular creations of the novelist, living types have already been pointed out that claim resemblance to them. Upon Miss Havisham, who is rich, a knot of greedy relatives found their great expectations, while her own expectations now are of the revenge she will take by training up the beautiful Estella to win and wring the hearts of men. She lives to see a piteous end to her sick hopes.

But let us turn to the book for a few extracts. In the opening scene we have at once the marshes out of which *Great Expectations* grew, and the beginning of the child's action which begat the convict's gratitude. The first chapter is with the convict on the marshes; the second is with Joe Gargery at the Forge. The delicacies of Joe's character are often suggested rather than told. We make out for ourselves the reason for his marriage with an orphan girl whom he saw left to rear by hand in her solitude an infant brother; nothing is urged upon us of the simple love and pity drawing him to take that desolate girl for his wife and adopt the infant Pip as his child. But we are told by himself why he leaves Mrs Gargery to develop into a shrew, to pull his whiskers and to knock his head against the wall as often as she will, without once using his blacksmith's arm or speaking one harsh word to quell her.... There is a subtle indication, we may observe, of the servile and broken wife that such a woman as Mrs Joe would have made – of the great weakness of her sort of domineering strength – in her dealing with Dolge Orlick, of whom she alone knew, though others suspected, that he had revenged himself upon her tongue by striking her down with a blow that doomed her to the short life of a helpless cripple.... Biddy again, who is mentioned in that extract, is a delightful instance of the delicacy with which fine womanly shades of the mind and character of a true-hearted working girl, wholesomely bent on the doing of her duty, can be blended with the natural turn of her word, and everywhere expressed while they are nowhere explicitly defined. Poor Biddy had kept shop at the village Dame School, and had taught Pip the first mysteries of letters. When Mrs Joe was made a cripple, the old woman who had kept the school was dead, and the orphan Biddy came to help the helpless woman at the forge.... Still more exquisite in the same way is the sketch of that long chat between Pip and Biddy.

The connexion of Pip's great expectations with the great old Bailey lawyer, and the ingenious blending of Newgate associations with Pip's fortunes, before many readers will have discovered any relation between Newgate and the source of his prosperity, we may note as another instance of the skill with which the unity of the story is preserved throughout. We may expect nothing from the fact that there was in the village by the marsh a stage-struck parish clerk with a theatrical delivery, but he comes to London as an actor, Pip looks in upon him one or twice at a minor theatre, and on one occasion this early history applied to the recognition of a second person who is among the audience, is of great value in the conduct of the tale to its catastrophe. When Pip becomes a pupil of Mr Matthew Pocket, whose wife, with a grandfather who ought to have been in the Peerage, was in her way a woman of great expectations and is not a blessing to her house, there are two fellow pupils, Startop and Bentley Drummle. They are not produced as detached sketches; each of these also becomes in his turn essential to the story. Even the audacious tailor's boy in the village, who mocks Pip in the street when he appears in his best clothes, has his own time and place for an important action necessary to the plot. But Mr Pumblechook does nothing. It is his part to be nothing while claiming to be everything; a servile flatterer of wealth for its own sake, the pompous and coarse pretender is there to represent the baser chorus of the world that will sing hymns even to a boy whom it has bullied in his poverty when he becomes, by no act of his own merit, a lad of great expectations in the way of cash.

We are tempted to quote largely from the wit and wisdom of this book, but it is in every reader's hand. Rich as it is in scenes vivid with life and truth, and in those phrases and sentences which occur only in what is written for more than one generation of readers, it is better that it should be read as it is being read, in its entirety. No other writer can construct a story with more skill than is shown in the construction of *Great Expectations*; and most certainly no other writer can unite with a natural presentment of life and character an equal force of original genius.

'Dickens's Comeback', *Saturday Review*, 20 July 1861, pp. 69–70.
Mr. Dickens may be reasonably proud of these volumes. After the long series of his varied works – after passing under the cloud of *Little Dorrit* and *Bleak House* – he has written a story that is new, original, powerful, and very entertaining.... It is in his best vein, and although unfortunately it is too slight, and bears many traces of hasty writing, it is quite worthy to stand beside *Martin Chuzzlewit* and *David Copperfield*. It has characters in it that will become part of common talk, and live even in the mouths of those who do not read novels. Wemmick strikes us as the great creation of the book, and his marriage as the funniest incident. How often

will future jokers observe, "Hulloa, here's a church; let's have a wedding." It is impossible not to regret that a book so good should not have been better. Probably the form in which it was first published may have had something to do with its faults. The plots ends before it ought to do. The heroine is married, reclaimed from harshness to gentleness, widowed, made love to, and remarried, in a page or two. This is too stiff a pace for the emotions of readers to live up to. We do not like to go beyond a canter through the moral restoration of a young lady. Characters, too, are entirely altered, in order to make the story end rapidly. Herbert, one of the most pleasing characters Mr. Dickens ever drew, starts as an amiable dreamy creature, incapable of business, and living on the vaguest hopes. But at the close of the tale it becomes necessary to provide for the hero. So Herbert comes out all at once as a shrewd, successful Levant merchant, and takes the hero into partnership. Villains, again, are sketched in and then smeared out again. Old Orlick, the gigantic lout of a blacksmith, commits every kind of atrocity, from breaking the skull of his mistress to purposing to burn the hero in a limekiln, and yet all we hear of him at the end is, that he is taken up for a burglary which forms no part of the story.... It is rather a story with excellent things in it than an excellent story.

Spectator, 20 July 1861, pp. 784–5.

The reader of *Great Expectations*, unless he has profited by his experience of Mr. Dickens's recent tales, is placed in much the same position as its hero. He has great and well-founded hopes at the beginning which are bitterly disappointed before the novel is half completed. The disappointment, however, is of an opposite kind. The reader is led to hope, when he begins the tale, that its course is to run continuously through that low life which Mr. Dickens describes with such marvellous accuracy and such delightful humour, to wind quietly among convicts and attorney's clerks, henpecked blacksmiths, and tailor's apprentices; here we find ourselves, and here we ardently trust we may remain, but the circumstances which raise Mr. Pip's hopes gradually depress ours; when his Ideal fairly enters the tale, we are discomforted, and when Mr. Dickens bursts into lyrics, melodrama, and recitative, we almost make up our mind finally to abandon the story, and are only tempted on by those indications of a flagging wing which suggest that the author must sink again before long into that vulgar life which his genius has thoroughly matured, out of that thin sentimental region where it is utterly paralyzed, or rather transformed into noxious rant.

The cause which renders Mr. Dickens's great genius so comparatively impotent in the more cultivated sphere of life and sentiment which he sometimes essays to paint, is not far to find. In the uneducated classes character is far more characteristically expressed, if we may use the expression, than in the higher. The effect of cultivation is to draw a certain thin semi-transparent medium over the whole surface of human nature, so that the effects of individual differences of character, though by no means hidden, are softened and disguised, and require, not so much a subtle discrimination to discern, as a subtler artistic faculty to delineate without falsification. The power of painting, by the turn of a phrase, by a transposition in a sentence, by a movement, by a mode of receiving or accosting another, the bias of a man's character, is a power apparently of a finer order, but really much less rare and remarkable than the intellectual instrument with which Mr. Dickens fascinates us. There are twenty or thirty writers, many of them ladies, who can use the former faculty to perfection. There is not one who can attempt to rival Mr. Dickens in his own field. The truth is, that to play upon an instrument that demands great delicacy, though it gives out little volume of sound, is far easier than to produce the highest effects from a coarser and rougher organ....

And his special power lies in the manipulation of such well-defined habits of thought, whether professional or otherwise, as mark themselves sharply on the outward bearing of men, and their broadest forms of speech. To these he can give an almost endless and illimitable variety; he will immerse and steep himself in them till he is thoroughly saturated, and then bring them into the most humorous contrast with all things human.... But he requires a habit of mind with a definite body to it, and this is so essential to him that he often mistakes the one for the other, and pounces upon some eccentric feature which he has noticed as if a class character could be extorted out of it, when it is quite incapable of yielding anything of the sort.... It is one of the disappointing traits in his recent tales that these mere tricks – the accidents, not the essence of human character – have taken the place of that large assemblage of minute, coherent habits which go to make up such a figure as Mrs. Gamp or Mr. Weller.... In this tale, we are sorry to say, and even in the better parts of it, this weakness abounds....

Mr. Dickens has made another mistake in the attempt which he has obviously made to construct a coherent tale, though it is obvious that his purpose has often wavered, and that many "undeveloped formations" have been finally abandoned before its close. His genius is not suited to a unity of plot. He needs the freedom to ramble when he will and where he will. The most successful of his works have uniformly been the most incoherent of tales. The truth is that he gets too much interested in his own plot, and forgets the characters in his interest in the story. What he does so powerfully cannot be undone under the strain of any exciting emotion. He is great when he accumulates details to illustrate such homely roundabout miscellaneous types of character as he loves most to sketch; but he is very small when he becomes lyrical, and he cannot deal with the destinies of his heroes and heroines without becoming lyrical....

If Mr. Dickens could only see how much he would gain if he could take a vow of total abstinence from the "Estella" element in all future tales, and limit himself religiously to vulgar life – we do not use the word in the depreciating sense – he might still increase the number of his permanent additions to English literature. This, *Great Expectations* certainly has not done.

Derby Mercury, Wednesday 24 July 1861, p. 6.
Mr. Pip is the hero of "Great Expectations," Mr. Charles Dickens' latest and best novel. True, in "Great Expectations" we have not a second Sarey Gamp, nor a second Samuel Weller. But we have a score of characters as original, as artistically

drawn, and more elaborately developed, than any our well-beloved author has before contributed to the world of literature.

When Pip was a boy he lived on the marshy banks of the Thames. His father and mother, his brothers and a sister, all lying in the cold wet churchyard, Pip lived with his only remaining sister who was married to a blue-eyed blacksmith, a gentle and loving quiet fellow. The sister was always in a "rampage" and so Pip led a very sorry life; he was the butt of every roughness and the victim of all unsisterly harshness. Pip's dwelling lay not far off the hulks and on a cold misty day he crosses an escaped convict who with terrible threats induces Pip to steal drink and victuals for him, which Pip takes on the following morning with a file to be used in freeing the escaped felon from a painful leg-iron. After a time Pip is called to visit a large house where a lady sits in darkened rooms with the cobwebs clinging all over the furniture, the walls, and the ceiling; where she herself sits day and night in a faded and torn bridal dress; and where upon a table stands the remains of a bride-cake at once the harvest and the home of innumerable spiders. The rich lady offers Pip work and by and by he goes regularly every week to play at cards with a proud young beauty, a companion to the disappointed bride, whose taunts make Pip discontented with his coarse, common hands and boots. Years pass on and at length a London lawyer calls on Pip and Joe and tells them the former has great expectations. The name of his benefactor is to be maintained a secret till he or she may disclose the truth, but it is evident that Pip and others see in Miss Havisham the great promise. Pip goes to London, dresses finely, keeps a page, contracts new and costly habits, forgets or rather shuns poor Joe and the quiet servant Biddy. He follows in thought the proud beauty who has bespoiled him of his heart and becomes a miserable disappointed heart-stricken fellow. His fortune-maker at length appears in the person of the convict for whom Pip committed his first felony and who was retaken after the felonious feeding. His presence at first is hateful to the proud youth but at length Pip sees the danger he runs in having returned to England (after amassing a fortune across the ocean) without leave. Months and months are spent in hiding the man and at length it is determined to attempt an escape to the continent. The attempt, however, fails, and, betrayed by a relentless enemy, the convict is again retaken but afterwards dies in Pip's arms from injuries received in the struggle. The proud, disdainful girl for whom Pip had despised the pure affection of the lowly Biddy marries a man he hates and thus his mortification is complete. The insight he has had into the houses of the wealthy, and the habits of those above his original station has disgusted him, and in that state of mind Pip returns to Joe and the blacksmith's home.

We have thus briefly sketched a very few of the more prominent movements in this admirable story to show the aim of the author. This aim appears to us higher and more noble than any of the intentions Mr. Dickens projected in his former works. The genius of the great Boz loves to have free scope untrammelled by plots and loves to roam about picking up exquisite bits of character here and there on the road through his works, and flinging about touches of humour, and exhibiting a deep insight into the human mind and the human heart; never forgetting the while his earnest desire to accomplish some valuable social lesson. In "Great Expectations" he deals very brave blows against the bugbear of modern society, discontent with one's natural position in life. He shows us in Pip an affectionate lad, a generous nature spoiled and thwarted by a desire to become rich. And how graphically he sketches the misery which follows the rise to fortune! We do not desire, even if we could, to place a complete idea of this fine work before our reader. We wish to lead them to the book itself, assured that they will thank us for the counsel, and assured too that it will sustain and enlarge the wide and deep affection for our master author. The village life, with which the story opens, contains sketches such as no other writer could have produced. Here is a description of A COUNTRY TOWN.... We think we know plenty of High-Streets like this. Another choice bit is Pip's encounter with Trabb's Boy after Pip returns to the village in his fine London dress.... Amongst the many very well drawn characters in "Great Expectations" are Magwitch, the convict; Jaggers, a great criminal lawyer; Wemmick, his clerk; Orlick, a rough blackguard; Mr. Wopsle, an ambitious parish clerk; and Mr. Pumblechook; all of whom will become as familiar as the creations which have distinguished "Pickwick," "Oliver Twist," and other productions by the same author.

Superfine spleen has been vented upon the late works of Dickens, but here is one that against all comers we hold to be deserving of an honest, cordial welcome, no less as the most finished and complete novel we have had from the same genial brain, than as a mighty lesson of the blessedness of content, and a great social benefaction.

Bury Times, Saturday 27 July 1861, p. 4.
The editor of the Athenaeum is not one of those who think Mr. Dickens's late writings inferior to his first. "Trying Mr. Dickens by himself," he writes, "we find in this his last tale as much force as in the most forcible portions of 'Oliver Twist' – as much delicacy as in the most delicate passages of 'David Copperfield' – as much quaint humour as in 'Pickwick.' In short, that this is the creation of a great artist in his prime we have felt from the first moment of its appearance, and can deliberately sign and seal the conviction, even though the catastrophe is before us, and though we have just been devouring the solution of 'Great Expectations.'

'General News', *Dundee, Perth, and Cupar Advertiser*, Tuesday 30 July 1861, p. 6.
Mr Charles Dickens's new work "Great Expectations" is said to be written with all his pristine vigour.

'GREAT EXPECTATIONS', *Morning Post*, Wednesday 31 July, 1861, p. 3.
Mr. Charles Dickens's position in literature is an old story now. He has been a popular author, very deservedly, for many years. There have been few popular authors concerning whom the undemonstrative British public has expressed anything so like enthusiasm, who has become an object of such personal interest to them. It is, therefore, much more unpleasant and disappointing to find Mr. Dickens guilty of undoing his own work and disintegrating his own renown, then to meet

with any ordinary subversion of expectations from any ordinary writer. The talent which deserved, and the industry which gained, such an eminence among English writers of fiction should have sufficed to maintain it; they should have preserved their possessor from as poor a conception and so slipshod a performance as "Great Expectations." Imagination is not less amenable to rules than any other faculty; though their nature differs, they are rules of taste rather than of law; and the writer who cannot subject his own productions to their influence displays a grave failing. An outrageously absurd book by a great writer may be regarded as a breach of the public confidence; it is in literature what a gigantic fraud is in commerce. It is ungenerous also; it is taking advantage of an assured position to do that carelessly and unconscientiously, by the doing of which with rigorous exactitude and pains such position has been acquired. It is not the first time that Mr. Dickens has betrayed his public; but in the other instances there were circumstances more or less extenuating. "Pictures from Italy," which is a now almost forgotten blot upon Mr. Dickens's literary reputation, was an admitted failure, because the writer, destitute of taste for art, or of the historical knowledge from which alone the power of enjoying antiquities or evoking associations can arise, departed from his true vocation, and lost himself in a labyrinth to which he possessed no clue. "Hard Times" was certainly not a success, because the author, whose political capacity is rather limited, and whose notions of social philosophy are shallow, flew much too high, and meddled with questions altogether beyond his grasp. Time, and several admirable works quite within his range, which is that of an imaginative writer whose appeals to feelings may be safely trusted, have condoned these offences. He has not aspired to teach authoritatively and dogmatically lately, and he has quizzed some abuses amusingly, and depicted some grave consequences pathetically, without volunteering to instruct the Legislature. But his present failure is more signal and more provoking than its predecessors, for it is a failure in his own line, and within his own limits.

"Great Expectations" is a book which offends against all the laws of probability, and outrages all the laws of execution; to it the famous lines so often quoted by the enemies of Gothic architecture might be aptly applied. It is full of

> "Rich windows which exclude the light
> And passages which lead to nothing."

It is a phantasmagoria of eccentricities, serving to display in their worst form those faults, which have been gradually increasing like a tide, in Mr. Dickens's style, and tending to efface all its highly-prized beauties. The grave demerit of this work lies not so much in its plot, which, though highly improbable, might have been carefully worked up into a fine story, and have claimed the more admiration from its bold and fanciful conception, but in the incongruous collection of monstrosities by whose agency the improbabilities are effected. The impression created by the story is similar to that derived from a prolonged gaze into a cabinet of Japanese curiosities, or of a visit to the harmless and incurable wards of the Bethlehem Asylum. Every one meets oddities, whether in or out of the "arm-chair," which

Charles Lamb declared the name placed an "oddity" in for life, but no one lives exclusively among oddities; no one has every event of his life brought about through their intervention, and every idea influenced by their eccentricities. The people who surround the hero of Mr. Dickens's new novel are as unlike men and women as are the Batrachian and Saurian monsters in the geological department of the Crystal Palace, with the important difference that such beings as the latter represent really did exist, while the former are impossible types. Mr. Dickens has indulged a morbid taste for eccentricities so much that this book has burst all bounds. Throughout the story the traces of perversions of former successes are painfully evident – wilful perversions they must be reluctantly called, as the writer, who has preserved his imaginative faculties, can scarcely be supposed to have entirely lost his critical ones. The uninstructed peasant, gifted with great tenderness of feeling and little grammatical accuracy of speech, has figured very happily indeed in many of Mr. Dickens's former works; in this, by dint of exaggeration on one side, and etiolation on the other, he becomes an absurdity of the first class. The unselfish kindness, the devotion, better than chivalrous, because springing from the heart, and not inculcated by the surroundings of Mr. Peggotty, are fine, racy, touching. The Yarmouth dialect in his mouth is both funny and appropriate. Similar questions are so caricatured in Joe Gargery, that all their meaning and effect are lost. He is a chuckle-headed, stupid lout, who maunders, rather than talks, in an impossible dialect, devoid of anything like the fun which the writer used to throw into such parts, and whose catchword "which I meantersay," is of such frequent recurrence, that really, if it were as brilliant as it is unmeaning, must have wearied the reader. In this book the mannerism (which has so overrun all the writer's works, and so infected numerous imitators, that he may be said to have attained the dubious eminence of a founder of a school of mannerism) is doubly oppressive, because it is not counterbalanced by any equally distinctive merit. It is a contemptible trick, because it is so extremely easy, every one can do it, just as every one can tell the card one has chosen, and then replaced in the pack. It is only the principle of "the nose that came down over the moustache, and the moustache that went up under the nose," liberally applied. Look at any of your friends attentively till you catch some little personal peculiarity, then describe it in flippant words, exaggerating it as much as possible; never mention the individual in question without repeating the phrase. There is the recipe, apply it to writing a novel, and you have the secret of the most "life-like" hits made by Mr. Dickens and his school. There is a degree of, no doubt, conscious impertinence about this grave defect in style, which is a ludicrous side of it. Mr. Dickens mentions some peculiarity of one of his people, and then, whole chapters afterwards recurs to it, and never seems to consider that the circumstance may not have struck his reader quite so forcibly as it has himself, and that, therefore, it is within the verge of possibility that the reference may not be intelligible. Mr. Wemmick, one of the least intolerable oddities of the book, is a flagrant instance of this trick. On his first introduction he is described as possessing a mouth like the slit in a letter-box, which is an obvious enough comparison; every one has seen people with mouths which would suggest the resemblance to duller observers than Mr. Dickens. But when he goes on to talk of Mr. Wemmick "opening his post-office" and "shutting his post-office" and then of his "posting his biscuit," the reader may fairly inquire not only wherein lies the wit of these constant references to a very ordinary comparison, but whether he can be considered bound to remember, "au pied de la lettre," every tittle of Mr. Wemmick's "signalement," so as to be prepared for the allusion a volume or so later. Then, again, among many other very silly arrangements made for the commonplace young person who succeeds to the "Great Expectations" is the hiring of a boy servant. This boy, "in bondage and in slavery, to whom I may have been said to pass my days," says Pip, is first called a "monster," and his "horrible requirements" of "a little to do" and "a great deal to eat" are commented upon; he is, in fact, the "transported page" of Dora and Doadey over again, and not wanted. But then he becomes "an avenging phantom," on which not very brilliant witticism a variety of changes are rung, until he is finally mentioned, long after, as "The Avenger," which is quite a tax on the reader's patience and memory. As to the offence which this sort of affected composition is against the rules of correct, not to say elegant, English, it is too patent to mention. And, indeed, Mr. Dickens has never subscribed to such rules; he has only ceased to render their systematic infraction excusable. Pip goes to Barnard's Inn on his arrival in London; and thenceforward Barnard does the duty in "Great Expectations" which St. Antoine did in "A Tale of Two Cities," with the difference that the latter is really expressive, a condensed conveyance of a great fact, and the former is as silly as it is incorrect. A reality is borne to the mind of the reader when he reads that "St. Antoine is up in arms," because the phrase is an elliptical form of saying, " The Faubourg of St. Antoine is up in arms," and that is a correct phrase; but when Pip looks out of his window, finds it is raining in London, and records the discovery thus – "An angel could not have concealed the fact that Barnard was shedding sooty tears outside the window like some giant of a sweep," Pip's biographer tries his readers a little too much. The fabrication of grotesque similes, devoid of proportion between their parts, and attractive only by their queerness, is a charlatanerie to which Mr. Dickens is only too prone to descend. The fine edge of his perception is wearing rapidly away. Humour is the most easily deteriorated gift a writer can possess. In his case its decadence has been rapid. Had he been endowed with wit it could not have suffered so much in the using; but he was only humorous, and now he is only grotesque. The low comedian is sinking into the clown.

The book resembles its name in one respect – it begins well and then disappoints. The first chapter is very good, fresh, vigorous, and interesting. It seizes on the attention of the reader in the way the former works of the same author did; indeed, it is more striking than any of his first chapters. It is in a plain, narrative style, and Pip's first interview with the convict, who, as the reader sees at once is to be his fate, may vie with anything Mr. Dickens has ever written. Mrs. Gargery is well drawn, and the first introduction of Joe is felicitous – his character is estimable all through; it is only the preposterous exaggeration which spoils it, the unnecessary loutishness, and the laborious unintelligibility. But the disappointment soon begins; the incorrigible weeds crop up. Of all the absurd phantasms conjured up by Mr. Dickens to encumber his pages, Mr. Wopsle and Mr. Pumblechook are the most uncouth, useless, and stupid. They are absolutely unnecessary to the action of the story, and entirely monstrous in themselves. There is not a gleam of fun in either of them; and the use made of Pumblechook (one of the writer's own special impossible names) to connect Pip with Miss Havisham, who is the prime and chief monstrosity of the story, is as clumsy a piece of handiwork as was ever turned out by the merest literary tyro. These people are oppressively useless and foolish; they say and do impossible things; they illustrate non-existent propensities and absurdities; they are so profoundly dull that they must have been a penitential exercise to their inventor. The story is like an undeveloped giant, one who has been suddenly stunted in his growth. After the fourth chapter it becomes a mere jumble of incongruities, among which Miss Havisham occupies the place of the green China dragon. This woman's character has no redeeming trait; she is such a foolish, senseless, fantastical, impossible humbug, such an unworthy subject for such a pen. The flighty follies of a turned brain become pathetic when they are united to the straying impulses of a wounded heart, no doubt, but to be interesting they must be true, they must touch some chord which vibrates in the heart of the reader. Miss Havisham's turned brain is simply contemptible; the story of it is such as a school girl might write, in trying to come at the romance of madness; it is altogether an ignorant conception of mental disease, as well as being characterised by an extraordinary absence of matter-of-fact. Supposing Miss Havisham possible and real, Miss Havisham would very soon have been removed from her deserted brewery to a mad-house, as Mr. Dickens has committed the indiscretion of providing her with male relatives who are not mad. The tawdry, ill-tempered woman, sitting by candle-light among her ragged and rotting bridal finery, her silly project of rearing an unknown female child to avenge her injuries on the male sex, and selecting as her first victim a blacksmith's boy whom she had never seen, and had only heard of through a man whom she had never seen, ordering this boy to "play," and alternating as to her own employments between trying jewels on the girl and being pushed round the room in a wheeled chair, offers altogether as puerile a creation of fancy as can be imagined. Nothing can be clumsier or weaker than her connection with the story throughout; she is made the vehicle of a mystification which stamps Pip as a fool from the minute it takes him in; and whenever her conduct is not utterly, sickeningly, foolish, it is false and mean. Mr. Dickens has been undecided in his dealings with the fate of this scarecrow. When Pip first goes to her house he gets nervous, and sees a kind of vision, to which two very silly pages are devoted, which, if they do not imply that the writer means Miss Havisham to hang herself, in the fullness of time, and Pip to see her do it, mean precisely nothing. Nevertheless, Miss Havisham is burned to death instead, which catastrophe, by the way, adds another to the list of violent deaths which began with Nancy, and ended with Sydney Carton. The author has been careless, also, in reference to Miss Havisham, as at the conclusion of the book Pip mentions that he has never seen her handwriting, and yet previously an important incident has been made to turn upon a note which he has received from her. Miss Havisham's relations are all utterly nonsensical, and have done duty before. Camilla is merely Mrs. Chick, without the excuse of a brother to be uneasy about. Sarah is the double of the equally grotesque Judy Smallweed. Mr. and Mrs. Matthew Pocket are Mr. and Mrs. Jelleby, the "mission" of the latter being replaced by an attachment to the peerage. As to Herbert and Clara they are Traddles, and the "dearest girl," much diluted, but still interesting, because such thorough, unselfish goodness can bear repetition – only such qualities can, though not the calling of overstrained nicknames, and the multiplication of small peculiarities. Herbert Pocket's calling Pip "Handel," because Pip was apprenticed to a blacksmith, and they are so harmonious together, is of that class of small wit which makes one cringe as if one's father had made an extremely bad pun before "company."

Pip himself is not badly drawn, allowing for the limited space of three volumes in which the blacksmith's boy has to become a gentleman and go through various adventures, and allowing for the extraordinary absence of comprehension of class distinctions for which Mr. Dickens is remarkable. Pip, having never been in other society than Joe's and the aesthetic servant girl's, except that of the insane Miss Havisham and the demoniacal Estella, is of course quite *en règle*, when represented as vivaciously criticising London, its buildings, and its institutions, finding himself at once at home in a gentleman's house, and drawing nice distinctions between the characters and manners of those with whom he comes in contact. Apart from this incongruity, which is after all allowable, and rejecting altogether the episode of Biddy, which is only to be matched in absurdity by the scene in which Florence Dombey, who could scarcely ever have seen tobacco or heard of rum-and-water, lights Captain Cuttle's pipe and mixes his grog. The individual Pip is an interesting character. His childhood is well described, his sensations about the convicts, indeed all that concerns the secret history of his life, kept away from the deformities of the Havisham and Estella episodes, is well done. The convict Magwitch is so finely drawn, is a conception so replete with talent, so full of the writer's picturesque skill in which this story is otherwise so deficient, and at the same time so original that it is surprising that it cannot redeem the book from failure. This man's life, in the little that is told of it (and therein there is masterly skill), this man's death in its utterly unaffected pathos, in its simple truth to one motive and idea, in its unspoken appeal to merciful judgement, and to human sympathy, is as forcible as beautiful, and as highly finished a piece of work as Mr. Dickens has ever turned out. It is a pity he cannot smash up the paltry, pretentious, vulgar gim-crackery in which this gem is set, by which it is almost hopelessly disfigured, and let it be seen as it is. The haste and want of finish of the story as it draws to a conclusion are perhaps inseparable from the way in which a serial is written, and as they do not blemish the one beauty of "Great Expectations," they are of little consequence. The scene of the attempted murder of Pip has the misfortune of not being original. Just such a scheme of vengeance and rescue was described by Mrs. Trollope, as taking place in a Virginian forest, which was a more likely locality than an English marsh.

It is not an uncommon mistake for men of mark to pride themselves on qualities which are not their greatest. Mr. Dickens seems to fall into this mistake. If he reflects on the beginning, the rise, and the progress of his renown, he may perceive that the cause of its decay is to be found in his persistence in the defects and disregard of the charms of his earlier style. The public can never be indifferent to a work from his pen; but his very popularity makes them exacting, and he must not disdain the assurance that he has fallen very far short of their "great expectations."

'Epitome of News, British and Foreign', *Louth and North Lincolnshire Advertiser*, Saturday 31 August 1861, p. 3.
We hear Mr Charles Dickens is at work upon another story, which will most probably be issued in the old serial form. His recent work is decidedly among the best we have had from his delightful pen, fully realising its title "Great Expectations."

'Notes from our London correspondent', *York Herald*, Saturday 31 August 1861, p. 8.
Mr. Dickens having concluded his last work, "Great Expectations," which I may say, in passing, has not fulfilled the popular expectation, for it is hardly worthy of being named in connection with his earlier volumes; and Sir Edward Bulwer Lytton being now in possession of *All the Year Round* for six months; who again is to be succeeded by Mr. Wilkie Collins for nine months, there is a rumour that Mr. Dickens is about to commence a new novel in his old style, in monthly shilling numbers, which will be published by Messrs, Chapman and Hall, Piccadilly.

London Daily News, Monday 2 September 1861, p. 2.
However much we may regret, for old associations' sake – associations now spreading over a quarter of a century – the abandonment by Mr. Dickens of his ancient form of publication in twenty monthly parts, it is not to be denied that in this, the last of his fictions, a peculiar excellence has resulted from the employment of a different mechanical shape and structure. If his former novels have excited our wonder by their elaborate and complex development of character, for which the ample space at the author's disposal afforded sufficient opportunity, "Great Expectations" claims our praise on distinct grounds – on those of concentrated plot and deep emotion. The story which is now given to the world in three post-octavo volumes, after already making the acquaintance of thousands of weekly readers in *All the Year Round*, is one of the best in point of construction which Mr. Dickens has ever written; and, though the exhibition of character is necessarily less elaborate than in the longer works (excepting in the case of Pip himself), the *dramatis personae* are instinct with life and truth. The main inconvenience of the autobiographical form of writing – viz, that the writer can only relate, excepting by way of spoken episodes, those scenes at which he himself was present – has been skilfully surmounted; and the book teems with incident and scenery, with varied personality and complicated action. Confined within its comparatively

small territory of three volumes, the whole hangs together with the cohesion of a veritable relation, and the reader is not permitted to lose his interest in the catastrophe because of the distance of the first step by which that catastrophe has been reached. It will be noted also by literary judges that a perfect oneness runs throughout the work, harmonising the very first and the very last chapter by a subtle community of atmosphere. We may say "of atmosphere" literally; for, as the story opens beneath the cold marsh mists of that bleak river-side country, with the wintry evening coming on, lonely and desolate, to the lonely boy who stands shivering at it, so it closes solemnly and sadly beneath the same mists of the same marshes, where the man who has associated them with so many sorrows and so many mistakes, comes in his solitude for the sake of the old, sad, sacred times. Here is the key-note of the book, struck in the very second and third pages.... Yes, there is that difference [between beginning and end] of added moonlight and starlight at the close; but in either case the marsh-fog is cold and heavy on the landscape, and on the spirit of the human onlooker. For this is a tale of life-long sorrow, of unsatisfied passion, and of many errors; and it is fitting that the tone of sadness which predominates over all other tones should continue in the final note. Grief such as Pip's does not permit of a sudden shifting of the scenes, and a jovial ending. "And they all lived happily ever after," though the best of conclusions for a fairy tale, where hero and heroine have nothing worse to encounter than a few score of dragons, an ogre or two, or a giant with three heads, will not do after those agonies of the soul of man and woman which makes the soul incapable of mere content, were it only out of reverence for the proud and golden attitude of its own suffering, its sorrowful knowledge, and its immortal hopes. For this reason it appears to us that Mr. Dickens has exhibited the instinct of a true artist in so ordering his story that when Pip returns to his native village with the intention of asking Biddy (once disregarded in the consuming splendour of Estella's beauty and majestic grace), to take pity on his desolate weariness, he finds Biddy just married to Joe. It is better a thousandfold that he should continue alone with his disappointment and his radiant vision, than that he should sink into the stagnation of a comfortable routine. In this respect, "Great Expectations" has all the completeness and ideality of a poem. Love unrequited, yet not without its reward, since in the end it purifies, exalts, and blesses, is the central thought of the whole story; and it is kept in view to the last.

There are men whom the shipwreck of the affections converts into savage cynics or desperate profligates; there are others whom the like misfortune calls to a higher and a larger life. Pip is of the latter class. We are accustomed, in that levity which is the natural reaction of sentimentalism and affectation – the Nemesis of a world of insincere poetry and conventional pretence – to regard as a good subject for merriment any ill-starred "affair of the heart" which may come to our personal knowledge. A jilted gentleman finds very little pity but that which is analogous with contempt; and no topic that can possibly be brought before a court of justice is so certain of exciting "roars of laughter," and of calling forth to the full the comic powers of counsel and judge, as a case of breach of promise of marriage. Yet disappointed affection is at the bottom of half the tragedies of life, and vitally influences the character of many individuals to the day of their death. Love, in the case of Pip, does more than influence his character; it creates and fashions it. It makes his weakness and his strength; leads him at first into selfishness, and ultimately into forgetfulness of self. From the moment when, as a mere boy, he sees the girl Estella in the gloomy old mansion where, in the perpetual light of tapers, she tends her crazed and unhappy guardian, he feels that his fate is bound to hers. He must be worthy of her beauty and refinement, though he tear himself from the loving hearts of his rough, ignorant, homely relatives and friends. He is ashamed of his coarse hands, and his thick boots, and his awkward manners; and he begins for the first time in his life to wish that Joe, the true gentleman in heart, were a little more of a gentleman in deportment. Grown older, and still clinging to his lofty passion, he slights the evident fondness of good, affectionate Biddy, and sees nothing on the flat marshes, on the leaden river, "on the sails of the ships, in the clouds, in the light, in the darkness, in the wind, in the woods, in the sea, in the streets," but Estella. And when the astounding news of his sudden enrichment comes upon him, and he goes up to London as a young man of "great expectations" and of considerable present means, love still continues his great tutor in selfishness. The development of his nature under these new conditions is profoundly true, and minute to the finest hair-strokes of human character, without at any time offending the laws of an autobiographical narration. He forgets Joe, who has watched over him with such tenderness from infancy; forgets his unfortunate bed-ridden sister; forgets Biddy; forgets the old forge and the sweet home memories. It is not that he is cruel or bad at heart; it is strength of passion, combined with deplorable weakness of will, that lies at the bottom of his selfishness; and the selfishness, by a subtle intuition of the writer, is made to take the aspect of a virtue, as it so often does. But the very passion that betrays him into this maze of error is in the end the glorious clue that leads him forth into the daylight of old regards and sympathies. As long as he thinks to win Estella, he has no thought for Joe or Biddy; but when the great blow of losing her comes on the top of other miseries, he turns again to them, not in the mere necessity for comfort, but because the pang of unrequited love has brought with it the knowledge of his own unworthiness, and has softened his heart where the hope of successful love had hardened it. The sudden gush of self-knowledge that bears down upon him sharply and fiercely when, recovering from the long delirium of fever, he finds Joe watching by his bedside, is touched with all that brief intensity of pathos for which Mr Dickens's writings are remarkable.... Equally true and beautiful is the little scene at the close, where Pip implores Joe and Biddy, the newly married, to forgive his old ingratitude.... We will not say that the companion figure of Estella is equal to Pip himself; but, granting the circumstances under which she has been brought up (and which in some particulars are difficult to grant), the character is true to nature, and very striking. Estella is a child of obscure origin, though on this point the progress of the story enlightens the reader in a very unexpected, startling, and dramatic way; and she has been educated by poor crazed Miss Havisham in a manner purposely designed to deaden the heart within her. For Miss Havisham has been deserted many years before on the morning of her wedding; and she has thenceforth shut herself up in the darkened house, and has devoted herself to the task of rearing this girl in such a way that she shall become a deliberate coquette, and revenge her patron's broken heart by breaking male hearts out of number. Singularly picturesque as are the details of the conception – the muffled, desolate old country house, the rotting marriage feast, the stopped clocks standing fatally at the exact minute when the tidings of the betrayal first arrived, the deserted brewery where all labour has been stopped too since the same date, and the weird old woman sitting in her ragged bridal finery in the midst of these ghostly influences – we cannot but regard this portion of the story as the least satisfactory, because the least truthful. The violence to probability is great; for (to say nothing of minor objections) it is inconceivable that Miss Havisham should choose a very young and very humble boy for making her experiments upon. Still, if we grant the circumstances – and we do grant them to the extent that a woman like Miss Havisham might desire to educate a girl into a species of avenging spirit for the general punishment of men – the character of Estella follows very naturally. We have heard it objected on feminine authority, which is a thing not to be lightly regarded on such a subject, that Estella is not natural because she is thoroughly heartless, which no girl ever was; but without entering on the larger proposition, we question the smaller. Estella is *not* thoroughly heartless, however much she may suppose herself to be so; for the very fact of her refusing Pip, and accepting the heavy brute Drummle, is a sign of something in her which, under good training, might have been developed into self-sacrifice, if indeed it be not self-sacrifice as it is. When Pip asks her if it can possibly be by her own act that she flings herself away on such a man, she retorts – "On whom should I fling myself away?" … And when, in the very last scene of all, after the death of Drummle, Pip and Estella encounter one another in the ruined garden of the now vanished house where Miss Havisham has lived and died, it becomes manifest that sorrow has exalted the one no less than the other.…

We may almost regard as a separate character from the man Pip, the boy who is father to that man, in the Wordsworthian sense of parentage. Mr. Dickens is always peculiarly happy in his delineation of children; and the child Pip is a masterpiece even for him. The mind of childhood in its simplicity and freshness, its ready belief of all things, its fancifulness, its conscience, its depth of feeling, its terrors, and its weaknesses, was surely never so wonderfully reflected, excepting in the same author's "David Copperfield." If a child could write an account of his own thoughts and emotions, with some power, supernaturally added, of looking down upon the whole mystery from the height of a man's mind, and with the acquired illumination of a man's experience, we could have nothing superior to those two pictures. Indeed, it is part of the secret of Mr. Dickens's genius, as it is of all artistic genius, that he has retained a large share of the child's nature in the midst of his mature life.

This is no less apparent in the conception of Joe Gargery than in that of the infantine Pip. Wonderfully subtle, humorous, and pathetic, in his inarticulate simplicity and nobleness of nature, is that gentlest of blacksmiths, that Christian

Tubal Cain. Joe is one of those fine specimens of human clay whose goodness proceeds from no self-conscious elaboration of principle, but from a sort of natural growth and harmonious development, like a flower from its stem. He knows nothing of ethics; can quote you no texts; would make the very worst of preachers, partly from excess of tenderness and charity, partly from sheer ignorance of any abstract proposition whatever; will drink his glass and smoke his pipe in the village tap-room; and, though the least quarrelsome of men, is ready for a round with any one whose insolence or ruffianism becomes unbearable. Yet his is a fitting type of the deeply religious man. His sense of right is true as an instinct; his affection, that of a woman; his moral strength, that of a hero. And then, how full of the best and finest flavoured comedy are the rough externals of the man – his awkward ways, his homely notions, his language ever bordering on the ridiculous, yet always saved from absolute absurdity by that grand, far-off ring of the gold of humanity which sounds forever in his speech! How we laugh at him, yet love him! And how thankful we should be to the genius which, in an age of cynicism and worldliness, can conceive such a type of all that makes the most intellectual cynicism and the most successful worldliness look small, and poor.

The grandest figure in the book, however, is that of the convict. Introduced in the first chapter as a forlorn, hunted, desperate creature, ready to do murder for a dinner, cowering about in his rags and broken chains, and shivering with the ague of the marshes into which he has escaped from the neighbouring hulks; he dies towards the end of the romance a softened, gentle human being, whose better nature has been aroused by kindness, and by the gratitude which kindness has awakened in him. The degrees by which this transformation is effected are finely shaded off, so that we see the man in the very process of the change that is being wrought in him. When first he comes back from Australia, bringing a surprise for the reader such as few even of the most experienced in these matters are likely to anticipate, he is still half a savage, though greatly improved from his first condition. The loneliness of the colonial prairies, where he has been tending sheep for many a year, is apparent in his wild and uncouth manners; and the ferocity of his previous life of crime breaks out at intervals. He eats in a rapid, ravenous, and noisy way, mumbling his food on one side like a dog; and his language is coarse and almost blasphemous. As the influence of Pip steals over him, and the real affection which he has conceived for the benefactor of his early years becomes deeper and deeper, his very manners change, and, though retaining his old deadly hatred of the villain Compeyson, to all else he is as gentle and placable as a child. The hard, rough, violent, perverted life even receives a touch of poetry on the eve of its setting, when Pip and Herbert Pocket are rowing the convict down the river, in the vain hope of getting him away from the penalty of re-capture he has incurred by coming back to England. Nothing can be more natural than the language put into the man's mouth on this occasion; and yet it glimmers with a ray of ideality, caught from the solemn and tender circumstances of the time....

Profoundly pathetic also is the death of this poor criminal in gaol; and all the previous incidents of the trial are struck upon the page with a reality that is at once broad and minute. The convict Magwitch is one of the most original of Mr. Dickens's conceptions, and one of the noblest, too, in the rugged force of its outlines, and the truly Christian moral it embodies.

We have briefly indicated the leading characters of the novel; but some of the subsidiary figures demand a word or two of notice. There are Mr. Jaggers, the lawyer, shrewd, watchful, and made up of legal cautions, reservations, and saving-clauses; Wemmick, his clerk, a man of a fine genial nature, oddly disguised by the necessities of his calling – a reproduction, to a great degree, of Panks in "Little Dorrit," but very delightful; the servile seedsman, Pumblechook; the pompous, but not ill-natured, parish-clerk and subsequent tragic actor, Mr. Wopsle; the good, honest fellow, Herbert Pocket, and his weak, impracticable parents; a capital sketch of a man whom the reader never sees, but whom he is made to hear – Old Bill Barley, sometime a ship's purser; and the village ruffian, Orlick. The last-mentioned of these characters is strikingly delineated in many respects, but his place in the story is not so clear as we could wish, and his motive for killing Joe's wife does not seem to us sufficient, nor, indeed, is it necessary to the tale that Mrs. Gargery should be killed at all.

The scenery is as excellently drawn as the characters. We have already alluded to the misty marshes which seem to form part of the very texture of the story. Suffice it here to say, that in a hundred places some brief touch of description, distinct and recognisable as a painting, brings the weary monotony and gloom of the fenny country before the eyes of the reader. Mr. Dickens never obtrudes his descriptions, but so links them with the action of the story, or the moods of mind of the chief persons, that they partake of the vitality of the whole dramatic conception. This is especially so in "Great Expectations." The work is the production of a genius which is at once mature and youthful; and it is calculated to give permanent delight to successive generations that are born to the inheritance of the English tongue.

Manchester Times, Saturday 14 September 1861, p. 3.
"Great Expectations," the latest, and, it may be added, among the cleverest of the stories that have appeared from the pen of Mr. Charles Dickens, is now publishing in the United States, and commanding a great sale. Messrs. Paterson [*sic*] of Philadelphia, it is said, gave Mr. Dickens £100 for a manuscript in advance of the English publication; and now, though other American publishers are offering pirated editions, Messrs. Paterson have the start, and are reaping the rewards of honourable enterprise.

Leeds Times, Saturday 21 September 1861, p. 6.
Most of the critics have spoken in laudatory terms of Mr. Dickens' last serial tale – "Great Expectations." Even the *Saturday Review*, which is usually so severe on the author of Pickwick, spoke favourably of his last production. We have read the story – so no doubt have many of our readers – and, despite the opinion of our fellow-workers of the fourth estate, are inclined to endorse the following estimate formed by our clever contemporary, the (London) *Guardian*: – Some dozen years

ago it would have been superfluous to analyse a story, published periodically and just completed, by Mr. Charles Dickens. All the world would have read it as it came out, it would have been an affront to his readers if a reviewer had ventured to assume their ignorance. But the great days of Pickwick and Nickleby and Oliver Twist have long melted into the past; their freshness has been dimmed, not only by time and later novelties, but by their author's own endless repetition of them. Many stories have been issued by him since, stamped with many degrees of good, bad and indifferent. They still command, no doubt, a considerable and an admiring audience; but it is something much smaller than the universal circle of English readers. We are making no improbable assumption if we suppose that a good many readers of the *Guardian* have never seen a line of "Great Expectations." It is – like David Copperfield, of which in many respects, though at a great interval, it reminds us – an autobiography; and it dates from the earliest period of the writer's life.... Such is the story. Our readers will see that it has its full measure of Mr. Dickens's usual faults. It is improbable and unnatural to the last degree. The caprice of the convict might be overlooked – though nothing is more unlikely than that a man, bred and educated as Magwitch is described to be, should exercise such disinterested self-denial on behalf of a distant and almost unknown object – since it is the keystone upon which the whole arch hangs, and without which the story could not have come into existence at all. But one such indulgence is all that an author can fairly be allowed to ask. He ought not to have tacked on to it the far more improbable and utterly unnatural episode of Miss Havisham and Estella. Nor is the plot, such as it is, so carefully worked out as it might have been. Compeyson, the arch-villain, who works all the back springs, is a mere name. We see nothing of him except the results. The human tools he works with are found ready fitted to his hand without explanation. Nor are his motives made clear. There seems no reason why he should not have arrested Magwitch instantly on his return, instead of waiting till he had nearly made his escape. And Estella's story is meagre in the extreme. It was hardly worth while to find a mother for her in Mr. Jaggers' housekeeper, if mother and daughter were not even going to be made acquainted with each other. Then again, Orlick, an inferior villain, is allowed to escape altogether, probably from sheer forgetfulness, since he is made the instrument of inflicting merited chastisement upon Pumblechook, a much more humble offender. But if the story has its faults, the scenes and characters have their merits. They are unusually free from that particular trick of Mr. Dickens, which consists of making a character by labelling a lay figure with some peculiar oddity, which serves henceforth as his special mark and distinction. Wemmick, Mr. Jaggers' clerk, is the only instance we can recall of this. He has a mouth which is described as being like the slit of a post-office – a comparison which does not hold good, since post-office slits have been made vertical – and is afterwards spoken of simply as the post-office; and he is continually talking of "portable property," and mentioning his old father under the appellation of "the Aged." But most of the other people are distinguished by more ordinary and less arbitrary marks. The first part which describes Pip's childhood in the marshes is decidedly good. Mr. Dickens has a knack in picturing boyhood, which has served him well in Oliver Twist, David Copperfield, and Paul Dombey, and does not fail him in Pip. He is always clever in minute painting, and the objects in the foreground of a child's mind always look so large as to justify very minute painting....

Westmorland Gazette, Saturday 14 September 1861, p. 6.
We must demur ... to the writer [of Temple Bar]'s incidental eulogy of what he calls "Mr Dickens's latest and most perfect work, *Great Expectations*." The wildest phantasmagoria of the absurd and unnatural that ever were collected together in any fictions of every day life are exceeded in the autobiography of "Mr Pip."

Kendal Mercury, Saturday 28 September 1861, p. 8.
[N]either Dickens's "Great Expectations" nor Bulwer's "Strange Story" equals in interest or popularity the "Explorations" by M. de Chaillu' [This was a book on 'the gorilla controversy' about whether gorillas are men or animals].

E.S. Dallas [unsigned review], *The Times*, 17 October 1861, p. 6.
Mr Dickens has good-naturedly granted to his hosts of readers the desire of their hearts. They have been complaining to him that in his later works he has adopted a new style, to the neglect of that old manner which first won our admiration. Give us back the old *Pickwick* style, they cried, with its contempt of art, its loose story, its jumbled characters, and all its jesting that made us laugh so lustily; give us back Sam Weller and Mrs Gamp and Bob Sawyer, and Mrs Nickleby, Pecksniff, Bumble, and the rest, and we are willing to sacrifice serious purpose, consistent plot, finished writing, and all else. Without calling upon his readers for any alarming sacrifices, Mr Dickens has in the present work given us more of his earlier fancies than we have had for years. *Great Expectations* is not, indeed, his best work, but it is to be ranked among his happiest. There is that flowing humour in it which disarms criticism, and which is all the more enjoyable because it deified criticism. Faults there are in abundance, but who is going to find fault when the very essence of the fun is to commit faults? ...

The method of publishing an important work of fiction in monthly instalments was considered a hazardous experiment, which could not fail to set its mark upon the novel as a whole. Mr Dickens led the way in making the experiment, and his enterprise was crowned with such success that most of the good novels now find their way to the public in the form of a monthly dole. We cannot say that we have ever met with a man who would confess to having read a tale regularly month by month, and who, if asked how he liked Dickens's or Thackeray's last number, did not instantly insist upon the impossibility of his getting through a story piecemeal. Nevertheless, the monthly publication succeeds, and thousands of a novel are sold in minute doses, where only hundreds would have been disposed of in the lump.... On the whole, perhaps, the periodical publication of the novel has been of use to it, and has forced English writers to develop a plot and work up the incidents. Lingering over the delineation of character and of manners, our novelists began to lose sight of the story and to avoid action. Periodical publication compelled them to a different course. They could not afford, like Scheherazade, to let the devourers of their tales go to sleep at the end of a chapter. As modern stories are intended not to set people to sleep, but to keep them awake, instead of the narrative breaking down into a soporific dulness [*sic*], it was necessary that it should rise at the close into startling incident. Hence a disposition to wind up every month with a melodramatic surprise that awakens curiosity in the succeeding number. Even the least melodramatic novelist of the day, Mr Thackeray, who, so far from feasting us with surprises, goes to the other extreme, and is at particular pains to assure us that the conduct and the character of his personages are not in the least surprising, falls into the way of finishing off his monthly work with a flourish of some sort to sustain interest.

But what are we to say to the new experiment which is now being tried of publishing good novels week by week? Hitherto the weekly issue of fiction has been connected with publications of the lowest class – small penny and halfpenny serials that found in the multitude some compensation for the degradation of their readers. The sale of these journals extended to hundreds of thousands, and so largely did this circulation depend on the weekly sale, that on the conclusion of a good story it has been known to suffer a fall of 40,000 or 50,000. The favourite authors were Mr J.F. Smith, Mr Pierce Egan, and Mr G.W. Reynolds, and the favourite subjects were stories from high life, in which the vices of an aristocracy were portrayed, now with withering sarcasm, and now with fascinating allurements. Lust was the *alpha* and murder the *omega* of these tales. When the attempt was made to introduce the readers of the penny journals to better authors and to a more wholesome species of fiction, it was an ignominious failure.... Mr Dickens has tried another experiment. The periodical which he conducts is addressed to a much higher class of readers than any which the penny journals would reach, and he has spread before them novel after novel specially adapted to their tastes. The first of these fictions which achieved a decided success was that of Mr Wilkie Collins – *The Woman in White*.... After Mr Wilkie Collins's tale, the next great hit was this story of Mr Dickens's to which we invite the attention of our readers. It is quite equal to *The Woman in White* in the management of the plot, but, perhaps, this is not saying much when we have to add that the story, though not impossible like Mr Wilkie Collins's, is very improbable. If Mr Dickens, however, chose to keep the common herd of readers together by the marvels of an improbable story, he attracted the better class of readers by his fancy, his fun, his sentiment. Altogether, his success was so great as to warrant the conclusion, which four goodly editions already justify, that the weekly form of publication is not incompatible with a very high order of fiction. And now there is being published, in the same periodical another novel, which promises still more. It is by one who of all our novelists is the greatest master of construction, and who knows how to keep an exciting story within the bounds of probability. The *Strange Story* which Sir Edward Lytton is now relating week by week, is not only interesting as an experiment in hebdomadal publication, it is doubly interesting as a scientific novel. Scientific novels are generally dull, dead things. Sir Edward Lytton undertakes the most difficult of all tasks – to write a scientific novel in weekly parts. It appears to be the greatest of all successes achieved by *All the Year Round*. Hundreds of thousands of readers rush to read 'the fairy tales of science and the long results of time' as recorded by Sir E.B. Lytton.

Great Expectations is republished as a three-volume novel. Mr Dickens, we believe, only once before published a three-volume tale – *Oliver Twist*. We mention the fact because the resemblance between the two tales is not merely the superficial one that they are both in the same number of volumes, but is also one of subject very much and of treatment. The hero of the present tale, Pip, is a sort of Oliver. He is low-born, fatherless and motherless, and he rises out of the cheerless degradation of his childhood into quite another sphere. The thieves got a hold of Oliver, tried to make him a pickpocket, and were succeeded in their friendly intentions by Mr Brownlow, who thought that he could manage better for the lad. Pip's life is not less mixed up with the ways of convicts. He befriends a convict in his need, and henceforth his destiny is involved in that of the prisoner. The convict in the new story takes the place of Mr Brownlow in the old, and supplies Master Pip with every luxury. In either tale, through some unaccountable caprice of fortune, the puny son of poverty suddenly finds himself the child of affluence. If we are asked which of the tales we like best, the reply must be that the earlier one is the more fresh in style, and rich in detail, but that the later one is the more free in handling, and the more powerful in effect. It is so, even though we have to acknowledge in the work some of Mr Dickens's worst mannerisms. For example, it is a mere mannerism that in all his tales there should be introduced some one – generally a woman – who has been confined indoors for years, and who, either from compulsion or from settled purpose, should live in dirt and gloom, never breathing the fresh air and enjoying the sunshine. A lady who has a whim of this sort is here, as in most of Mr Dickens's tales, the blind of the story. Making every allowance, however, for repetitions, the tale is really worthy of its author's reputation, and is well worth reading.…

These few quotations are taken from the first two volumes. When Mr Dickens gets into the third he is driven along by the exigencies of the story, and he can no longer afford to play with his subject. The interest is still sustained, but it is of a different kind. We might quote whole passages of eloquent writing and passionate dialogue, but readers, we dare say, will be better pleased with the sort of extracts we have given. The public insist upon seeing in Mr Dickens chiefly the humourist; and, however great he may be in other directions, they count all as nothing beside his rare faculty of humour. To those who may not be satisfied with a work of this author's unless humour superabounds most, we can heartily commend *Great Expectations*.

Birmingham Gazette, Saturday 26 October 1861, p. 6.
While on literary matters, I may mention that by an eccentric bibliopolic arrangement now becoming common, Charles Dickens's story of "Great Expectations" is out in three volumes, and in the hands of thousands of readers by this time – although the

story is not finished in *All the Year Round*. Any candid critic must praise it; for it is one of the cleverest and most artistic books he has ever written, the ease, neatness, and elegance of the style being in advance of anything he has yet produced with, perhaps, the sole exception of "David Copperfield."

London Daily News, Monday 4 November 1861, p. 2.
Dickens's Great Expectations has already reached a fifth edition, a proof that his earlier style, to which he has reverted, has not lost its hold upon the public. One of his disciples, Mr. Anthony Trollope, has a work ready for the press – a collection of tales, which will be published by Chapman and Hall.

'Mr Dickens's Last Novel', *Dublin University Magazine*, December 1861, pp. 685–93.
If the title of Mr. Dickens's last novel could fairly be taken to mean more than a slight foreshadowing of the plot therein developed, we could not easily bring ourselves to congratulate the author on a hit so curiously unhappy as that which a playful fancy will be prone to lay to his account. Of those who may have had the boldness to expect great things, even in these latter days, from the growing weakness of a once mighty genius, there can be few who have not already chewed the cud of disappointment bitter in proportion to the sweetness of their former hopes. Doubtless there were some good easy souls who saw in "Hard Times" and "Little Dorrit" either the fitting outcome or the momentary eclipse of bygone triumphs won by the pen of "Boz." In "A Tale of Two Cities," friendly critics of the latter class seemed to discover flashes of something that might, by courtesy, be taken for the well known brilliance of other days. But, after all, how many of those who have helped to carry "Great Expectations" into a fourth or even fifth edition, entered on the reading of it with any serious hope of finding in Pip's adventures a worthy pendant to those of Pickwick or Martin Chuzzlewit? Would it not be far nearer the truth to say, that nine persons out of ten have approached these volumes with no other feeling than one of kindly regard for the most trivial utterances of an old favourite, or of curiosity, half painful, half careless, to see what further ravages time might have yet in store for the mental frame of a novelist already past his prime?

To ourselves, indeed, the title of the book suggested something utterly at variance with the mood of mind in which we sat down to read the book itself. Expecting little, we gained on the whole a rather agreeable surprise. Our last effort at reading a new novel by the author of "Pickwick," had left us stranded high and dry among the midmost chapters of "Little Dorrit." Thenceforth nothing could tempt us into renewing our olden intercourse with a writer whose pen had lost so large a share of its olden cunning, until the perusal of some half dozen conflicting criticisms on his latest performance aroused within us an amused desire to ascertain for ourselves, how far the more flattering opinions had overshot the bounds of literal truth. After a careful reading of "Great Expectations," we must own to having found the book in most ways better than our very small expectations could have foreboded. But, in saying this much, we are very far from endorsing the notion that it comes in any way near those earlier works which made and which alone are likely hereafter to keep alive their author's fame. The favourite of our youth still stands before us, in outline but little changed, the old voice still sounding pleasantly in our ears, the old humour still peeping playfully from lip and eye; but time, flattery, and self-indulgence have robbed his phrases of half their whilom happiness; the old rich humour shines wan and watery through an ever-deepening film of fancies farfetched or utterly absurd; while all the old mannerisms and deformities that once seemed to impart a kind of picturesque quaintness to so many neighbouring beauties, have been growing more and more irredeemably ungraceful and pitilessly obtrusive.

In judging of this new work, however, it is best not to look back too far along the line of its forerunners. Popular authors in these days live fast. A few years of such astonishing success as Mr. Dickens began long since to enjoy were little likely to effect no change for the worse in the outflowings of a genius naturally weak to withstand the dangerous spells of popular admiration. It would be doing him scant justice to rank his last novel with any of those which lifted him into his present leadership in the realm of letters. The best of racehorses will break down with too frequent running at too early an age; and novel-writing, at too high a pressure, is sure, in the long run, to tell its own tale. Some authors there are on whom the hand of time and the shocks of chance may have fallen lightly; but their number in these days is not large, and to their number clear-seeing criticism must shrink from adding the name of Mr. Dickens. But in refusing to place him on his old level, let us give him all credit for what he has really done. Compared with works such as "Bleak House" and "Little Dorrit," the one before us certainly claims a much higher place in our regards than either of the two just named. With all its faults it has the merit of being less wearisome, less weak in structure, less scarred with politics and pretension, less bedizened with finespun sentiment and groundless sarcasm. The story itself, however absurd in outline and fantastic in details, moves on with a livelier, firmer tread, dawdling indeed through much of the second volume, but only, as it were, to save itself for the grand rush of startling incidents that fill so many pages of the third. And the characters also, however strange to our experience of any other world than that of farce or popular fiction, seem to have been wrought out with more of the old workmanlike skill, and lighted up with freer touches of the old laughter-begetting humour, than the author, if we are not mistaken, had contrived for many years past to show forth.

To a reader ignorant of his earlier works and tolerant of all extravagances, if only they can tickle his fancy or keep his interest in full play, "Great Expectations" would offer a plenteous stock of enjoyable or exciting passages. Take for granted the truthlikeness of his portraiture, and you cannot but admire the clearness with which he conceives, and the consistency with which he works it up. After a little, the most critical reader resigns himself to the passing witchery, and begins to believe in Magwitch, Gargery, Miss Havisham, almost as heartily as their creator himself might be supposed to do. Each character speaks a language of its own, and behaves, however farcically, in its own peculiar fashion. Round each there circles a distinctive atmosphere made up of the humorous, dashed, more or less largely, with the sentimental or the frightful. Of food for laughter, for compassion, for eager curiosity, there is here no lack, if once you can lay aside your own ideas of what is fit and probable, and enter without reserve into the spirit – wild, whimsical, outrageous though it often be – of an entertainment got up by the oldest, yet still the first of our living humourists. Taken up in this manner, the book will easily commend itself to any reader wishful of wiling away a lonely evening by his own fireside. If with the pursuit of mere emotional enjoyment he can blend never so little of a critic's taste for reading his author's own character, the pleasure to himself will be all the greater, and the time devoted to it will not have been spent in vain.

The very first lines of the book give the keynote to its general character, and also to one of the writer's most marked peculiarities.... Here you at once feel is a novel meant to contain a good deal of funny writing after the pattern which so many copyists have done their worst to make too familiarly known. In this case, however, we have gotten at least the general article turned out of the old original workshop. Inferior as it may be to some earlier samples, it bears the stamp of no 'prentice hand. Little Pip's absurd speculations about his dead kindred resemble nothing so much as the childish fantasies of a Copperfield or a Paul Dombey. In their very extravagance there is just enough of likelihood to impart a keener edge to our enjoyment of the humorous surprises therein revealed; while none but their actual author would have been held excusable for putting into a child's brain fancies at once so laughably original and so ingeniously absurd – fancies which are only kept within the pale of things possible by the belief that he who has thus depicted them was surely capable in his childhood of having conceived the like.

More clearly farcical, nor less thoroughly characteristic, is the passage alluding to the hero's name. Fancy, in the first place, such a surname as Pirrip in real life! Among all the names we have ever heard of, is there one so gibberingly unmeaning as this? But Mr. Dickens is here seized only with a worse attack of his old weakness for the funniest sounding and least possible words that ever were hashed out of our English alphabet. Pirrip, Gargery, Wemmick come not unnaturally after Nickleby, Chuzzlewit, Micawber, Meagles, and a dozen more with which we are all familiar. They all help to show by what small tricks their inventor would heighten the impression already made on us by his eccentric humour, much as some popular comedian might raise an additional laugh by making faces now and then aside at his audience. For the same reason are we so often reminded that Pip was brought up by hand, that Wemmick's mouth was like a post-office, that Mr. Jaggers had a trick of biting his finger at you, and a way of washing the dirt of his daily business off his hands at frequent intervals. But in Pip's case there was the further amusement of twisting a funny name out of one less funny, as "Boz" had once been tortured out of "Moses." Or rather, it may be, that by an inverted process was Philip Pirrip found to be involved in Pip. Anyhow we have here a clue to the weaker side of Mr. Dickens's humour, to that unsoundness, whether of feeling or culture, which flaws even his finest conceptions, to that wild love of farce and caricature which, growing up with him from the earliest of his author-days, has certainly not decayed with the growth of his literary greatness.

His genius being always extravagant and his humour essentially comic, that extravagance must generally take a farcical turn. As Sydney Smith could not help being witty, so the author of "Pickwick" cannot help continually writing broad farce. For all his other excellences this is the one department in which he has gained the doubtful honour of a foremost place. Many even of his serious passages are tainted with a strong infusion of funny caricature. His best descriptions, whether of things or people, smell of unmistakable farce. His fancy fastening on the ridiculous side of things, brings it out into a prominence as absurdly overdone as Mr. Doyle brings out the heads and faces in his wonderful caricatures of English life and manners. Had chance not turned him into a writer of serial stories, he might have furnished the theatres with a long succession of farces and melodrama that would have driven all rivalry out of the field. There is hardly a character of his painting in which this tendency does not more or less prevail. To the delightful unreality of Sam Weller, Dick Swiveller, or Mark Tapley, we have not the heart to object; nor could such a being as Mrs. Nickleby have been drawn effectively without some admixture of the farcical. But if every character in a novel is more or less flavoured with farce, shall we call such novel a striking picture of real life? And in Mr. Dickens's many volumes how many characters would a fair critic deem wholly true to nature or to any reasonable conception of natural chances? In "Great Expectations," at any rate, the natural is largely overlaid by the farcical. Joe Gargery, Mr. Jaggers, the Convict, Pumblechook, Miss Havisham, Wemmick, which of these is exempt from tokens of their parent's besetting weakness? Some fibres of human interest run through them all: in some of them we are drawn for the nonce to believe almost as earnestly as the child believes in her pet doll; but even in our kindliest moments nothing can tempt us wholly to forget that their humanity is at best a theatrical caricature. Most nearly natural is the likeness of dear old Joe, the patient husband of a termagant wife and the stealthy playmate of her little fatherless brother. But from this fair-haired, blue-eyed Hercules of a blacksmith the taint of farcicality spreads ever darker and deeper, until in the portrait of Estella's crazy guardian it seems to cover all things with a hue as strangely misleading as the reflection of a healthy human face in an ill-made time-disfigured looking glass.

The extravagance of Mr. Dickens's nature often leads him to harp too often on the same string, to spin too fine a thread out of even his happiest ideas. Having, for instance, got so much fun out of Pip's dead belongings, he presently, without seeming excuse, returns to the charge, and makes Pip launch out into yet wilder fancies than before in his childish effort to grasp the full meaning of "Georgiana Wife of the Above." The murderous-looking casts in Mr Jaggers's room are everlastingly grinning, scowling, or otherwise unpleasantly reminding us of their hanged originals. Why should Mrs Pocket be always throwing "grandpapa's grand-daughter" in our teeth? Whatever grains of humour might have suggested the likening of anybody's mouth to a post-office, their effect is wholly lost in the tiresome frequency with which that likeness is pointed out, until poor Wemmick cannot eat his dinner without being said to post it. So, too, among other bits of illustrative humour touching the Convict's first appearance to little Pip, we are told that as he limped his way in fetters over the churchyard brambles and nettles, he looked, in Pip's young eyes, "as if he were eluding the hands of the dead people, stretching up cautiously out of their graves to get a twist upon his ankle and pull him in." Perhaps the most daring stretch of fancy in the whole book is the account of little Pip's frightened pleading to the face of a black ox, seen through the white marsh-mists, whom his guilty conscience mistook for some minister of punishment come to accuse him of his unwilling theft. In this merciless pumping-up of grotesque or ridiculous fancies Mr. Dickens recalls the similar weakness of an otherwise different writer, whose sickly straining after sentimental subtleties marred the great literary merits of "Transformation." But Mr. Hawthorne's whimsies could hardly go down with any but the sickliest of American school-girls, while those of Mr. Dickens will often evoke an irrepressible laugh from English boys and men who can sometimes allow themselves to feel like boys.

The first part of "Great Expectations" is, perhaps, the most redolent of its author's own manner. There is something of the old weird power in the opening interviews between Pip and the runaway convict on the marshes and in the churchyard. The description of Pip's home leads out into a very amusing sketch of Mrs. Gargery, the cross-grained sister, who revenges herself for the trouble of bringing Pip up by hand by perpetually taunting him with the fact, and treating him to such frequent tastes of "Tickler," that the poor little fellow saw no reason to doubt that he was indeed brought up by hand. Pip's kind friend, Joe Gargery, seemed, also, to be brought up in the same fashion, to judge by the lady's constant habit of seizing him by the whiskers, and beating his head against the wall – treatment which disturbed the calmness of Joe's temper as little as it harmed the surface of his skull. Joe and Pip being brothers in misfortune, become fast friends, and fortify each other by secret looks, and signs, and whispers, whenever Mrs. Gargery is "on the rampage" … There is vigour, too, in the description of the midnight chase after the runaway convicts; and our early dislike of Mr. Pumblechook is well sustained by the further development of his disagreeable tendencies at various periods of Pip's life. Overlaid as it is with the broadest caricature, his character keeps essentially true to itself, whether we see him worrying Pip with arithmetical questions, all through his breakfast, or slavering him with maudlin entreaties for the honour of shaking his hand, or slandering him all over the town as ungrateful to his earliest benefactor.

Wherever Joe Gargery makes his appearance, some pages of pleasant reading are sure to await us. His character seems to be wrought out with the same kindly affection that drew Mark Tapley and Newman Noggs. His battle with the brute Orlick teaches us to respect the mighty strength which all his wife's outrageous worrying can never provoke him, for one moment, to use against her … the simple, manly, faithful-hearted blacksmith approves himself as one of nature's truest noblemen – a being whose soul, but for its great humility, might have looked down on Pip's from a far loftier height than that whence Pip himself, in the heyday of his social preferment, seemed to regard his awkward, quaint-spoken friend of yore....

Biddy, too, with her quiet thoughtfulness of the folk at the forge, seems like another of those sweet, simple flowers that bloom now and then to gladden the byways and hollows of human life.... About Pip himself, the apparent hero of his own story, we hardly know what to say. As long as he remains at the forge, trying to teach Joe his letters, or seeking to enlarge his own stock, first under Mr Wopsle's great aunt, and then under that stage-stricken hero himself, he still maintains in our eyes somewhat of the interest first evoked by his meeting with the terrible convict in the dreary church-yard by the marsh.... But time and good fortune, combined with the weakness that mars all Mr. Dickens's attempts at painting the social life of the more polished classes, go far to efface our first impressions, and make us wonder whether the original Pip might not have died in early boyhood, leaving some worthless substitute to trade thenceforth on his good name. Anyhow Pip's acquaintance with Estella seems gradually to turn him into as feeble a snob as ever was palmed off on the novel reader for a hero. Under the blighting influence of Satis House, his character grows as shadowy as the greatness of his own expectations proves at last to be. The growth of his mad love for a girl of mere moonshine, melts away his manlier qualities, and renders him weakly ungrateful alike to his first and his latest benefactor. Between his departure for London in the character of a new made gentleman and the reappearance of Abel Magwitch, the story of his life is a broad waste of sluggish unreality, relieved once or twice by a bit of green oasis in the form of a visit from Joe Gargery, or of an evening spent at Walworth in the company of Pip's quaint friend Wemmick. After a time, indeed, the march of events brings him once more nearer to our human sympathies; but even then we are anxious far less about himself than about the rough-mannered, kind-hearted outcast, whose invincible longing to look upon a gentleman of his own making, tempts him to dare the risk of discovery, and consequent death, by coming back to the land from which his judges' doom had banished him forever. If Mr. Dickens had tried his best to portray the idle young man of Barnard's Inn as a mere weak-minded snob in fine clothing, he could not have succeeded better than he has perhaps unwittingly done. It may be that a love so foolish as that of Pip for Estella would weaken the fibres of never so brave a heart, and that a youth just new to the enjoyment of wealth and personal freedom would for the moment fling away all remembrance of his former friends. But Pip's tiresome maundering about his sweetheart, his consciously prolonged avoidance of poor Joe, and his morbid loathing of the kind but coarse-mannered wretch to whom his rise in the world is wholly due, seem to our thinking as little needed for the working out of the first conception of Pip's character, as they are likely to increase our interest in a hero whose claim thereon was never of the clearest. Repentance comes, indeed, to him at the last, but by that time our attention is fixed on far more notable objects; and in the whirl of incidents that wind up the story, we hardly care to know whether the nominal is to end his days in a debtor's prison, to pine abroad a poor lonely bachelor, or to marry in good time the young lady who has meanwhile given herself away to a worthless rival.

Far more boldly, if not more naturally drawn, is the figure of Abel Magwitch, the convict who frightens Pip at the outset of the tale. The shivering famine-stricken savage limping away on that wild marsh has a heart within him that appeals to ours from the moment we hear that click in this throat.... Amid the softening spells of that sick room from which the poor bruised patient felon will never go to the gallows outside, we, too, may learn, like Pip, some lessons of humility and loving-kindness which shall bear good fruit in after days.

Of Pip's London friends, Herbert Pocket is perhaps the most natural, but Wemmick is certainly the most entertaining. On the latter, and his master Jaggers, the author seems to have expended an equal amount of his happiest comedy, and his broadest farce.... The other characters in the story belong either to farce or melodrama, or a mixture of both.... In the management of his story Mr. Dickens seems to have aimed at engrafting on his own faulty methods the yet faultier subtleties of Mr. Wilkie Collins. Novelists of the latter type seem to fancy that the art of story-telling lies in the weaving of sheer riddles, the putting together of puzzles that claim attention from their intricacy alone. Into this rut the author of "Great Expectations" has evidently floundered with results in their own way remarkably successful. "The Woman in White" may henceforth hang her head before a greater than she.... On the whole, to us, not expecting very great things, this novel has proved an agreeable surprise. More compact than usual in its structure, it contains a good many striking passages, a few racy and one or two masterly portraits, a story for the most part cleverly sustained and wrought out to no lame or disjointed issues. In his characters, Mr. Dickens repeats himself least of all living novelists – a virtue which time has not yet impaired, and on which too great a stress can hardly be laid. Those in his present work are for the most part not more distinct from each other than from any to be found in former works. His plot, like his characters however improbable, has a kind of artistic unity and clear purpose, enhanced in this case by the absence of much fine-drawn sentiment and the scarcity of surplus details. If the author must keep on writing novels to the last, we shall be quite content to gauge the worth of his future essays by the standard furnished to us in "Great Expectations."

'Dublin University Magazine – December', *Dundee Courier and Daily Argus*, 3 December 1861, p. 4.

The 'Dublin University,' being an Irish magazine, it is not a legitimate ground of complaint that occasionally a large portion of its space is occupied with Irish subjects. It is so occupied this month and although these articles ... are likely to interest on the other side of the St George Channel, they do not prove very attractive in this. Generally, however, the present number of the 'Dublin University' is a good one. There is a well-written review of Mr Dickens's "Great Expectations," but we must take exception to the disparaging estimate which the writer has formed of the later works of the novelist. They are not equal to his first, and, for an obvious reason, the later works of few novelists are equal to the first, but he must be a rather unusual reader who could lay down even "Little Dorrit" at its "hindmost chapters."

[John Moore Capes and J.E.E.D. Acton], the *Rambler*, January 1862, pp. 274–6.

[W]ith all his faults, we should be puzzled to name Mr. Dickens's equal in the perception of the purely farcical, ludicrous, and preposterously funny, though not so much now, perhaps, as in the days when he had not adopted the stage trick of putting some queer sayings into his characters' mouths, and making them utter it on every possible occasion. It is by a partial flickering up of this bright gift that "Great Expectations" has proved an agreeable surprise to so many of his readers. The story is as exaggerated and impossible as any he ever perpetrated; it is uncomfortable, too, and abounds with those tedious repetitions to which he has become so grievously addicted. Mr Jaggers is always biting his forefinger; Provis begins his speeches with a stereotyped phrase. But there is some very good fun in the story, nevertheless; not jovial, not hearty, not Pickwickian indeed, but really comic, and sufficient to excite a pleasant quiet laugh on a dull winter-day. Wemmick, the lawyer's clerk, who lives in a cockney castle at Walworth, and fires off his gun at sundown every night, is a conception, barring the last characteristic, worthy of Dickens's happiest days. The walk to the wedding is delicious. And, on the whole, then, we may rejoice that even in Mr Dickens's ashes still live his wonted fires. Perhaps, if he would lie fallow for a year or two, and let his thoughts range at will, and eschew everything that is tragic, sentimental, or improving, especially in his particular line of improvement, we need not despair of seeing a still more lively reproduction of the delightful absurdities with which he charmed his readers a quarter of a century ago.

'Mr Dickens's "Great Expectations"', *Dundee Advertiser*, Wednesday 29 January 1862, p. 4.
When Dickens's "Tale of Two Cities" appeared we alluded to it as a most dismal specimen of a "Dismal Literature," and expressed a hope that he would revert to his first and best Pickwickian style. His recent story "Great Expectations," is, we are glad to observe, thoroughly Pickwickian.

'Our London Letter', *Elgin Courier*, Friday 14 March 1862, p. 5.
Assuredly … Sir Edward Lytton has beaten both Mr Wilkie Collins and Mr Charles Dickens on their own ground. The improbable plots of "The Woman in White" and "Great Expectations," are as nothing compared with the dose of mystery which the Right Honourable Baronet has shaken up for his participants to swallow. The truth possibly is, that the form of publication adopted, almost compels a writer of fiction rather to study the popular taste, than to adhere to the high principles of his art.

[Mrs Margaret Oliphant], 'Sensational Novels', *Blackwood's Magazine*, May 1862, pp. 574–80.
So far as 'Great Expectations' is a sensation novel, it occupies itself with incidents all but impossible, and in themselves strange, dangerous, and exciting; but so far as it is one of the series of Mr. Dickens's works, it is feeble, fatigued, and colourless. One feels that he must have got tired of it as the work went on, and that the creatures he called into being, but who are no longer the lively men and women they used to be, must have bored him unspeakably before it was time to cut short their career, and throw a hasty and impatient hint of their future to stop the tiresome public appetite. Joe Gargery the blacksmith alone represents the ancient mood of the author. He is as good, as true, patient, and affectionate,

as ungrammatical and confused in his faculty of speech, as could be desired; and shields the poor little Pip when he is a child on his hands, and forgives him when he is a man too grand for the blacksmith, with all that affecting tenderness and refinement of affection with which Mr. Dickens has the faculty of making his poor blacksmiths and fishermen much more interesting than anything he has ever produced in the condition of a gentleman. Near Joe's abode, however, dwells a lady who is intended to have much more influence upon the fortunes of the hero than his humble protector. Here is the first sight of Miss Havisham, and her surroundings, as they are disclosed to little Pip and the reader....

This is fancy run mad. As the story progresses, we learn that this poor lady, who is perfectly sane, much as appearances are against her, has lived in this miraculous condition for five-and-twenty years.... In this ghastly company lived a pretty young girl called Estella, whom Miss Havisham had reared with the avowed intention of avenging her own wrongs against men in general by breaking as many hearts as possible. The unlucky little Pip is the first victim selected. He is brought there to be operated upon in the special hope that he may learn to love Estella, and by her means have his heart broken – though the unfortunate little individual in question has no connection whatever with the breaking of Miss Havisham's heart, nor any other title to be considered as a representative of male humanity. If startling effects were to be produced by any combination of circumstances or arrangement of still life, here, surely was the very scene for a sensation. But somehow the sensation does not come. The wretched old heroine of this masquerade is, after all, notwithstanding her dire intentions of revenge upon the world, a very harmless and rather amiable old woman, totally incapable of any such determined folly. Estella grows up everything she ought not to grow up, but breaks nobody's heart but Pip's, so far as there is any evidence, and instead of carrying out the benevolent intentions of her benefactress, only fulfils a vulgar fate by marrying a man without any heart to be broken, and being miserable herself instead. Here there is the most perfect contrast to the subtle successes of "The Woman in White." Mr. Dickens's indifference or languor has left the field open to his disciple. With the most fantastic exaggeration of means, here is no result at all achieved, and no sensation produced upon the composed intelligence of the reader. The shut-up house does not deceive that wary and experienced observer: he waits to see what comes out of the bridal dress of twenty-five years' standing, and its poor occupant; and as nothing in the least startling comes out of either the one or the other, declines to be excited on the subject. The whole of this scene, and of the other scenes which follow in this house, and the entire connection between Miss Havisham, Pip, and Estella, is a failure. It is a mere piece of masquerading which deceives nobody, and carries to the utmost bounds of uninteresting extravagance that love of the odd and eccentric which has already brought Mr. Dickens to occasional misfortune in his long and well-deserved round of success.

Very different, however, is the darker side of the story. The appearance of the escaped convict in the squalid and dismal solitude of the marsh – the melancholy landscape with that one wretched figure embodying the forlorn and desolate sentiment of the scene – is perhaps as vivid and effective a sketch as Mr. Dickens ever drew. It is made in fewer words than usual, done at a breath, as if the author felt what he was saying this time, and saw the scene too vividly himself to think a full development of every detail necessary to enable his reader to see it also....

After another very vivid picture of the same marshes under the wild torchlight of a convict-hunt, this horrible figure disappears out of the book, and only comes to life again at the end of the second volume, when, as Pip's unknown benefactor, the mysterious secret friend who has made the young blacksmith a gentleman, he re-emerges, humanised and horribly affectionate, out of the darkness. The young fellow's utter despair when he finds himself held fast in the clutches of this man's gratitude and bounty – compelled to be grateful in his turn while loathing the very thought of the obligation which he has been unwittingly incurring – is very powerfully drawn, and the predicament perhaps as strange and frightful as could be conceived.... The sudden change which thus clouds over a hitherto harmless and aimless existence; the precautions necessary to keep the stranger safe; the gradual concentration of all interests into this one; the way in which, when hunted and in danger, the unfortunate young hero grows first tolerant, then anxious, and at last affectionate, to his strange and uncongenial friend, – is carefully done, and contains all there is of interest and excitement in the book. It is a struggle against an unseen enemy – always an exciting spectacle; and the fact that it is not the imperilled criminal himself for whom we are principally concerned, but the generous young men who have devoted themselves to save him, refines the contest, and gives it an interest less coarsely tragical.... Perhaps most readers will make sure of what is going to happen to Abel Magwitch before they retire to their peaceful pillows, but once there, the returned convict will not haunt them.... Mr. Dickens has this time made nothing but a narrative, powerful, indeed, but not pictorial, and from which we cannot quote any one incident sufficiently vivid and distinct to concentrate the attention of the reader....

The secondary persons of this book, however – almost entirely separated as they are from the main action, which is connected only in the very slightest way with the rest of the story – are, so far as they possess any individual character at all, specimens of oddity run mad. The incredible ghost, in the wedding-dress which has lasted for five-and-twenty years, is scarcely more outré than the ridiculous Mrs. Pocket.... Of the same description is the ingenious Mr. Wemmick, the lawyer's clerk, who lives in a little castle at Walworth, and calls his old father the Aged, and exclaims, 'Hulloa! Here's a church – let's go in!' when he is going to be married. Is this fun? Mr. Dickens ought to be an authority in that respect, seeing he has made more honest laughter in his day than any man living, and called forth as many honest tears; but we confess it looks exceedingly dull pleasantry to us, and that we are slow to accept Mr. Wemmick's carpentry as a substitute for all the homely wit and wisdom in which Mr. Dickens's privileged humorists used to abound. Besides all this heavy sport, there is a sensation episode of a still heavier description, for the introduction of which we are totally unable to discover any motive, except that of filling a few additional pages – unless, perhaps, it might be a desperate expedient on the part of the author to rouse his own languid interest in the conduct of the piece. Otherwise, why Pip should be seduced into the clutches of the senseless brute Orlick, and made to endure all the agonies of death for nothing, is a mystery quite beyond our powers of guessing. And again Mr. Dickens misses fire – he rouses himself up, indeed, and bethinks himself of his old arts of word and composition, and does his best to galvanise his figures into momentary life. But it is plain to see all along that he means nothing by it; we are as sure that help will come at the right moment, as if we saw it approaching all the time; and the whole affair is the most arbitrary and causeless stoppage in the story – perhaps acceptable to weekly readers, as a prick of meretricious excitement on the languid road, perhaps a little stimulant to the mind of the writer, who was bored with his own production – but as part of a narrative totally uncalled for, an interruption and encumbrance, interfering with the legitimate interest of the story, which is never so strong as to bear much trifling with. In every way, Mr. Dickens's performance must yield precedence to the companion work of his disciple and assistant. The elder writer, rich in genius and natural power, has, from indolence or caprice, or the confidence of established popularity, produced, with all his unquestionable advantages, and with a subject admirably qualified to afford the most striking and picturesque effects, a very ineffective and colourless work; the younger, with no such gifts, has employed the common action of life so as to call forth the most original and startling impressions upon the mind of the reader. The lesson to be learned therefrom is one so profoundly improving that it might form the moral of any Good-child story. Mr. Dickens is the careless, clever boy who could do it twice as well but won't take pains. Mr. Wilkie Collins is the steady fellow, who pegs at his lesson like a hero, and wins the prize over the other's head. Let the big children and the little perpend and profit by the lesson. The most popular of writers would do well to pause before he yawns and flings his careless essay at the public, and to consider that the reputation which makes everything he produces externally successful is itself mortal, and requires a sustenance more substantial than a languid owner can be expected to give.

'Literary Notices: Blackwood's Magazine', *Birmingham Gazette*, Saturday 3 May
     1862, p. 3.
Then comes an article on "Sensation Novels," in which Mr. Wilkie Collins's "Woman in White" is acknowledged to be great as a work of art, the weak point being that we cannot bring ourselves to hate that consummate villain Fosco. Of "Great Expectations" the writer of the article says that, so far as it is a sensation novel it occupies itself with incidents all but impossible, and in themselves dangerous and exciting; but, so far as it is one of the series of Mr. Dickens's works, it is feeble, fatigued, and colourless.

'Literature' [a review of *Blackwood Magazine*'s review], *Nottinghamshire
     Guardian*, Tuesday 6 May 1862, p. 3.
In "Sensation Novels" we have a discriminating comment on the class of literature which is now most in favour. Mr. Dickens comes in for some reprehension for the carelessness he has latterly evinced in his writings, and *Blackwood* endorses

the opinion, which most readers have already formed, that the master has been surpassed by the pupil – the "The Woman in White," of Wilkie Collins is infinitely superior to the "Great Expectations" of the conductor of "All the Year Round."

Northampton Mercury, Saturday 7 June 1862, p. 6.
The love of the marvellous is an inherent characteristic of the human mind; and, although, in its lower and extravagant phases it may be regarded as one of the weaknesses of our mental nature, tending, by its indulgence, to lower, to deteriorate and to becloud our perceptions, yet, in some of its modifications, in its better phases, in its higher tendencies, it constitutes one of the many admirable qualities which, in combination, raise the human intellect so infinitely above the level of the lower animals; and constitute the distinction between the rational and the irrational creature. In its better aspect, we find the love of the marvellous oftentimes supplying an impulse to the explorer, the discoverer, the man of science, and the inventor…. It makes so popular tales such as "The Woman in White" by Collins, "Great Expectations" by Dickens, and the "Strange Story" by Bulwer.

'Our Library Table: Great Expectations', *The Ladies' Cabinet of Fashion, Music and Romance*, August 1861, pp. 218–20.
If Mr. Dickens's name did not stand alone on the title-page, we should be disposed to attribute much of the conception – even some of the execution – of this story to his friend and fellow-writer, Mr. Wilkie Collins. For a long time now these novelists have been accustomed to write together. The Christmas numbers of "Household Words," jointly produced by them, showed year by year a gradual assimilation of the two styles. At first the difference was broad and marked; the least critical of us could assign to each writer his own chapters. But, after a Christmas or two, readers began to be puzzled in such investigations. Which was Mr. Dickens and which was Mr. Collins came to be decided mostly by the choice, not the conviction, of the critic. No longer we wondered at the monstrous joining together of black fish and beautiful woman: the mermaid had disappeared, and if the physiologist could still detect in the delight of gods and men, a suspicion of the fishy fins and tail, he confessed that those anomalous members had been reduced to their lowest possible rudiments. That this assimilation of the two styles was a great gain to the joint story is evident enough. Whether the influence of the one writer upon the other, when exhibited in works written separately, is a gain or a loss, it would occupy more than the space at my disposal here to discuss. The influence of Collins upon Dickens was very much greater than that of Dickens upon Collins. If we compare this last book with the early sketches of Boz, we see how great is the change, and further that this change is all in the direction of the Romantic school of which Collins is the English chief. Collins's books on the other hand show simply a steady progression in the one line which his genius had marked out for him. Dickens's influence upon him is to be found only in treatment and phrase – in a spice of sentimentalism, in a solemn aping of jocularity utterly repugnant to his manner of thought – never in conception either of story or character. Still, though we attribute much of the

change in Dickens's writing to Collins's influence, we must allow that the change is by no means in opposition to his own genius, and that his bias in this direction would have showed itself had Collins never written. Dickens began by professing an extreme naturalism. In his earliest sketches and in Pickwick, he describes only such scenes as came under his own notice. The lower classes of life, the ordinary places and events and characters – these he sets before himself as models from which to paint. To say that he painted these most untruly is to say only a truism stale to everybody now. We all know his manner of observation. Seizing upon some external point or trait in a man (Wemmick's post-office; Jaggers's finger-biting, hand-washing, boot-creaking; Joe's whisker-feeling; Mrs Gargery's apron; the same now as thirty years ago), and never getting deeper in than that, likening it to something strange, and ever after mistaking that to which he has likened it for the thing itself, and flying off into the most astonishing metaphorical rambles – we all know this manner by heart; and we all know that his characters are not men but funnily-painted puppets, though sometimes a human truth is spoken out of their wooden mouths which startles us as if a stock or stone had spoken. Professing extreme naturalism, he was the most unnatural of writers. Professing to draw on the most familiar portion of the world around him, he lost his way and got into a world which was the most extravagant burlesque of that he had left behind, a region whose inhabitants habitually made harlequins and pantaloons and clowns of themselves, where pantomimic transformations were continually occurring, things becoming men and men things, and one thing becoming another, until all was chaos. The closest of observers, he was the worst of describers. The distant hills of the landscape he looked upon were as near to him as the pebbles under his feet – he saw the grass grow upon their ridges, and strove to paint the growing of it. He had the keenest sense of a certain harmony and likeness between all things in heaven and earth; but trying to express it, instead of showing how all things were parts of a universal whole, he made each other than it was. That a writer, when attempting to copy the commonest phrases of life, should be betrayed by his imagination into inventing an altogether ideal world, with inhabitants unreal as the shadows in Plato's cave, is a fact that would seem at once to separate him broadly from the naturalists. Dickens's first fame, as it seems to us, was a pseudo fame. He will never live because of his truthful representations of nature, or because of his insight into human character, or because of his photographs of the manners and customs of the time. So long as his books do live it must be from other and even opposite causes. His original wit and talent of grotesque and exaggerated description caught the public ear by their strangeness at first; and people instantly attributed to him a power of depicting low life, because they happened to be low-life puppets who were exhibited in this new species of writing. But among thoughtful persons his fame will rest by no means on his talent for describing simple nature high or low, but on his literary art. We must pass on to the book in hand. Briefly let us write that, comparing "Great Expectations" with the "Sketches by Boz," we should pronounce "Great Expectations" to be the legitimate offspring of Dickens's true genius, and the sketches to be mere abortional fruit of an immature tree. In the legends introduced into his earliest works, in "Oliver Twist," in "A Tale of Two Cities," we may trace, step by step, the over-mastering of false naturalism by native romanticism. However much Wilkie Collins has influenced him, it has not been against but with the grain. This romance of "Great Expectations" is a little too much like "The Woman in White." It would be difficult to point out the precise points of resemblance. If analyses of both plots were placed side by side we should find that that of the later book was even carefully rendered different from that of the earlier. Still the stories are of the same kind, and affect us in the same manner.... The readers of "All the Year Round" must begin to feel this painfully. The plot runs thus.... Now we cannot praise this plot. The queer coincidences with regard to Estella, her papa and mamma, cannot be put down as anything but most impossible absurdities. The account of jilted Miss Havisham and her wedding-cake is stolen bodily out of Mr. Wilkie Collins's brains. For all this, the story goes well. The suspense of the last volume cannot be surpassed. A man who can make us hold our breath cannot be denied literary skill. Let us bow to that, and let others discuss the absurdities, each for himself. As for the characters, those who know Mr. Dickens's ideal world, and can translate the ghosts thereof into the real flesh and blood of this world, will discover in Mr. Jaggers a notable creation; also in Joe Gargery they will discover some glimpses of a human soul that will be like enough to blind their eyes with tears. The book as a story is utterly inferior to "A Tale of Two Cities." The lovers of fun will find but little facetiousness in it; but to those who respect the magical art which can stir their blood by mere words, this book will seem to have in it elements of a higher success in that art than Mr. Dickens has yet achieved.

American Reviews

Reproduced by kind permission of the Serial and Government Publications Division of the Library of Congress, Washington, DC.

'New publications', *New-York Daily Tribune*, 25 August 1861, p. 2.
No one of the former productions of Mr. Dickens is richer in the peculiar qualities which have given him such a wide and solid popularity than the present remarkable creation of his genius. Without falling back on his own steps, and reproducing in a new form the characters with which the whole reading world is familiar, he follows out the path in which he has won such brilliant renown, and exhibits a series of fresh illustrations of the kind of individualities which his pen delights to represent, and of the walks of life in which all the affinities of his intellect make him completely at home. The personages in this story bear the evident marks of their paternity; they show a strong family likeness to the extensive gallery of portraits with which the name of Charles Dickens has become identical; they are drawn for the most part from a layer of society with which his readers have no special sympathies; and regarded as individuals, they are not precisely of the stamp whose acquaintance the warmest admirers of the author would be solicitous to cultivate. Nor does the plot in which they are made to figure attract by the natural sequence of its

events; it presents a succession of wild improbabilities; and although conducted with more than Mr. Dickens's usual finesse, it carries invention to the extreme borders of legitimate romance.... [The final scene concerning Pip and Orlick] is, perhaps, the most powerful of any in the work, and fully proves that Mr. Dickens has lost none of the accustomed vitality which infuses such natural blood and heat into such big delineations of a great catastrophe.... We purposely abstain from furnishing our readers with any inkling of the methods by which the denouement of the plot is reached, but they may obtain from our rapid sketches a general idea of the prompt and ingenious artifice of its management. The story is marked by the hatred of pretense and affectation – the sympathy with young, and obscure, and even criminal life – the quick perception of the comic phases of character and society – and the occasional touches of tragic pathos, which so happily distinguish the productions of Mr Dickens from the wearisome crowd of modern novelists. In humour the present work is less admirably successful than most of his popular masterpieces. It abounds in grotesque and hilarious comparisons, but they more frequently take the character of broad farce than is common even with the rollicking sallies of the author. Thus, after the boy Pip had been dosed by the beneficent Mrs. Joe with a nauseous cup of tar water, he remarks that "At the best of times so much of this elixir was administered to him as a choice restorative, that he was conscious of going about *smelling like* a new fence." … Dickens, however, would not be himself without the use of some such safety-valves which permit the escape of the farcical fancies which crowd every convolution of his brain. His true humour constantly flashes out through the inimitable platitudes of Mr. Pumblechook, the droll conceptions of Wemmick, and the infantile good-heartedness of honest, burly, long-suffering Joe Gargery.

Nashville Union and American, 24 March 1861, p. 3.

Harper, we see, has taken his readers deep into Dickens' new story of "Great Expectations" as well as continuing with "A Day's Ride" by Charles Reade [*sic*], with any quantity of illustrated literature and American and European intelligence. Thank you, gentleman; call again.

'The now-publishing novels of Dickens and Thackeray', *Cincinnati Daily Press*, 10 April 1861, p. 1.

The two greatest novelists of the present age are simultaneously engaged in the task, fascinating alike to reader and writer, of creating – no other word will express the idea – characters which promise to live prominently in the world of fictional personages. Thackeray, in his *Adventures of Philip*, and Dickens, in his *Great Expectations*, are each following out in a different way the same idea; each giving us the history of a young man, and at the same time showing in vivid colours the peculiar style of their writing. Thackeray's hero, Philip, belongs to good society and hob-nobs with gentry and nobility. Dickens' hero is a very poor little boy who works in a blacksmith's shop, and knows no more of fashionable life than he gleans from a visit to a rich lame old maid for whom he does some service.

The young years of Philip are but briefly told, while from the moment he launches into society all his actions are minutely described. But Dickens, with that inimitable skill and delicate feeling which so characterizes his young people, dwells with care and pleasure on the child life of his hero. In this, indeed, there is a marked difference between the two novelists. Thackeray has no little folks, while Dickens would be celebrated had he never given us an adult character, and were known to the reading world only by Little Nell, by the boy David Copperfield, or by the greatest creation of this class, little Paul Dombey.

New York Times, 13 November 1860, n.p.
The New-York correspondent of the Philadelphia Press writes: "I have seen at HARPERS' the opening pages of DICKENS' new serial, Great Expectations, the first chapters of which will be issued in the Weekly on Wednesday next. They pay him for it £1,125. It is to run through nine months, and each number will be published here about a week in advance of its publication in England. JOHN MCLENAN is at work on the illustrations. The HARPERS have also secured, for £600, the early sheets of the Cornhill Magazine, which is to contain a new story by THACKERAY. This will be published in the magazine. The Magazine will likewise soon contain new tale by the author of Adam Bede – one of the tenderest, truest, and most fascinating of story-tellers.

Great Expectations promises to be one of the cleverest things DICKENS has done. Its opening is very brilliant. His last work, A Tale of Two Cities, was entirely unique, showing a vein he had not hitherto worked, and it will hold its place in our literature as one of the most vivid and impressive of all literary illustrations of history. It combined the romance, the terror, the pathos of the French Revolution, as no other book except Carlyle's History. The new work will strike a livelier key."

'New Publications', *New York Times*, 23 September 1861, n.p.
In regard to DICKENS' last work – Great Expectations – almost as many different opinions prevail as it has readers. But whatever opinions may prevail relative to the literary merits of the work, one can be entertained as regards the form in which it is just issued by JAMES G. GREGORY. Of the edition, of which the two volumes before us form part, we have before spoken in such terms and at such length as to render any further mention almost superfluous. The quality of the paper, the clearness of the type, and the beauty of the binding, render each successive volume of the series a work of wonder, as well as a thing of beauty destined to remain a joy forever. In the illustration of Great Expectations, however, we fancy that DARLEY has not quite done justice to himself. He was hurried, perchance; or it may be that he has been sacrificed by the engraver. As in the matter of cooks and meats, it is often that designers and engravers are furnished by different powers.

Edwin P. Whipple, 'Reviews and Literary Notices: Great Expectations by Charles Dickens', *Atlantic Monthly*, September 1861, pp. 380–82.
The very title of this book indicates the confidence of conscious genius. In a new aspirant for public favor, such a title might have been a good device to attract

attention; but the most famous novelist of the day, watched by jealous rivals and critics, could hardly have selected it, had he not inwardly felt the capacity to meet all the expectations he raised. We have read it, as we have read all Mr. Dickens's previous works, as it appeared in instalments, and can testify to the felicity with which expectation was excited and prolonged, and to the series of surprises which accompanied the unfolding of the plot of the story. In no other of his romances has the author succeeded so perfectly in at once stimulating and baffling the curiosity of his readers. He stirred the dullest minds to guess the secret of his mystery, but, so far as we have learned, the guesses of his most intelligent readers have been almost as wide of the mark as those of the least apprehensive. It has been all the more provoking to the former class, that each surprise was the result of art, and not of trick; for a rapid review of previous chapters has shown that the materials of a strictly logical development of the story were freely given. Even after the first, second, third, and even fourth of these surprises gave their pleasing electric shocks to intelligent curiosity, the *dénouement* was still hidden, though confidentially foretold. The plot of the romance is therefore universally admitted to be the best that Dickens has ever invented. Its leading events are, as we read the story consecutively, artistically necessary, yet, at the same time, the processes are artistically concealed. We follow the movement of a logic of passion and character, the real premises of which we detect only when we are startled by the conclusions.

The plot of "Great Expectations" is also noticeable as indicating, better than any of his previous stories, the individuality of Dickens's genius. Everybody must have discerned in the action of his mind two diverging tendencies, which, in this novel, are harmonized. He possesses a singularly wide, clear, and minute power of accurate observation, both of things and of persons; but his observation, keen and true to actualities as it independently is, is not a dominant faculty, and is opposed or controlled by the strong tendency of his disposition to pathetic or humorous idealization. Perhaps in "The Old Curiosity Shop" these qualities are best seen in their struggle and divergence, and the result is a magnificent juxtaposition of romantic tenderness, melodramatic improbabilities, and broad farce. The humorous characterization is joyously exaggerated into caricature, – the serious characterization into romantic unreality. Richard Swiveller and Little Nell refuse to combine. There is abundant evidence of genius both in the humorous and the pathetic parts, but the artistic impression is one of anarchy rather than unity.

In "Great Expectations," on the contrary, Dickens seems to have attained the mastery of powers which formerly more or less mastered him. He has fairly discovered that he cannot, like Thackeray, narrate a story as if he were a mere looker-on, a mere "knowing" observer of what he describes and represents; and he has therefore taken observation simply as the basis of his plot and his characterization. As we read "Vanity Fair" and "The Newcomes," we are impressed with the actuality of the persons and incidents. There is an absence both of directing ideas and disturbing idealizations. Everything drifts to its end, as in real life. In "Great Expectations" there is shown a power of external observation finer and deeper even than Thackeray's; and yet, owing to the presence of other qualities, the general impression is not one of objective reality. The author palpably uses his observations as materials for his creative faculties to work upon; he does not record, but invents; and he produces something which is natural only under conditions prescribed by his own mind. He shapes, disposes, penetrates, colours, and contrives everything, and the whole action is a series of events which could have occurred only in his own brain, and which it is difficult to conceive of as actually "happening." And yet in none of his other works does he evince shrewder insight into real life, and a clearer perception and knowledge of what is called "the world." The book is, indeed, an artistic creation, and not a mere succession of humorous and pathetic scenes, and demonstrates that Dickens is now in the prime, and not in the decline of his great powers.

The characters of the novel also show how deeply it has been meditated; for, though none of them may excite the personal interest which clings to Sam Weller or little Dombey, they are better fitted to each other and to the story in which they appear than is usual with Dickens. They all combine to produce that unity of impression which the work leaves on the mind. Individually they will rank among the most original of the author's creations. Magwitch and Joe Gargery, Jaggers and Wemmick, Pip and Herbert, Wopsle, Pumblechook, and "the Aged," Miss Havisham, Estella, and Biddy, are personages which the most assiduous readers of Dickens must pronounce positive additions to the characters his rich and varied genius has already created.

Pip, the hero, from whose mind the whole representation takes its form and colour, is admirably delineated throughout. Weak, dreamy, amiable, apprehensive, aspiring, inefficient, the subject and the victim of "Great Expectations," his individuality is, as it were, diffused through the whole narrative. Joe is a noble character, with a heart too great for his own powers of expression to utter words, but whose patience, fortitude, tenderness, and beneficence shine lucidly through his confused and mangled English. Magwitch, the "warmint" who "grew up took up," whose memory extended only to that period of his childhood when he was "a-thieving turnips for his living" down in Essex, but in whom a life of crime had only intensified the feeling of gratitude for the one kind action of which he was the object, is hardly equalled in grotesque grandeur by anything which Dickens has previously done. The character is not only powerful in itself, but it furnishes pregnant and original hints to all philosophical investigators into the phenomenon of crime. In this wonderful creation Dickens follows the maxim of the great master of characterization, and seeks "the soul of goodness in things evil."

The style of the romance is rigorously close to things. The author is so engrossed with the objects before his mind, is so thoroughly in earnest, that he has fewer of those humorous caprices of expression in which formerly he was wont to wanton. Some of the old hilarity and play of fancy is gone, but we hardly miss it in our admiration of the effects produced by his almost stern devotion to the main idea of his work. There are passages of description and narrative in which we are hardly conscious of the words, in our clear apprehension of the objects and incidents they convey. The quotable epithets and phrases are less numerous than in

"Dombey and Son" and "David Copperfield"; but the scenes and events impressed on the imagination are perhaps greater in number and more vivid in representation. The poetical element of the writer's genius, his modification of the forms, hues, and sounds of Nature by viewing them through the medium of an imagined mind, is especially prominent throughout the descriptions with which the work abounds. Nature is not only described, but individualized and humanized.

Altogether we take great joy in recording our conviction that "Great Expectations" is a masterpiece. We have never sympathized in the mean delight which some critics seem to experience in detecting the signs which subtly indicate the decay of power in creative intellects. We sympathize still less in the stupid and ungenerous judgements of those who find a still meaner delight in wilfully asserting that the last book of a popular writer is unworthy of the genius which produced the first. In our opinion, "Great Expectations" is a work which proves that we may expect from Dickens a series of romances far exceeding in power and artistic skill the productions which have already given him such a pre-eminence among the novelists of the age.

Bibliography

Primary Sources

Anon., *The Cinema, Its Present Position and Future Possibilities: National Council of Public Morals* (1917; New York: Arno Press and the New York Times, 1970).

Anon., *Dramatic Index, covering articles and illustrations concerning the stage and its players in the periodicals of America and England and including the dramatic books of the year*, 43 Vols. (Boston: F.W. Faxon, 1909–1949).

Bagehot, Walter, 'Charles Dickens', in *Literary Studies by the late Walter Bagehot*, Vol. 2, ed. by Richard Holt Hutton (London: Longmans, Green and Co., 1879).

Barnes, Walter, *A Study Guide to the Critical Appreciation of the Photoplay Version of Charles Dickens' Novel Great Expectations* (New York: Published for the National Council of Teachers in English, Bureau of Publications, Teachers College, Columbia University, 1934).

Barry, Iris, 'What the Public Wants', *Daily Mail*, 21 November 1925: 8.

Chesterton, G.K., *Chesterton's Biographies: Charles Dickens* (1906; Kelly Bray: Stratus Books, 2001).

———, *Appreciations and Criticisms of the Works of Charles Dickens*, illustrated edition (1911; Gloucester: Dodo Press, 2008).

Dickens, Charles, *Great Expectations*, introduction by George Bernard Shaw (New York: Limited Editions Club, 1937).

———, *Great Expectations*, abridged by H. Oldfield Box (London: Hodder and Stoughton Classic Fiction, 1955).

———, *Letters of Charles Dickens*, ed. Kathleen Tillotson and Graham Storey, 11 Vols. (Oxford: Clarendon Press, 1965–97).

———, *Great Expectations*, ed. Margaret Cardwell (Oxford: Oxford University Press, 1998).

———, *Great Expectations*, ed. Edgar Rosenberg (New York: W.W. Norton & Co., 1999).

———, *The Dent Uniform Edition of Dickens' Journalism*, Vol. 4: 'The Uncommercial Traveller' and Other Papers 1859–70, ed. Michael Slater and John Drew (London: J.M. Dent, 2000).

———, *The Manuscript of Great Expectations* (Cambridge: Cambridge University Press Library Collections, 2011).

———, *Great Expectations*, introduction by Sarah Phelps (London: Random House/BBC Books, 2011).

Forster, E.M., *Commonplace Book*, ed. by Philip Gardner (London: Scholar Press, 1985).

Forster, John, *Life of Charles Dickens*, Fireside Edition (London: Chapman and Hall, 1872).

Gilbert, W.S., *Great Expectations: A Drama in Three Acts with Prologue* (no publisher, 1871).

Guinness, Alec, *Great Expectations*, playscript (no publisher, 1943).

Hardwick, J.A., *Comic and Sentimental Songbook* (London: Diprose & Bateman [?], 1861).

Kitton, Frederic George, *The Dickensiana: A Bibliography of the Literature Relating to Charles Dickens and his Writings* (1886; New York: Haskell House, 1971).

———, *Dickens and his Illustrators Cruikshank, Seymour, Buss, 'Phiz,' Cattermole, Leech, Coyle, Stanfield, Maclise, Tenniel, Frank Stone, Landseer, Palmer, Topham, Marcus Stone, and Luke Fields. With twenty-two portraits and facsimiles of seventy original drawings now reproduced for the first time* (London: Redway, 1899).

Lipard Barclay, G., ed., *The life and remarkable career of Adah Isaacs Menken, the celebrated actress: An account of her career as a danseuese, an actress, an authoress, a poetess, a sculptor, an editress, as captain of the 'Dayton light guard,' as the wife of the pugilist John C. Heenan, and of 'Orpheus Kerr'* (Philadelphia: Barclay, 1868).

Lewes, G.H., 'Dickens in Relation to Criticism', *Fortnightly Review*, 11 (February 1872): 141–54.

Mansfield, Katherine, *Journal of Katherine Mansfield*, ed. by J. Middleton Murry (London: Constable, 1927).

Newbolt, Henry, *The Teaching of English in England: being the report of the Departmental Committee appointed by the President of the Board of Education to inquire into the position of English in the educational system of England* (London: His Majesty's Stationery Office, 1921).

O'Brien, Frank M., *The Story of the Sun, New York, 1833–1928* (New York: D. Appleton, 1917).

Pascoe, Charles Eyre, *The Dramatic List: A Record of the Performances of Living Actors and Actresses of the British Stage*, 2nd ed. (London: David Bogue, 1880).

Scott, Charles Augustus Shafto, *My Unknown Friend: A Drama, in Three Acts. Being a Dramatized Version of the Novel 'Great Expectations,' by the Late Charles Dickens*, Dicks' Standard Plays, Number 412 (London: John Dicks, no date).

Schreiber, Lady Charlotte, *Extracts from Her Journal 1853–1891*, ed. by the Earl of Bessborough (London: John Murray, 1952).

Stevenson, R.L., *The Letters of Robert Louis Stevenson* ed. by Bradford A. Booth and Ernest Mehew (New Haven and London: Yale University Press, 1994).

Win Faxon, Frederick, ed., *Dramatic Index, covering articles and illustrations concerning the stage and its players in the periodicals of America and England and including the dramatic books of the year*, 43 Vols. (Boston, MA: F.W. Faxon, 1909–1949).

Wood, Ellen (Mrs Henry), *East Lynne*, introduction by Sally Mitchell (New Brunswick, NJ: Rutgers University Press, 1984).

Secondary Sources

Acker, Kathy, *Great Expectations: A Novel* (New York: Grove Press, 1982).

Ackroyd, Peter, *Dickens* (London: Sinclair-Stevenson, 1990).

Adair Fitz-Gerald, Shafto Justin, *Dickens and the drama: being an account of Charles Dickens's connection with the stage and the stage's connection with him* (London: Chapman and Hall, 1910).

A.E.B.C., 'The Screen version of *Great Expectations*', *Dickensian*, 31 (Winter 1934): 102.

Afnan, Elham, 'Imaginative Transformations: *Great Expectations* and *Sunset Boulevard*', *Dickensian*, 94 (Spring 1998): 5–12.

Allardyce Nicoll, J.R., *A History of Late 19th-century Drama 1850–1900*, Vol. 1 (Cambridge: Cambridge University Press, 1946).

———, *A History of English Drama 1660–1900* (Cambridge: Cambridge University Press, 1979).

Allingham, Philip V., 'The Illustrations for Great Expectations in Harper's Weekly (1860–61) and in the Illustrated Library Edition (1862): "Reading by the Light of Illustration"', *Dickens Studies Annual*, 40 (Spring 2009): 113–69.

———, and Irina Gredina, 'The Countess Vera Sergeevna Tolstaya's Russian Language Adaptation of *Great Expectations* (1895)', *Dickensian*, 105 (Summer 2009): 122–34.

Andrews, Malcolm, *Charles Dickens and His Performing Selves* (Oxford: Oxford University Press, 2006).

Anon., 'When found', *Dickensian*, 31 (Spring 1935): 81.

Aronofsky Weltman, Sharon, '"Can a Fellow Be a Villain All His Life?": *Oliver!* Fagin and Performing Jewishness', *Nineteenth-Century Contexts*, 33 (2011): 371–88.

Aschkenasy, Nehama, 'Agon's The Dickensian Moment: "Baya'ar uva'ir"', *Journal of Modern Jewish Studies*, 2 (2003): 174–90.

Balio, Tino, ed., *The American Film Industry* (Madison, WI: the University of Wisconsin Press, 1985).

Baston, Jane, 'Word and Image: The Articulation and Visualization of Power in *Great Expectations*', *Literature/ Film Quarterly*, 3 (1996): 322–31.

Bawden, Liz-Anne, ed., *The Oxford Companion to Film* (Oxford: Oxford University Press, 1976).

Beetham, Margaret, 'Open and Closed: The Periodical as a Publishing Genre', *Victorian Periodicals Review Special Issue: Theory*, 22, ed. by Laurel Brake and Anne Humpherys (1989): 96–100.

Behr, Edward, *The Complete Book of Les Misérables* (New York: Arcade Publishing, 1989).

Benjamin, Walter, 'The Work of Art in the Age of Mechanical Reproduction', in *Illuminations: Essays and Reflections*, ed. by Hannah Arendt; trans. by Harry Zohn (New York: Random House Schocken Books, 1968).

Bigsby, Christopher and Don B. Wilmeth, eds., *The Cambridge History of American Theatre*, Vol. 2: *1870–1945* (Cambridge: Cambridge University Press, 1999).

Bolter, Jay David, and Richard Grusin, *Remediation: Understanding New Media* (Cambridge, MA: MIT Press, 1998).

Bolton, Philip H., *Dickens Dramatized* (London: Mansell, 1987).

———, *Women Writers Dramatized: A Calendar of Performances from Narrative Works Published in English to 1900* (London and New York: Mansell Publishing, 2000).

Brake, Laurel, Bill Bell and David Finkelstein, eds., *Nineteenth-Century Media and the Construction of Identities* (Basingstoke: Palgrave Macmillan, 2000).

Briggs, Asa, *The History of Broadcasting in the United Kingdom*, Vol. 2: *The Golden Age of Wireless 1927–1939* (Oxford and New York: Oxford University Press, 1995).

Brogan, Hugh, *The Penguin History of the USA*, New Edition (London: Penguin, 1999).

Brooks, Peter, *The Melodramatic Imagination: Balzac, Henry James, Melodrama, and the Mode of Excess* (New Haven, CT: Yale University Press, 1995).

———, *Reading for the Plot: Design and Intention in Narrative* (Cambridge, MA: Harvard University Press, 1992).

Brownlow, Kevin, *David Lean* (London: Richard Cohen Books, 1996).

Butler, Ivan, 'Dickens on the Screen', in *Film Review 1972–73*, ed. by F. Maurice Speed (London: W.H. Allen, 1972).

Butt, John and Kathleen Tillotson, *Dickens at Work* (London: Methuen, 1968).

Callow, Simon, *Charles Dickens* (London: HarperCollins, 2012).

Cardwell, Sarah, *Adaptation Revisited: Adaptation and the Classic Novel* (Manchester: Manchester University Press, 2002).

Carey, Peter, *Jack Maggs* (London: Faber, 1997).

Clayton, Jay, *Charles Dickens in Cyberspace: The Afterlife of the Nineteenth Century in Postmodern Culture* (Oxford: Oxford University Press, 2003).

Clifford, Jo, *Great Expectations by Charles Dickens: Adapted for the Stage* (London: Nick Hern Books, 2012).

Cohen, Jane R., *Charles Dickens and His Original Illustrators* (Columbus, OH: Ohio State University Press, 1980).

Collins, Philip, *Charles Dickens, the Public Readings* (Oxford: Oxford University Press, 1983).

———, ed., *Charles Dickens: The Critical Heritage* (Abingdon and New York: Routledge, 1986).

Cooke, Lez, *British Television Drama: A History* (London: BFI, 2003).

Corrigan, Timothy, ed., *Film and Literature: An Introduction and Reader* (London: Routledge, 2012).

Crowther, Andrew, *Gilbert of Gilbert and Sullivan: His Life and Character* (Stroud: The History Press, 2011).

Davis, Paul B., 'Dickens, Hogarth, and the Illustrations for *Great Expectations*', *Dickensian*, 80 (Autumn 1984): 130–43.

———, *The Life and Times of Ebenezer Scrooge* (New Haven, CT: Yale University Press, 1990).

————, *Charles Dickens A to Z: The Essential Reference to His Life and Work* (New York: Facts On File, 1998).

DeBona, Guerric, *Film Adaptation in the Hollywood Studio Era* (Champaign, IL: University of Illinois Press, 2010).

Denning, Michael, *Mechanic Accents: Dime Novels and Working-Class Culture in America* (New York and London: Verso, 1987).

Diakonova, Nina, 'Russian Dickens Studies, 1970–1995', *Dickens Quarterly*, 12 (1995): 181–6.

Dobie, Ann B., 'Early Stream-of-consciousness writing: *Great Expectations*', *Nineteenth-Century Fiction*, 25 (March 1971): 405–16.

Dolin, Tim, 'First Steps Towards a History of the Mid-Victorian Novel in Colonial Australia', *Australian Literary Studies*, 22 (2006): 273–93.

Donahue, Jo, ed., *The Cambridge History of British Drama*, Vol. 2: *1660–1895* (Cambridge: Cambridge University Press, 2004).

Douglas, Susan J., *Listening In: Radio and the American Imagination* (Minneapolis, MN: University of Minnesota Press, 2004).

Douglas-Fairhurst, Robert, *Becoming Dickens: the Invention of a Novelist* (Cambridge, MA and London: Harvard University Press, 2008).

————, 'Among the Greats', *Guardian Review*, 29 September 2011: 6.

Dubrez Fawcett, F., *Dickens the Dramatist on Stage, Screen and Radio* (London: W.H. Allen, 1952).

Eaton, Marcia Muelder, 'Laughing at the Death of Little Nell: Sentimental Art and Sentimental People', *American Philosophical Quarterly*, 26 (October 1989): 269–82.

Eaton, Michael, '*The Dickensian* goes to the Cinematograph', *Dickensian*, 101 (Winter 2005): 233–9.

Eddy, Spencer L. Jr., *The Founding of the Cornhill Magazine* (Muncie, IN: Ball State Monographs No. 19, 1970).

Edwardson, Mickie, 'James Lawrence Fly's Report on Chain Broadcasting (1941) and the Regulation of Monopoly in America', *Historical Journal of Film, Radio and Television*, 22 (2002): 397–423.

Eisenstein, Sergei, 'Dickens, Griffith, and the Film Today', in *Film Form: Essays in Film Theory and The Film Sense*, trans. and ed. by Jay Leyda (New York: Meridian Books, 1957).

Ellis, Thomas, 'The Literary Adaptation – an Introduction', *Screen*, 23 (1982): 3–5.

Fielding, K.J., 'The Piracy of Great Expectations', *Notes and Queries* (November 1955): 495–6.

————, 'The Critical Autonomy of *Great Expectations*', *Review of English Literature*, 2 (1961): 75–88.

Fischler, Alan, 'Love in the Garden: Maud, Great Expectations, and W.S. Gilbert's Sweethearts', *Studies in English Literature, 1500–1900*, 37 (Autumn 1997): 763–81.

————, 'The Descent of Darwinism: W.S. Gilbert and the Evolution of *Great Expectations*', *Dickensian*, 98 (Summer 2002): 101–12.

Ford, George H., *Dickens and His Readers: Aspects of Novel Criticism Since 1836* (New York: W.W. Norton, 1965).

———, 'Dickens in the 1960s', *Dickensian*, 66 (May 1970): 170–71.

Fraser, Robert, *Book History through Postcolonial Eyes: Rewriting the Script* (Abingdon and New York: Routledge, 2008).

Frick, John W. Jr., *Uncle Tom's Cabin on the American Stage and Screen* (Basingstoke: Palgrave Macmillan, 2012).

Friedman, Stanley, 'The Complex Origins of Pip and Magwitch', *Dickens Studies Annual*, 15 (1986): 221–31.

Genette, Gérard, *Palimpsests: Literature in the Second Degree* (Lincoln, NE: University of Nebraska Press, 1997).

Giddings, Robert, Keith Selby and Chris Wensley, *Screening the Novel: The Theory and Practice of Literary Dramatization* (Basingstoke: Macmillan, 1990).

———, 'Boz on the Box: A Brief History of Dickens on British Television', *Dickensian*, 103 (Summer 2007): 101–15.

———, and Erica Sheen, eds., *The Classic Novel from Page to Screen* (Manchester and New York: Manchester University Press, 2000).

———, and Keith Selby, *The Classic Serial on Television and Radio* (Basingstoke: Palgrave Macmillan, 2001).

Gillman, Susan K. and Robert L. Patten, 'Dickens: Doubles: Twain: Twins', *Nineteenth-Century Fiction*, 39 (March 1985): 441–58.

Glavin, John, *After Dickens: Reading, Adaptation and Performance* (Cambridge: Cambridge University Press, 1999).

———, ed., *Dickens on Screen* (Cambridge: Cambridge University Press, 2003).

———, *A Library of Essays on Charles Dickens: Dickens Adapted* (Burlington, VT: Ashgate, 2012).

Gledhill, Christine, ed., *Home Is Where the Heart Is: Studies in Melodrama and the Woman's Film* (London: BFI, 1987).

Glover, David and Scott McCracken, eds., *The Cambridge Companion to Popular Fiction* (Cambridge: Cambridge University Press, 2012).

Gluchowski, Krzysztof, 'Dickens and Poland', *Dickensian*, 98 (Spring 2003): 44–51.

Gomery, Douglas, *The Hollywood Studio System* (New York: St Martin's Press, 1986).

Grams, Martin Jr., *Radio Drama: A Comprehensive Chronicle of American Network Programs 1932–1962*, 2 Vols. (Jefferson, NC: McFarland, 2008).

Grass, Sean, *Our Mutual Friend: A Publishing History* (Burlington, VT: Ashgate, 2014).

Greenblatt, Harmon, 'David Lean Production', *Dickens Magazine*, 1 (2001): 8–9.

Gross, John and Gabriel Pearson, eds., *Dickens and the Twentieth Century* (London: Routledge and Kegan Paul, 1962).

Guinness, Alec, *My Name Escapes Me: The Diary of a Retiring Actor* (London: Hamish Hamilton, 1996).

———, *Blessings in Disguise* (London: Penguin, 1997).

Hagan, John, 'Structural Patterns in Dickens' *Great Expectations*', *English Literary History*, 21 (March 1954): 54–66.

———, 'The Poor Labyrinth: The Theme of Social Injustice in Dickens's *Great Expectations*', *Nineteenth-Century Fiction*, 9 (December 1954): 169–78.

Hajkowski, Thomas, *Studies in Popular Culture: The BBC and National Identity in Britain, 1922–53* (Manchester: Manchester University Press, 2010).

Haldane-Lawrence, David, 'Charles Dickens and the World of Opera', *Dickensian*, 107 (Spring 2011): 5–21.

Hammerton, J.A., *The Dickens Picture-Book: A Record of the Dickens Illustrators* (London: the Educational Book Co., 1912).

Hammond, Mary, 'Hall Caine and the Melodrama on Page, Stage and Screen', *Nineteenth Century Theatre and Film*, 31 (Summer 2004): 39–57.

———, 'The Multimedia Afterlives of Victorian Novels: The Readers Library Photoplay Editions in the 1920s', *Nineteenth Century Theatre and Film*, 37 (December 2010): 28–44.

———, and Shafquat Towheed, eds., *Publishing in the First World War: Essays in Book History* (Basingstoke: Palgrave Macmillan, 2007).

Hammond, Michael, *The Big Show: British Cinema Culture in the Great War 1914–18* (Exeter: Exeter University Press, 2005).

Hanbery Mackay, Carol, 'A Novel's Journey into Film: The Case of *Great Expectations*', *Literature/Film Quarterly*, 13 (1985): 127–34.

Harper, Henry J., *The House of Harper: A Century of Publishing* (New York: Harper & Brothers, 1912).

Harper, Sue, 'The Representation of Women in British Feature Film, 1945–1950', *Historical Journal of Film, Radio and Television*, 12 (1992): 217–30.

Hartnoll, Phyllis, ed., *The Oxford Companion to the Theatre* (Oxford: Oxford University Press, 1951).

Hatfield, Charles, *Alternative Comics: An Emerging Literature* (Jackson, MS: University Press of Mississippi, 2005).

Hibbert, Christopher, *Charles Dickens: The Making of a Literary Giant* (Basinstoke: Palgrave Macmillan, 2009).

Hilmes, Michael, ed., *The Television History Book* (London: BFI, 2003).

Hobsbawm, Eric, *Age of Extremes: The Short Twentieth Century 1914–1991* (London: Abacus, 1995).

Hodges Holt, Shari, 'Dickens from a Postmodern Perspective: Alfonso Cuarón's *Great Expectations* for Generation X', *Dickens Studies Annual*, 38 (2007): 69–72.

Hollington, Michael, ed., *The Reception of Charles Dickens in Europe*, 2 Vols. (London and New York: Bloomsbury, 2013).

Hook, Andrew, *F. Scott Fitzgerald: A Literary Life* (Basingstoke: Palgrave Macmillan, 2002).

Hume, Kathryn, 'Voice in Kathy Acker's Fiction', *Contemporary Literature*, 42 (Autumn, 2001): 485–513.

Hung, Eva, 'The Introduction of Dickens into China: A Case Study in Target Culture Reception', *Perspectives: Studies in Translatology – Special issue: Chinese Translation Studies*, 4 (1996): 29–41.

Jacobs, Lea, *The Decline of Sentiment: American Film in the 1920s* (Berkeley, Los Angeles and London: University of California Press, 2008).

J.G., '*Great Expectations* realised', *Dickensian*, 55 (September 1959): 139.

Johanningsmeier, Charles A., *Fiction and the American Literary Marketplace: The Role of Newspaper Syndicates in America, 1860–1900* (Cambridge: Cambridge University Press, 1997).

John, Juliet, *Dickens and Mass Culture* (Oxford: Oxford University Press, 2010).

Jones, Lloyd, *Mister Pip* (London: John Murray, 2008).

Jordan, John O. and Robert L. Patten, eds., *Literature in the Marketplace: Nineteenth-Century British Publishing and Reading Practices* (Cambridge: Cambridge University Press, 1995).

Jordan, John O., ed., *The Cambridge Companion to Charles Dickens* (Cambridge: Cambridge University Press, 2001).

———, 'Global Dickens', *Literature Compass* 6 (2009): 1211–23.

———, and Nirshan Perera, eds., *Global Dickens* (Burlington, VT: Ashgate, 2012).

Joshi, Priya, *In Another Country: Colonialism, Culture and the English Novel in India* (New York: Columbia University Press, 2002).

Kaplan, Fred, *Dickens: A Biography* (London: Hodder & Stoughton, 1989).

Kosok, Heinz, *The Theatre of War: The First World War in British and Irish Drama* (Basingstoke: Palgrave Macmillan, 2007).

Koszarski, Richard, *An Evening's Entertainment: The Age of the Silent Feature Picture, 1915–1928* (Berkeley: University of California Press, 1990).

Kuhn, Annette, 'Cinema-Going in Britain in the 1930s: Report of a Questionnaire Survey', *Historical Journal of Film, Radio and Television*, 19 (1999): 531–43.

Kujawska-Lis, Ewa, 'The Transformations of Charles Dickens in Early Socialist Poland', *Literature Compass*, 10 (April 2013): 396–405.

Lansbury, Coral, 'Charles Dickens and His Australia', *Journal of the Royal Australian Historical Society* (June, 1966): 115–27.

———, 'Terra Australis Dickensia', *Modern Language Studies*, 1 (Summer, 1971): 12–21.

Law, Graham, *Serialising Fiction in the Victorian Press* (Basingstoke: Palgrave Macmillan, 2000)

Leavis, F.R. and Q.D. Leavis, *Dickens the Novelist* (London: Chatto and Windus, 1970).

Ledger, Sally and Holly Furneaux, eds., *Charles Dickens in Context* (Cambridge: Cambridge University Press, 2011).

Lee, Klaudia Hiu Yen, 'Cross-Cultural Adaptation of the Dickensian Spatiality: The Case of *Little Dorrit*', *English: Journal of the English Association*, 62 (2013): 6–21.

Leighton, Mary Elizabeth and Lisa Surridge, 'The Plot Thickens: Toward a Narratological Analysis of Illustrated Serial Fiction in the 1860s', *Victorian Studies*, 51 (Autumn, 2008): 65–101.

Leiter, Samuel L. and Holly Hill, eds., *Encyclopaedia of the American Stage* (Westport, CT and London: Greenwood, 1985).

Lenlow, Elbert, *Reader's Guide to prose Fiction: An Introductory Essay, with Bibliographies of 1500 Novels Selected, Topically Classified, and Annotated for Use in Meeting the Needs of Individuals in General Education* (London and New York: A. Appleton-Century, 1940).

Leonard, Hugh, *Great Expectations: a Play, adapted from the novel by Charles Dickens* (London and New York: Samuel French, 1998).

Litvack, Leon, 'Dickens, Australia and Magwitch, Part I', *Dickensian*, 95 (Spring 1999): 24–50.

———, 'Dickens, Australia and Magwitch, Part II: The Search for *le cas* Magwitch', *Dickensian*, 95 (Summer 1999): 101–27.

Mackenzie, Hazel and Ben Winyard, *Charles Dickens and the Mid-Victorian Press, 1850–1870* (Buckingham: University of Buckingham Press, 2013).

Malik, Rachel, 'Horizons of the Publishable: Publishing in/as Literary Studies', *English Literary History* 75 (2008): 707–35.

———, 'Stories Many, Fast and Slow: *Great Expectations* and the Mid-Victorian Horizon of the Publishable', *English Literary History*, 79 (2012): 477–500.

Mankowitz, Wolf, *Mazeppa: The Lives, Loves, and Legends of Adah Isaacs Menken: A Biographical Quest* (New York: Stein and Day, 1982).

Marill, Alvin H., *More Theatre: Stage to Screen to Television*, Vol. 1: *A–L* (Metuchen, NJ & London: Scarecrow Press, 1993).

May, Elaine, ed., *Webster's Guide to Charles Dickens: Novels and Film and Television Adaptations* (Baldwin City, KS: Webster's Digital Services, 2011).

Mazzeno, Laurence W., *The Dickens Industry, Critical Perspectives 1836–2005* (Rochester, NY and Woodbridge, Suffolk: Camden House, 2011).

McFarlane, Brian, *Novel to Film* (Oxford: Oxford University Press, 1996).

———, *Screen Adaptations: Great Expectations, the Relationship between Text and Film* (London: Methuen, 2008).

———, and Anthony Slide, eds., *Encyclopaedia of British Film* (London: Methuen, 2003).

McParland, Robert, *Charles Dickens's American Audience* (Plymouth: Lexington, 2010).

Meckier, Jerome, *Innocent Abroad: Charles Dickens's American Engagements* (Lexington, KY: University Press of Kentucky, 1990).

Moretti, Franco, *Atlas of the European Novel 1800–1900* (New York and London: Verso, 1998).

Morgentaler, Goldie, 'Meditating on the Low: A Darwinian Reading of *Great Expectations*', *Studies in English Literature 1500–1900*, 38 (Autumn, 1998): 707–21.

Morley, Malcolm, 'Stages of *Great Expectations*', *Dickensian*, 51 (Spring 1955): 79–83.

Mukherjee, Ankhi, 'Missed Encounters: Repetition, Rewriting, and Contemporary Returns to Charles Dickens's *Great Expectations*', *Contemporary Literature*, 46 (Spring 2005): 108–33.

Musselwhite, David, *Partings Welded Together: Politics and Desire in the Nineteenth-Century English Novel* (London: Routledge, 1987).

Nicholson, Norman, *Wednesday Early Closing* (London: Faber and Faber, 1975).

Noonan, Michael, *Magwitch* (New York: St. Martin's Press, 1982).

Nowell-Smith, Simon, 'The "Cheap Edition" of Dickens's Works (First series) 1847–1852', *Library*, 22 (Sept. 1967): 245–51.

O'Gorman, Francis, ed., *The Cambridge Companion to Victorian Culture* (Cambridge: Cambridge University Press, 2010).

Parfait, Claire, *Uncle Tom's Cabin: A Publishing History* (Burlington, VT: Ashgate, 2006).

Paris, Michael, ed., *The First World War and Popular Cinema: 1914 to the Present* (New Brunswick, NJ: Rutgers University Press, 2000).

Paroissien, David, 'Dickens and the Cinema', *Dickens Studies Annual*, 7 (1978): 68–80.

———, *The Companion to Great Expectations* (Robertsbridge, Sussex: Helm Information Ltd, 2000).

Parrinder, Patrick, *Nation and Novel: The English Novel from Its Origins to the Present Day* (Oxford: Oxford University Press, 2006).

Patten, Robert L., *Charles Dickens and His Publishers* (Oxford: Oxford University Press, 1978).

———, *Charles Dickens and "Boz": The Birth of the Industrial-Age Author* (Cambridge: Cambridge University Press, 2012).

Petrie, Graham, 'Dickens, Godard and the Film Today', *Yale Review*, 64 (December 1974): 185–201.

———, 'Silent Film Adaptations of Dickens Part 1: From the Beginning to 1911', *Dickensian*, 97 (Spring 2001): 7–21.

———, 'Silent Film Adaptations of Dickens Part II: 1912–1919', *Dickensian*, 97 (Summer 2001): 101–15.

———, 'Silent Film Adaptations of Dickens Part III: 1920–1927', *Dickensian*, 97 (Winter 2001): 197–213.

Plotz, John, *Portable Property: Victorian Culture on the Move* (Princeton NJ: Princeton University Press, 2009).

Pointer, Michael, *Charles Dickens on the Screen: the Film, Television, and Video Adaptations* (Boston, MA: Scarecrow Press, 1996).

Powell, Kerry ed., *The Cambridge Companion to Victorian and Edwardian Theatre* (Cambridge: Cambridge University Press, 2004).

Pucci, Suzanne Rodin and James Thompson, eds., *Jane Austen and Co.: Remaking the Past in Contemporary Culture* (Albany, NY: University of New York Press, 2003).

Read, Piers Paul, *Alec Guinness: The Authorised Biography* (London & New York: Simon & Schuster, 2003).

Rider Haggard, H., *Rural England: Being an Account of Agricultural and Social Researches Carried Out in the Years 1901 & 1902*, Vol. 2 (1902; Boston: Adamant Media, 2001).

Roe, Sue, *Estella: Her Expectations* (Brighton: Harvester Wheatsheaf, 1982).

Rose, Jonathan, *The Intellectual Life of the British Working Classes* (New Haven and London: Yale University Press, 2001).

Sadrin, Anny, *Great Expectations* (London: Unwin Hyman, 1988).

———, 'French Studies on Dickens Since 1970', *Dickens Quarterly*, 12 (1995): 187–98.

———, ed., *Dickens, Europe and the New Worlds* (London and New York: Macmillan and St. Martin's Press, 1999).

———, '"The Tyranny of Words": Reading Dickens in Translation', in *Dickens: the Craft of Fiction and the Challenges of Reading: Proceedings of the Milan Symposium*, ed. by Rossana Bonadai, Clotilda de Stasio, Carlo Pagetti and Alessandro Vescovi (Milan: Edizioni Unicopli, 2000).

Sasaki, Toru, 'Translating *Great Expectations* into Japanese', *Dickensian*, 107 (Winter 2011): 197–201.

Savin, Maynard, *Thomas William Robertson: His Plays and Stagecraft* (Providence, RI: Brown University Press, 1950).

Schatz, Thomas, *The Genius of the System: Hollywood Filmmaking in the Studio Era* (New York: Metropolitan Books, Henry Holt & Co, 1988).

Schickel, Richard, *D.W. Griffith and the Birth of Film* (Pavilion Books: London, 1984).

Schlicke, Paul, *Dickens and Popular Entertainment* (London: Unwin Hyman, 1985).

———, ed., *Oxford Reader's Companion to Dickens* (Oxford: Oxford University Press, 1999).

Secord, James, *Victorian Sensation: The Extraordinary Publication, Reception, and Secret Authorship of Vestiges of the Natural History of Creation* (Chicago, IL: University of Chicago Press, 2001).

Sedgwick, John, 'The Market for Feature Films in Britain, 1934: A Viable National Cinema', *Historical Journal of Film, Radio and Television*, 14 (1994): 15–36.

———'Film "Hits" and "Misses" in Mid-1930s Britain', *Historical Journal of Film, Radio and Television*, 18 (1998): 333–51.

Shattock, Joanne and Michael Wolff, *The Victorian Periodical Press: Samplings and Soundings* (Leicester and Toronto: Leicester University Press and the University of Toronto Press, 1982).

Singer, Ben, *Melodrama and Modernity: Early Sensational Cinema and Its Contexts* (New York: Columbia University Press, 2001).

Slater, Michael, *Charles Dickens* (New Haven, CT, and London: Yale University Press, 2009).

Smith, Grahame, *Dickens and the Dream of Cinema* (Manchester and New York: Manchester University Press, 2003).

Smith, Walter E., *Charles Dickens: A Bibliography of His First American Editions 1836–1870* (New Castle, DE: Oaknoll, 2012).

Socolow, Michael, 'Psyche and Society: Radio Advertising and Social Psychology in America, 1923–1936', *Historical Journal of Film, Radio and Television*, 24 (2004): 517–34.

Staples, Leslie C., 'Great Expectations Realised', *Dickensian*, 43 (1947): 79–81.

Stokes, Melvyn and Richard Maltby, eds., *Hollywood Abroad: Audiences and Cultural Exchange* (London: BFI Publishing, 2004).

Stoneman, Patsy, *Brontë Transformations: The Cultural Dissemination of Jane Eyre and Wuthering Heights* (Brighton: Harvester Wheatsheaf, 1995).

Storey, Gladys, *Dickens and Daughter* (1939; London: Haskell House, 1982).

Sutcliffe, Allan, 'Dickens in the Music Hall: Part 1', *Dickensian*, 106 (Summer 2010): 101–17.

———, 'Dickens in the Music Hall: Part 2', *Dickensian*, 106 (Winter 2010): 207–26.

Sutherland, John, *Victorian Fiction: Writers, Publishers, Readers* (Basingstoke: Palgrave Macmillan, 1995).

Taylor, A.J.P., *English History 1914–1945* (Harmondsworth: Penguin, 1973).

Taylor, Beverly, 'Discovering New Pasts: Victorian Legacies in the Postcolonial Worlds of *Jack Maggs* and *Mister Pip*', *Victorian Studies*, 52, Special Issue: Papers and Responses from the Seventh Annual Conference of the North American Victorian Studies Association, held jointly with the British Association for Victorian Studies (Autumn 2009): 95–105.

Taylor, Miles and Michael Wolff, eds., *The Victorians Since 1901: Histories, Representations and Revisions* (Manchester: Manchester University Press, 2001).

Tharaud, Barry, 'Great Expectations as Literature and Film', *Dickensian*, 87 (Summer 1991): 102–10.

Tomalin, Claire, *Charles Dickens: A Life* (London: Penguin, 2011).

Tompkins, Jane, *West of Everything: the Inner Life of Westerns* (Oxford and New York: Oxford University Press, 1993).

Vasey, Ruth, *The World According to Hollywood 1918–39* (Exeter: Exeter University Press, 1997).

Vlock, Deborah, *Dickens, Novel Reading, and the Victorian Popular Theatre* (Cambridge and New York: Cambridge University Press, 1998).

Waller, Philip, *Writers, Readers, and Reputations: Literary Life in Britain 1870–1918* (Oxford: Oxford University Press, 2006).

Watts, Alan S., 'Why Wasn't *Great Expectations* Illustrated?' *Dickens Magazine*, Series 1, Issue 2 (no date): 8–9.

Wearing, J.P., *The London Stage: a calendar of plays and players*, Vol. 2: *1930–1939* (Metuchen, NJ & London: Scarecrow Press, 1990).

Wellens, Oscar, 'The Earliest Dutch Translations of Dickens (1837–1870): An All-inclusive List', *Dickensian*, 97 (Summer 1997): 126–32.

Worth, George J., 'Great Expectations: A Drama in Three Stages (1861)', *Dickens Quarterly*, 3 (December 1986): 169–74.

Wynne, Deborah, '"We Were Unhealthy and Unsafe": Dickens's *Great Expectations* and *All the Year Round*'s Anxiety Stories', *Journal of Victorian Culture*, 5 (2000): 25–59.

———, *The Sensation Novel and the Victorian Family Magazine* (Basingstoke: Palgrave Macmillan, 2001).

Zambrano, Ana Laura, 'The Charles Dickens Show and Great Expectations Comes To Television', *Dickens Studies Newsletter*, 6 (March, 1975): 24–8.

Index